INSIGHT GUIDES
GREEK ISLANDS

Contents

THE BEST OF GREEK ISLANDS: TOP ATTRACTIONS

From elegant Old Towns, dizzyingly perched cliffside monasteries and ancient sites steeped in history, to a reviving dip in a thermal spring and basking on the deck of your own yacht.

△ **Corfu Old Town**. Eminently strollable, this town is indisputably Greek – but Latinate in style with its slatted Venetian shutters, canal-tile roofs, intimate squares and celebrated arcades, nestled between two giant fortresses. See page 130.

◁ **Panagía Hozoviótissa Monastery**. Improbably wedged into a cliff above Amorgós's southeast coast, this monastery greatly impressed Le Corbusier on his 1911 visit. It is still the spiritual centre of the Cyclades. See page 185.

▷ **Classical Temple of Aphaea**. The juxtaposed colonnades of this temple on Aegina seem straight out of an M.C. Escher drawing; the piney hilltop site is everything you'd expect for an ancient sanctuary. See page 154.

△ **Santoríni.** Sailing into the bay of Santoríni is one of Greece's great experiences: broken pieces of an ancient volcano's rim — Santoríni and its attendant islets — trace a gigantic circle around the deeply submerged caldera, whitewashed villages clinging to the black cliffs around. See page 191.

▽ **Lésvos.** This island has more thermal springs than any other Greek island, thanks to its volcanic core; the Ottoman-era and domed Loutrá Géras on the eponymous gulf is the most user-friendly of several. See page 223.

△ **Ermoúpoli.** Elegant yet lived in, contrasting marble pavements with colourful houses, Unesco-recognised Ermoúpoli on Sýros was founded by Hiot refugees and is the Cyclades' tip-of-the-hat to the Belle Epoque. See page 171.

△ **Skópelos Hóra.** Exquisitely preserved, it seems to exist in a 1980s time-warp, but in the best sense: old-fashioned shops, atmospheric arcades and a generous sprinkling of churches. See page 203.

△ **Agíou Ioánnou tou Theológou Monastery on Pátmos.** Founded in 1088, this monastery transcends the cruise-ship crowds besieging it with vivid frescoes, a rich treasury and unique architecture. See page 279.

▽ **Haniá Old Quarter.** An unusual combination of the Ottoman and Venetian distinguishes this port, a double bay with ample eating, drinking and people-watching opportunities. See page 300.

▽ **Ionian islands.** Flotilla-sailing between the islands is the best choice for novices; conditions are milder than in the open Aegean, but the scenery is every bit as gorgeous, and characterful anchorages are close together. See page 84.

THE BEST OF GREEK ISLANDS: EDITOR'S CHOICE

The Greek Islands' museums, festivals, culinary specialities, beaches and hiking trails... here, at a glance, are some recommendations to help you plan your journey.

The island of Sámos is host to some fine beaches.

BEST MUSEUMS

Museum of Modern Greek Art, Rhodes. The most important collection of 20th-century Greek art outside of Athens. See page 243

Vathý Archaeological Museum, Sámos. Exquisite small Archaic-era objects from the local Hera sanctuary, plus an enormous *kouros*. See page 232

Museum of Asian Art, Corfu. World-class collection, embracing China, Afghanistan and all in between, assembled by three Greek diplomats. See page 131

Theophilos and Thériade Museums, Lésvos. Over 50 works by 'primitive' local artist

Theophilos, next door to Greece's finest modern art collection, amassed by his patron Thériade. See page 224

Iráklio Archaeological Museum. Showcases the best Minoan frescoes and artefacts; should re-open in full by 2014. See page 287

Archaeological Museum, Kálymnos. State-of-the-art museum highlighting the island's Hellenistic and Roman past, featuring statues of Asklepios and a bronze matron in mint condition. See page 271

Minoan vase, Iráklio Archaeological Museum.

BEST FESTIVALS

See pages 46 & 56.
Easter on Hydra. Fishermen carry the *Epitáfios* (Bier of Christ) into the water to bless the boats.

15 August at Ólymbos, Kárpathos. Exemplified by tables for communal feasting and music on *lýra*, *tsamboúna* and *laoúto*.

St Spyridon Procession, Easter Saturday, Corfu. The relics of the island's patron saint go walkabout

in the Old Town to honour his past miracles.

Carnival on Skýros. Derived from pagan revels, this features outrageously costumed revellers performing the "Goat Dance" over four weekends preceding Lent.

Santoríni International Music Festival, Firá. Two weeks of classical music in September, by top-notch international performers.

Easter celebrations on Hydra.

BEST LOCAL SPECIALITIES

Marinated anchovy fillets.

See pages 69 & 74

Pickled caper greens, Nísyros. The "national shrub" of this volcanic islet gets the vinegar treatment, thorns and all.

Genuine thyme honey. Scrub-covered islands like Kálymnos, Foúrni

and certain Cyclades produce the purest – dark and strongly aromatic.

Tzitzírafa, Alónissos. Pickled wild pistachio shoots, gathered in spring – superb by themselves or in a salad.

Kalatháki féta, Límnos. Small, drum-shaped sheep-milk cheese with telltale wire-mould marks; blissfully creamy.

Gávros marinátos, Léros. Marinated anchovy fillets, headed and boned; an ideal *oúzo* partner. There's also *koliós marinátos* (mackerel), equally delicious.

Noúmboulo, Corfu. Succulent smoked pork sirloin fillet. Expensive but addictive.

BEST BEACHES

Egremní, Levkáda. This west-coast paradise just pips two adjacent rivals for the Ionian crown. See page 140

Pláka, Náxos. Dune-backed and part naturist, this stretches for 5km (3 miles) to other, wilder beaches. See page 189

Soúda, Crete. The most protected and scenic of many beaches near

Plakiás, fed by a palm-tree-lined stream. See page 301

Evgátis, Límnos. Stream-fed fine blonde sand framed by volcanic pinnacles, and with Agios Evstrátios islet to look at. See page 221

Velanió, Skópelos. A superb, long, pine-backed pebble stretch, the delight of naturists. See page 204

Idyllic Egremní beach, Levkáda.

Tables with a view, Hydra.

BEST HIKES

Egiáli to Hóra, Amorgós. This five-hour traverse takes in Hozoviótissa Monastery and sweeping sea views en route. See page 184

Northwest coast, Sámos. A path along this verdant coast links Potámi Bay and Drakéï village via the Seïtáni beaches, still home to monk seals. See page 233

Gorge of Samariá, Crete. This slashes through the White Mountains and its descent is an unmissable

activity on Crete. See page 304

Kálymnos. Bare, craggy Kálymnos has some of the best walking in the Dodecanese, with old paths linking villages and remote chapels. See page 271

Alónissos. This island the Sporades offers loop-walks through Kastanórema ravine from coastal Agios Dimítrios, or around Melegákia with its country chapels. See page 205

Hiking on the island of Amorgós, Cyclades.

The Knights' castle overlooks the flat-roofed houses of Líndos, on the east coast of Rhodes.

Santoríni, famous for its whitewashed villages and blue-domed churches.

The exquisite natural harbour at Líndos, on the east coast of Rhodes.

The blue balconies and tall, white houses of Mandráki, Nísyros.

THE GREEK ARCHIPELAGO

The Greek islands have fascinated European travellers since the Grand Tourists first passed through during the 18th century.

Páros windmill.

The Greek islands rank among the most alluring realms in the Mediterranean – indeed the world. Clean, cobalt-hued seas, beaches of all sizes and consistencies, the availability of a range of sophisticated water sports and up to eight reliably sunny months a year ensure a winning combination. With recent infrastructure changes and a sharpening up of the tourism "product", the vivid, rough-and-ready country which first attracted large numbers of artists, writers and the generally bohemian during the 1960s has finally come of age.

Thankfully, even with development, the Greek islands will never become a type of Switzerland-on-Aegean. Despite inducements from the EU, of which Greece has been a member since 1981, (and the most recent pressure to change owing to the severe economic crisis) the islanders stubbornly insist on their right to be Greek. Modernity, as manifested by proper espresso coffee machines and bank ATMs, is often only superficial. Pride in traditions is still evident to varying degrees. This goes hand in hand with an awareness of politics and history to put to shame that in most of jaded Northern Europe.

Tsambíka bay, Rhodes.

Indeed, a healthy historical consciousness comes with the territory due to all the islands having had a turbulent past. Never powerful enough – except, briefly, Crete – to rule themselves, but too strategically sited to be ignored by adventurers en route to richer pickings, the islands were fated to suffer a dizzying succession of invaders and foreign rulers, each of whom left an indelible legacy in terms of monuments, cuisine, language and culture in general.

Perhaps the biggest surprise for new visitors to the archipelago – "chief sea", the age-old term for the Greek islands – is the sheer variety of what, from the map, looks like a homogeneous portion of the Mediterranean. Ranging from the small, arid islets of the central Aegean, with their poster-cliché Cubist houses, to the fertile, forested giants, whose high mountains even carry a frosting of snow in the right season, there is no such thing as a stereotypical Greek island.

The streets of Firá, Santoríni.

ISLAND MENTALITY

Greece has over 60 permanently inhabited islands.
Despite their superficial similarities, each has a
distinct identity and an often unique history.

I t's one of those words that psychiatrists
might use to trigger an automatic response
from a patient stretched on the couch.
Say "island" and childhood recollections of
Robinson Crusoe may spring to mind. Often,
islands are associated with escape from a complex universe into a private, more manageable
world that offers individuals control over their
own destiny. Crusoe becomes comfortable in
his prelapsarian paradise, and it's a surprise,
when rescue is at hand, that he doesn't tell his
saviours to push off.

"Greek island" would probably add some
specific touches to the imagery: a cluster of
dazzlingly white buildings against a shimmering sea, donkeys bearing their burdens against
a backdrop of olive groves, small circles of
weather-beaten fishermen bent over their nets,
jolly tavernas full of *retsína, moussakás,* shattered
plates and background music from *Never on
Sunday* and *Zorba the Greek.* Accurate in part
until the 1980s, perhaps, but any generalisation
about the Greek islands – anything more ambitious than the staringly obvious – would almost
certainly be wrong.

Inter-island relations

Although islands are classified as members of
one group or another, each has a strong sense
of separate identity and invariably an idiosyncratic history to back it up. Often, neighbouring
islands exhibit mutual resentment bordering
on loathing (though islands separated by two
or three intervening ones are at least neutral
about each other if not actively cordial). Visitors would seldom be aware of this unless they
made a point of going down to the local café
and chatting to the men ensconced there. Con-
ditioned by long winter nights when nothing

Carrrying a heavy load on Skiáthos island.

ILLEGAL SUBSTANCES

The apparently tolerant attitude towards tourist
behaviour in Greece does not extend to recrea-
tional drug use, and islands like Íos, Ikaría or
Crete with a youth clientele or counter-cultural
reputation are subject to close undercover sur-
veillance. Although customs searches of EU arrivals very rare, on the whole, it's wise to err on the
side of extreme caution in other respects. The
legal system is largely based on a presumption of
guilt, with up to 18 months in remand until
charges are brought, and typical sentences for
even small amounts of cannabis for personal use
can be two to three years.

much happens, they have developed the knack of holding forth on any subject under the sun, and a new audience is welcome. Taxi drivers, ticket agents and your landlords can be similarly garrulous.

The reasons for fraught inter-island sentiments may be current, as in smaller islands (eg Ikaría) perceiving the inhabitants of a larger, favoured provincial neighbour (Sámos, in the case of Ikaría) as overbearing. Or they may be of long-standing bad blood that has arisen from a variety of causes: rivalry in fishing or sponge-gathering (think Karpathians' views on the rapa-

climate is unhealthy, the houses barely fit even for animals, the water undrinkable, the beaches uncomfortable. For example, many Corfiot jokes revolve around the supposedly dim, rustic Paxiots to the southeast. You shouldn't take such stories or opinions too seriously (often those propounding them don't): they are great fun, and the opportunity to move between neighbouring islands in order to compare notes should be savoured. It is almost axiomatic that if two islands were to strike the curious visitor as being practically identical, those islands would necessarily be at opposite ends of the Aegean.

Greek smile.

cious Kalymnian fleets); abductions and forced marriages generations back; or participation in a long-ago rebellion against the Ottomans, at their neighbour's behest, with disastrous consequences (as happened to the Hiots, goaded by the Samians). Even a proven historical incident will be given a different spin or even disputed by neighbours. Skiathots proudly describe the burning of much of their main port in August 1944 as German reprisal for persistent, patriotic resistance activities; tell that to a Skopelot and the reply might be "They have to find some excuse for why their town is so ugly!"

Almost everywhere, you will be assured that "those people" (just on or over the horizon) are untrustworthy, inhospitable or worse, that the

Apart from the natural tendency for small island communities to be staunchly independent, there is a historical basis for their individualism – an outgrowth of centuries of self-sufficiency enforced by neglect or outright abuse by overlords. Since Neolithic times, the islands have been tossed around like loose pebbles in the cultural tides that have surged to and fro through the eastern Mediterranean, and none has emerged from that experience quite like any other.

Intruders

Momentous events were taking place on some of the Cyclades as early as 6500 BC, and accelerated there some three millennia later with the advent of the Bronze Age. At about the same time, settlers from the Middle Eastern coast landed with the skills which developed into the Minoan civilisation.

To look at the history of Corfu, for instance, merely from the 7th century AD, is to pick up the chronicle of invasions a long way down the line. Nevertheless, the record from that date reveals an amazing cavalcade of intruders to the island. All of them have left some kind of legacy, even if finding traces today would require more diligent research than most visitors care to conduct while on holiday. Dedicated scholars could probably assemble a jigsaw, with pieces

population retreated when danger threatened. The defences did not always keep determined pirates like Khair-ed-din Barbarossa out, but they did mean that the pirates had to make an effort instead of lazily helping themselves to 10 years of stored harvests or all the eligible virgins when they happened to be cruising by.

Stepping stones

Crete, Límnos, Samothráki, Thásos, Sámos, Kós and Rhodes have the richest and most thoroughly documented sites for historically minded visitors, but on any island there is

The Temple of Lindian Athena in Líndos, Rhodes.

still extant on Corfu, that would reflect each and every one of these waves.

The evidence does not necessarily consist of archaeological ruins or excavated objects. Corfu extrapolated from one small chapter of its convoluted history an abiding passion for cricket, albeit played with local variations which would raise the eyebrows of traditionalists in England. The same epoch bequeathed to both Corfu and its tiny neighbour Paxí a taste for *tzíntzi býra* (ginger beer) – though again, scarcely recognisable as such to an Edwardian Englishman.

Other islands received almost as much unwanted outside attention as Corfu. Piracy was a perennial problem, hence the number of collective fortifications *(kástra)* to which the island

FOREIGN OCCUPIERS

Corfu's history is a saga of occupation by foreign powers, each of whom left a mark. From the 7th century, the island was ruled successively by Greeks (the Byzantine Empire), Normans, Greeks (the Despotate of Epirus), Sicilian Angevins and Venetians, the latter for over 400 years. Then it was the turn of France, then Russia, Britain and Greece. The Serbian army and government-in-exile stayed peacefully here during 1916, while Italy occupied Corfu briefly in the 1920s and again during World War II. After Italy capitulated in September 1943, Germany became the last foreign occupier, until their evacuation in autumn 1944.

bound to be something to pick over, even if it isn't mapped. A good tip for amateur archaeologists would be to ask themselves where, taking into account security, prevailing winds, terrain, water supply etc, they themselves would have chosen to build something – and then start looking for evidence of past peoples.

The topographical differences among the islands are worth considering. If some islands look like mountain peaks, it is because, basically, they are – much of the area now covered by the Aegean was once a solid land bridge between the Balkan peninsula and Asia Minor, which

Washing clothes the traditional way on Páros.

became submerged completely only at the end of the last Ice Age, leaving only the summits exposed. The seabed around the islands can drop precipitously to 3,500 metres (11,600ft) in places, for example east of Crete. Closer to Asia Minor, the sea is generally much shallower, but even here the Aegean, quiet and bather-friendly one moment, can be transformed into a lethal cauldron within the space of an hour or two.

Anyone hiring a boat on holiday should never leave port without consulting the islanders. For thousands of years, lives have depended on accurate weather predictions, and local lore handed down is often more reliable than official forecasts on meteorological websites or via other electronic media.

Ways and means

If the purpose of a visit to the islands is nothing more than to settle on a stretch of agreeable beach and live (relatively) cheaply, visitors should be lucky on both counts. Greece has several thousand (mostly uninhabited) islands altogether, and these, plus the mainland shores, add up to technically the longest coastline of any country in Europe. Basic commodities, including certain accommodation categories and ferry tickets, have regulated prices; though the adoption of the euro in early 2002 led to stiff hikes well beyond inflation, the ongoing economic crisis saw accommodation prices in many areas frozen at summer 2009 levels, comparing well to other Mediterranean destinations.

Expensive exceptions include Corfu Town, Rhodes, Mýkonos, Páros and Santoríni. Whatever the local businesspeople may think in private of the antics of their visitors, they tend to be stoical about them in public and continue to pocket the money. Zákynthos (ground zero for youth boozing) and Mýkonos (a gay mecca) in particular would not have been allowed to develop as they have under the puritanical 1967–74 dictatorship, when even topless sunbathing was discouraged. However, since the 1980s if not earlier, what bathers choose to wear or discard has been a matter of personal choice, and there is usually at least one beach on every island where nudity is tolerated, if not officially so.

The best way to enjoy the islands is to arrive with a certain attitude. By all means, begin by uncritically enjoying the vistas seared into the senses by island holiday brochures – the white buildings set against a shimmering sea, the donkeys on a backdrop of olive groves, and so on. Then, when the novelty wears off, or perhaps earlier, examine each island as if it were an onion, and start stripping off the skins. If not a long-standing dispute about fishing rights, some other unexpected aspect is certain to be revealed.

How to strip the onion is a large part of what this book is about. It hopes to show by example, as no book will ever be written that says everything about 10,000 (or even 100) islands. The learned Helidoros once tried to set down everything of note about Athens's Acropolis, as it existed in the 2nd century BC. Fifteen volumes later…

THRACIÆ PARS oggi ROMANIA

CONSTANTINOPOLI Bizantium olim et Stambul

Nicopoli

Nesstria

Braca

Buthenium lacus

Maximianopoli

Beryssa et Arpera et Abdera

Cicones

Doriscus campus

Bebryce

Traianopoli et Zirines et

Maronea et Sci

Bisstones

Selybria et Salumbria

Scutari

Caledona

Nicomedia
Comidia
li Nicor et
Unigimid et Ischmit

G. à Nicomedia

Stretto di Costantinopoli et Bospheros Thracius

Radisto et Piranthe Rhedastus

MARE DI MARMARA
olim
PROPONTIS

Chizico Lot Cyzicus

I. à Prote

Iruich

Mowanspolus

Burgia Bursa
et Prousa et Prusa et
Olympium

Marmora I. et Proconnesus
Neuris et Elaphonesus

Bursi
Prousio ét

Ancira

Gallipoli

Anatolia Propria

Mysia Minor

Lampsaco et Lampsacus

Li Dardanelli
Sesto et Abida

ANATOLIA

Chizasso

Tasso I. et Thassus et Æria

Samandrachi
et Samus et Samothrace

Molchino

Stalimene et Palvoca

Mudra

Lembro I. et Imbrus

Cape Grego et
Marmana Prom.

Sigæum Prom
oggi Cape di Giannizari

Tenedo I.

Troia

Mysia Maior

Andramiti et
Andramyttium

Gurmania et Caicus

Pergamo et Pergamus

Piscopie et
Como Castri et
Cume et Cumas

ARCIPELAGO

oggi

MAR BIANCO

anticamente

ÆGÆVM MARE

Pelagnesi I. et Alonesus

Seraquino et Peparethus I.

Sciro I. et Scyrus

Cia Insula

Metelino I.
olim Lesbos

Molino et
Mytilene

Spiero Del
Pino

Scio
Colira et
Spalar

Smirne et
Smyrna

Argenna et
Phocea

Vecchia vecchia
et Phocea

Sar-cham

Sarabat o aqua

Ephesio

Cari-si
et Lydia

ASIA MINOR

Scio I. et Chiur et Chios

Chios o Chies et Cassris

ICARIVM MARE

Andro I. et Andres

Tino I. et Tenos

Nicaria I.
et Icaria

Samo

Samo I. et Samus

Rocho I.

Dragonisi

Aidinelli

Delos grande et Rhene

Micolo I. et Miconus

Stapoda I.

Fermiace I.

Molasso et Miletus

Insulæ Cyclades

Caura et Exiopolia

Dili ò piccola De los, ò le Scuole
di Delos, Iagia et Ortygia

Sirna I. et Syrus

Mandria I.

Lero I. et Leria

CARIA

Thermia I.
et Cythnur

Nicsia I. et Naxus

Datch I.

Palmosa o Patino
et Patmos

Agatonisi I.

Doris

Pariol et Paros

Capra I. et Claro

Morgo I. et Amorgus

Pirai I.

Zinara I.

Capra I.

Lango et
Coricosa

Alero et Halicarnasso

Sesino I.
et Seriphus

Rachia I.

Namio I. et Anaphe

Zenora I. et Gyaros

Leuita I. et Lebinthus

Lango I. et Cos

Nero et Rio

Sifano I. et Siphnus

Argentiera I.
et Cimolus

Poluno I.
Sicandro I.
et Cimolus

Camena I.

Sorpe I.

Nisari I.
et Nisyros

Piscopia
et Tilos

Iola di Rodi et Rhodus

Sicalo I.
et Cithnus

Milo I. et Melos

Nio I. et Ios

Gierra I.
et Ihera

Percello I.

Zafania I.

Deonia I.

Limonia I.
et Telos

Carchi o Chalce I.

Rodi
et Rhode

Annia I.

Remonia I.

Fetoni I.

Sporades Insulæ

MARE MYRTOVM

Stampalia I. et Astypalea

Redi
et Rhe

Tiresia I. et
Therasia

Santorini o S. Erini
et Thera Insula

Plana I.

Scarpanto I. et Carpathus

Aprenni I.

Spada et Cianum pr.

MARE DI CANDIA ol. CRETICVM Mare

Standia I. et Dia

Louo I.

MARE DI SCARPANTO olim Carpathium Mare

Cassio I. et Cassus

S. Teodoro
Louo Ins.

C. Molaca

C. Sassono
et Dion. pr.

Candia

C. S. Zuane
et Zephyrion pr.

Sipalonga

Loopetro

C. Sidero

CANDIA olim CRETA

Retimo

Milo

Tamen Padia

Maglia

C. Salomoni
et Samenium pr.

Palocastro
et Itium

Scala
Miglia d'Italia
Leghe comuni di Francia
Leghe comuni di Germania
Leghe d'un hora de camino

DECISIVE DATES

c. 3000 BC
First Bronze Age cultures in Crete and the Cyclades.

2600–1450 BC
Minoan civilisation flourishes on Crete until tsunami from huge volcanic eruption on Thera devastates north coast. Subsequently, many Cretan palaces destroyed by fire related to civil strife.

c.1400 BC
Mycenaeans occupy Crete and Rhodes, establish a trading empire, devise Linear B – the first written Greek.

12th century BC
"Sea Peoples" from beyond the Black Sea invade islands, destroying Mycenaean civilisation but bringing Iron Age technology with them.

1150–800 BC
"Dark Ages": cultural and economic stagnation. Refugee Mycenaeans (known as Ionians) settle on Aegean islands and in Attica.

c.770 BC
Contact with Phoenicians and Egyptians spurs a revival of Greek cultural life. Phoenician alphabet adopted.

750 BC onward
Rise of first city-states, foremost among them Athens, Sparta and Corinth.

546–500 BC
Persian Empire expands to control Ionian Greek cities on Asia Minor's west coast. Under Darius the Great, Persians conquer many Aegean islands.

490–479 BC
Persian invasions of Greek mainland repulsed by united Greeks led by Spartan army and Athenian navy. Ionian cities freed from Persian rule.

Classical and Hellenistic Ages

477–465 BC
Athens establishes Delian League comprising islands and cities in Asia Minor. Islands attempting to secede are brutally suppressed by Athens.

454 BC
The League's treasury is moved from Delos to Athens. Effectively, the islands are now part of an Athenian Empire. "Golden Age" of Classical Athens.

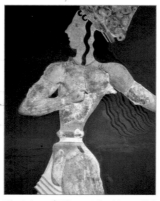

The Prince of Lilies or Priest-king Relief in the Palace of Knossós, Crete.

431–404 BC
Peloponnesian War leaves Athens defeated and weakened.

338 BC
Greek city-states defeated by Philip II of Macedon.

336–323BC
Philip succeeded by son Alexander, who extends a transient empire as far as India.

323 BC
On Alexander's death, this empire is divided between his generals. Greek islands mostly run by Egyptian Ptolemies.

Romans and Byzantines

197–146 BC
Romans defeat Macedonian Antigonids and annex Greece.

3rd/4th centuries AD
Christianity spreads; barbarian raids from north.

330
Co-emperor Constantine establishes Constantinople as his capital.

391–5
Theodosius I outlaws paganism and Olympic Games banned. Roman Empire splits into two, Latin West and Byzantine East.

824–961
Arabs occupy Crete until Emperor Nikiphoros Phokas retakes island.

1080–1185
Normans from Sicily invade or raid Greek islands.

1204
The Fourth Crusade: Constantinople temporarily taken by Latins. Venetians

claim the Ionians, Cyclades and Crete.

1309
Knights Hospitallers of St John occupy and fortify the Dodecanese, especially Rhodes.

1344–1478
Genoese assume control of north Aegean islands.

1453
Ottoman Turks capture Constantinople, renamed Istanbul and made capital of Ottoman Empire.

1462–1523
Aegean islands taken over in stages by Ottoman Turks.

1649–69
Ottoman conquest of Crete, which the Venetians lose.

1797–1814
Napoleonic French, then Russians, occupy Ionian islands.

1814–64
British rule in Ionian islands.

Independence and After

1821–9
War of Independence against Ottomans.

1830–32
At peace conferences, Ottomans cede Évvia to Greeks, but keep Dodecanese, northeast Aegean and north mainland.

1834
Athens becomes capital of Greece, replacing Návplio.

1864
Ionian islands ceded to Greece.

The aftermath of an Italian air raid on Corfu Town, April 1941.

1898
Crete becomes an independent principality within the Ottoman Empire.

1909–10
Army revolts against political establishment in Athens allow Eleftherios Venizelos to form new government. Venizelos intermittently PM until 1935.

1912–13
Balkan Wars: Greece takes Crete, northeast Aegean islands and Macedonia. Italy occupies Dodecanese.

1917
Greece belatedly enters World War I on Entente side.

1919–22
Asia Minor campaign ends in catastrophic defeat. Expulsion of Greek civilians from Turkey. Greek possession of western Thrace confirmed.

1940–1
Greece rebuffs Italian invasion and fights with Allies until invaded by Nazi Germany.

1944
Greece is liberated by Allies.

1946–9
Civil War between Greek government and Communists opposed to restoring monarchy.

1947
Dodecanese joined to Greece.

1967–74
Greece ruled by junta of right-wing colonels; King in exile.

1974
Colonels deposed; republic established.

1981
Andreas Papandreou's PASOK party forms first leftist government. Greece becomes full member of EEC (now EU).

2004
Centre-right New Democracy wins elections; Athens hosts the Olympic Games.

2008–9
Riots in response to police killing an Athens youth. George Papandreou leads PASOK to victory in 2009 elections.

2010–11
Greece's finances revealed as insolvent after decades of mismanagement. Papandreou resigns in favour of unelected "unity" government. Two bailout packages offered by international lenders at the cost of austerity measures.

2012
Two inconclusive elections produce a three-party coalition mandated to negotiate better aid terms from the lenders.

2013
Economic outlook barely changes, but tourism figures improve markedly.

The famous Phaistos Disc, a highlight of Iráklio's Archaeological Museum.

WAVES OF INVADERS

The history of Greece, and especially its islands,
is inextricably linked to the sea. It is largely a
chronicle of foreign conquerors and occupiers.

What distinguishes the course of Greek history from that of her Balkan neighbours is the impact of the sea. The sea diffuses cultures, transfers peoples and encourages trade – and until our own times it was invariably a swifter means of transmission than overland. Nowhere in Greece is the sea as inescapable as on the islands.

The poverty of the thin island soil has forced inhabitants to venture far afield for their livelihood. At the same time, the islands have been vulnerable to foreign incursions, whether by Arab pirates, Italian colonists or modern tourists. All have played their part in transforming local conditions; some have had an even wider impact. Phoenician traders, for example, appear to have brought their alphabet, which the Greeks then adopted and changed, to the islands during the early Geometric period. At the same time, Egyptian influence was leading island sculptors to work in stone. It is no coincidence that the earliest examples of monumental Greek sculpture are all to be found on the islands.

On Crete, the Bronze Age had produced the first urban civilisation in the Aegean: this was the age of the Knossos and Phaistos palaces, erected in the centuries after 2000 BC. Other islands such as Thera (today Thíra or Santoríni) also flourished at this time. Thucydides' account of how King Minos of Crete established his sons as governors in the Cyclades and cleared the sea of pirates certainly suggests considerable Cretan control of the Aegean. The Aegean was not to be dominated by a single sea power for another millennium until the rise of the Athenian Empire.

Economic growth

Before this, however, communities of Greeks had begun to flourish on most of the islands,

An inaccurate artist's view of the Colossus of Rhodes.

IMPERIALISM IN ACTION

The Italian occupation of the Dodecanese under Mussolini imposed the draconian prohibitions of an imperialist regime, intent on "Italianising" the islands and islanders. Secret police stamped out nationalist activity; the Orthodox religion had no official status from the late 1920s; the blue-and-white colours of the Greek flag were prohibited in public; and only Italian could be used in public from 1936 – slogans such as *Viva il Duce, viva la nuova Italia imperiale!* were daubed on the walls of recalcitrant shopkeepers. During the 1930s, many islanders emigrated to the Greek mainland, Egypt, southern Africa and America.

exploiting local quarries and mines, and developing indigenous political systems. Some communities achieved considerable wealth, notably on Siphnos (today Sífnos), whose gold and silver mines had made her inhabitants reputedly the richest citizens in the Cyclades by the 6th century BC. Some reflection of this wealth can be seen in the ruins of the marble treasury which Siphniots dedicated to Apollo at Delphi.

It was in the 6th century, too, that the inhabitants of Thera began to mint their own coinage, a physical manifestation of the

Dionýsios Solomós, the Ionian poet whose Hymn to Freedom was adopted as the national anthem after Independence.

island's powerful status in the Aegean. At one point Thera's influence was to extend not only to Crete, Melos (Mílos), Páros and Rhodes, but as far west as Corinth and as far east as Asia Minor.

During the 5th century BC, the islands' independence was curtailed as Athens used anti-Persian fears to manipulate the Delian League. This had been formed in 478 BC as an alliance between equal partners to form a strong naval power in the Aegean. But Athens soon controlled the League and used its resources in a series of wars against rivals such as the naval city-state of Aegina (Égina). It was Athenian intrigues with the Corinthian colony on Corfu, however, that led to the Peloponnesian War

which was ultimately to cripple – and break – Athens forever.

During the Hellenistic period the islands remained turbulent backwaters, prone to internecine struggles which made them easy prey for their more powerful neighbours. By the beginning of the 2nd century BC, Rome had established herself in the Aegean; Crete became the centre of a province that included a part of North Africa.

Under Roman guidance roads were laid, aqueducts constructed, new towns and grand buildings erected. Despite this prosperity, the Aegean as a whole remained a Roman backwater. Little is known of conditions of life in the islands either then or after AD 395, when they passed under the control of the Eastern Roman Empire. Only with the onset of the Arab raids in the 7th century does the historical record become more complete.

With the decline of Roman power in the Mediterranean, the islands faced a long period of instability: for more than a millennium they were attacked by invaders from all points of the compass. From the north, briefly, came the Vandals and Goths; from the south, the Arabs, who established themselves on Crete in 824 and proceeded to plunder the rest of the Aegean for over a century. From the west came Normans in the 11th century, followed by the Genoese and Venetians; finally, from the east came the Ottoman Turks, who succeeded in dominating almost all of the islands in the Aegean between the 15th and 18th centuries.

Other groups, too, played minor roles – quite apart from powers such as the English, French and Russians, who all shared an interest in the Greek islands. The impact of these various peoples on the islands was complex and tangled, making it awkward to generalise about the historical experiences of the islands themselves. Only by considering the main island groups individually may things fall into place.

The Ionian Islands

On the eve of the 1821 Greek uprising, an English traveller to Corfu noted: "The natural weakness and position of the Ionian islands, and all their past history, demonstrate that they must ever be an appendage of some more powerful state; powerful at sea and able to protect them as well as to command." Situated close to the

Greek mainland, and vital staging-posts on the voyage from Western Europe to the Levant, the Ionian islands were perhaps inevitably a focus of constant conflict.

Corfu had suffered brief attacks during the 5th century from Vandals and Goths, the destroyers of the Roman Empire in the West, but it was not until the Eastern Empire lost its possessions in southern Italy that the Ionian islands again became vulnerable to invasion. This time the predators were the Normans. At the time when William the Conqueror was establishing Norman control over England,

(which intermittently captured Levkáda) down to 1797, when Napoleonic forces ousted the Venetians.

During these four centuries, the Ionian islands were ruled by local nobility and by administrators sent out from Venice. The influence of the Republic was felt in the introduction of cash crops such as olives and currants, in the repressive regime under which the peasants worked and in the Italian language which the nobility affected to speak. At first Venetian rule was energetic – so that, for example, after Ottoman raids had left Zákynthos virtually

A watercolour of Itháki harbour.

Robert Guiscard, Duke of Apulia, defeated the Byzantine army and its emperor, before dying of a fever on Kefaloniá. His nephew Roger, King of Sicily, occupied Corfu in 1146 and held it for six years.

Although notional Byzantine allies, the Venetians soon proved to have territorial ambitions of their own. After the sack of Constantinople in 1204 during the Fourth Crusade, the Ionians were parcelled out among noble Venetian families, who in fact never took control of these islands, which swung between renewed Norman-Sicilian rule and that of the Despotate of Epirus. Not until 1386 did the Ionians come under direct Venetian rule, which continued through a succession of Ottoman attacks

SO CALLED 'TURKS' ON CRETE

The Ottoman conquest of Crete was helped by the Venetian rulers having antagonised the islanders in various ways. Subsequently, few Anatolians actually settled on Crete; most of the local so-called Turks were Cretan converts to Islam, who did so to enjoy a higher civil status and who never even bothered to learn Turkish. These "Turks" made up as much at 40 percent of the population in the main north-coast towns. Mosques were limited in number, and many of the converts were adherents of the Bektashi dervish order. The Cretan origins of these "Turks" gave to the repeated Orthodox uprisings the bitter nature of a civil war.

uninhabited in the late 15th century, vigorous resettlement policies soon created the basis for new prosperity. Zákynthos (Zante to the Venetians) had only 36 families in 1485, but 752 families by 1516, and her revenues increased forty-fold in 30 years thanks to the introduction of these valuable crops.

By the 18th century Venice had lost her possessions in the Aegean and the Peloponnese; in the Ionian Sea, the Venetian-held islands were ravaged by pirates operating from Paxí and the Albanian coast; internally, blood feuds and political assassination made life precarious.

Detail of an embroidery from Skýros, probably from the 17th century.

The end of Venetian rule was bloodless: when the French invaders arrived, they discovered the fortress guns rusting and the garrison without any gunpowder. Napoleon himself had written in 1797 that "the great maxim of the Republic ought henceforth to be never to abandon Corfu, Zante…." But within two years, the Napoleonic forces had antagonised the locals by suppressing the Orthodox Church, and a joint Ottoman-Russian force established the puppet, semi-autonomous Septinsular Republic, which lasted just eight years until the French retook the islands, introducing more constructive reforms until forced out by the British in 1814 after Waterloo.

Sir Thomas Maitland, the first Lord High Commissioner, in the words of a Victorian historian, "established a Constitution which, possessing every appearance of freedom, in reality left the whole power in his hands". But it could not satisfy the islanders' desire for freedom from foreign rule, a desire that intensified after the creation of the Kingdom of Greece in 1832. In 1864 Britain ceded the Ionian islands to the modern Greek state, a condition stipulated by the new King George I for taking the throne.

The Cyclades, Sporades and Saronic Gulf islands

The Cyclades, unlike the Ionian islands, were a commercial backwater: main trade routes passed via Crete and the eastern Aegean islands to Smyrna and Aleppo. While they remained a lure to pirates, they were never of comparable interest to major powers. Until the rise of the seafaring Italian city-states in the 11th century, most trade in the Aegean was in the hands of Greeks.

However, the weakness of the Byzantine navy was underlined by a series of Arab raids against the islands and the Greek mainland. By the 12th century a British chronicler noted that piracy had become the curse of the Aegean: many of the islands were abandoned, while others – Skýros in the Sporades, for example – became pirate lairs.

The sack of Constantinople in 1204 brought new masters to the Aegean. The unimportance of this group of islands to them meant that the Venetians were content to leave the task of occupying them to minor nobility. Of these, the most successful was Marco Sanudo, a nephew

FOREIGNERS IN THE IONIANS

After 1797, when the French and British took successive control of the Ionian islands, they found a society very different to their own. Wheeled transport was virtually unknown on several islands owing to the appalling roads, and the priests opposed the French introduction of the potato on the grounds that this was the apple with which the serpent had tempted Eve in the Garden of Eden. At the same time, the inhabitants of the islands were demanding western European amenities. The British obliged by bringing improved roads, aqueducts and, with a touch of the public-school love of team sports, the game of cricket.

of the Doge Enrico Dandolo, who equipped eight galleys at his own expense and sailed to the Aegean where he founded the Duchy of Náxos in 1207.

Náxos itself became the capital of a fiefdom of 10 surrounding islands, and on it Sanudo built a castle, erected a Catholic cathedral and provided solid fortifications for the town. Other adventurers helped themselves to islands such as Ándros and Thíra (Santoríni). The Ghisi family obtained Tínos and Mýkonos, as well as the Sporades islands, establishing a dynasty which clashed with the Sanudi until both were overwhelmed by the Ottoman navy in the 16th century. The Duchy of Náxos lasted over 350 years and only ended with the death of Joseph Nasi, the Sephardic Jewish favourite of Selim II, upon whom the sultan had bestowed the islands after their capture.

But the exceptional longevity of the Duchy of Náxos should not obscure the turbulence of life in the Aegean in these centuries. Piracy had increased in the late 13th century, with Greek corsairs from Monemvasiá or Santoríni, Sicilians and Genoese – and had caused, for example, the inhabitants of the island of Amorgós to emigrate en masse to Náxos, whose fertile interior was relatively inaccessible.

In the 14th century Catalan mercenaries, brought in for the conflict between Venice and Genoa, ravaged some of the islands, raided others and even occupied Aegina (Égina) for some decades. Ottoman troops landed on Náxos and took 6,000 captives. The Ottoman forces often consisted of recent converts to Islam, and were led by renegade Aegean Greeks such as the notorious brothers from Lésvos, Khair-ed-din and Amrudj Barbarossa.

Local rulers began to complain of depopulation: Ándros had to be resettled by Albanian mainlanders; Íos, virtually uninhabited, was replenished by families from the Peloponnese. Astypálea was repopulated in 1413 by Cycladic colonists, abandoned in 1473 and only inhabited once more after 1570. During the 16th century, the islands suffered a series of attacks by the Ottoman navy and by mid-century Venetian influence was on the wane. Within 50 years, most of the islands had been brought under the sultan's rule, though Tínos only succumbed as late as 1715.

Conditions of life did not improve under Ottoman rule. Piracy, famine and fatal disease remained the perennial problems. In the 18th century the plague decimated the islands on four separate occasions, continuing into the next century, well after this scourge had died out in most of Europe. Thus the Ottomans, like their predecessors, were forced to repopulate.

Often the new colonists were not Greeks. The Frenchman Joseph Pitton de Tournefort reported in the early 18th century that most of the inhabitants of Andíparos were descended from French and Maltese corsairs. He also noted that villages on Ándros were "peopled only by Albanians, dressed still in their tradi-

A 1795 watercolour showing the unfinished Temple of Apollo, Náxos.

tional style and living their own way, that is to say with neither creed nor law".

It was the Albanians who were to play a major role in the struggle for Greek independence. Waves of Albanians had been colonising the islands of the Aegean since the 14th century. They were concentrated on the Saronic islands – the eminent Koundouriótis family, for example, moved from Epiros to Hydra around the year 1580. By the late 18th century, Hydra, with a largely Albanian population, possessed one of the largest and most powerful shipping fleets in the Aegean, which played a prominent role in the War of Independence.

The importance of these islands was underlined by the choice of Aegina (Égina), for a short time, as the first capital of the new Greek state. Refugees flocked here when it was the seat of government, only to leave again when it was replaced by Návplion, on the mainland. When Edouard About visited the town in 1839 he reported it "abandoned – the homes that had been built tumbled into ruins, the town once more became a village; its life and activity fled with the government".

The northeast Aegean islands

Although the east Aegean islands shared the experience of Arab raids with the Cyclades, the

The sea battle of Sámos, one of the first clashes in the War of Independence; watercolour from 1824.

two areas developed differently as the rivalry between Venice and Genoa increased after the Fourth Crusade. As allies of the resurgent Byzantine Empire against her Latin enemies, the Genoese were given trading rights in the Black Sea and granted permission to colonise (and garrison) the eastern Aegean.

> *Italianate family names provide linguistic evidence of Venetian rule in the Cyclades, while Catholic communities have also survived: Náxos has many small, double-naved country churches for both Catholic and Orthodox use.*

A Genoese trading company controlled the mastic plantations of Híos from 1346, that year also seeing occupation of Ikaría and Sámos. In 1355 Lésvos passed into the hands of the Gattelusi family, who eventually extended their control to Thásos, Límnos and Samothráki. However, as in the west Aegean, the power of the Ottoman navies simply overwhelmed these local potentates, and with the fall of Híos in 1566 all the islands of the east Aegean passed into Ottoman hands.

Lésvos had been conquered by the Ottoman Turks as early as 1462, and most of the inhabitants emigrated. In 1476 the inhabitants of Sámos fled to Híos, but returned to the deserted island after 1562. Belon du Mans, who visited the island around 1546, wrote: "It is striking that an island like Sámos must remain deserted. The fear of pirates has rendered her uninhabited so that now there is not a single village there, nor any animals" (an exaggeration, as a few primitive hamlets remained in the mountains). Despite these islands' proximity to the mainland, they attracted only a small number of Muslim colonisers, and the bulk of the population remained Greek, supplemented by immigrants from the Balkans and Anatolia. Only on Lésvos were Muslim settlers to be found farming the land; elsewhere they stayed close to the towns.

The 1821 insurrection had variable support in these islands. Sámos was the most fanatic supporter of the revolution. The Samians landed as agitators on Híos where, in 1822, the Ottomans brutally suppressed a rather half-hearted revolt. Fustel de Coulanges wrote in 1856: "Any person aged more than 32 years whom one meets today on Híos was enslaved and saw his father slaughtered."

It was little consolation to know that the massacre on Híos, melodramatically painted by Delacroix, had aroused the attention of European liberals, and strengthened philhellenic sentiment. Refugees fled westwards, transporting the island's traditional *loukoúmi* (Turkish delight) industry to Sýros in the Cyclades, whose port of Ermoúpoli became the busiest port in the new Greek state. Other refugees settled in Alexandria, Trieste, Marseilles and as far north as Amsterdam.

Elsewhere in the east Aegean, the changes were just as great. The Ottoman authorities were only able to suppress the uprising with

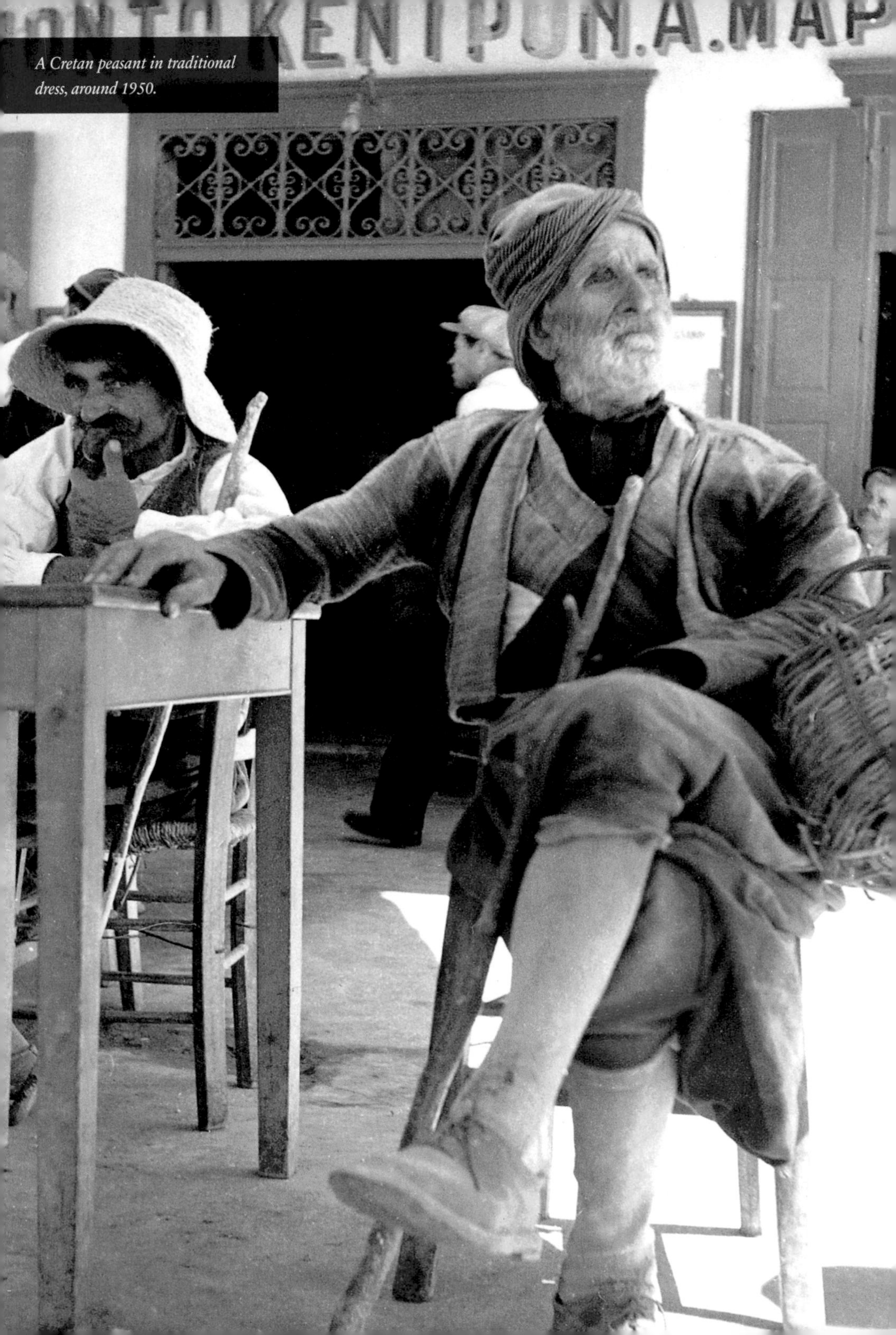

A Cretan peasant in traditional dress, around 1950.

THE ISLANDS TODAY

The 20th century was a political roller-coaster for Greece and its islands, alternating between monarchy, military dictatorship and republicanism.

The islands did not all become part of independent Greece at the same time. Only the Cyclades, the Sporades and Evvia (Euboea) formed part of the original state after the peace treaties of 1830–2. At the insistence of about-to-be King George I, a Danish prince (and – more to the point – because they were no longer considered of strategic value), the Ionian islands were ceded by Britain to Greece in 1864.

The other major additions resulted from war. Crete and the northeast Aegean islands became part of Greece in 1913 after the First Balkan War, except for Samothráki which was joined in 1922, along with mainland Thrace. The Dodecanese islands were freed from Italian occupation by World War II and formally incorporated into Greece in 1948 after a year's Greek military government. Since several of the islands were wealthy ports at a time when Athens was still a village, it is scarcely surprising that their influence on cultural developments in the new state was disproportionate to their size and overall population.

In politics, the Hydriot families of Voulgaris and Koundouriotis, the Metaxas clan in the Ionians, the Samian Themistoklis Sofoulis, not to mention the Cretan Eleftherios Venizelos – in many ways the founder of the modern Greek state – all typified the vigour which the islanders brought to the political scene. Greek literature and music were marked by the Ionian islands' close links with Italy – personified in Zakynthian poet Dionýsios Solomos, whose *Hymn to Liberty* became the words of the national anthem; Corfiot Nikolaos Mantzaros actually wrote the tune – while many Aegean islands were the birthplace of musical stars in rebetic and folk genres (see page

A pelican once started an inter-island feud between Mýkonos and Tínos.

61). Skiáthos bred the important fiction writers Alexandros Papadiamantis and his cousin Alexandros Moraitis; Corfu nurtured writer Iakovos Polylas; Lésvos has produced the Nobel Prize-winning poet Odysseas Elytis, the regional writer Stratis Myrivilis and the "primitive" painter Theóphilos; while Crete, not to be outdone, produced in literature and letters a figure to match Venizelos – Nikos Kazantzákis.

The islands' economic influence has also been profound, especially before the Balkan Wars of 1912–13 added the fertile regions of northern Greece to the impoverished state, and again in recent decades with the increasing traffic in tourists. The shipping fleets of the Aegean islands, exports of currants from Zákynthos and Kefaloniá, olive oil from Lésvos and Crete, salted fish from various east Aegean islands, and emigrant remittances from islanders scattered across the globe – from Canada to Australia to Florida – have all helped bolster the country's economy.

Islands for outcasts

But islands have long had other uses, too. Límnos, under Ottoman rule, was used as a place of exile for political offenders. Henry Tozer, who

Civil-war political prisoners await their fate.

visited the island in 1884, learnt that a former grand vizier had been living there for eight years and was "almost forgotten at the capital", while an extreme instance of isolation was Gávdos islet off Crete. According to Spratt, an English vice-admiral distinguished for his *Travels and Researches in Crete* who visited in 1865, its inhabitants did not see a boat for months on end, while he himself disembarked among naked swimmers who, to his Victorian eye, were "primitive in their habits and ideas… a mixed and degenerate race".

The Greek central government also found the islands useful as prisons, both for regular criminals in large compounds on Aegina (Égina) and Corfu and, more ominously, at

The fortress islet of Spinalónga, off the northeast coast of Crete, after a long career as Venetian citadel and Muslim village, was used as a leper colony until the late 1950s.

certain times for political opponents. On Aegina, what was built as an orphanage under the new Kapodistrias government in the late 1820s soon became an important prison (now closed pending restoration as a potential museum), and the originally British-built jail on Corfu, now well short of humane requirements, is still used.

During the 1930s the Metaxas dictatorship sent its political opponents – as well as social misfits like the *rebétes* (see page 63) – to forbidding, isolated islands such as Folégandros, Síkinos and Amorgós. During the Civil War (1946–9), in which the left-wing forces which had strongly resisted the occupying Nazis and Fascists were suppressed, the uninhabited island of Makroníssos just off the southeastern coast of Attica was home to a vast, bleak prison camp for political detainees, while Ikaría, neighbouring Foúrni, Límnos and its tiny satellite Agios Evstrátios were used for house arrest of Communists

The colonels, who ruled Greece with a heavy, sometimes brutal hand from 21 April 1967 until 24 July 1974, continued the tradition, incarcerating their political opponents in Makroníssos, Gyáros, Léros and Amorgós, as well as the regular prisons on Aegina and

BACKWARD-LOOKING COLONELS

The military junta that ruled Greece from 1967 to 1974, under the leadership of Colonel George Papadopoulos, was driven by a mixture of self-interest and retrograde nationalism. The colonels – from peasant or lower middle-class backgrounds – largely recycled the ideology of the 1930s Metaxas regime, embodying provincial reaction to a new world of urban consumers. They wanted a return to traditional morality and religion, censored the press and suppressed intellectual debate, while closing the frontiers to bearded, long-haired or mini-skirted foreigners – at least until they realised the implications for Greece's tourist trade.

Corfu. On occasions, particularly on Amorgós and Corfu, the islanders managed to circumvent military security and give the political prisoners some support.

Incomers and emigrants

Since the late 1950s most islands have experienced the erratic but inexorable growth of tourism, a trend initiated when Greek shipowners began to acquire islands for their own private use. When Stavros Niarchos and Aristotle Onassis continued their competition by respectively buying the islands of

as multiplied and/or improved airports and airlines.

The counter to this influx has been a steady flow of emigration from the islands. Between 1880 and 1920 or thereabouts, most Greek emigrants were from the mainland. For various reasons, large numbers of islanders did not follow until the 1950s: would-be island emigrants were constrained by the availability of transport and their own awareness of the wider world, and, in the case of islands like the northeast Aegean group and the Dodecanese, by citizenship status (Ottoman, Italian) which made obtaining

Shipping magnate Aristotle Onassis and his first wife Tina.

Spetsopoúla just off Spétses in the Saronic Gulf and Skorpiós beside Levkáda in the Ionian Sea, they set an ideal which innumerable tourists have tried to follow in finding their own island paradise.

Mýkonos, Rhodes, Skiáthos and Corfu were the first to see large numbers of summer visitors, but the trend has spread to virtually all the inhabited islands. If a ship goes there, there will be tourists, and the luxury of what they will find varies more or less according to the island's accessibility. For both visitors and island residents, the biggest changes since the 1970s have been the increasing availability of hydrofoils, catamarans or "high-speed" ferries, more expensive but far faster vessels, as well

POST-JUNTA POLITICS

After the junta collapsed in 1974, a referendum terminated the monarchy. The new conservative PM Constantine Karamanlis secured entry into the EEC, which Greece joined in 1981. That year, Andreas Papandreou's PASOK party won elections to form Greece's first socialist government. Scandals brought defeat in 1989, but with no real alternative offered by centre-right Néa Dimokratía (ND), PASOK regained power from 1993 to 2004 when ND again took office. Five years later PASOK was re-elected, though Andreas' son George resigned in 2011 in favour of a technocratic interim government that preceded the current three-party coalition.

passports and permission to enter countries such as the US awkward.

Moreover, several islands prospered after being incorporated into the Greek state. Sýros, for example, became the most important port and manufacturing centre in Greece in the first few decades after 1830. Even after the rise of Piraeus (Pireás) it remained an important centre, whose standing may be gauged by the fine 19th-century villas and warehouses of its capital Ermoúpolis. On other islands, such as Mílos, Thásos and Náxos, the late 19th century was a period of rapid exploitation of mineral resources.

Sokrátous, the main commercial artery in Rhodes' Old Town.

By World War I, however, much of this activity had slowed down, and emigration both to Athens and abroad was increasing, taking advantage of improved transport and communications. In Athens and Piraeus, newcomers from islands formed closely knit communities, each with its own affinity clubs and cafés – recreated islands of familiarity in the urban sprawl. With the collapse of international trade between the world wars, the trend slowed for several decades, but gathered pace once more with the European "miracle" of the post-war years. Many islanders moved to Sweden, France, Holland and West Germany, as well as to South Africa, Rhodesia, Australia and North America.

Improved communications

By the 1960s, road and rail links between Greece and Western Europe began to be modernised. So too were links between the islands and the mainland: the first seaplane connection with Rhodes had been established as early as 1927 by the Italians, but it was only in the 1960s that aerial links between Athens and the Aegean became significant; many airports on the border islands were built in the mid-1960s amidst the first major Cyprus Republic crises, and doubled as military air-bases. At the same time, relatively modern, faster car ferries were introduced, replacing vintage rust-buckets which could take almost twice as long for the same trajectory. On the islands themselves, dirt – then paved – vehicle roads appeared, often for the first time, in some cases displacing local boat services (such as, for instance, Haniá to villages of Crete's southwest coast).

Improved communications not only opened up the closed island societies, but also exposed their local economies – which had survived World War II mostly by subsistence farming – to a new world of export and import. Trucks could now be loaded with agricultural produce on Crete, say, and then be driven directly up from Piraeus to markets in northwestern Europe. The return flow was (and still is) consumer delights: household appliances, cars, motorbikes, clothes and inevitably plastic junk from the Far East.

A new balance has been established since about the 1970s. During the warm months at least, many islands appear to be thriving, what with the crowds disembarking from boats and clogging the village streets, and with their actual and official populations (compiled from voter registration rolls) more or less matching. With the advent of modern transport, weekend visits by internally emigrated islanders (or second-home owners) have become feasible almost year-round. But the bustle is often illusory.

Limits to full-time island life

The stark reality is that keeping Greece's islands viable for year-round habitation – especially the smaller, remoter ones – is an uphill task, inevitably involving subsidies (EU or national) that are increasingly difficult to come by in the current political and economic climate. Financial assistance can mean everything from preferential VAT rates for border-zone islands (now abolished), state-of-the-art fibre optic cables, or offering intrinsically uneconomical ferry routes. Despite the optimistic picture of improved transport painted above, it's a constant battle to maintain links with the mainland; Olympic Airways and its successor Olympic Air steadily reduced flight frequencies to most islands, with competitors not taking up the slack. Shipping companies also cherry-pick the most profitable routes to

(and to a lesser extent Thessaloníki, Pátra and Vólos). On a smaller scale, this proves true within large islands too – the four major coastal towns of Crete have done a good job of emptying the villages of their hinterlands in recent decades.

The main three reasons for leaving can be summarised as employment opportunities (severely reduced outside of the tourist season), health care and educational facilities. With some sterling exceptions, state hospitals on the islands leave much to be desired – for instance, if they can manage it, Corfiots shun

A café frequented by the locals of Plomári, Lésvos's second town.

the largest islands, grudgingly providing often irrational schedules (see page 312) to other destinations while trousering large subsidies for the privilege. Eastern border islands like Sámos or Lésvos once flourished as transshipment points within the Ottoman Empire, but in more recent times indeed languish literally and figuratively at the end of the line, a status only likely to be relieved in the improbable event that Turkey joins the EU.

But this logistical summary can only hint at the everyday feeling of being marooned in the Aegean, so pleasant to short-term visitors but evidently irksome to islanders who have found it increasingly difficult to resist the black-hole-like gravitational pull of Athens

their own, brand-new but understaffed, hospital in favour of the vastly superior teaching hospital attached to Ioánnina University on the mainland. Before the advent of helipads suitable for medical evacuations on the smaller islands, those taken suddenly, severely ill were as good as doomed.

There are decent universities on Crete (Réthymno and Iráklio), Corfu and the east Aegean, where the University of the Aegean has its faculties deliberately scattered over Lésvos, Híos, Sámos, Léros and Rhodes to spread employment opportunities and inject life into communities during winter. But again they're competing with the higher-learning colossi of Athens, Thessaloníki, Pátra, Ioánnina and

On the larger forested islands, wildfires remain a constant fear – and temptation to unscrupulous developers and their hired arsonists.

Vólos. Most mainland-bred doctors and public-school teachers consider island positions a short-term, hardship posting (paid extra as such) away from the bright lights – even if there are those conscientious and/or eccentric exceptions, repeatedly signing up to staff a

Compare and contrast the islands by hopping from one to the other.

clinic on a *vrahonisída* (rocky outcrop). As for bright, ambitious islanders who have worked and studied abroad or on the mainland, they rarely return unless forced to by economic or family circumstances.

Left-leaning politics

In national politics, on average the islands are slightly left of centre (in the case of Lésvos, Ikaría, Crete and some of the Ionians, communist or nearly so), with somewhat less support for neo-fascist Golden Dawn than elsewhere. Besides his native Crete, Venizelos received staunch initial support from all the northeast Aegean plus Corfu, this political

affiliation still reverberating four generations on. The Cyclades and Dodecanese, as permanent net beneficiaries for every sort of subsidised programme, in the past generally plumped for PASOK as the party most likely to provide them, though in 2012 ND was the top finisher there. But despite their illustrious contributions to Greek leadership and territorial aggrandisement, today's islands are unlikely ever to swing a close election – these are typically decided in suburban precincts of Athens or Thessaloníki – and their relative (un)importance was aptly symbolised by the late 2007 subsuming of the Ministry of the Aegean into that of the Mercantile Marine, prior to two more mergers and downgradings in 2009–10. Even during the late 2008/early 2009 youth rioting, which convulsed Athens following the shooting of an unarmed 15-year-old boy by an Athens policeman, barely a ripple registered in most island towns other than some anti-establishment graffiti.

Coming together over conservation

One concern that most islands do share with the mainland – in fact to an enhanced degree owing to fragile ecosystems – is conservation and development policy. Limited water supplies are constantly outstripped, especially on the smaller islands, to such a degree that the tanker-boat is a routine sight in summer. Despite the economic downturn, purpose-built villa projects pitched at both Greeks and foreigners proliferate, the worst-planned ones amounting to visual pollution as well as putting pressure on water resources.

The future of the islands is, much as some Greeks might resent it, bound up with foreigners. Ignoring for the moment landed refugees (see page 54), settled immigrants – for the most part Albanians – make up an increasing proportion of the workforce, especially in the building trades (they also outnumber the native-born population in some neighbourhoods). Yet since the millennium direct, non-charter, nine-months-of-the-year air links between Northern Europe and Corfu, Iráklio and Rhodes – with more destinations likely to appear – attest to the burgeoning numbers of expats and holiday-home owners who also help keep local economies going.

Horse carrying a heavy load on Hydra, where cars are banned.

RELIGIOUS FESTIVALS

Greek religious festivals – and there are many – celebrate saints' days and other events in the religious calendar with devotion and high spirits.

Greek island life is punctuated year-round by saints' days and religious festivals, or *panigýria*. As there are about 150 major saints in the Orthodox calendar, there's an excuse for a party most weeks of the year.

Easter is the most important festival, seven weeks after the pre-Lenten carnival. Colourful and noisy, traditional services mark the Resurrection, from humble chapels to sumptuous monasteries.

During *Megáli Evdomáda* (Holy Week), churches are festooned in purple velvet ribbons. On Maundy Thursday, Pátmos monks re-enact Christ's washing of his disciples' feet prior to Gethsemane. On Good Friday an *Epitáfios* (Bier of Christ) is decorated by women in each parish and paraded solemnly through the streets at dusk. In some islands an effigy of Judas is filled with fireworks and burnt, on Friday or Saturday.

On Easter Saturday, before the 9am Próti Anástasi service, church decoration changes to red and white ribbons. At midnight all is plunged in darkness as the priest lights the first candle from the holy flame representing the light of the world, and intones: "*Hristós anésti*" (Christ has risen) as the flame is transmitted to the entire congregation to light their candles. The moment is marked by deafening fireworks and more – on Kálymnos they throw dynamite from the cliffs, on Híos rival parishes rocket each other's steeples. Back home, everyone plays a form of conkers with eggs dyed red on Maundy Thursday, then breaks the Lenten fast with *magirítsa* soup made from lamb's offal, lemon and rice.

On Easter Sunday a lamb or kid is barbecued outdoors, with the usual music and dancing.

Candles burning bright in the beautiful 6th-century Ekatondapylianí church (Our Lady of Hundred Doors) on Páros.

In the early hours of Easter Sunday after the midnight service, churchgoers, here on Aegina, head home in candlelit processions.

Icons are paraded during the celebrations for Lambrí Tríti (Easter Tuesday) in Olymbos, the remote mountain village on Kárpathos, in the Southern Dodecanese.

On Skýros, performers adorned with pelts, kidskin masks and loops of livestock bells perform their annual 'goat dance'.

CELEBRATING ALL YEAR ROUND

Greeks mix piety and pleasure with gusto for all their festivals, from the most important to the smallest fair. The biggest religious event after Easter, the Dormition of the Virgin *(Kímisis tis Panagías)* on 15 August, draws Greeks home from across the globe. After a liturgy on 14 August evening, the icon of the Virgin is paraded – often with brass bands playing funeral dirges – prior to a communal feast which can last for days. Celebrations are especially spectacular in Ólymbos, Kárpathos, with dazzling costumes, special dances and traditional songs.

Seasonal festivals on the islands honour everything from sponges to sardines to snakes, and national holidays like *Óhi* ("No") Day (28 October) have patriotic parades marking Greece's reply to Mussolini's surrender ultimatum.

Celebrations usually occur the night before the actual feast day; everyone in the community attends, from babies to elders. The main liturgy is on the day, at churches hung with pennants and decked in cut foliage.

Hard-boiled eggs, dyed red to symbolise the blood of Christ, are cracked in a conkers-like game at Easter.

Resplendent in their ceremonial garb, Greek Orthodox priests on Pátmos come together for the Easter ceremony.

Militínia, Cycladic Easter cakes with goat's cheese filling.

Waiting for custom in Parikiá, Páros.

PEOPLE AND IDENTITIES

An attachment to the ancestral village, awareness of
seasonal and diurnal rhythms dictated by climate,
and an assumed equivalence between Orthodoxy and
Greekness typify the character of islanders.

Roughly 10 percent of Greece's population resides in the islands, nearly half in towns of over 5,000 inhabitants – which means that the stereotypical rural idyll, even (or especially) in the remotest spots, is fading fast.

Historically, Greeks rarely moved far from their *patrída*, or home province. But the mid-20th century saw a sort of seasonal transhumance established between one's native village and the big city, usually Athens, accordingly nicknamed *To Megálo Horió* (The Big Village). If the island in question is close enough to the town migrated to, weekend visits are feasible; otherwise, the *patrikó spíti* (ancestral family home) may only be occupied in high summer, typically from mid-July until the new school term around 11 September. On arrival, dead bugs and dust are swept out, paint brushes and awnings deployed, repairs commissioned, barbecues lit, and positions taken on plastic terrace chairs, all with remarkable speed. Sadly, since 2009 the daunting costs of round-trip ferry transport for a car and four or five persons means that many island houses lie permanently vacant.

Work and leisure

Until spiralling debt and expenses plus the current economic crisis dictated more nose-to-the-grindstone attitudes, most Greeks reckoned that they worked to live, not the other way around. Even in winter, when there is less need for a siesta, the midday *mikró ýpno* time is still sacred, to be spent over a long lunch with family, friends or business associates. The summer climate, meanwhile, dictates that people who work outdoors, in agriculture or the building trade, begin a single shift just after dawn and knock off by 3pm.

Nationwide and regional chains may be spreading rapidly – specifically supermarkets,

Taking refreshment at Iráklio's market, Crete.

homewares, office furniture, computers and electronics – but many island businesses are still small, family-owned and staffed. This helps disguise unemployment as underemployment, and permits various fiddles concerning pension contributions.

Sunday remains very much a day of rest, and at weekends warm weather prompts a mass exodus towards the beaches, which often have lively "all-day" bars complete with loud music. Despite recent laws dictating that nightspots should close by 2am, at weekends at any rate this is widely winked at: nights in island towns are long and loud, though with less motorcycle traffic than before owing to fuel costs, and with yet more noise (from car horns especially) when a favoured athletic team, or political faction, wins a contest. Earlier, at dusk, the local military band might march down the quay playing tunes not necessarily martial, and not necessarily in tune either, prior to lowering the flag.

Even in these pinched times, every sizeable island makes an effort to organise some sort of summer festival. This will include folk dancing, theatre and above all concerts with big-name stars, pitched as much at seasonally returned islanders as at foreigners (or more so). But the most authentic entertainments arguably won't be experienced at such organised events, but at

often happens in Anglo-Saxon countries. Very early on, children are inculcated into the routine of late nights out at the taverna, either as toddlers asleep in a pram parked by the chairs, or as older kids playing tag around the tables. They are spoken to – and expected to converse up to their abilities – as adults, which accounts in part for the tremendous (over-)confidence of kids and teenagers. Not too many shrinking violets here: in an often rough-and-tumble culture like that of Greece, assertiveness is a survival skill.

Individual families tend to be small. Like Spain and Italy, Greece has negative native

Taking a wander in Skiáthos Town.

tavernas. These can serve as informal showcases for Greek music and lyrics, the latter stemming from a rich mid-20th century tradition in poetry which spawned two Nobel laureates, Odysseas Elytis and George Seferis. A small group of men (or women), maybe a bit tipsy, will interpret well-loved songs accompanied by unamplified *bouzoúki*, guitar and accordion: the intimate *ta tragoúdia tis paréas* (songs with one's oldest friends).

Children, families, gender roles

Children are adored – arguably spoilt, especially boys – and expected to behave like children; yet at the same time they are not allowed to determine adults' schedules, or kept segregated, as so

population growth, with a birth rate well below replacement level at roughly 1.4 kids per couple. Much of this is a reaction to impoverished times before the 1960s when four or five siblings growing up in a single room was the norm. Now it's considered shameful to have more offspring than you can properly educate

Progonoplixía (ancestor fixation), crediting all and everything to the ancient Greeks – neatly embodied by dad Gus in My Big Fat Greek Wedding – is the flip side to xenomanía, a fetishisation of foreign consumer goods, music and foodstuffs.

and set up with a house of their own (the D-word, "dowry", is used circumspectly since the practice of demanding it per se was outlawed in the 1980s). Abortion is widely resorted to, with surprisingly little comment from the Orthodox Church.

Nipagogía (crèches) certainly exist, a worthwhile legacy of the first PASOK government, but one suspects they are used to full capacity only in the biggest towns and cities and by the most harassed of working parents. Elsewhere, grandmothers are perennially available childminders, a role assumed with relish. Through-

Food symbolism – and consequences

Food and eating is not just a pretext for sociability, or proof of maternal virtue, but is highly symbolic and integral to a sense of identity. *Kólyva* (food for the dead, made up of varying proportions of grain, breadcrumbs, nuts, pomegranate seeds and raisins), for instance, forms an essential part of periodic memorial services for the departed, symbolically keeping the deceased linked to the living. Food-related terms are used as diagnostic, affectionate or insulting tags: an older relative will scoop up an adorable infant

Triangles of sticky baklavá are boxed up for a customer at this Ionian delicatessen in Levkáda Town.

out the day there will be to-ing and fro-ing with foodstuffs and/or child in hand between the houses of the various generations.

The legal status of women was significantly upgraded by PASOK reforms, and many women (like former mayor of Athens, then foreign minister Dóra Bakogiànni and Communist Party head Aléka Paparíga) are now prominent in public life. Most, however, are still caught up in the bind of both having to work – if only in a family business – and fulfil traditional mother and wife roles. That said, men's attitudes have changed since the relatively recent, macho 1970s: happily seen in public pushing a pram or carrying children, they've even been rumoured to change a nappy or two.

and exclaim *"Ná sé fáo!"* ("Good enough to eat!"); sleek, spoilt children (especially male), presumably overfed from infancy in the belief that a plump toddler is a healthy one, are dubbed *voutyrópeda* ("butter-kids"); coddled, 20-something offspring of either gender, still taking their laundry to be done at the parental home (actually they will probably still be living there until marriage or a job in another town), are deemed *mamóthrefti* ("mother-fed"). Since their attempted 1940 invasion, Italians are *makaronádes* ("macaroni-eaters" – though the Greeks eat just as much pasta), while Asia Minor refugees were long derided as *giaourtovaptisméni* ("yoghurt-baptised", after that Anatolian staple little known in Greece before the 1920s).

You'll notice that many people are, to put it diplomatically, plump. Greece perennially jostles in EU statistics with Malta and the UK for the crown of Most Overweight Population. This is a consequence, in part, to uncomfortably close memories of hunger, especially during World War II and the Civil War, as well as a diet enjoining the consumption of bread *and* potatoes/rice/pasta *and* oil with every meal.

Mortified by this ranking (especially in the run-up to hosting the 2004 Olympics), the islands are now well sown with gyms and rather more dubious slimming salons, while increasing

> Bread is fraught with symbolism – chunks of leavened loaves comprise the andídoron, blessed and distributed to church congregations, while to refuse it at a taverna or shared table is considered deviant at best.

In 1944, the numerous Jewish communities of the islands were wiped out with the exception of those on Zákynthos, though they elected to depart en masse for Israel after the war and the 1953 earthquake. Refugees from Asia Minor

Baptismal font at Ekatonpylianí Church, Páros.

numbers of Lycra-clad cyclists and joggers sporting MP3 players brave the hazardous road verges.

Orthodoxy, Hellenism and minorities

Before the recent influx of immigrants (see pages 54), Greece, the islands included, was remarkably homogeneous, not to say parochial, in being Greek Orthodox in religious affiliation. About the only exceptions were a significant community of Armenians in Iráklio, Crete – who have been there since they accompanied Nikiphoros Phokas on his reconquest of the island from the Arabs in AD 961 – the Catholics of the Cyclades (concentrated in Sýros and Tínos), and the Maltese-descended Catholics of Corfu.

were far less important than on the mainland – in the Ionian islands their settlement was actively resisted – although these communities are noticeable on Thásos, Límnos, Lésvos, Híos, Sámos and especially Crete, where most north-coast towns had Muslim populations before 1923.

Even for those who rarely set foot in a church, "Orthodox" is considered synonymous with "Greek"; there seems little place in the national discourse for Jews, Catholics and Protestant sects such as Jehovah's Witnesses, let alone Muslims. The 50,000 native Catholics (plus about 150,000 foreign resident ones) are particularly vociferous on the legal disadvantages of being a *xénon dógma* or foreign creed, unrecognised compared to the established Church.

Island communities are largely Greek Orthodox.

New Immigrants

With its frontier islands doubling as a gateway to Europe, Greece is struggling to control the mounting tide of illegal immigration.

An August evening on tiny Agathonísi, remotest of the Dodecanese, and the quay hosts 150 people preparing to bed down rough for the night: the last three days' 'harvest' of illegal immigrants, landed

An illegal immigrant and his child arrive on Crete following rescue by the Greek coastguard.

here after a clandestine sea-crossing from Turkey, guarded by just two gendarmes. Mostly men but also some women and children, they are not apt to cause trouble – which explains the few guards – for they have so far got what they want: entry into Europe.

The crowd is largely from Iraq, Syria, Afghanistan and Pakistan, but some sub-Saharan and north Africans can also be seen. The migrants don't talk much to strangers, except to ask to change US dollars for euros, or enquire where they can buy a phone card to call relatives back home. Despite appearances, they are rarely completely destitute – money is usually concealed from the rapacious people-smugglers who demand thousands to get each individual to, through, and out of Turkey.

Every summer, the *akritiká nisiá* (frontier islands) off the Turkish coast act as an irresistible magnet for illegal immigration until winter storms halt the passage. Greece has demanded that Turkey stem the flow, and accept for deportation illegal immigrants proved to have come via Turkey. But given the low pay of most Turkish port officials, bribes from captains for turning a blind eye to departing boats have the desired effect – when the local police aren't themselves moonlighting as smugglers. Despite a June 2012 re-admission protocol signed between the EU and Turkey to repatriate them, Turkey typically accepts barely 10 percent of the annual Greek applications to return illegal migrants.

Survival of the fittest

Walking across Agathonísi, you'll spot discarded life-vests and synthetic drip-dry clothing inappropriate to summer conditions, plus the occasional deflated rubber raft on the shore: unscrupulous captains, wary of being detained by the Greek coastguard, dump their human cargo in international or Greek waters, well short of Agathonísi, and race back to Turkey. An alternative is launching the migrants in overloaded rafts with just a compass and a baulky engine, leaving West Africans who know something of the sea in charge. Refugees have become aware of these tactics, and are prepared to paddle or swim for land if close enough, or else wait to be fished out of the Aegean by the Greeks as required by law. Drownings occur regularly even in good weather, but it's amazing that there aren't more, considering that the coastguard is as likely to swamp the rafts or drive them back into Turkish waters. What you won't find amongst the debris, or on the migrants themselves, are any ID, SIM cards, clothing labels or bus tickets that would prove where they're from or where they have passed through – making it impossible for Greek authorities to repatriate them legally, and obliging them (by the terms of the Dublin Regulations) to prevent them escaping to other EU states.

The next afternoon the local ferryboat *Nísos Kálymnos* departs with all 150 refugees sitting quietly at the back of the upper sun-deck, cordoned off from holiday-makers by marine rope. On arrival at Pátmos, they're lodged temporarily at the police station until the midnight mainline ferry arrives from Rhodes to take them away to Athens and further processing. Many locals resent even this brief stopover – *"Dióhni ton tourismó"* ("It drives out tourism"), they say – on their smart island much more used to cruise-ship passengers than ragged refugees.

"Processing" means shelter, meals and medical examinations for just three days at a score of receiving centres scattered across Greece – most established against strenuous local opposition – after which migrants are served with a deportation order giving them a month to leave the country. Most disappear into the huge refugee underground, ripe for the attentions of Golden Dawn (read on). Others apply for political asylum, giving them six to 24 months' residence while their case is reviewed. Less than 1 percent are accepted; Greece views asylum-seeking as economic migration by the back door.

The EU's highest immigrant ratio

Versus a native population of 10.4 million, Greece has around 1.4 million immigrants – only about 600,000 of them legalised through various amnesties between 1998 and 2005. This is the highest ratio in the EU, in what previously had been a monochrome culture; unsurprisingly immigrants have become a major social and political issue.

Most established and numerous are the nearly 1 million Albanians, who arrived mostly in the early 1990s; but there are also Bengalis, Afghans, Pakistanis, Chinese, Somalis, Lebanese, Iranians, Syrians, Egyptians, Filipinos, Iraqis, West Africans and nationals of various non-EU Central European states (these are the largest groups).

The ongoing economic crisis, plus illegal immigration, has fuelled the rise since 2011 of Golden Dawn (Hrysí Avgí), the most violent and brazen of Europe's neo-Nazi parties, with significant police toleration and even membership. Their platform can be summarised by their graffito "Work for Greeks only." Despite being severely cracked down on in 2013 following the murder of a Greek public figure, vigilante actions against both legal and illegal immigrants, and breaches of parliamentary decorum, Golden Dawn might still finish in third place were elections held now. They have flourished in a society where racist or discriminatory attitudes and laws were long common. In particular, non-EU immigrants hoping to be self-employed must prove investment of 60,000 euros, no matter how small the business – a ludicrous figure. Thus many refugees never escape being roving pedlars of fake designer bags, sunglasses and pirate DVDs. As one pro-immigrant non-governmental organisation's leaflet ironically

put it, "Our grandparents refugees, our parents emigrants, and we – xenophobes and racists?"

There were about 57,000 recorded illegal migrants in 2012, about the same as in 2011 and 2010, perhaps a quarter of these entering via the border islands. In 2009 Greece received a 13.7 million euro grant from the EU to secure its frontiers, including 3.2 million euros to beef up the coastguard, but little of this helped upgrade reception facilities – many police thought that this would just attract more migrants, though those arriving on Sámos are lodged in a designated holding centre, opened in 2008 at the behest of the UNHCR, which had condemned as

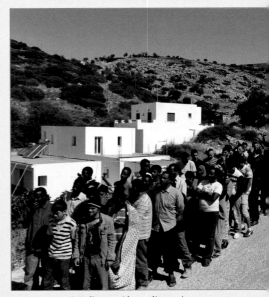

Immigrants wait in line outside a police station on Agathonísi in May 2009.

inhumane the prior detention facility in an old officers' club. The sun-baked, hillside camp, built on a former army firing range and dubbed "Guantánamo" locally, often exceeds its capacity of 600.

Overall, the official response to the illegal immigrants has been substandard, in breach of various UN and EU regulations. Given the local crisis, the Greek construction and agricultural industries no longer need cheap undocumented labour, one result of which has been, near the docks of Pátra and Igoumenítsa, periodic impromptu camps of immigrants hoping to stow away on boats to Italy. "Greece is not really Europe," many say, their sights set firmly on Italy, Spain, Sweden or England, where they often already have relatives in residence.

RELIGION

The degree of religious faith in the countryside, where many beliefs and acts of devotion are little changed since before the advent of Christianity, contrasts sharply with opinions on the all-too-human Church itself.

The Orthodox Church still exerts a noticeable influence over contemporary Greek life, especially on the smaller islands, and even the most worldly, sceptical families will have religious services for the critical rites of marriage, baptism and funerals. Yet there's a marked disconnect between private devotion and beliefs (some little changed since pagan times), and public disparagement of the Church, which has suffered a sharp loss in prestige since the 1960s.

Historical background

In 1833, the Church in newly independent Greece was detached from the Constantinople Patriarchate and made autocephalous, but controlled by the Ministry of Education and Religion, which paid the salaries of priests and bishops (both ministry and this civil-servant status endure). As Greece expanded, territories incorporated after 1912 remained subject to the Ecumenical Patriarchate, which at times produced friction with the Athenian archbishop. Although the Church ran many charitable programmes for refugees and war orphans during the mid-20th century, its reputation suffered badly under the junta, which most clerics endorsed (with a few honourable exceptions). After the 1974 restoration of democracy, the Church was downgraded from state institution to just Greece's established religion; during the first PASOK term, civil marriage was legalised.

Despite notional subordination to a secular ministry, however, no government ever managed to bring Orthodox institutions to heel. The most serious attempt, during 1987–8, saw incumbent Education/Religion Minister Andonis Tritsis make a stab at thorough reforms, specifically urging lay participation in elections for all Church offices and the expropriation of

Colouring the everyday – devotional architecture in Firá, Santoríni.

surplus ecclesiastical property. When thwarted by Andreas Papandreou himself, Tritsis resigned on principle – from the party as well – and was soon elected Mayor of Athens as an independent.

The next kerfuffle occurred in 2002 when, in accordance with EU directives, the government proposed to omit religious affiliation from identity cards. Led by combative, controversial Archbishop of Athens and All Greece, Khristodoulos, the faithful unavailingly marched in the streets against this godless innovation; a compromise bill to make declaration of creed optional foundered.

But this was as nothing compared to the consecutive scandals which erupted during 2004 and 2005, so lurid you couldn't make them up:

monasteries as hotbeds of homosexual intrigue; embezzlement by the Archbishop of Attica (jailed for six years and defrocked); smuggling of rare icons; bribing of judges (one of whom absconded). Greek media comics like Lakis Lazopoulos and Tzimis Panousis mercilessly satirised the clerical foibles – all of which made the attempted prosecution by a Church deacon (with Khristodoulos' connivance) of veteran musicologist and folk musician Domna Samiou, for singing bawdy carnival songs on state TV, that much more pathetic a diversion.

Still rumbling on are scandals emanating from two Mount Áthos monasteries: Esfigménou's refusal to recognise the current patriarch and a resultant lengthy campaign by other Athonite monks and the Greek state to eject its tenants, and a rigged real-estate swap between Vatopedíou and the government, greatly to the latter's detriment, as well as undermining of the Cypriot banking system, with Vatopedíou's abbot briefly jailed for fraud and embezzlement. Some might say parishioners are getting poor value from their tax-paid clerics. Amidst the ongoing economic crisis, the first serious murmurings against the Church's tax-exempt status are finally being heard.

A bedrock of belief

The old adage that organised religion need not have much to do with spirituality or belief is amply borne out by Greek everyday life, especially in rural areas. In the countryside, you will notice hillside chapels and roadside shrines (*proskynitária*), built in fulfilment of a vow of thanks (for supernatural assistance) to the patron saint. Inside are more votive offerings: the *támmata*, flat metal or 3D wax images representing the nature of the favour granted, such as a healed body part or a longed-for baby.

Saints are considered intercessors for the faithful: real, hovering personages in contrast with the remote deity. Icons, which form the core of Orthodox worship, are not just two-dimensional images but conduits to the "other side" which the saint inhabits. They are emblems of the parish, village or island, paraded with honour on feast days to bestow blessings and receive homage in return. The unseen world has both benevolent and menacing aspects: saints are occasionally still glimpsed in their chapels by the pure of heart, while sermons advise the wearing of crucifixes around the neck, considered vulnerable to demonic attack.

Though birthday parties for children are on the increase, traditionally Greeks only marked *giortés* (saints' name days), which celebrate Orthodox baptismal names. Even people named for pagan or mythological personalities are given a "Christian"

> *Priests have long been the focus of a superstition at odds with their social status. Meeting one on the street was supposed to be exceedingly unlucky; many men dispelled the jinx by discreetly touching their testicles.*

Monastery of the Panagía, Hydra.

moniker, and a baby is usually christened after one of its four grandparents. Someone will say "*Giortázo símera*" (I'm celebrating today) – which in the case of a popular name like Ioannis or Eleni can mean a quarter of the village holding open house for friends to drop by – to which the proper response is "*Hrónia pollá*" (Many years, or in other words, many happy returns).

Devotional fasting may be on the wane in towns, but it is still prevalent in rural areas, especially during the days of "Great Lent" (before Easter), the first two weeks of August, and "Little Lent" (the time before Christmas). A whole range of foodstuffs is forbidden then, which has had a marked effect on Greek cuisine (see page 69).

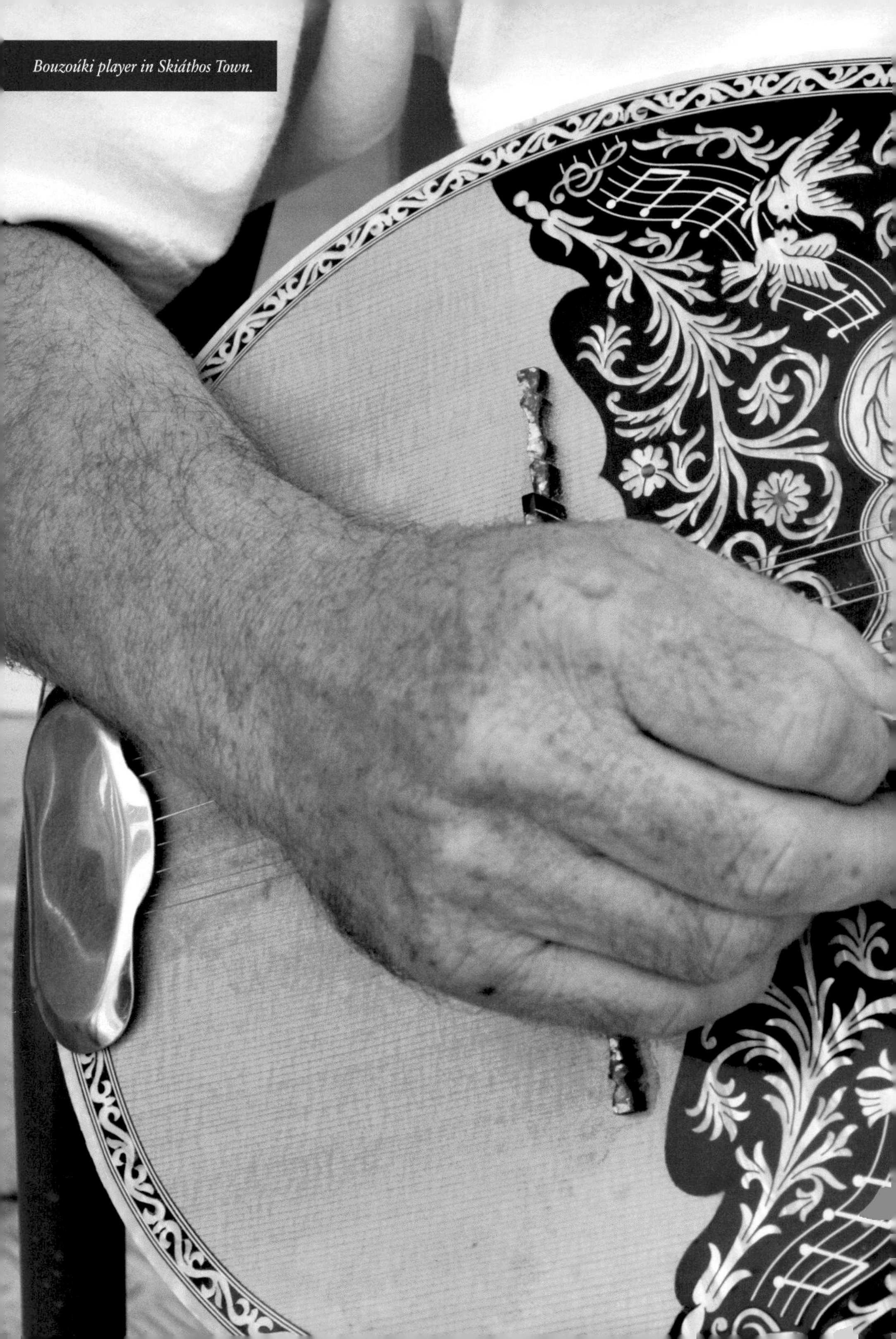

Bouzoúki player in Skiáthos Town.

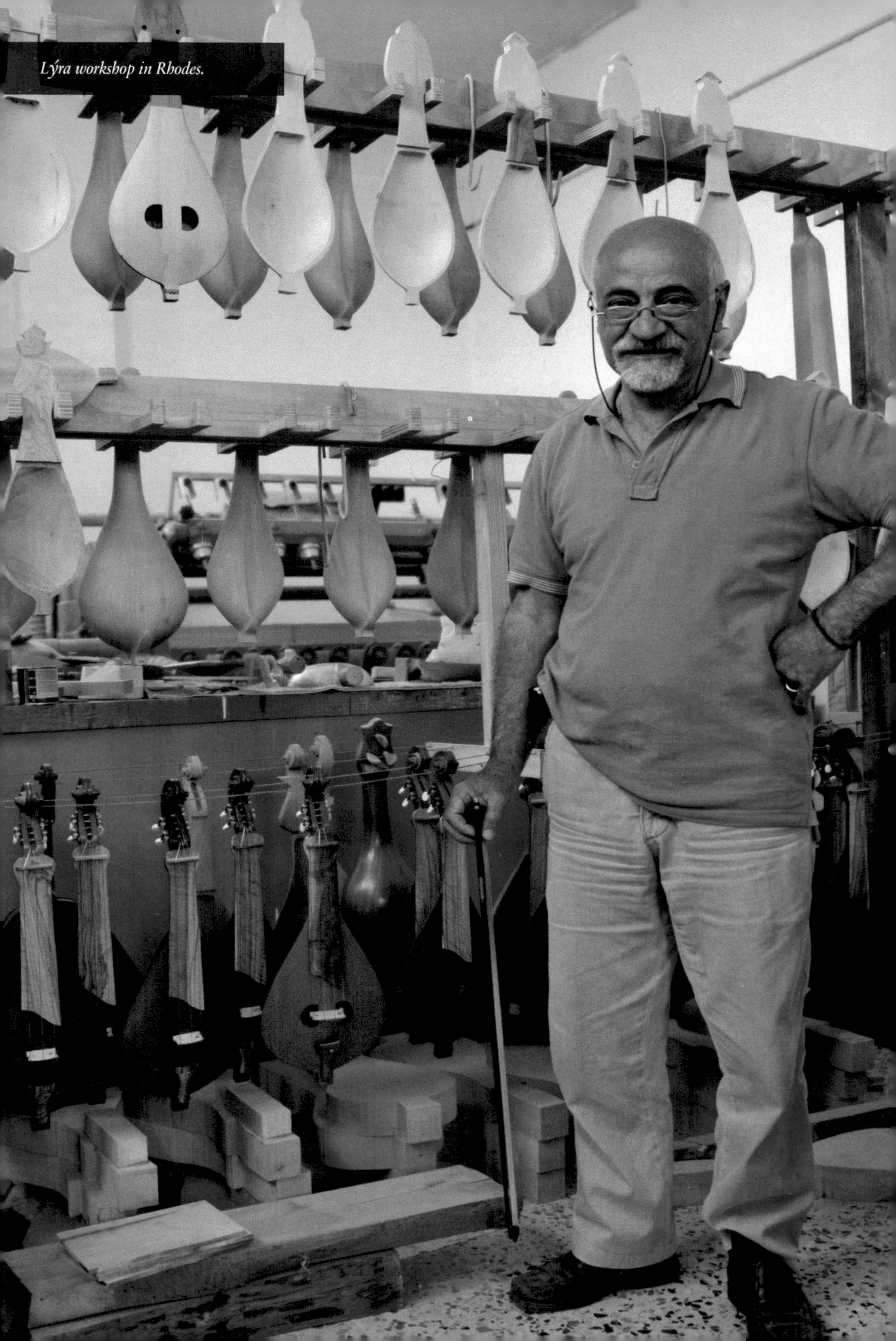
Lýra workshop in Rhodes.

DEBUNKING THE BOUZOÚKI

Like the islands themselves, Greek music has been influenced by many neighbouring cultures, which gives it a richness and complexity far beyond the confines of stereotypical *bouzoúki* instrumentals.

The visitor is ambling along some photo-genic island harbour at sunset, looking forwards to a meal of grilled octopus washed down with a little *oúzo*. What better way to complete the image than with some background music on the *bouzoúki*? After all, isn't *bouzoúki* music the quintessence of all things Greek?

Well, yes and no. Those familiar soundtracks for Manos Hatzidakis's *Never on Sunday* and Mikis Theodorákis's *Zorba the Greek*, sold ad nau-seam in instrumental cover versions from resort souvenir stalls, have effectively closed foreign minds to anything else of value in Greek music.

What the big record companies push on inex-perienced foreigners, in catalogue sections cyni-cally labelled "*Touristiká*", is merely the tip of the iceberg, a snapshot of a brief period in the early 1960s which coincided with Greece's emergence as a mass-tourism destination. While the origi-nal compositions, arrangements and recordings skilfully distilled elements of Greek music into a cinema-friendly form, the offcut remixes adul-terated for foreign tastes – with titles like *Disco Bouzouki My Love* (sic) – are another matter.

Diverse influences

Greece deserves the cliché image of a musical crossroads and collecting-basket, with a range of diverse influences inside a deceptively small country; even a small selection of CDs will give some idea of Greece's rich musical tradi-tions. The *bouzoúki* stereotype has obscured the Aegean music hidden away behind *sky-ládika* (roadhouse-type venues) with their heavy amplification. Acoustic *nisiótika* or island music has an altogether cleaner, gentler sound, and against the odds has mounted a modest come-back since the 1980s. In the Cyclades especially

Folk musicians of times gone by.

(of all Greek territories the least affected by the invaders – see page 30), it's very much *sui generis*, displaying only some Italian influence.

Rhythms, often in unconventional time signatures, are lilting and hypnotic; melodies, traditionally executed on violin, bagpipes and *laoúto*, the fretted folk lute, are exquisite. The lyrics, tokens of a more innocent time, grap-ple with eternal island concerns – the sea that claimed a loved one, the mother who wonders if her sons will ever return from exile, fishing or farming days interrupted by the festival of a beloved saint – but occasionally verge on the poetically surreal.

Various members of the Náxos-born Koni-topoulos clan are the ones you're most likely to hear, but a younger performer with frankly better musicanship and new original compositions is fiddler Nikos Ikonomidis, a native of Skhinoússa, near Amorgós. Particularly prized are archival recordings of Anna and Emilia

> *Some modes do not start with do–re–mi (C–D–E), like the Western major scale, but do–do sharp–mi (C–C#–E). Violins on the islands are still sometimes tuned à la Toúrka, D-A-D-G, rather than the standard tuning with E on top.*

Beautifully crafted bouzoúkis for sale.

Hatzidaki, a mother-daughter team from the Dodecanese, and singing sisters from Kós, Anna Karabesini and Efi Sarri. On Crete, performers to look out for include Vasilis Skoulas, the idiosyncratic Psarandonis, and (on historical recordings) Stelios Foustalieris. In the Ionian islands, the Italian heritage is evident in Neapolitan-style *kantádes*, sung in four-part harmony, and often accompanied by mandolin, violin and guitar tuned to Western scales.

Compositions and instrumentation (the *sandoúri* or hammer dulcimer, or brass bands) of Asia Minor enrich the repertoire of the northeast Aegean islands and the Dodecanese. Meanwhile, the long vocal introductions to Cretan songs bear traces of North African and Arab music.

Structure and social context

Most traditional Greek music is either pentatonic (five notes in the scale) or based on a modal system used in musics of the Middle East. The *októehos* system at the basis of Byzantine ecclesiastical chant, however, was not (as many nationalists assert) descended from ancient Greek music, but from the modes of Jewish or secular melodies from ancient Palestine; its greatest composer was 5th-century Syria's Romanos O Melodos.

Greece's lyrics were never divorced from music as in the West, where for example opera librettos were commissioned separately. Since antiquity both have been inseparable, and in recent decades musical settings of poetry – or high-quality, purpose-written lyrics – have constituted some of Greece's most powerful music. Much-esteemed lyricists of poetic calibre include Kostas Virvos, Manolis Rasoulis, Nikos Gatsos and Manos Eleftheriou. The enthusiastic Greek website www.stixoi.info contains tens of thousands of song lyrics, including translations into foreign languages. Instrumental music remains a relative rarity, while unaccompanied voice still features in women's laments, *tis távlas* (table songs), *tis strátas* (road songs) and epics such as the medieval Cretan *Erotókritos*.

Like all folk music, *nisiótika* were not originally conceived as entertainment but were integral to religious festivals, weddings, funerals or work. Unfortunately, on the more touristed islands it's become almost impossible to hear genuine acoustic music – count yourself lucky if you're invited to a soirée with traditional instrumentation.

Greek rhythms, American blues?

Unlike Western metres in units or multiples of two, three or four beats, the Greeks seem to have matched their musical rhythms to the cadences of their poetry since the age of the Homeric hexameter; catchy 5/8, 7/8, 9/8 and even 11/8 time signatures are common in Greek traditional music. The composer Mimis Plessas (1924–), a jazzman also responsible for numerous Greek movie soundtracks, remembers a 1953 jam session with American jazz trumpeter Dizzy Gillespie. Plessas had no trouble fingering a nimble 7/8 rhythm on the piano – and promptly lost Dizzy. "I can't do it, something's missing," said the great jazzman. Less convincingly, Plessas claimed: "Imagine the field cry of the black man transported to Greece – that's what Greek music is."

Plessas was not the first to have simplistically found similarities between the American blues and Greek song – especially *rebétika*, the genre foreigners are most likely to gravitate towards. Originally, this was the semi-clandestine music of a particular segment of the Anatolian refugee population which flooded into Athens, Piraeus and Thessaloníki after the disastrous 1919–22 Greco-Turkish War, and the compulsory exchange of religious minorities between the two nations.

Hardcore urban *rebétika* superficially resembles the blues in origins and preoccupations – poverty and social exclusion, disease, the allure of drugs and idleness, faithless women, thwarted love – and its practitioners (the *rebétes*) and lyrics were persecuted and censored during the 1930s. Westernising Greeks despised, and still despise, its "oriental" roots, but one can safely say that *rebétika* existed in some form around the east Aegean coast and the Black Sea for decades before that. By the 1950s, however, *rebétika* became "domesticated" and incorporated into mainstream Greek music. In 1953 Manólis Hiótis marked the demise of the original rebetic style by adding a fourth string to the *bouzoúki*, allowing it to be tuned tonally rather than modally – thus spawning *laïká* and *elafrolaïká*, the urban "popular" styles heard on the radio countrywide.

This was just one aspect of the ongoing postwar Westernisation of Greece, with the local musical scene arrayed in two opposing camps: adherents of traditionally derived styles versus those who forsook roots music for imported jazz/cabaret, symphonic and rock models.

The state of the art

Then-Communist Theodorákis, after his 1964 *Zorba* outing, shunned Byzantine/rebetic/traditional sources completely in favour of Western quasi-symphonic works and film music. Generally, the political Left historically condemned apolitical, escapist styles such as *rebétika* and *laïkó*, attempting at one point to "raise mass consciousness" with recycled *andártika*, wartime resistance anthems.

> There is substantial overlap between *nisiótika* and *rebétika*: many composer-musicians hailed from the islands, including Markos Vamvakáris of Sýros and Giorgos Katsaros from Amorgós, with cross-pollination between the genres.

More thoughtful musicians attempted to bridge the high–low culture gap with hybrid styles: the *éntekno* or "artifice" music of Crete-born Yannis Markopoulos, where traditional instruments and themes were used within large-scale compositions of great emotive power; a succession of guitarist singer-songwriters, led by Dionysis Savvopoulos and Nikos Papazoglou, who challenged the supremacy of the ubiquitous *bouzoúki* with modern lyrics too, giving rise to Greek folk-rock; and revivalists such as Cretans Haïnides and Loudovikos ton Anogion, who countered rock-drum-kit-and-electrification of

A bouzoúki-playing busker in Athens.

live traditional performances with updated, rearranged standards and original compositions.

Rebétika enjoyed a revival after the fall of the junta, which had tried to ban it, although the fad – most pronounced among urban intellectuals – has long since waned. Re-issue recordings now mainly target a foreign audience, many first exposed to the genre by Stavros Xarhakos' and Nikos Gatsos' soundtrack to the 1983 film *Rebétiko*.

But "pure" *laïkó* and *nisiótika*, despite being looked down on by educated Greeks (especially overseas students), refuses to die. It's a perennial scenario in Greece, where a Westernised cultural elite keeps busy attempting unsuccessfully to banish "low-class" habits.

AEGEAN ARCHITECTURE

Traditional architecture and town planning on Aegean islands is a response both to the environment and local history between the 13th and 19th centuries; today Islanders much prefer the qualities of more modern homes.

The development of both architecture and town profiles across the Aegean was spurred by several factors. By the late 12th century, Byzantine power had declined considerably, and the Venetians took advantage of this to divert the Fourth Crusade to Constantinople in 1204, smashing the central authority which until then had ruled all the islands. The Cyclades and Sporades in particular were parcelled out to Venetian nobles and adventurers, while in the course of the following centuries the crusading Knights of St John and the Genoese established themselves in the Dodecanese and northeast Aegean respectively. After various attempts, the Venetian Republic acquired sovereignty of the Ionian islands in 1386, and the main towns that evolved on Zákynthos, Corfu and Kefaloniá conformed very much to the example of Venice itself, with high, tottering, louvre-shuttered townhouses as well as Baroque churches giving onto vast piazzas.

Ermoúpoli balconies, Sýros.

Anti-piracy measures

Piracy became rife in the Aegean, and most coastal settlements were abandoned in favour of inland or at least elevated towns known as the *hóra* ("the place"), from which hostile ships could be sighted from a distance and appropriate measures taken. Cycladic and Sporadic villages featured zigzagging lanes and cul-de-sacs, with the purpose not only of acting as wind baffles, but so as to confuse intruders, who (not knowing the maze-like street plan) could more easily be trapped and dispatched.

The ultimate anti-raider defence was the *kástro*, a usually rectangular compound with gated access, the backs of the contiguous

The doorways of kástra all faced inwards, with upper storey entrances reached by arpeggios of parallel staircases.

houses substituting for conventional curtain walls. Some, but not all, *kástra* are originally Venetian-planned and built; others are adapted from Byzantine or even ancient sites. The best examples, still inhabited, are located on Andíparos, Sífnos, Náxos, Folégandros and Síkinos. The *kástra* at Kímolos (which was founded by a Greek Orthodox trader under Ottoman rule) and Astypálea were effectively abandoned after World War II, while Skáros on Santoríni and Kástro on Skiáthos were both deserted by the mid-19th century, after the Barbary corsairs had been suppressed by the French in 1833.

The Dodecanese and northeast Aegean had no *kástra* per se – except arguably the mastic villages on Híos – but towns grew up at the base of proper Genoese or Knights' castles, or on Pátmos around a fortified monastery.

Materials, styles, structures

Construction of houses both humble and grand was drystone (without mortar), using were supported by intertwined *fíthes*, gnarled but extremely strong trunks of a local juniper species, covered with a perpendicular series of canes and finally a layer of *pateliá*, special earth tamped down with a roller.

> Rhodes Old Town is an instance of Western military engineering and grid planning based strongly on the ancient city, and doesn't really count as vernacular architecture.

Panagía tou Pýrgou church, a diminutive landmark on Skópelos.

local rock, though recycling ancient masonry was common, and plaster rendering the rule on village-centre dwellings. On small islands, walls were (and still are) whitewashed regularly for hygienic reasons, to impart texture with built-up coats, and to enhance heat reflectivity. Steps and walkways were also outlined in whitewash to aid night-time travel – invaluable before the era of streetlamps. Flat roofs served both for drying crops like figs or grapes, and to collect rainwater for cisterns; in the *kástra* they served a military purpose, as defenders could move rapidly on them from one threatened side of the settlement to another. Given a lack of deciduous hardwood, these flat roofs (and any upper floors)

Wooden balconies and railings are typical of many ports in the Cyclades and Dodecanese; during former times they were often made of *katráni*, a durable cedar imported from Asia Minor – now it is probably tropical hardwood. Ornate, wrought-iron fanlights and railings are a feature of many islands, particularly Kálymnos, Léros and the northeast Aegean.

Houses on the larger Dodecanese, and most of the northeast Aegean, tended to eschew whitewashing, opting either for bright colour (especially on Kálymnos), pointed bare masonry (Lésvos and Límnos) or painted lath-and-plaster upper storeys – notably on Sámos and Thásos – identical to that found across the mainland Balkans.

Building for all purposes

Multi-roomed houses around a courtyard emerged in the 19th century, replacing the one- or two-room modular houses typical of *kástra*; Cretan townhouses with courtyards date from the Venetian occupation. Neoclassical ornamentations and methods – including

> Churches often owed their existence to a private vow, and they remained in the same family for generations.

Windmill on Páros.

pitched roofs with canal- or pan-tiles, as well as the ironwork noted previously (see page 65) – became common after Greek independence.

Churches, many of them diminutive and incorporated seamlessly into the fabric of a village, were built in a similar style to secular buildings (though usually with vaulted roofs). Monasteries, especially isolated rural ones, had similar architecture but were always walled – both in accordance with Orthodox doctrine, in other words to mark them apart from "the world", and as a practical measure to deter piracy. Belfries and bell-walls, the star of many a postcard, are relatively recent, Western-influenced introductions: during Ottoman times there were restrictions on the ringing of

church bells lest they offend Muslim sensibilities, though this proved less true in homogeneously Christian islands like the Cyclades.

Certain communal constructions were vital to a largely self-sufficient rural economy: domed ovens suitable for bread and roast meat alike, windmills to process the summer grain harvest (when the *meltémi* wind was conveniently at its height) and watermills – found on Kéa, Andros, Skiáthos, Skýros, Náxos and Kýthnos, as well as islands with more obvious, strong streams like Sámos, Lésvos, Ikaría and Crete.

The benefits of whitewashing include heat reflectivity.

Some watermills have ended up outlasting windmills in terms of usage, working right up until the 1980s. Their profile, usually with a sluice preceding a staged descent tower, is unmistakable. Windmill construction and repair was a special trade, and hardwood tree trunks suitable for the main shaft had to be imported from mainland forests; walls might be over one metre (3ft) thick to support the tremendous stresses imparted through the masts.

Rectangular dovecotes, introduced by the Venetians as a feudal privilege, are restricted to Tínos (which has almost 1,200 of them), Ándros, Mýkonos and Sífnos. Stone-slab niches and vents in geometric designs adorn a leeward side of the structure.

Improved conditions within the Ottoman Empire from the late 18th century onwards fostered the growth of a Christian bourgeoisie, something evident in the opulent shipowners' mansions on Hydra and Spétses, plus others on a less grand scale at Límni, Evvia and on Andros. The same era saw the appearance of multi-storey, semi-fortified tower-mansions around Mytilíni (Lésvos), structures with few parallels on other islands, though plenty on the mainland.

The 19th-century industrial warehouses of the larger east Aegean islands like Lésvos, Híos and Sámos, typically devoted to the olive-milling,

– deemed cramped, dark and insanitary – are left to those nostalgic Athenians and foreigners foolish enough to purchase them for renovation. When locals deign to remain in an old house, they typically deface it with mass-produced aluminium windows and doors, and flanged, so-called *romaïká* tiles which arguably make many communities look like a southeast Asian slum when seen from above (unless the settlement has been declared *diatiritéo* – under a conservation order).

A stab at checking the spread of inappropriate styles and materials was made in 2001 when

The Aquarium – colonial Italian architecture on Rhodes.

leather-tanning or distilling trades, constitute a special case in both style – derived from similar structures in Asia Minor, just across the water – and size, with typically 80cm (2.5ft) thick walls rather than the 50cm (1.5ft) thickness almost universal for dwellings across the Aegean.

Modern adulterations

Sadly, none of the foregoing seems to interest many of today's islanders, especially those on the larger islands. Like most Greeks, their dream is of a modern rural villa or at least free-standing house amidst gardens or fields, with wraparound balconies, fireplaces doubling as space heaters and, above all, easy car access and parking. Traditional village-centre houses

Rarely are there any subsidies available to support those islanders who do wish to employ the invariably more expensive, labour-intensive traditional techniques.

then-Minister of the Aegean, Nikos Sifounakis, promulgated rules for building on the smaller, more picturesque islands – but not on any of the larger ones, where too many voters would have been antagonised. These restrictions, even where still in force, have been complemented or even substituted by those of the very powerful state archaeological service, which effectively controls areas like the Cycladic *kástra*, Sými and Rhodes Old Town.

Bringing in the catch in Livádia harbour, Tílos.

FOOD AND DRINK

Renewed pride in traditional regional recipes, a change in restaurant cooking habits and the advent of a quality wine industry have all done wonders for Greek cuisine.

Greek restaurant fare long had a poor reputation amongst foreign visitors. Casserole dishes *(magirevtá)* were saturated in oil, overcooked and served lukewarm; resinated wine was likened to paint stripper; leafy greens and seafood were severely limited in summer. Unless they travelled off-season, or were invited to eat by a family, visitors were apt to form a frankly libellous impression of local cuisine.

Eating in Greece at the dawn of tourism was constrained by the interrelated factors of poverty, religious strictures and the unforgiving Mediterranean environment, not to mention feelings of shame about "peasant" culture. Until the 1960s, most people ate meat just a few times a month and at major holidays – not just for financial reasons, but because of Church-mandated abstention from meat and cheese which, for the devout, could total several months of the year. A range of *nistísima* or fasting foods had evolved, many of them the so-called *laderá* or "oily" dishes comprising stewed or rice-stuffed fresh vegetables, and pulses; those ladles of olive oil, along with chunks of bread, also conveniently quelled hunger pangs. Piping-hot food was actively believed to be bad for you. Bread was made partly or wholly from barley, easy to grow on the more barren islands, and equally easy to turn into long-keeping *paximádia* (rusks).

Snails emerging from hibernation after the first rains, *volví* (bitter wild hyacinth bulbs), various kinds of *hórta* (radicchio, notchweed and chicory) gathered from a hillside, *ftéres* (fern sprouts), *glystrída* (purslane) sprigs weeded from the summer garden: such were the wild foods much sought after by resourceful country-dwellers. But this kind of "granny" fare collided head-on with returning Greek emigrants and their Western, fast-food tastes, and a simultaneous

A simple aubergine dish in Santoríni.

tendency to give tourists what they seemed to want, not threatening "ethnic" food. Thus souvláki and chips ruled unchallenged for decades.

Slow food redux

The late 1980s saw a rehabilitation and upgrading of traditional Greek cooking. Increased prosperity and travel or study overseas had broadened culinary horizons, while under the post-junta PASOK governments there was certainly an anti-Western backlash and increased pride in Greekness. But growing nostalgia for the *patrída* (rural homeland), and the loosening of country cooking's association with grinding poverty, were more powerful forces. Crete, with its long growing season and rich wild flora, became a main focus for this renaissance. Cookbooks multiplied – Myrsíni Lambráki's *Hórta*, telling one what to do with every variety of edible wild plant, went through dozens of printings – while celebrity TV chefs emerged. Restaurants and *ouzerís* began to update home-style recipes, emphasising fresh, locally sourced, seasonal ingredients, sensible cooking times and minimised use of oil, allowing intrinsic food flavours to emerge. The most *nouvelle* restaurants were (and are) dubbed *koultouriárika* – "highbrow" –often a bit precious in their menus, slimline portions and prices. But those

chips are for tourists only. Minced meat appears in such *magirevtá* as *lahanodolmádes* (stuffed cabbage leaves), *giouvarlákia* (rice-and-mince-balls in egg-lemon sauce) and *yaprákia* (stuffed vine leaves) – the latter more commonly found as its vegetarian version, *gialantzí* ("liar's") *dolmádes*. *Píttes* (turnovers) can similarly be stuffed with *nistísima* or a meat/cheese filling.

Mezédes or *orektiká* (starters) are frequently meat-free: *fáva* (claimed best on Santoríni) is yellow split peas puréed, then served with chopped onions, lemon wedges and olive oil, while *mavromátika* (black-eyed peas) are boiled

Atmospheric bar in Skiáthos Town.

survivors that succeeded in providing value left a lasting mark on the eating-out scene.

The basics

Despite the waning of strict fasting and more disposable income, vegetables remain the backbone of island cuisine. Tasty *nistísima*-compliant favourites include all manner of *hórta* drizzled with oil and lemon juice, fresh *koukiá* (broad beans – abundant during Lent), *anginátes alá políta* (artichoke hearts, carrots, dill and potatoes), *briám* or *tourloú* (ratatouille) of courgettes, aubergine, tomatoes, garlic and onion, and stewed lentils or chickpeas. Potatoes, hand-cut daily into chips or medallions, are still the hallmark of a good restaurant; Belgian pre-pack

THE IDEAL VS THE REAL

While researching *Heirs to the Greek Catastrophe*, her classic 1970s study of an Asia Minor refugee community near Piraeus, anthropologist Renée Hirschon learned that a "good" housewife's worth was demonstrated by her presence in the kitchen, slaving over labour-intensive dishes involving lots of rolling out of filo dough, canning, stuffing and baking – slow food *avant la lettre*. Quick fried or grilled dishes were dismissed by her informant as *tis poutánas to faï* or "whore's food", the sort of snacks that a prostitute might whip up between clients. Ironically, perhaps, such recipes are the staples of many contemporary *ouzerí* menus.

and then served chilled, garnished with onion and parsley. *Taramosaláta*, *tzatzíki* and *melitzanosaláta* will be familiar from a thousand overseas kebab houses, but in the islands no outfit with an eye to its reputation will decline to make these in-house to a notably chunky consistency; pre-purchased catering packs are for touristy tavernas or "snack bars" only.

Although *horiátiki*, or peasant's salad, is the summer mainstay, between October and April salads are more diverse – cabbage with grated carrot early in winter, followed by medleys of lettuces, rocket, radishes, spring onions and dill.

are for grating, grilling or frying, crumbly (like *dermatísio*) for stuffing, soft (like the sweet *myzíthra*) for spreading or spooning. *Saganáki* is any suitable cheese, fried, or alternatively any cheese-based sauce.

Meat and fish

In terms of meat, pig is big, coming in budget form as *apáki* (Cretan cured pork, leanest from a piglet) or *loukánika* (sausages), for which every island has its own recipe, from the long, skinny ones of Sfakiá on Crete to the chunky, coarse-grained ones of Ándros. Cold piggy snacks mean

Starters of féta cheese and fáva, which is made from puréed yellow peas and similar to pease pudding.

Perhaps surprisingly, Greeks are Europe's top per capita cheese-eaters. *Féta* – for which Greece has secured European court rulings protecting its "registered trademark" status – is the most famous of numerous varieties, which range from soft to hard, sweet to sharp. Cow, goat or sheep milk are used alone or in unpredictable combinations. Hard cheeses (like *kefalograviéra*)

Certain shellfish must be eaten alive to avoid poisoning: petalídes (limpets), gyalisterés, kydónia (cockles), kténia (scallops) and petrosolínes (razor clams). If they twitch when drizzled with lemon juice, they're alive.

pikhtí (brawn), air-dried salami (especially from Levkáda) or succulent *noúmboulo* from Corfu. More ubiquitous are *souvláki*, *gýros* (pork slices cut from a dense-packed, side-cooked cylinder) *brizóla* (pork chops) and *pansétta* (spare ribs, not belly bacon as elsewhere). On bigger islands with extensive flocks, there may be local *soúvla* or *exohikó*, various spit-roasted cuts of lamb, goat or pork. Lamb and goat are more common from April to autumn.

Non-farmed scaly fish is as expensive in Greece as elsewhere in the Mediterranean. You're usually better off choosing humbler, seasonally available species than the bream and sea bass familiar from Northern European supermarkets. East Aegean and Dodecanese islands near the nutrient-rich river mouths of Anatolia and Dardanelles have the best choice. The profile changes from spring, with the last of the shrimp and sole, to early summer's swordfish and *marídes* (pickarel), to the deliciously flash-fried *atherína* (sand smelt) and *gávros* (anchovy), plus grillable *sardélles* (sardines) and *koliós* (mackerel) later in summer. The last two also make excellent marinated *mezédes*. Other affordable seafood includes grilled or stewed octopus and cuttlefish. Once poor people's food, now trendy and expensive, are sea urchin roe and *foúskes*, a bizarre Dodecanesian invertebrate which tastes much like oysters.

barely quaffable, some are great. *Retsína* (wine flavoured with pine resin) is offered nationwide, but it travels poorly and bottled (as opposed to barrelled) *retsína* for many is an oxymoron; the best stuff comes from Attikí, around Athens.

Oúzo, the national aperitif, is distilled from grape-mash residue left over from winemaking, and then flavoured with aniseed or fennel; strength is typically 40–48 percent alcohol. The best island labels come from Lésvos, Híos and Sámos. Unflavoured variants of *oúzo* include *tsípouro* (on Thássos and the Sporades), and *rakí* or *tsikoudiá* (Crete).

Try the humbler, seasonally available species of fish.

Do try the local wines.

Island drinks

Another motor for the makeover of Greek cuisine was the emergence from the late 1980s onwards of a quality wine industry, overseen by foreign-educated Greek oenologists. Owing to limited bottling capacity – many microwineries don't exceed 15,000 bottles annually – most premium wines are unknown outside Greece, but they can be as good (and expensive) as French, Italian or southern hemisphere rivals. The best island wines are reckoned to hail from Límnos, Rhodes, Sámos, Santoríni, Híos, Kefaloniá and Crete. There's been keen interest in reviving heirloom grape varieties. Conversely, the Greek culinary renaissance included new-found esteem for bulk wines, which had nearly disappeared. Some are

THE GREEK BEER SCENE

The apparent variety of Greek beers is deceptive. One holding company controls 95 percent of the market, dominated by fairly insipid foreign brews made under license, particularly Amstel and Heineken; the best label from this near-monopoly is Alfa. Worthy, distinctive-tasting independents are Vergina, brewed in Komotiní (including a strong red and a wheat beer), Fix (nationwide) and numerous microbreweries, especially Craft (Athens), Brinks (Réthymno) – in equally good dark and blonde varieties – Donkey (Santoríni), Septem (Evvia), Magnus Magister (Rhodes), Nissos (Tínos) and Corfu Beer.

EATING YOUR WAY ROUND THE ISLANDS

Traditional Greek food is better than its reputation, especially if you ignore what's offered to tourists and seek out traditional local dishes.

Anyone who has experienced tourist menus of chicken and chips or microwaved *moussakás* can be excused for believing that Greece isn't the place for culinary delights. So for a taste of real Greek cooking, follow the locals to backstreet tavernas. The food at such traditional places, geared for a lunch-hour clientele, more than compensates for any lack of fancy decor. If communication is a problem, take a look at what's cooking and point at what you want. Ordering this way is accepted practice.

You'll soon find there's more to Greek cuisine than *souvláki* and *taramosaláta*. Vegetables like fresh runner beans, okra or butter beans, cooked in olive oil and tomato; hearty fish soups; cheese, leek or spinach pies with a feather-light filo pastry; cuttlefish with spinach; rabbit stew; courgette flowers stuffed with rice and fried in batter – the islands offer dishes for all tastes. There are plenty of vegetarian options because of the many fast days in the Orthodox calendar.

Regional variations reflect island history and foreign occupations. Many dishes have strong Italian and Turkish influences. You'll find pastas and pilafs, plus vegetable recipes like *briám* and *imám baïldí*, their foreign names absorbed into Greek menus.

From the *krasotýri* of Kós, the *sofríto* (veal casserole) of Corfu to the *fourtália* omelettes of Andros, every island has its speciality. Some may seem strange – *foúskes* (a marine invertebrate) or *kokorétsi* (spit-roasted offal) are not for the faint-hearted – but prove to be delicious. If all else fails, *horiátiki*, the classic Greek village salad, with feta, olives, peppers, cucumber and tomato, takes some beating.

Pasta and wine on the beach in Levkáda.

Fresh fish and roasted vegetables in Santoríni. The fish and seafood in the Aegean is delicious but scarce, so prices can be high.

Marinated anchovies make for a tasty starter.

Each island has its version of oúzo.

AND SOMETHING TO DRINK?

You can drink anything in Greece from cocktails to local firewater. *Oúzo*, the national aperitif turns harmlessly milky when water is added. It's usually drunk with olives or other starters *(mezédes)*. If you prefer wine, *retsína* (white wine flavoured with pine resin, *right*) is an acquired taste, ranging from lightly to heavily scented. The best labels are Georgiadi and Malamatina, both from Thessaloníki.

Popular inexpensive bottled wines include Tsantali and Boutari, available nationwide in reds, whites and rosés, or Zítsa bulk wine from Ípiros, For something better, go for Tsantali Agioritiko in white and red, Papaïoannou reds or any white from Límnos. Try also premium island wines like Gentilini Robola white from Kefaloniá, Voultsos on Zákynthos, Economou or Lyrarakis from Crete, Methymneos from Lésvos, Hatziemmanouil from Kós, Triandafyllou rosé from Rhodes, Ariousos from Híos or Ktima Argyrou or Sigalas from Santoríni.

After dinner try Greek brandy, Metaxa, which comes in three starred grades (five is best). Any *kafenío* (coffee bar) will serve up Greek coffee – *skéto* (without sugar), *glykó* (sweet) or *métrio* (medium). Decent espressos/ cappuccinos or filter coffees are steadily displacing a prior fixation with bad instant formulas.

Grilled octopus is an affordable seafood meal.

Kataífi is made from a vermicelli-like pastry of shredded filo dough, filled with chopped nuts and drenched in honey syrup.

Save space for dessert, they are usually very rich…

CRUISING ROUND THE ISLANDS

Greeks have sailed between the islands for thousands of years. Today it is possible to follow in their wake, on anything from day-trips to all-inclusive luxury cruises.

Having over 60 inhabited islands means having ships to serve them, and Greece has a long shipping tradition. Anyone who has sailed the Aegean, where white cruise-ship superstructures rival the dazzling sun itself, knows the affinity Greeks have for their boats.

The giants of the past, such as Aristotle Onassis and Stavros Niarchos, are no longer with us, and their successors keep a much lower profile. They are there, however: hundreds of Greek shipping companies operating out of 1 sq km (0.4 sq miles) of office blocks in the port city of Piraeus and overlooking the seafront at Aktí Miaoúli, where suited office-workers rub shoulders with burly crewmen headed for the NAT (seamen's social fund) building.

Despite economic turmoil, owners remain emotionally committed to their businesses. In terms of satisfaction, little can equal gazing out of one's air-conditioned headquarters and watching one's ship come in. The same feeling must have prompted the great 18th-century captains of Hydra and Spétses to build their *arhondiká*, or mansions, facing out to sea.

The transportation of goods to and from the Greek islands is fundamental to their economies. For visitors to the country, however, best is the pleasure of being cargo, the joys of cruising.

Which cruise to choose?

The most frequent voyages in Greece are one-day cruises. A typical one-day cruise from Piraeus or Paleó Fáliro is an excellent introduction to the Greek islands. You will visit the 5th-century BC Temple of Aphaea

Boat trip to Skiáthos.

(*Aféa*) on Aegina, one of the finest in all Greece; at Póros you will pass through the narrow straits with the town's tile-roofed houses towering above the ship on one side and extensive lemon groves on the other, mainland side; in Hydra you will stroll through the beautiful little town arrayed around the harbour.

There are also one-day cruises from Iráklio, Crete, to Santoríni – sailing into that remarkable caldera is one of the highlights of Aegean travel.

There are also three-to ten-day cruises, most of them operating out of Piraeus, though some worthwhile eight-day cruises operate out of Rhodes or Crete. One of the best

Examine itineraries carefully before you book. You want to cover long stretches of open sea after dark, with overnights or late-night stays only in interesting ports like Návplio, Mýkonos or Pátmos. Many cruises are just too rushed.

outfits for this is Seafarer (www.seafarercruises. com), with a variety of itineraries on medium-sized motor or sail-assisted yachts capable of anchoring in smaller, less visited ports of the Cyclades and Dodecanese. Variety Cruises (www.varietycruises.com) has similar offerings out of Piraeus, Rhodes and Crete.

International cruises

For longer, international cruises, it's wise to opt for a surviving company using medium-capacity craft (under 1,000 passengers) which – while perhaps not up to the luxury standards of transatlantic or Caribbean cruises – are usually small enough to manoeuvre into most chosen harbours, and do not dwarf their destinations like the towering new generation of gin palaces. They constitute the best way to see the most interesting ports in the eastern Mediterranean and Black Sea, in reasonable comfort and with good food.

A typical three-day cruise starts from Piraeus, taking in Mýkonos, Kuşadası (for Ephesus) in Turkey, Pátmos, and either Rhodes or Crete; four-day cruises will definitely include all of the ports just noted, plus Santoríni, whereas a one-week cruise will stretch up to Istanbul too. Ten-day cruises forsake Turkey (except for Ephesus) in favour of add-ons to Katákolon (for ancient Olympia), Corfu, Kefaloniá, Sicily and Genoa in Italy, plus Marseilles. It's also possible to circle much of the Black Sea coast in nine days, stopping at Varna (Bulgaria), Yalta (Russia), Trabzon and Samsun (Turkey) as well as Istanbul and Kavála in northern Greece. More rarely, there are seven-day cruises taking in Cyprus and Israel, with stops in Santoríni and Mýkonos.

Politics at sea

As with all things Greek, there is a political dimension, hingeing on the word *cabotage*. Cabotage is an international legal term meaning, as far as Greek shipping companies

are concerned, a monopoly on all lines connecting Greek domestic ports. Many foreign ships have historically cruised Greek waters with passengers they brought from outside, and returned to some port outside Greece, but cabotage long protected Greek cruise companies from foreign competition in Greek waters.

By European Union decree, this nautical monopoly was supposed to cease, for EU-registered ships at least, in 2004. Since then, in theory, the market was incrementally opened, with many existing Greek ships improved and

The Dodecanese islands make for a dramatic backdrop to a cruise.

brand-new ships brought into service to stave off competition. It certainly brought about a number of mergers and rationalisations to enable survival in trying times.

Greek governments are fond of imposing regulations, often impenetrable, usually expensive, upon every aspect of life imaginable, including Greek shipping. Many Greek shipowners long responded by registering their ships under a cheaper flag of convenience (usually Malta, Liberia or the Caymans). Finally, with the lifting of cabotage in late 2011, such foreign-registered ships (along with lots of Italian-flagged ones, in particular Costa Cruises) could at last cruise between the Greek islands.

Sun, clean seas and sand (or shingle) have made for a winning tourist formula.

The best topographical hiking maps, covering most islands listed, are published by Anávasi (www.anavasi.gr) in Athens; otherwise variably good local maps and guide booklets exist.

On the sea

With gold or silver medallists at the 2000, 2004 and 2008 Olympics, windsurfing has the cachet in Greece that cycling has in France. While it might seem windy – and

Just about every island visitor gets into the Aegean, though perhaps not quite to the extent of inter-island swimmers, who think nothing of an afternoon's crawl back and forth amongst the smaller Cyclades lying between Náxos and Amorgós; many tours are organised here by SwimTrek (www.swimtrek.com). Sea kayaking is a slightly less strenuous way of covering much the same territory and visiting otherwise inaccessible coastal formations. The rewards are subtle but tangible, like glimpsing brightly hued kingfishers perching on sea-level rocks in autumn.

Hiking trail along the coast of Skiáthos.

boards are on offer – almost everywhere, only certain resorts have the right combination of exposure and onshore topography to be world-class. Indeed, sites like southern Kárpathos, Prassonísi on Rhodes and Vassilikí on Levkáda do host annual European tournaments; but Kamári on Kós, Agios Geórgios on Náxos, Kokkári on Sámos and Paleohóra on Crete will be more than enough for beginners and intermediates to handle. Kitesurfing, where devotees standing on a small board are propelled very quickly by a parabolic kite controlled with four lines, is like windsurfing on steroids. Frequently launched into the air, kitesurfers are the skateboarders of the sea.

Under the sea

Scuba-diving has been slow to take off in Greece, owing to historical restrictions on the practice: so much archaeological wealth is assumed still to be submerged that the government has generally denied applications to authorise new dive zones for fear of antiquity theft. In 2008, after years of lobbying, existing schools managed to have the list of allowable venues greatly expanded, especially around Rhodes, Skiáthos and Alónnisos, and more venues should be opened once the painfully slow process of archaeological surveying is completed. The most reputable schools are on Skiáthos, Alónnisos, Léros, Kálymnos, Mýkonos, Náxos, Mílos, Corfu (Paleokastrítsa),

Kefaloniá, Sámos and Rhodes. Don't expect a tropical profusion of fish – the Aegean is far too exploited for that. The attraction lies rather in caves, tunnels and other formations, as well as in sedentary marine life. Léros, with its World War II wrecks and debris from the battle of autumn 1943, is arguably the most interesting spot.

The sailing scene

Sailing is a rewarding way of exploring this country of islands, whether in your own yacht, in a chartered boat or as part of a flotilla.

The clear waters of Skiáthos.

While the package holidaymaker and the independent island-hopper are forced to rely on the ferries and their often idiosyncratic timetables in order to travel among the islands, yachties enjoy a remarkable degree of independence – except, of course, from the winds. Sailing around Greece is not over-complicated by bureaucracy, but some paperwork, unfortunately, is unavoidable – namely transit logs for the boat, and a crew list with full names and passport numbers.

Chartering, now a fundamental part of the sailing scene in Greece, began throughout the islands in the mid-1970s; it was the idea of an enterprising group of British boat-owners who decided that they had had enough

of miserable English summers and wanted holidays in the sun. This type of sailing is increasingly prevalent and has done much to encourage the development of marinas and improved facilities. Increasing numbers in recent years have seen a spread of poorer-quality boats, but most reputable charter companies supply yachts that are renewed every five years or so. They are designed for holidays in the sun and equipped to a luxurious standard with deep freezes, deck showers, snorkelling equipment and even a pair of thick gloves to handle the anchor chain.

Making the right choice

It's important to match experience with the correct type of charter. Inexperienced sailors should select a flotilla holiday where a group of yachts cruise as a fleet, under the instructive eye of a lead boat crew. If you are an experienced sailor, you may want to arrange a "bareboat" charter, in which you act as your own skipper. If you can afford a crewed charter, you can simply relax on deck and leave all the sailing, boat handling, cooking and bureaucracy to paid hands.

Whether you're taking your own yacht to Greece or chartering, the range of sailing areas is large and your choice should take account of varying local weather conditions.

The recognised sailing season is from April to October, when the skies are mostly clear; temperatures vary between 23° and 38°C (70s and 90s degrees Fahrenheit) in July and August. Winds throughout the Aegean Sea tend to be from the north. The most talked-about weather

FLY THE FLAG

All charter vessels must sail under the Greek flag (and a Turkish courtesy flag if you cross the maritime border), even if the yacht is hired from a foreign company. It is best to charter from one of the larger companies, which will prepare the charter agreement and are better organised at helping you through the process of leaving the marina. Keep the boat's papers, including the crew list, accessible: you'll have to present them to the port authorities in any harbour you dock in. If you are going to "bareboat", at least two of the crew must have sailing qualifications that need to be brought along to satisfy the authorities.

phenomenon is the *meltémi*, a steady north wind which can affect the entire Aegean, and can reach Force 7 to 8 on the Beaufort scale in midsummer. It's a capricious wind, typically appearing around mid-June and dying down in late September. Usually the *meltémi* arises just before or after midday and calms with sunset, but can arrive without warning and blow for as little as one hour or for as long as one week. Yachtsmen must take care not to be caught on a lee shore, and should be aware that the *meltémi* can cause an extremely uncomfortable steep, short sea.

the Dodecanese as the most difficult waters in which to sail.

Sailing in the Dodecanese has the additional problem of the nearby Turkish maritime border. The Turks insist that anyone sailing in their waters must clear customs at one of their ports of entry. The border is policed at sea and it is therefore unwise to enter Turkish waters unless you intend to enter Turkey officially.

Weather reporting in Greece is generally good. Virtually every Greek evening newscast is followed by a weather report which someone can translate for you (though the graphics

When choosing a sailing area, bear in mind the varying local weather conditions.

Occasionally the hot, damp, southeasterly sirókos wind, often carrying reddish dust from North Africa, will blow hard across the southern Aegean and Ionian – but it doesn't last long.

In the northern Aegean the *meltémi* blows from just east of north and, further south towards the Cyclades and Crete, predominantly from true north. By the time it reaches Kárpathos, Rhodes and other southerly Dodecanese, this wind has gathered even more strength and is from the northwest. Its local violence has persuaded some charter companies to classify

are obvious), and port authorities will be well informed. If you have a laptop or tablet device, and proximity to a Wi-fi zone (increasingly common in marina cafés), log on to www.meteo. gr or www.poseidon.ncmr.gr, the latter with useful wind-and-waves graphic profiler; www.sailingissues.com is another useful site.

The Saronic Gulf and the Ionian Sea offer the gentlest sailing conditions, mainly because the islands are relatively close to each other (and to the mainland) and because the *maístros*, the more northwesterly variant of the *meltémi* in the Ionian, is usually weaker. The *maístros* tends to blow only in the afternoon, when the heat of the Greek mainland accelerates the wind off the sea.

Despite this variety of local winds, Greek seas are often quite windless, so yachtsmen should be prepared to motor. Whatever the conditions, you should always protect yourself against the sun and the increased glare off the water – which can produce temporary blindness.

The greatest appeal of the Greek islands is the solitude offered by their remoteness. The green islands of the Ionian are a frequent first-choice venue for a number of reasons. The shelter among the many islands offers safe cruising, but if you want more lively conditions, a trip in the open waters to the west of

where, almost without exception, mooring is stern or bow to the quay.

Moving east from the Saronic Gulf, the influence of the *meltémi* becomes stronger, and it is not until you travel north of Évvia to the Sporades that you find dependable shelter in any weather – each island here has a protected, south- or southeast-facing harbour. Beyond Skýros to the northeast lies the open, and generally wild, Aegean, with little casual sailing owing to the great distances involved. From the Sporades, most skippers make for the inlets and peninsulas of the Halkidikí peninsula, east of Thessaloníki.

Yachts moored in Mandráki harbour, Rhodes Old Town.

Levkáda (Léfkas) and Kefaloniá will provide marvellous sailing. Easy anchorages and safe village moorings are within a few hours' sail of each other throughout these islands. The best time to sail here is definitely during spring and autumn: August sees Italian yachtsmen pouring over from Italy, clogging up the numerous but small harbours.

The Saronic Gulf is a favourite haunt of yachtsmen, beingso close to Piraeus. The little island of Angístri, off Aegina, has some lovely coves; Póros, Hydra and Spétses have attractive town harbours as well as quieter anchorages; and the east coast of the Peloponnese is unjustly underrated. In mid-season it will be difficult to find a berth at the town quays

MARINAS AROUND THE ISLANDS

The biggest concentration of marinas is near Athens and Piraeus, though these are not particularly attractive. Other major marinas among or near Greek islands are at Kalamariá, just outside Thessaloníki; at Gouviá, an hour's sail north from Corfu Town; and at Corfu Town itself. The marina at Levkáda is right in town, just off the canal. In the Dodecanese, there's a marina at Mandráki on Rhodes, (more suited to larger yachts), plus ones on Kálymnos and (the largest) on Léros. The large marina at Pythagório (Sámos) is ideal as an end point for a one-way itinerary. All these marinas make excellent staging posts/charter bases.

Island Hopping

The pleasures of travelling from one island to another using Greece's interlinking ferry routes are numerous, but it pays to be prepared.

First there's the never-ceasing view – a bas-relief pattern on a blue base of low, mysterious summits. Plus, there are unique opportunities to "visit" other islands besides your destination – 15 minutes observing a port from top deck can reveal much about a place and its people. Reunions, farewells and the redistribution of a warehouse's worth of goods take place just below the rear railing. Is that a piano or an ice-cream freezer being offloaded? Is that cheeping coming from an embarking truck with a battery farm of chickens?

Without thorough advance checking, however, it's easy to experience the worst aspects of island-hopping in the form of missed connections, being stranded, or even sailing straight past the intended island with no way back for two days.. Even ferry journeys that go according to plan can be lengthy, not to mention nerve-racking rather than restful: if the boat reaches your small, remote destination at 2am, it's your responsibility to wake up – set your alarm! – and get off.

The *meltémi* is a fact of Greek summer life, unaffected thus far by global climate change. When winds are too strong, ships are delayed or kept in port. If you are depending upon ferries to take you back to Athens for your flight home, leave at least one full day's leeway. Athens has its pleasures; missing your flight home does not.

Hydrofoils and larger catamarans which carry cars play a significant role in inter-island travel. They are twice as fast as conventional ferries – ideal if time is limited – but also twice as expensive, and not without other disadvantages. Neither "cats" nor hydrofoils provide much of a view, and both are far more sensitive to bad weather than conventional boats. A good compromise are *tahyplía* or "high speed" ferries (especially Blue Star's), which cost little more than the old tubs but sail a good deal more quickly. Hydrofoils have also been known to stay in port rather than depart simply because there were not enough passengers to justify the trip.

Routes and schedules

Classic ferry itineraries include the central Cyclades circuit (Mýkonos, Páros, Náxos, Íos and Santoríni), the Argo-Saronic line (Póros, Hydra, Spétses), and the major Dodecanese route (Pátmos, Léros, Kálymnos, Kós and Rhodes). Less popular are the western Cyclades arc (Kýthnos, Sérifos, Sífnos and Mílos), the main Sporades islands (Skiáthos, Skópelos, Alónnisos), and the link between Rhodes and Crete via Hálki, Kárpathos and Kásos. In the Ionian islands, it's easy to travel between Levkáda, Itháki and Kefaloniá. Besides Piraeus, the most important

Safety prevails.

mainland ports are Lávrio, Rafína, Thessaloníki, Kavála, Vólos and Pátra; on the islands, Páros, Sámos, Rhodes and Kós are useful regional hubs. The most comprehensive, up-to-date sources of ferry schedules is the website of the Greek travel agents' manual, Greek Travel Pages (www.gtp.gr), or alternatively www.openseas.gr. Peripheral, subsidised lines – the so-called *agonés grammés* – often have user-hostile schedules, either with uncivilised departure/arrival times, unhelpful frequencies (departures on two consecutive days, then nothing for five), or both. The ministry which pays shipowners handsome subsidies does not seem to stipulate in exchange the provision of rational, tourist-friendly timetables.

The domesticated goat.

ISLAND WILDLIFE

The diverse island landscapes support a varied collection of flora and fauna. Birds in particular, both resident and migrant, bring delight to ornithologists.

Arrive at a mid-Aegean island in the heat of summer and you may feel you've inadvertently stumbled upon a remote outpost of the Sahara. Arid brown countryside sheds clouds of dust each time the hairdryer wind blows, and the only surviving plant life is in carefully nurtured village window-boxes.

Visit in spring, however, and the picture is an entirely different one. Lush greenery and brightly coloured flowers cover the plains and hillsides, and even waste ground becomes garden.

The first seedlings and bulbs sprout shortly after the first autumn rains. Growth gathers pace through the cool but partly sunny winters; a few weeks into the new year, flowers start to bloom in the far southeast. Rhodes, Kárpathos and eastern Crete are followed in succession by western Crete, then the Cyclades and the eastern Aegean. Spring arrives in the Ionian islands and the north Aegean as summer appears in Rhodes.

As plants lead, so other wildlife follows. The number of insects increases, and the insect-eaters flourish; food chains gear up for a spring and early summer of proliferation.

Local fauna

Before mankind first settled in the region, the Greek islands had a mixture of forest, some tall, impenetrably dense *maquis* vegetation, and much *garrigue*. The latter (*phrýgana* in Greek) consists of low shrubby bushes which are often spiny, resisting both the grazing of animals and the bare legs of walkers. Mixed together with the shrubs are fragrant herbs, colourful annuals and, enjoying protection under those spines, fragile orchids.

Butterflies are conspicuous from spring to autumn.

It's a myth that man and his flocks destroyed a verdant Greek Eden of continuous woodland: some larger islands had populations of wild plant-munching animals – such as deer – long before any human arrivals. Native grazers led to the flora's evolution of discouraging defences – spines, foul tastes – which armed it well for the comparatively recent introduction of domesticated sheep and goats. (See also page 92.)

Reclusive mammals

Wild mammals occur on the islands, but most are secretive. Crete has its ibex-like wild goat or *agrími* (also called the *krí-krí*), a shy inhabitant of the White Mountains. Amid fears of its demise from over-hunting, some animals were transferred to the island of Día, near Iráklio, where they flourished and multiplied – ironically eliminating the rare native plants.

Elsewhere, the largest mammals are the badger, and the jackal of the eastern Aegean and Corfu, but the one you are more likely to see is the stone marten. This resembles a dark-brown ferret, long, slim, agile and fast-moving, sighted both during the day and in headlights crossing roads at night. They are frequent victims of the taxidermist's art, and many tavernas have one stuffed on display.

a variety of species from Africa. Their final destination will probably be much further north, but the Greek islands may be their first landfall after the Mediterranean crossing. Both black and white storks migrate through Greece, nesting on the way. Individ-

> On Skýros there is a very small wild horse, a unique breed thought to be that depicted on the frieze of the Parthenon; less than 150 pure-bred specimens survive.

The white pelican, or Pelecanus onocrotulus.

Most other mammals are small: field rats (common on Corfu and Sámos), rabbits or hares, wild mice, and a variety of bats that can move from island to mainland and vice versa.

The National Marine Park northeast of Alónissos is an important haven for the Mediterranean monk seal – the most endangered of all the world's seals. About 55 of a total world population of less than 400 live here. Between islands, look out for common dolphins shadowing ferries.

A birdwatcher's paradise

While mammal-watchers may find themselves underemployed, the birdwatcher should not be. The spring migration brings

ual flamingos may turn up anywhere there is a salty coastal pool, but you should visit Lésvos, Sámos and Límnos to see them nesting in quantity between December and March (though since 2007 their flight patterns have favoured touchdown in western Greek wetlands instead).

Much smaller, but most colourful, are the crested pink, white and black hoopoe, the bright blue-and-brown roller, and the multicoloured bee-eater – the latter two highly visible in May. For many ornithologists, raptors – hawks, vultures, Bonelli's eagles and Eleonora's falcons – prompt the biggest thrill, although numbers of the latter two species are down on Tílos, owing to decline in the populations of rock partridges and passerines, respectively their favourite prey.

Larger species inhabit mountain areas, especially on Crete, where gorges and cliffs provide secure nesting and the requisite isolation. Spectacular griffon vultures, sometimes in large flocks, patrol the skies in search of dead livestock, soaring effortlessly on broad wings the size of a door. The much scarcer lammergeier has narrow wings, the ultimate flying machine in its search for bones – or tortoises – to drop onto rocks and break open.

Reptiles and insects

The most abundant reptiles are lizards, some 21 species, of which the Balkan green lizard is perhaps the most conspicuous. Bolder and more stockily built is the iguana-like agama, sometimes called the Rhodes dragon, though it's also found on Corfu and several Aegean islands. Unlike others, this greyish rough-skinned lizard, when disturbed, will often stay around for a few minutes to check out the danger. Worth special note are the geckos (three species, the most common the so-called "Turkish"), which cling harmlessly to your hotel-room wall.

Tortoises occur on many islands, though surprisingly not on Crete. Once gathered in tens of thousands for the pet trade, they now lead safer lives wandering noisily through the underbrush, especially during spring migration. Their freshwater aquatic relatives, the terrapins, favour streams with bare muddy banks for sunbathing.

Marine loggerhead turtles are decreasing in numbers as their nesting beaches are lost to tourism. They used to breed widely on Crete, Kós and Rhodes – now they are restricted to a few beaches on Kefaloniá, Zákynthos and possibly corners of Crete and southeastern Rhodes.

Snakes often cause alarm, but most are harmless, and all prefer to be left alone. Locals tend to overreact and attack any snake they see, though this is actually the best way to increase the chance of being bitten. Poisonous vipers do occur on some of the Ionian, Cycladic and east Aegean islands – they usually have a zigzag pattern down the spine, and move rather lazily.

Mosquitoes may seem the commonest insects at night, but Corfu is noted for its springtime fireflies, little flashing beacons that drift over damp fields and hedges after dark. Paler lights in the hedgerows are wingless glow-worms. During the day, butterflies are obvious, often in great quantity and variety. Some of the large hawk-moths may be seen during the day – the hummingbird hawk-moth, like its namesake, relies on superfast wingbeats to hover at flowers as it feeds.

Noisier are the huge, glossy blue-black carpenter bees which spend much of their time looking for suitable nesting sites, usually a hollow cane or utility pole. Noisiest of all

A stone marten clambers atop a fallen branch.

is the cicada, basically an overgrown aphid, which perches – usually on a pine tree – and keeps up a deafening racket, which is the typical soundtrack of the Mediterranean to some. Despite their size and volume, they are well camouflaged, so surprisingly hard to see. African locusts are really giant grasshoppers, though they never pillage in devastating swarms this side of the Mediterranean.

Praying mantids keep their barbed forearms in a position of supplication until an unwary insect moves nearby – then the mantid becomes a hungry atheist. Even the male of the species is devoured as he romances the female, his substance helping to nourish the next generation.

THE ISLANDS IN BLOOM

The Greek islands are at their most colourful in spring and early summer, when every hillside and valley is bedecked with glorious flowers.

Greece in spring is a botanist's (and photographer's) dream. Some 6,000 species of wild plant grow in mainland Greece and the islands, and in the spring (February to May) visitors may enjoy a magnificent cornucopia of flowers and fragrances.

Hillsides resemble giant rock gardens, while brilliantly coloured patches of untended waste ground outdo Northern Europe's carefully tended herbaceous borders with ease. Winter rains, followed by a bright, warm, frost-free spring, produce a season's blooming compressed into a few spectacular weeks before the summer's scorching heat and drought become too much. By late May or early June the flowers are done, the seeds for next year's show are ripening, and greens are fading to brown to match the tourists on the beaches.

Except in the cooler, higher mountains, most plants go into semi-dormancy to survive the arid summer. The first rains of autumn, as early as mid-September, but usually mid-October, tempt a few autumn bulbs into flower but also initiate the germination of seed plants that will grow and gather strength during the winter in preparation for the following spring when their flowers will again colour in the waiting canvas of the hills and valleys.

The richness and diversity of the flora are due in part to the islands' location between three continents – Europe, Asia and Africa – partly to the Ice Age survival in temperate Greece of pre-glacial species, and partly to the wonderful variety of habitats. Limestone, the foundation of much of Greece, is a favoured home for plants, providing stability, minerals, water supply and protection.

Pretty thorned poppies on the beach.

A typical Santoríni church awash with colour.

Wild artichokes are painfully spiny to prepare for the pot, but their delicate flavour is much prized by Greek country folk over the spineless cultivated variety, and accordingly they command a price premium.

A happy bee.

BEETLES, BEES AND BUTTERFLIES

The profusion of flowers and plants provides food for an equal profusion of insects. Butterflies are conspicuous from spring to autumn, including the swallowtail, whose equally colourful caterpillars feed on the leaves of common fennel. Its larger, paler and more angular relative, the Scarce Swallowtail, despite its name, is even more abundant.

Look for clouded yellows and paler cleopatras, reddish-brown painted ladies and southern commas, white admirals and a myriad of smaller blue butterflies.

Butterflies, bees and day-flying hawk-moths tend to go for flowers with nectar, while beetles and flies go for the pollen. Some bugs even take advantage of the heat accumulated in the solar cup of many flowers in order to warm up their sex lives.

The leaves of plants feed armies of insect herbivores, which themselves are eaten by more aggressive insects. Some of the omnivorous Greek grasshoppers and crickets are as happy munching through a caterpillar, or even another grasshopper, as the grass it was sitting on.

The hills are alive – sunshine, colour and quantity mark the spring flowering of the islands, as here on Lésvos in mid-April.

Spanish broom (Spartium junceum) splashes low hillsides with yellow blooms in May.

Wild flowers along the road in Rhodes.

ISLANDS OUT OF SEASON

The onset of winter and the disappearance of tourists bring sudden, dramatic changes to Greek islands small and large.

I t is only when the charter flights have ceased for the year that the real character of many islands staggers out of its unseasonable estivation. Larger islands can absorb a deluge of visitors without having to adopt an entirely different identity. A visitor arriving in Crete in October would not discover, as may happen on a tiny Cyclade, that the post office was working a nine-hour week, matching boat arrivals, with daily operation not set to resume until the following spring. It is difficult to overstate the distorting impact of an island population measured in hundreds being swamped by four or five times as many people.

Quick change

Superficially, the change into hibernal uniform is swift. Migrant waiters, kitchen staff and scooter-hire personnel depart to look for winter jobs elsewhere. Awnings over beachside cafés are rolled up and stowed, tourist-oriented shops boarded up; beaches are suddenly bereft of their loungers and umbrellas.

An ancient provider of winter warmth on Ikaría.

A good sign that the islanders have literally found their feet again, after grinding summer schedules, is the resumption of the evening promenade or *vólta*, a quasi-formal ritual stroll in which small groups file from one end of a locally prescribed route to the other, and back again. Among them are the elderly and disabled, seldom seen in public during the season. However, in a few large, untouristy towns, such as Híos port, the *vólta* continues year-round.

The *vólta* makes visible all kinds of island machinery in motion. Orthodox priests, symbols of a notional propriety largely eclipsed by the summer heathens, reassert their magisterial presence among the faithful. Office-holders and petitioners in island politics fall into step

beside the mayor for a peripatetic conference.

If municipal elections (formerly in mid-autumn, but in May as of 2014) are imminent, the preliminary promenade-plotting will develop into campaigns complete with mobile sound trucks and launching of fireworks by the winners. Various religious festivals involve street processions, the mayor and priests conspicuously linked in secular-clerical solidarity at the head of an enthusiastic brass band.

The locals have to buy food and other supplies, so corresponding shops remain stocked (if not always with the same product lines as in summer). But no island is completely self-sufficient, and storms can play havoc with already reduced ferry services. Consequently, shelves go temporarily bare, and butane canisters for stoves and heaters may run out because the gas tanker-boat can't safely anchor opposite the fuel depot.

In calm seas, the fishermen sail at dusk and return at dawn but, for the rest of the male population, the longer nights are the cue to bring out the playing cards (or occupy themselves in other ways… Kastellórizo in particular has a huge quota of children, around 40 for its small adult population of about 200). Officially, no money changes hands, but substantial fractions of the summer takings surge back and forth. That said,

Locals playing backgammon in Skópelos.

the days when islanders in the seasonal tourism trade could spend all winter gambling away the proceeds are long gone: living costs have rocketed, pensions have been savagely cut, and now everybody has to have a second (and maybe third) enterprise to tide them over until spring.

Winter residence

Landlords don't expect to earn rent in winter, so out-of-season visitors will find prices negotiable. Prime accommodation near the sea may be worth a slight premium while the water is still at a tolerable temperature – for the hardy, until December, and then again from April on. It's worth asking about vacant farmhouses; these have the simultaneous advantages of privacy, as

well as neighbours popping around with eggs, greens and a bottle of local wine.

If outdoor conditions are an important criterion, southerly islands like Crete and Rhodes are marginally warmer and brighter. All across the Aegean, however, winter winds can cut to the bone, and houses not built specifically for the summer trade are more likely to have some form of heating. On more vegetated islands, the shriek of chainsaws in autumn heralds the stockpiling of firewood, the best of which are olive prunings (generated the previous year after the November-to-March olive harvest). A basic, cast-iron wood stove is affordable; energy-efficient models a worthwhile step up. Even assuming a cosy interior, when rain runs in muddy torrents down village lanes, many expats discover the limits of their love for Greece.

An insider's view

The English novelist Simon Raven spent the winter of 1960 on Hydra looking into "what goes on when winter comes, when the last epicene giggle has hovered and died in the October air". He decided he was among a bunch of atavistic pirates who, happily engaged in making money during the summer, reverted in winter to the old distrust of strangers who used to come only to spy on their illicit booty.

Hydra has since acquired a considerable number of full-time expats and, assuming the Hydriots never read what Raven wrote, he would probably feel more comfortable among them now. But one of his conclusions stands the test of time: only in winter can one discern what an island is really like.

WINTER VENUES

On islands such as with a large student popula-tion, such as Corfu, Samos, Lésvos and Crete, October to May sees the emergence of afford-able, quasi-improvised nightlife: Latin-dance evenings at beach bars that can be enclosed against the weather, cinema clubs screening art-house fare, fancy-dress parties for the Carnival season. Many tavernas which spend the tourist season playing Zorba instrumental soundtracks on an endless loop now host qual-ity live acoustic music-for-Greeks two nights a week, with modest or no markup on often much-improved food.

Olive groves on Syros.

Pythagório harbour, Sámos.

Skiáthos Kástro, the abandoned
16th-century capital of the island.

Kitesurfing on Levkáda.

Emborió harbour on Hálki, the island's only settlement.

INTRODUCTION

A detailed guide to all the island groups,
with their principal sites clearly cross-
referenced by number to the maps.

The cove of Lalária, Skiáthos.

The poet Odysseas Elytis once said: "Greece rests on the sea." It's an observation that few countries could claim with such authority. Some 25,000 sq km (10,000 sq miles) of the Aegean and the Ionian seas are covered by islands, the exact number of which has, in characteristic Greek fashion, been subject to dispute. There may be 3,000 islands and islets, of which 167 are inhabited; a more realistic total is 2,000, with fewer than 70 inhabited.

The definition of "inhabited" is open to interpretation, too. Does a tiny *vrahonisída* (rocky islet), bare save for one shepherd and 20 goats, count as uninhabited? Can an island that is totally deserted except for pilgrimages made annually to a small chapel at its summit claim to be inhabited?

The truth is perhaps immaterial; both visitors and inhabitants are more interested in sea and sky than in facts and figures. What is indisputable, however, is the sheer variety of landscape and experience behind the familiar images.

This is what we attempt to show here; islands with an ancient past and a modern outlook, the complex choices and the pure, simple pleasures. In order to accommodate everything implied in the phrase "a Greek island", we have devoted space to islets such as Ágios Evstrátios and Télendos, as well as to well-known giants like Crete and Rhodes and holiday favourites such as Corfu and Mýkonos. We do not ignore the

Day-trippers departing.

familiar, popular islands, but explore them with typical Insight thoroughness, to grasp the true heart of the place behind the tourist clichés.

So welcome aboard the ferry – and don't be fazed by spelling variations you will encounter on notices or road signs. We have tried to be consistent in transliterating place names, but the Greeks themselves are notoriously variable when rendering their language into Roman characters. For more on the Greek language, see the *Travel Tips* section at the back of this book.

BULGARIA
Kărdžàli
Edirne
BLACK SEA
İstanbul
áma
Xánthi
Komotiní
TURKEY
Keşan
avála
Liménas
Alexandroúpoli
Marmara Denizi
onikós
Thásos
Kavakköy
pos
Bandırma
Bursa
SOS
Samothráki
Áthos
Fengári
1611
Thermá
(Loutrá)
Athos
2033
Thrakikón Pélagos
Çanakkale
honía
Gökçeada
Abide
Mýrina
Límnos
Ayvaçık
Edremit
Balıkesir
E
C
E
Ágios
Evstrátios
Giourá
Pipéri
Mólyvos
sos
Sporádes
Mytilíni
Lésvos
Plomári
Akhisar
TURKEY
Skýros
Skyros
Psará
ba)
Paralía Kymis
Híos
İzmir
Híos
Urla
Pyrgi
Çeşme
Karystos
A
E
G
E
A
N
Sámos
Vathý
(Sámos)
Aydın
Denizli
Ándros
Karlóvassi
Ikaría
Ándros
Foúrni
Ág.
Kírykos
Agathonisí
Kéa
Tínos
Giáros
Arkí
Milâs
Muğla
Kýthnos
Ermoúpoli
Sýros
Tínos
Lipsí
S
Mýkonos
Pátmos
E
Cyclades
Léros
Sérifos
A
Páros
Náxos
Kálymnos
Bodrum
Sífnos
Náxos
Andíparos
Kós
Kós
Kímolos
Síkinos
Íos
Amorgós
Kéfalos
Fethiye
Mílos
Folégandros
Nísyros
Sými
Astypálea
Dodecanese
Tílos
Ródos
Kaş
Santoríni
(Thíra)
Anáfi
Sýrna
Hálki
Mt Atávyros
1215
Megísti
(Kastellórizo)
Líndos
Kritikó Pélagos
Ródos
(Rhodes)
Kárpathos
niá)
Réthymno
(Rethimno)
Iráklio
(Heráklion)
Kríti (Crete)
Kásos
Arkádi
Ida
(Psiloritis)
2456
Plakiás
Ágios
Nikólaos
Bitía
Hora
Sfakion
Knossós
Zákros
Ag.
Galini
Ierápetra
Gávdos

Greek Islands

0   50 km

0   50 miles

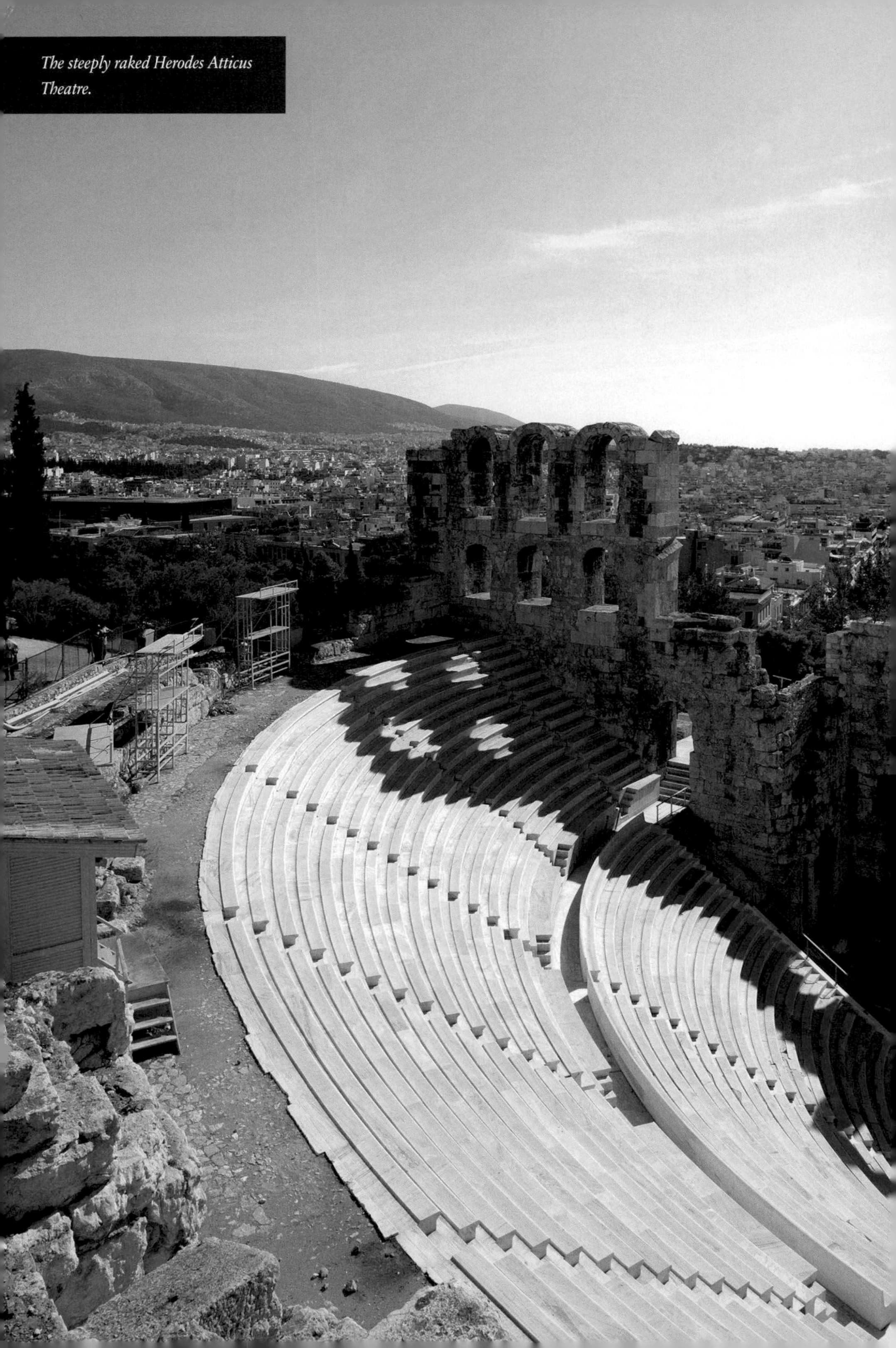

The steeply raked Herodes Atticus Theatre.

ATHENS STOPOVER

Large and hectic, sometimes spectacular, always exhilarating, Athens can be simply exhausting. But if you have a day or two to look around, there's plenty to see.

Athens was suddenly designated capital of the new Greek state after the War of Independence, and despite diligent Bavarian attempts at town planning – largely disregarded – it never mellowed into a venerable old age. Since the post-1923 influx of Greek refugees from Asia Minor, Athens has grown haphazardly and rapidly, with incongruent juxtapositions of old and new, such as a faded neoclassical mansion, still with a garden, ensconced between modern office blocks, its windows hermetically closed against the traffic roar. A whole raft of infrastructure projects completed before the 2004 Olympics – most notably the efficient metro system – have made this brash, sometimes plain ugly capital much more liveable.

Branching off from the frenzied central arteries are the less congested minor veins of the city; most apartment blocks have balconies or full-sized verandas, where you glimpse half-clad Athenians emerging from their afternoon siesta to read the paper, water their plants, or eat their evening meal. The hot weather makes open-air life a necessity, or at least open-window life, as prime-time television draws folk indoors.

Ancient Athens

If your time in Athens is limited, it makes sense to start with the premier

monuments dating from Ancient Athens's "Golden Age", the 5th century BC. Seen from the right angle, driving or walking along below, the **Acropolis** ❶ (summer Mon–Fri 8am–8pm, Sat–Sun 8am–3pm;winter shorter hours; charge) can still make the grimy concrete fade into insignificance. Climb up in the early morning, when crowds are thinnest, and a strip of blue sea edged with grey hills marks the southwestern horizon.

The **Propylaia**, the official entrance to the Acropolis built by Mnesikles

Main Attractions

Parthenon
Temple of Olympian Zeus
Pláka quarter
Acropolis Museum
Benaki Museum
Byzantine and Christian Museum
National Archaeological Museum
Museum of Popular Musical Instruments

Shopping around Sýndagma.

Supporting the porch of the Erechtheion, the Caryatids' faces still bear the pigments of ancient "make-up".

The Parthenon, viewed from the Erechtheion.

Theseus forgot to change his signal-sail from black to white, is the small, square temple of **Athena Nike**, finished in 421 BC, and recently completely rebuilt.

The scaffolded **Parthenon** looks a bit like a stonemason's workshop, just as it must have done in the 440s BC when it was under construction as the centrepiece of Pericles' giant public works programme. Some of his contemporaries thought it extravagant, accusing Pericles of dressing his city up like a harlot. In fact, the Parthenon celebrates Athena as a virgin goddess and the city's protector. Her statue, 12 metres (39ft) tall, and made of ivory and gold plate to Phidias' design, used to gleam in the dim interior. In late antiquity it was taken to Constantinople, where it disappeared.

The **Erechtheion**, an elegant, architecturally complex repository of ancient cults going back to the Bronze Age, was restored around the millennium. Completed in 395 BC, a generation after the Parthenon, it once contained the supposed tomb of King Kekrops, mythical founder of the ancient Athenian royal family.

around 430 BC, was cleverly designed with imposing columns to impress people coming up the hill. Parts of its coffered stone ceiling, once painted and gilded, are still visible. On what was once the citadel's southern bastion, from which King Aegeus legendarily threw himself off when his son

THE PARTHENON

Hundreds of blocks of marble have been levered down from the Parthenon, to replace the rusting iron clamps inserted in the 1920s with non-corrosive titanium ones (rust made the iron clamps expand, cracking the stone). The restorers have also collected and identified some 1,600 chunks of Parthenon marble scattered all over the hilltop. Many of these were blown off in the 1687 blast caused by a Venetian artillery shell igniting Ottoman munitions stored inside the temple. Once they have been painstakingly replaced, about 15 percent more of the building will be on view. New blocks cut from near the ancient quarries on Mount Pendéli, the source of the original 5th-century BC stone, will be used to fill the gaps, and fade within a few years to more closely match the original masonry.

The Caryatids now supporting the porch are modern copies; four surviving originals (one is missing, one is in the British Museum) are prize exhibits in the **Acropolis Museum** (see page 113). In Ottoman times, the Erechtheion was used by the city's Ottoman military commander as a billet for his harem.

On the south side of the Acropolis lies the **Theatre of Dionysos ❷** (summer Mon–Fri 8am–8pm, Sat–Sun 8am–3pm; winter 8.30am–3pm; charge). Surviving marble seating tiers date from around 320 BC and later, but scholars generally agree that plays by Aiskhylos, Sophokles, Euripides and Aristophanes were first staged here at 5th-century BC religious festivals. A state subsidy for theatregoers meant that every Athenian citizen could attend these events.

Herodes Atticus, a wealthy Greek landowner and Roman senator, built another theatre on the south slope of the Acropolis in the 2nd century AD: the steeply raked **Herodes Atticus Theatre ❸** (better known as the Iródio), which is now used during the Hellenic Festival for performances of popular or classical music and ballet.

Earlier in the 2nd century AD, Roman Emperor Hadrian, a fervent admirer of classical Greece, erected an ornate **arch** marking the spot where the classical city ended and the provincial Roman university town began. Little of this Roman city can be seen beneath the **National Gardens**, or the archaeological area behind the towering columns of the **Temple of Olympian Zeus ❹** (Stíles Olymbíou Dioú; daily, summer 8am–7pm, winter 8am–3pm; charge), but recent excavations indicate that numerous Roman buildings stood in this area, at least as far as the **Panathenaic Stadium** (Kallimármaro), refurbished by Herodes Atticus. Work on the temple had been abandoned in around 520 BC when funds ran out, but Hadrian finished the construction and donated a statue of Zeus as well as one of himself.

As the Acropolis was mainly used for religious purposes, while the ancient Greek **Agora ❺** (daily, 8am–3pm ; charge) was employed for most other public activities – commercial,

TIP

The main tourist information office (EOT) is in a purpose-built building at the base of pedestrianised Dionysiou Areopagítou. It provides free maps of Athens and the islands, ferry timetables and museum schedules. There's also a branch in the airport.

The Féthiye Tzamí, an Ottoman mosque on the edge of the Roman Forum.

Agora finds. The completely intact **Hephaestion**, the Doric temple opposite (alias the Thisseion), is rather clunky compared to the Parthenon.

A 1st-century BC astronomer, Andronikos of Kyrrhos, designed the picturesque **Tower of the Winds** ❻ (Aerides; daily 8.30am–3pm), a well-preserved marble octagon within the scanty remains of the **Roman Agora** (daily 8.am–3pm; charge). The tower is decorated with eight relief figures, each depicting a different breeze, and once contained a water-clock.

One block north of the tower stand the remains of what is known as **Hadrian's Library** (daily, 8am–3pm; charge), and is actually an enormous multi-purpose cultural centre built around a colonnaded courtyard.

City streets

The heart of the modern city lies within a triangle defined by **Platía Omónias** (Omónia Square) in the north, **Platía Syndágmatos** ❼ (Sýndagma Square) to the southeast and **Monastiráki** to the south. Except for a few narrow cross-streets, this is

Art souvenirs in Pláka.

political, civic and educational. Today it looks like a cluttered field of ruins, but the reconstructed **Stoa of Attalos**, a 2nd-century BC shopping mall, is a refreshingly cool place to linger and houses a worthwhile museum of

a car-free area, which has taken on a new lease of life. **Ermoú** is now a long pedestrian walkway with reinvigorated shops (albeit some vacant with the crisis) and refurbished facades, enlivened by pavement buskers and push-carts. Except when a rally or riot is taking place on nearby Sýndagma, this an attractive area to wander in the evening. Be prepared for some extravagantly coloured, witty and often polemic graffiti – Athens is perhaps the most heavily "decorated" city in Europe.

Monastiráki has a tourist-pitched market selling a weird assortment of objects, where collectors of kitsch will find much to interest them. Across Ermoú, Psyrrí district has more workshops and more practical items on sale. The old **Varvákios covered market**, a 19th-century gem roughly halfway between Monastiráki and Omónia, is the city's main meat and fish market, crowded with shoppers milling between open stands displaying fish, seafood and every variety of poultry and meat you could imagine.

Pláka, the city's oldest quarter clustering at the foot of the Acropolis, has been restored to its former condition (or rather, to a fairly good reproduction of it), with motor vehicles prohibited (for the most part), 19th-century houses refurbished and streets tidied up. It is now a delightful, sheltered place in which to meander, full of small beauties: look out for half a dozen Byzantine churches, two Ottoman mosques, several museums and the 4th-century BC **monument of Lysikratos**.

Byzantine Athens is fairly well represented with mostly 11th-century churches – besides a dozen in Pláka, there are several others huddling below street level in the shadow of taller, modern buildings. They are still in constant use: passers-by slip in to light a yellow beeswax candle, cross themselves and kiss an icon in near-darkness before returning to the noise outside. One of the most handsome is **Agii Theodóri** ❽ just off Klavthmónos Square, built on the site

of an earlier church, in characteristic cruciform shape with a tiled dome and a terracotta frieze of animals and plants. **Kapnikaréa** in the middle of Ermoú has an apsidal fresco of the Virgin Platytéra by the distinguished neo-Byzantine painter Photis Kontoglou, while the 12th-century **Mikrí Mitrópoli** (Small Cathedral) next to its garish successor features extensive external bas-relief masonry recycled from all previous eras. The huge, domed **Church of Sotíra Lykodímou** on Filellínon Street was bought by the Tsar of Russia in 1847 and completely rebuilt by 1856 to serve the city's growing Russian Orthodox community.

Athens's museums

Top of the agenda for rushed visitors is likely to be the **Acropolis Museum** ❾ (Tue–Sun 8am–8pm, Fri until 10pm; charge), a few hundred metres south of and below the Acropolis rock. While decidedly retrograde-modern when seen from the outside, inside the building is arrayed to duplicate the experience of ascending the Parthenon's various levels. A

The Tomb of the Unknown Warrior, by Sýndagma Square, is guarded by Evzónes, elite soldiers in traditional mountain costume.

ramp – reproducing the approach to the Propylaia – leads up from the ground floor to an intermediate one, home to all the free-standing statuary (and much more) displayed in the cramped old museum, including the four original Caryatids still in Greece, revealing an Archaic ideal of femininity in their earrings, tresses and crinkled, close-fitting dresses. The top floor has been built exactly to mirror the arrangement of the friezes of the Parthenon, clearly visible through windows – those originals that Greece retains pointedly abut plaster casts of the roughly 60 percent residing in the British Museum, with the clear implication that they ought to be returned.

The **Benaki Museum** ❿ (www. benaki.gr; Wed, Fri, Sat 9am–5pm, Thur 9am–midnight, Sun 9am–3pm; charge), at the National Gardens' northeast corner, houses an eclectic collection of treasures from all periods of Greek history – including jewellery, costumes, the recreated interiors of two rooms from a Kozáni mansion, and two icons attributed to El Greco in the days when he was a Cretan painter called Doménico Theotokópoulos. The beautifully laid-out galleries make this one of the most attractive museums in the city. There are always worthwhile temporary exhibits in a special gallery.

The privately endowed **Museum of Cycladic Greek Art** ⓫ (www.cycladic. gr; Mon, Wed, Fri 10am–4pm, Thur 10am–8pm, Sat 10am–3pm; charge) nearby features the beautiful prehistoric white marble figurines dismissed as barbaric by Belle Epoque art critics but numbering Picasso and Modigliani among their admirers. They come from graves in the Cycladic islands, but scholars are still uncertain of their purpose (see also page 180). There are also numerous worthwhile temporary exhibits, some held in the adjoining neoclassical Elena Stathatou mansion-annexe.

The **Byzantine and Christian Museum** (www.byzantinemuseum.gr; Tue–Sun summer 8am–8pm, winter 9am–4pm; charge) across busy Vassilísis Sofías, originally occupied a mock-Florentine mansion built by

Admiring excavations under the Acropolis Museum.

the eccentric philhellene Duchess de Plaisance. Exhibits, dating from the early Christian period to 13th-century Attica frescoes, now reside in an impressive modern wing, subterranean yet bright and spacious, and include the 7th-century AD Hoard of Mytilene well-displayed and informatively labelled.

The **National Archaeological Museum** ⓬ (www.namuseum.gr; Mon 1.30–7.45pm, Tue–Sun 8am–6.45pm; charge) holds the city's most important collection of ancient artefacts. Highlights include the stunning gold work of the Mycenaean trove, more prehistoric Cycladic art, the Andikythera mechanism (an intricate astronomical computer 15 centuries ahead of its time), the Akrotiri frescoes (see page 192) and major bronze sculptures, including the wonderful Poseidon found off the coast of Évvia.

Of the many small Pláka exhibitions two of the best are the **Folk Art Museum** (Tue–Sun 9am–4pm; charge) at Kydathinéon 17, with a reconstructed room full of murals by naïve Lésvos artist Thephilos; and the

Museum of Popular Musical Instruments (Tue and Thur–Sun 10am–2pm, Wed noon–6pm; free), in a fine neoclassical mansion at Diogénous 1–3. The collection here, curated by Greek ethnomusicologist Phivos Anogiannakis, features just about every traditional instrument ever played in Greece, with archival photos and listening posts to round out the experience. The museum shop sells CDs of folk recordings, particularly of island music, while the garden hosts worthwhile evening concerts all summer.

With extra time available, you should take in some of the city's excellent private art galleries, which have multiplied since the millennium despite dire economic straits. The main **Benaki Museum annexe** just off our map at Pireós 138 (Thur and Sun 10am–6pm, Fri–Sat 10am–10pm) has consistently good temporary exhibits (often photographic), as does the **Theoharakis Foundation** just off Sýndagma at Vasillísis Sofiás 9 (www.thf.gr; daily 10am–6pm, until 8pm Thur–Fri; charge). Just a block or so behind, at Kriezótou 3, is perhaps the best Athens

art museum for the uninitiated: the **Hadjikyriakos-Ghikas Gallery** (Wed–Sun 10am–6pm; charge), technically yet another annexe of the Benaki. It's somewhat misnamed – while indeed installed in the former home of the great painter, with his top-floor residence and atelier preserved as at his death in 1994, most of the many galleries honour (with intelligent labelling) just about everybody who was anybody in 20th-century Greek cultural life, including architects, cartoonists and photographers as well as painters.

Athens by night

Not least because of roasting summer temperatures, Athenians are decidedly nocturnal. Even during the small hours the main streets are never entirely deserted, which makes Athens one of the safer cities in which to walk at night, although metro pickpocketing, muggings and car break-ins are on the rise. Lost night-time sleep is made up for with a long afternoon siesta (*never* telephone an Athenian – or any Greek or that matter – between 2.30pm and 6pm).

Both informal (bar-based) and organised nightlife is still fairly lively and long despite the economic pinch. The original central district for this was Psyrrí, just beyond Monastiráki (with which it shares a metro station). Accounts of hip Psyrrí's demise in popular lore are greatly exaggerated, but it is true that the margin of trendiness and gentrification spreads steadily outward and further northwest, encompassing the formerly dismal, rust-belt neighbourhoods of Gázi, Rouf, Keramikós, Metaxourgío and Votanikós.

Hot venues, for cutting-edge arts events as well as music, change regularly – consult a listings website or a local friend. But durable examples include Pireós 260, a converted factory behind the School of Fine Arts that's a popular Hellenic Festival venue, or Avlea in Votanikós, hosting quality Greek music events at realistic drinks and admission prices. There are also a half-dozen well-loved summer cinemas to be found in the central districts of Thisío, Petrálona, Kolonáki and Exárhia.

Stunning displays at the Byzantine and Christian Museum.

Coping with Piraeus

Most visitors only go to Piraeus to catch a ferry, but this bustling port does offer some points of interest.

Piraeus is a city in its own right. Although unabashedly industrial/commercial, with few concessions to the numerous tourists who pass through, it's worth allowing some extra time for it before or after a seagoing journey, even if there are few echoes of *Never on Sunday* these days. (The underworld moved to Athens during the puritanical colonels' dictatorship. Since then, successive mayors have been elected on a "smarten up Piraeus" platform.)

Get there well before sailing time so that you have half an hour or so to arrive at your departure quay in good time as ships leave promptly. The departure quay is often very remote although a shuttle bus does run. You also need to allow time to buy a ticket; if you have a car or want a sleeping berth, this should be organised days (in peak season, a week or more) in advance.

The easiest way to get to Piraeus from central Athens is on the metro. Take line 1 and allow around 45 minutes' journey time from Sýndagma. From Athens Airport, express bus X96 takes about 90 minutes to reach the main quay at Piraeus, as long as there is no traffic.

To the right quay

Your ticket agent will tell you which quay your ferry departs from. They are numbered E1 to E10 going around the main basin clockwise. As a general guide: boats to the Cyclades depart from quays E5–E7 opposite the metro station; direct boats to Crete leave from E4, along Aktí Kondýli on the northeastern side of the port; catamarans and hydrofoils to the Argo-Saronic islands depart from E9, along Aktí Miaoúli, while slow car ferries to the same destinations go from E8 next to Karaïskáki Square; the Dodecanese are served both from E10, at the far end of Aktí Miaoúli, and from E1, way across the harbour, with most northeast Aegean sailings from E2.

Cosmopolitan Piraeus

The radical cosmopolitanism for which Piraeus was famous 2,500 years ago still exists – immigrants are conspicuous, and leftist deputies are regularly returned to parliament – but few remains survive. Those that do comprise a stretch of elegant 4th-century BC wall that runs beside the coast road beyond Zéa Marína, and an ancient amphitheatre which backs onto the **Archaeological Museum** (Tue–Sun 8.30am–3pm; charge) at Hariláou Trikoúpi 31. It is well worth visiting if you have time, although it is a very long walk from Quay E10.

Its prize exhibits are two bronze statues found in 1959; a magnificent 6th-century BC *kouros* (idealised figure of a young man), that is known as the Piraeus Apollo; and a 4th-century helmeted Athena, looking oddly soulful for a warrior goddess, as well as another 4th-century BC bronze of Artemis.

Statuary at the Piraeus Archaeological Museum.

THESSALONÍKI STOPOVER

With several airlines serving the city from various points in the UK, and a network of onward domestic flights, Thessaloníki has become a feasible gateway to the islands.

Main Attractions
Archaeological Museum
Agios Dimítrios church
Agía Sofía church
Kástra district
Modiáno market

The White Tower was added to the Roman-Byzantine walls by the Venetians.

Modern apartment blocks characteristic of many Mediterranean seaside cities predominate. But a century ago, the skyline consisted of minarets rising above a tile-roofed town picturesquely climbing between medieval ramparts to an upper quarter. When more than half of this was destroyed by the Great Fire of August 1917, British and French architects accompanying the Allied expeditionary forces were commissioned to produce a new city plan; surviving Art Deco buildings enhance the wide boulevards they designed. But the fire spared much, and after years of neglect, this architectural heritage has been signposted and selectively renovated.

A brief history

Thessaloníki was founded in 315 BC by Macedonian king Kassander; it became an important halt on the Roman **Via Egnatia** between the Adriatic and the Hellespont. Saint Paul visited, and wrote two Epistles to the Thessalonians; Christianity (and the city)

got further boosts from the Byzantine emperors Theodosius (who issued his edict banning paganism here) and Justinian, who began new churches to supplement those adapted from Roman structures. Despite hostile raids, earthquakes, fires and adjacent malarial swamps, Thessaloníki prospered.

After 1500, many Sephardic Jewish refugees from Iberia settled here at Ottoman invitation, lending Salonika – as they called it – its defining trait until 1912, when they still constituted over half the population of 140,000, making it the largest Jewish city of that era. In 1943, 70,000 remained to be deported by the Nazis; fewer than 1,000 remain today.

After 1923, Thessaloníki epitomised a Greek refugee town: in absolute numbers, Athens had more, but by proportion of population, Thessaloníki contains more citizens with Anatolian ancestry than anywhere else in Greece.

After years in Athens' shadow, Thessaloníki has come into its own, with innovative venues occupying historic buildings, its native musicians (such as Nikos Papazoglou or Sokratis Malamas) frequently at the forefront of Greek song. The early November Film Festival is a major event on the European cultural calendar.

Downtown Thessaloníki

Platía Aristotélous Ⓐ is the hub of downtown, extending inland towards the ancient Agora and church of Agios Dimítrios. There are plenty of cafés and *ouzerís*, both outdoors and tucked into nearby buildings.

On the easterly seafront, behind the landmark White Tower, the **Archaeological Museum Ⓑ** (www.amth. gr; summer Mon 10.30am–8pm, Tue–Sun 8am–8pm, winter Tue–Sun 8.30am–3pm; charge), displays sumptuous Macedonian, Hellenistic and Roman finds from the entire region. Just beyond, the splendidly laid out **Museum of Byzantine Culture Ⓒ** (www.mbp.gr; summer Mon 10.30am– 8pm, winter Mon 8.30am–5pm, Tue– Sun 8.30am–3pm; charge, combined tickets available), displays artefacts from the Early Christian period (4th– 7th century) through to the Middle Byzantine period (8th–12th century).

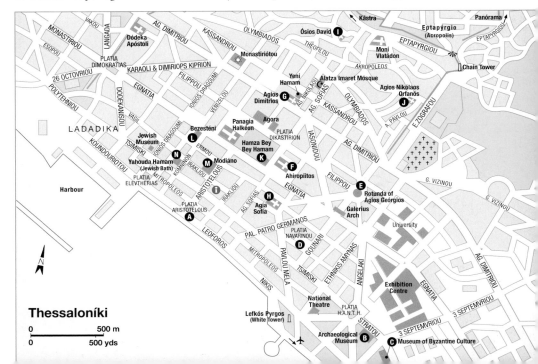

Thessaloníki

0   500 m
0   500 yds

FACT

During Ottoman rule, most Byzantine churches were converted into mosques, and their interiors coated in whitewash. Once removed after 1923, in many cases brilliant mosaics were found underneath.

At **Platía Navarínou** (D), Roman Thessaloníki is exposed as the excavated **Palace of Emperor Galerius Caesar,** who martyred the city's patron saint, Demetrius, in AD 305. Nearby survives part of Galerius's triumphal **arch**, squirming with intricate reliefs, erected over the Vía Egnatía in AD 297 to celebrate a victory over the Persians.

The other significant Roman relic is the **Agios Geórgios Rotunda** (E) (Tue–Sun 8.30am–3pm), northwest of the arch. Intended as Galerius's mausoleum, this is a rare circular Roman structure, later serving as a church, then a mosque. Glorious if hard-to-see 4th-century wall mosaics hide high up inside; the truncated minaret is the city's last standing one.

Byzantine Thessaloníki

More Byzantine churches survive in Thessaloníki than in any other Greek city. The earliest examples are clear adaptations of the colonnaded Roman basilica. Near the Agora stand 5th-century **Ahiropíitos** (F) (with fine mosaic patches under the arches between ornate columns) and its contemporary,

Inside the vaulted Bey Hamam.

Agios Dimítrios (G) (Mon 12.30–7pm, Tue–Sat 8am–8pm, Sun 10.30am–8pm), the largest church in Greece.

Agios Dimítrios is the city's main church, founded on the site of his martyrdom, and almost entirely rebuilt after the 1917 fire. Six small mosaics of the 5th to 7th century, featuring the saint, appear near the altar. The fire revealed a crypt thought to be adapted from the Roman baths where Demetrius was imprisoned.

South of Ahiropíitos is 8th-century **Agía Sofía** (H) (Holy Wisdom; daily 7am–1pm, 5–6.30pm), built in conscious imitation of its namesake in Constantinople. Its dome contains a vivid Ascension mosaic.

The steep alleys of **Kástra** lie about a 20-minute walk from the seafront. Since the 1980s, this once poor and despised neighbourhood has been renovated and now teems with trendy tavernas and cafés.

Tiny 5th- or 6th-century **Ósios Davíd** (I) church (Mon–Sat 9am–12 noon and 4–6pm; donation) is hidden up here. Its western end has vanished, but nost so an outstanding apsidal

mosaic depicting the vision of the Prophet Ezekiel of Christ Emmanuel, shown as a beardless youth seated on the arc of heaven, surrounded by Evangelical symbols.

Other churches uphill from the Vía Egnatía date from the 13th and 14th centuries. Financial constraints meant that frescoes, rather than mosaics, were their preferred ornamentation. By far the best of these is **Agios Nikólaos Orfanós** ❶ (Tue–Sun 8.30am–2.45pm).

Ottoman and Jewish Thessaloníki

The Ottomans, after their 1430 conquest, converted most churches for worship; thus there are as many civic buildings as purpose-built Ottoman mosques. Worthy 15th-century specimens include the graceful **Alatza Imaret Mosque** at the base of Kástra – around the corner from the **Yeni Hamam**, restored as an events venue – and the dilapidated **Hamza Bey Mosque** ❸ on Via Egnatia. It has yet to get the same treatment as the nearby **Bezesténi** ❶, a refurbished six-domed covered market now tenanted by luxury shops. The **Bey Hamam** (Mon–Fri 11am–8pm, Sat noon–5pm), dating from 1444, has stalactite vaulting over the entrance and inside.

By contrast, there are few traces of Thessaloníki's Jewish past, owing to the 1917 fire and the Nazi destruction of cemeteries and synagogues in 1943–44. Centrepiece of the vast central bazaar, selling everything from wooden furniture to live poultry – is the covered **Modiáno Market** ❹, a fish, meat and produce hall named after the Jewish family that established it. While barely half-occupied today, the Modiáno still supports authentic, atmospheric *ouzerís*.

Close by, the Louloudádika Hamam or Flower-Market Bath was also known as the **Yahouda Hamam** ❺ or Jewish Bath; the Jewish clientele is gone, but the flowers are still outside. On nearby Agíou Miná, the **Jewish Museum of Thessaloníki** (www.jmth. gr; Tue–Fri, Sun 11am–2pm, Wed, Thur also 5pm–8pm; charge) presents the history of the Jewish community in Thessaloníki.

TIP

For atmospheric bars and clubs, head for Ladádika, the former red-light district and port quarter behind the passenger ferry terminal.

THE CITY WALLS

Thessaloníki's seafront **Lefkós Pýrgos** (White Tower; www.lpth.gr; Tue–Sun 8.30am–3pm), effectively the city's logo, was a Venetian addition to the Roman-Byzantine walls. The 1826 massacre of unruly Janissaries here earned it the epithet "Bloody Tower". The Greeks whitewashed it from 1912 to 1985 – thus the new alias. A spiral staircase emerges at the crenellated roof terrace, affording fine views.

A vanished curtain wall leading inland from here past the university linked the White Tower with the **Chain Tower**, the northeastern corner of the fortifications; beyond it lies the **Eptapýrgio** (Yedi Küle in Turkish), the Seven Towers Fortress, long a jail, on the northeastern corner of the old walled **acropolis**.

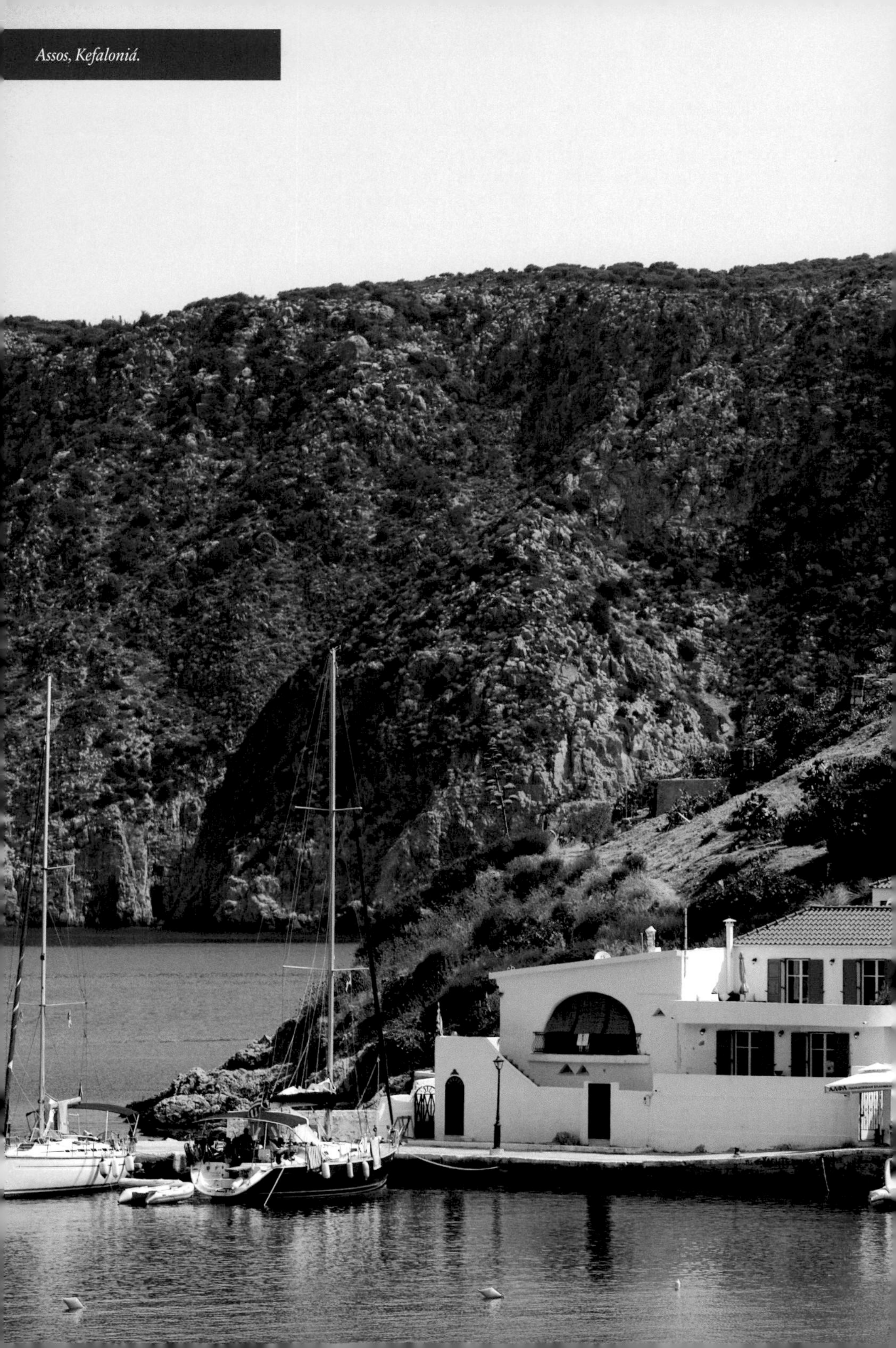

Assos, Kefaloniá.

Cape Skinári, Zákynthos.

THE IONIAN ISLANDS

Corfu, Paxí, Levkáda, Itháki, Kefaloniá,
Zákynthos, Kýthira.

Waiting patiently for that lift.

The islands of the Ionian Sea just west of Greece are dubbed the Eptánisa – "seven isles". However, the seventh, Kýthira, lies south of the Peloponnese and, while sharing history, culture and architecture, remains isolated from the other six islands.

During the 8th and 7th centuries BC, colonists from Corinth occupied the most northerly Ionian islands; two centuries later Corfu's rebellion against Corinth helped start the Peloponnesian War. The Ionians have since had many overlords, but the Venetian period left the most indelible mark. Artists, craftsmen and poets were sent to Venice for their education, returning home with a cosmopolitan perspective. Today, thanks to regular links with Italy, the islands still have a distinctly Italian flavour, most obviously in their cuisine and music.

Heavy rainfall makes the Ionians among the greenest of Greek archipelagos. Olive groves and vineyards are reminders that agriculture still plays a role in the economy. But this same unsettled weather has ruined many a holiday: from mid-September until late May, storms can wash out beach outings without warning. But escape to the mainland (or neighbouring, sunnier islands) is easy. There are several daily buses to Athens, regular seasonal ferries between Levkáda, Kefaloniá and Zákynthos, and flights between Athens or Thessaloníki and Corfu, Kefaloniá and Zákynthos (as well as peripheral flights between them).

North Itháki.

Today the Ionians are beset not by invaders (other than tour companies) but by earthquakes, the most recent serious one in 1953. Casualties were high and the beautiful Venetian-built capitals of Kefaloniá and Zákynthos were flattened. Reconstruction began almost immediately, though with different emphases. The Zakynthians recreated their Venetian town plan, albeit in reinforced concrete, while Ithacans rebuilt houses faithfully in the old style. Except in the central business district, the pragmatic residents of Argostóli in Kefaloniá put up makeshift buildings; a few unmodernised ones still remain.

CORFU

Few places have been exploited for tourism as much as Corfu. Yet away from the package-tour resorts there is much to savour in this beautiful verdant island.

Strategically poised where the Ionian Sea becomes the Adriatic, just off the mainland, Corfu (Kérkyra) has always been coveted, with a turbulent history of invaders and rulers. There's evidence of habitation dating back 50,000 years, but Corfu enters history as "Korkyra" in 734 BC, when it was colonised by ancient Corinth. By the mid-7th century BC, Korkyra was a major, independent naval power, siding in 433 BC with Athens against Sparta (and Corinth), triggering the Peloponnesian War. After 229 BC, the island fell under relatively uneventful Roman dominion.

Nearly eight centuries of Byzantine rule from AD 395 brought stability and prosperity, but latter years saw incursions and periods of domination by various groups: "barbarians", the Norman-Angevin Kingdom of the Two Sicilies, the Despotate of Epirus, and the Venetians. Weary of misrule and pirate raids, the Corfiots themselves asked to be put definitively under the protection of Venice, which obliged in 1386 – and stayed for 411 years, successfully outlasting two Ottoman sieges and leaving a rich legacy of olive groves. Napoleon dissolved what remained of the Venetian Empire in 1797, and the French held the island until 1814 (except for the eight-year interregnum of the

Ottoman/Russian-controlled "Septinsular Republic"). The British took over in 1814, staying for 50 years until all the Ionian islands were ceded to Greece as a sweetener for George I's ascent of the Greek throne.

During World War I, Corfu and Vídos islet were the final destination of a retreating, defeated Serbian army; a museum and cenotaphs from that era remain. In the next world war, the city suffered extensive damage in 1943 under a German bombardment to displace the Italian

Main Attractions

Listón
Néo Froúrio
Andivouniótissa Museum
Paleá Períthia
Erikoussa islet
Angelókastro
Ágios Geórgios Págon beach

Corfu signs.

occupiers, who had surrendered to the Allies; during their brief but brutal stay, the Nazis rounded up and deported Corfu's significant Jewish community, resident here since Venetian times.

A multicultural capital

Corfu Town, known as **Kérkyra** ❶, occupies a peninsula on the east coast. "Corfu" is a corruption of *koryfo*, or "peak", there being two such on a Byzantine/Norman-fortified outcrop much altered as the **Paleó Froúrio** (daily, summer 9am–7pm, winter 9am–4pm; charge) by the Venetians during the 15th and 16th centuries, when they cut a canal to make the citadel an island. The more complete **Néo Froúrio** to the west (same hours; charge) is strictly Venetian, and offers superb views over the town, cradled between the two forts.

With its tottering, multi-storeyed Venetian-style apartments, and maze-like lanes ending in quiet plazas, the Old Town constitutes a *flâneur*'s paradise; it was tidied up prior to hosting a 1994 EU meeting, but you wouldn't know it. Vacant bomb sites still yawn near the Néo Froúrio, and many main thoroughfares are blighted by touristic tat, but

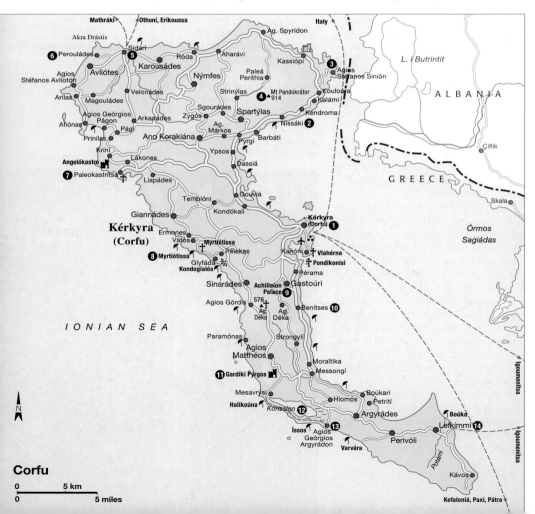

Corfu

0   5 km

0   5 miles

the backstreets remain surprisingly unspoilt, festooned with washing-lines and echoing to pigeon coos. The elegant counterpoint to this is the **Listón**, built by the French as a replica of the Rue de Rivoli in Paris. The name refers to local aristocrats listed in the Venetian *Libro d'Oro*, with sufficient social standing to frequent the arcades.

The Listón faces the Spianáda (Esplanade), a large and grassy open space cleared by the Venetians to deprive attackers of cover. At pricey Listón cafés you can order *tsintsibíra* (ginger beer), an enduring British legacy; other legacies include cricket, played idiosyncratically on the Spianáda, and the Victorian cemetery at the edge of town, still used by the 7,000-strong UK expat community.

The Spianáda is also the focus for Orthodox Easter celebrations, among the best in Greece. On Good Friday eve, each parish parades its *Epitáfios* (Christ's Funeral Bier) accompanied by uniformed brass bands, playing funeral dirges. On Saturday morning the relics of local patron saint Spyridon go walk-about, and then the tunes get jollier as townspeople shower special pots and crockery from their balconies to banish misfortune. The Saturday midnight Resurrection Mass finishes with fireworks launched from the Paleó Froúrio.

Both music and Saint Spyridon are integral parts of Corfiot life. Until destroyed by Nazi incendiary bombs, Corfu had the world's largest opera house after Milan's La Scala, and premières of major works took place here; there are still regular classical music performances and thriving conservatories. Spyridon, after whom seemingly half the male population is named "Spyros", was actually an early Cypriot bishop whose relics ended up here after the fall of Constantinople. Credited with saving Corfu from several disasters, his casket is processed four times yearly from his 16th-century shrine a block back from the Listón.

Unmissable sights

The town's two must-see indoor sights are the **Museum of Asian Art**

Beach fun.

(Tue–Sun 8.30am–3.30pm, may open later in summer; charge), a collection housed (together with excellent changing exhibits) in the British-built Palace of Saints George and Michael, plus the **Andivouniótissa (Byzantine) Museum** in Mourágia district (Tues–Sun 8.30am–3pm; charge), a medieval church crammed full of unusual icons of the 15th to the 18th centuries, many of them painted by refugee Cretan artists who came here after the fall of Venetian Crete in 1669. The **Archaeological Museum**'s (closed until 2015) star exhibit is the massive Gorgon pediment from a temple of Artemis at Paleopolis, but the more detailed pediment of a Dionysiac symposium, complete with the god, acolyte and lion, equals it. Both came from excavations in **Mon Repos estate** (daily 8am–7.30pm; free), where there are not only other ruined temples and an early Christian basilica, but also the **Paleópolis Museum** (daily 8am–c.3pm; charge), which holds worthwhile exhibits. Just south of this at **Kanóni** are the photogenic islets of **Vlahérna**, with

a little monastery and causeway to it, and **Pondikonísi**, said to be a local ship petrified by Poseidon in revenge for the ancient Phaiakians helping Odysseus. North of Corfu town, served by launches from the old port, forested **Vídos** island was the final destination of a retreating defeated Serbian army (a museum in Corfu Town, and cenotaphs at various spots remain from that era) and has good beaches plus a taverna.

The north of the island

Northwest of town are busy resorts such as **Kondókali**, **Komméno**, **Dassiá** and **Ypsos**, used by both Greek and foreign visitors, though **Barbáti** is probably the first beach you would stop for. The coast between **Nissáki** ❷ and **Agios Stéfanos Sinión** ❸ fancies itself a mini-Riviera, with smart villas – there are hardly any hotels – and secluded pebble coves. But mass tourism takes over again at **Kassiópi**, important in antiquity but now with only a crumbled castle. Up the slopes of 914-metre (2,300ft) **Mount Pandokrátor**

The 13-century Angelókastro.

❹ nestles **Paleá Períthia**, a well-preserved Venetian-era village. Back on the coast, little-frequented beaches between Kassiópi and **Aharávi** are pleasant alternatives to overdeveloped **Róda** and **Sidári** ❺ From Sidári ply the most reliable boats to the three small inhabited Diapóndia islets: **Mathráki**, **Othoní** and **Eríkoussa**. Mathráki is the wildest and least developed, Eríkoussa the most visited, thanks to its sandy beaches and proximity.

Northwest-coast beaches beyond Sidári are superior, beginning at quieter **Perouládes** ❻, continuing through **Agios Stéfanos Avliotón**, Arílas and **Agios Geórgios Págon**, the latter being the best of this series. Beyond **Kríni** looms the shattered but superbly set Byzantine-Angevin **Angelókastro**, guarding the approach to the beautiful double bay of **Paleokastrítsa** ❼, now oversubscribed; best admire it from above, at Theotókou monastery, or from the cafés in **Lákones** village.

Beyond here, beaches resume at **Ermones**, but either **Myrtiótissa** ❽, small but beloved of naturists,

or bigger **Kondogialós,** with lots of amenities, are better, while **Agios Górdis** is a backpackers' paradise. Inland, **Pélekas** has famous coastal panoramas and sunsets, which prompted Kaiser Wilhelm II to build a special viewing platform.

The Achilleion Palace is stuffed with over-the-top statuary.

The south of the island

Inland and south of Kérkyra, near Gastoúri, stands the pretentious **Achilleion Palace** ❾ (daily, Apr–Oct 8am–7pm, Nov–March 8.45am–3.30pm; charge), built in 1890–91 for Empress Elisabeth of Austria, then acquired by Kaiser Wilhelm II after her assassination in 1898. It once housed a casino, has hosted EU meetings, and is now a museum of kitsch. **Benítses** ❿ has seen its heyday come and go, though the village itself is quite attractive and is getting a new lease of life thanks to a new marina completed in 2012; **Moraïtika** and **Messongí** are by contrast busier, but local beaches are better.

Inland, roads visit what is seemingly another island, winding around **Agii Déka** hill (576 metres /1,890ft), with the uninhabited monastery of Pandokratóra near the summit. Due west of Messongí is the **Gardíki Pýrgos** ⓫, a crumbling octagonal Angevin castle in a curious lowland setting. The castle road continues to the fine **Halikoúna** beach at the northwest end of the **Korissíon** lagoon ⓬, a protected nature reserve and a magnet for birdwatchers. From the nearby hill village of **Agios Matthéos**, you can reach another sandy beach, **Paramónas**.

Back on the main trunk road, Argyrádes gives access to the north-coast villages of **Boúkari** and **Petrití**, which have low-key facilities owing to a lack of good beaches. In the opposite direction lies **Agios Geórgios Argyrádon** ⓭, developed during the 1990s for mass tourism, with only splendid **Íssos** beach, a mecca for windsurfers, to its credit. The Corfiots have deliberately quarantined the Club 18–30 set at **Kávos**. The underrated, second-largest town on Corfu, **Lefkímmi** ⓮, goes about its business just inland, seemingly oblivious to its raucous neighbour; the Lefkimians visit the beach at Boúka, the mouth of the river picturesquely bisecting Lefkímmi.

The southern end of the Corfu Trail is found nearby at the ruined monastery of **Panagías Arkoudílas**, poised on Cape Asprókavos above some idyllic, deserted beaches.

The photogenic islet of Vlahérna, with its little monastery.

Working the Land

Traditional farming methods are still used on many islands, with the economic crisis prompting a back-to-the-land movement after years of rural depopulation.

The silver-leafed olive trees that grace the Aegean landscape form an integral part of island life. Olive oil has long formed a staple part not only of the Greek diet, but the local economy. Even urban families have olive groves, gathering their own olives to take to a local mill. Depending on variety and locale, harvesting – either raking from the trees or collecting from black mesh nets that also mark the scenery – occurs between October and January, with pruning (the wood is a highly prized fuel) soon after.

For most full-time island farmers, agricultural produce is for local use only, with non-mechanised techniques enforced by hilly terrain, though roto-tillers have now replaced ploughing teams. The striking patterns of irregular fields result from the division of land to form inheritances and marriage dowries. A typical farming community consists of 10 to 100 close-packed houses, their small yards containing chickens and the occasional pig. Most villages now have at least dirt-road access, power lines (or solar panels) and perhaps some fixed phones, but water supply can be a problem.

A large-scale goat- or sheep-herder may have 100 to 500 animals; he concentrates on producing kids or lambs for the peak periods of Easter and summer. In the cooler months, most herders collect wild foliage for both bedding and fodder. By contrast, there's the elderly widow with a few goats and fields, working them on her own. In spring, animals are taken to graze in fairly remote pastures.

Crops and methods

Small-scale farmers supplement the family diet with lentils, broad beans and chickpeas, fruit and vegetables. During spring and summer, ubiquitous vegetable patches produce (in this order) potatoes, beans, tomatoes, courgettes, peppers, melons and aubergines – in return for considerable investment in time and effort, but not always pesticides or fertilisers. Subsistence farmers unable to spend on these products make a virtue of necessity by producing de facto organic crops.

During early summer, grain – especially barley – is still often reaped by hand with a sickle, laid out in situ to dry, and then threshed. This is usually done by machine, especially on larger islands such as Rhodes, Kós and Límnos, but on a few remote, rugged islands, a team of mules or donkeys is still walked over the crop strewn on the threshing cirques (*alónia*) to smash the husks with their hoofs, prior to winnowing and sieving.

Traditional farming methods are disappearing however, sporadic EU subsidies notwithstanding. The youth exodus from the villages to towns or the mainland to find work, plus competition with other EU farmers, have spelt doom for labour-intensive methods, as numerous overgrown fields and crumbled terraces attest. One positive outcome of the ongoing economic crisis is a reversal in this migration: many younger people, unable to survive in the city, are returning to live rent-free in their ancestral village, in some cases to take up farming. The main hope for the agricultural sector is to increase value through official organic certification – difficult when your olive groves are aerially sprayed without your consent against the destructive *dákos* fly – or the marketing of speciality cash-crops such as almonds, pine-nuts and kumquats.

The oil-producing olive grove, at the heart of both the local economy and of the Greek diet.

Agios Dionýsios in Zákynthos.

SOUTHERN IONIAN ISLANDS

Everything here, from architecture to food, has been influenced by the Italians, who continue to arrive in large numbers each August. Yet in recent years Brits, and central Europeans, are as or even more numerous.

axí (Páxos), the smallest of the seven main islands of the Ionian archipelago, is 90 minutes by conventional boat from Corfu (Kérkyra) – half that time by hydrofoil. Hilly and green, it has rugged west-coast cliffs, several sea-caves and various pebble beaches. Paxí figures little in ancient history and mythology, when it was uninhabited, though Tim Severin's *The Ulysses Voyage* identifies the Homeric spring and dell of Circe as the modern one beside the late Byzantine church of Ypapandí, in the far north. Paxí acquired extensive olive groves and served as a hunting reserve for the Corfiot Venetian aristocracy, but was only systematically populated as of the 15th century. The gnarled olive trunks, their shimmering leaves like coins tossed in the breeze, are emblems of the island, and provided the main livelihood before tourism – Paxiot oil ranks among the best in Greece, and has won many international medals. Dwellings, from humble cottages to baronial mansions, are tucked into hollows out of sight, and out of reach of the *maïstros*, the prevailing northwest wind; only during modern times have villas with sea and coast views appeared.

All boats dock at the small capital, **Gáïos ❶**, arrayed fan-like around its main square and sheltered by the two islets of **Agios Nikólaos** and **Panagía**,

with, respectively, a Venetian castle and small monastery. Gáïos preserves narrow streets and a few grand 19th-century buildings with Venetian-style balconies and shutters, plus most island shops, though tavernas are undistinguished.

Paxí's single main road meanders northwest, through the olive groves and tiny hamlets consisting of a few houses, and perhaps a *kafenío* at main junctions. Locally sold walking guides point you along a maze of old walled paths, dirt tracks and paved

Fishermen on Levkáda.

Southern Ionian Islands

0   10 km
0   10 miles

lanes, which provide the best way to see the island. Reached by a side road, **Longós** on the northwest coast is the most exclusive resort, flanked by the popular beaches of **Levréhio** and **Monodéndri**, the latter with road access. The "motorway" ends at **Lákka ❷**, beloved of yachts and the majority of landbound tourists, with a better choice of food and lodging; small beaches like **Orkós** lie within walking distance.

The northeast coast of **Andípaxi** (Andípaxos) islet shelters the two excellent beaches of **Vatoúmi** and **Vríka**, well known to day-trippers in summer but idyllic off-season. Only in summer, when several tavernas operate, do a dozen people live here; Andípaxi's vineyards produce a heavy red wine favoured for local festivals, and a lighter tawny white.

Levkáda (Léfkas)

Like Évvia, Levkáda is barely an island, joined to the mainland by a floating drawbridge over a canal. Greeks seasonally crowd the place, glad to find an island exempt from the prices and weather-whims of a ferry crossing. Yet Levkáda feels like the Ionian, with standard Venetian influences on speech and cuisine, the imposing fort of Santa Maura by the bridge, plus spear-like cypress and bright yellow broom in May carpeting the steep hillsides. Kefaloniá may be higher, but Levkáda has a more rugged landscape, which has preserved rural lifestyles in the hill villages; the older women still wear traditional dress, while local crafts and foodstuffs are avidly promoted.

Levkáda Town ❸ faces the canal and the lagoon enclosed by the Gýra sandspit; local topography provides safe mooring for numerous yachts on the southeast quay. Of all Ionian capitals, it's the most pedestrian-friendly; much of the central area is off-limits to cars. The municipal axis is Ioán-nou Melá, which beyond lively Platía Agíou Spyrídonos becomes Wilhelm Dörpfeld, in honour of the early

20th-century German archaeologist who attempted to prove that Levkáda was in fact Homeric Ithaca. He is again duly revered in the excellent **Archaeological Museum** (Tue–Sun 8.30am–3pm; charge), with well-labelled exhibits on ancient religion and daily life. Also notable are several ornate Italianate churches dating from the late 17th or early 18th century, where arched windows, artwork of the Ionian School and Baroque relief work sit oddly beside post-earthquake belfries modelled on oil derricks.

Levkáda is the homeland of 20th-century poet Angelos Sikelianos, and Lafcadio Hearn, a 19th-century short-story writer who immortalised supernatural Japan, born here to Greek and Irish parents. There are cultural links between the island and Japan, and streets commemorate both men.

Heading down Levkáda's east coast, the little port-resorts of **Lygiá** and **Nikiána**, with pebble coves and fish tavernas, are the first places to prompt a stop. They are calmer and quieter than **Nydrí** ❹, 20km (12 miles) south of Levkáda opposite a

mini-archipelago of four islets. The view out to them is the reason Nydrí has been earmarked for package-tourist development, since local beaches are frankly mediocre. Until the 1970s it was a tiny fishing village, where Aristotle Onassis used to pop over for dinner from Skorpiós, his private island; there's a statue of the man on the quay now named for him, but no trace of exclusivity lingers, and his daughter finally sold Skorpiós in 2013.

Levkáda balcony.

The one conventionally inhabited satellite island, **Meganísi**, accessible by daily ferry, is an increasingly ill-kept secret; yachters already appreciate its quiet bays and attractive villages. The best escape for landlubbers lies 3km (2 miles) inland, where the **Roniés Waterfalls** prove suprisingly impressive, and indicative of abundant water at the heart of Levkáda.

Beyond Nydrí, Dörpfeld excavated extensively at Stenó, and is buried on the far side of sumpy **Vlyhó** bay. The island ring road curls past Mikrós Gialós pebble bay and Sývota yacht harbour before descending to **Vassilikí** ❺, 40km (25 miles) from town,

Lunch by the lagoon in Levkáda Town.

one of Europe's premier windsurfing resorts. Boat tours are offered around Cape Levkátas – where Sappho legendarily leaped to her death – to spectacular west-coast beaches, also accessible by roads of varying steepness. Southernmost **Pórto Katsíki** ❻ stars on every third postcard of Levkáda; **Egremní** and **Gialós** are less frequented, while panoramic **Atháni** village has the closest tourist facilities. Further on, **Drymónas** is the most architecturally preserved settlement on the island, while **Kalamítsi** has an eponymous beach and "shares" **Káthisma**, Levkáda's longest strand, with **Agios Nikítas** (Aï Nikítas). The only port actually on the west coast has become a relatively upmarket resort, though worth avoiding in peak season. Beyond Agios Nikítas's own little beach, **Pefkoúlia** stretches north to the headland dividing it from **Agios Ioánnis**, the nicest section of Gýra beach, with its abandoned windmills.

Journeys inland thread through the half-dozen **Sfakiótes** hamlets occupying a fertile upland, where churches with Venetian-style belfries may be seen. The usual destination is **Karyá**, even higher and cooler, with a thriving crafts tradition and a vast central *platía* shaded by several giant plane trees.

Ithaca (Itháki)

Evidence that Itháki actually was the ancient home of Odysseus, wandering hero of Homer's *Odyssey*, is hardly conclusive, but this hasn't discouraged a local Homeric "heritage industry", with numerous streets and businesses named for characters in the epic, and modest archaeological sites assiduously signposted as putative locales for various episodes.

Most ferries dock at the cheerful capital, **Vathý** ❼, occupying the head of a long bay. Though badly damaged by the 1953 earthquake, many buildings survived, while others were tastefully rebuilt with traditional architectural elements. There are more tavernas and *kafenía*, especially along the quay, than in any other port town of this size. Several pebble beaches, pleasant, if not Itháki's best, lie close by; this is an island ideally sized for scooter exploration and walking.

Hiking Mount Enos, Kefaloniá.

THE ODYSSEUS TRAIL

Odyssean sites near Vathý include the **Bay of Phokrys** (now Fórkynos), the **Cave of the Nymphs**, the **Spring of Arethoúsa**, and ancient **Alalkomenae** (Alalkoméni). Having landed at Phokrys, it is said, Odysseus climbed up to the cave and hid various gifts given him by King Alkinoös of the Phaeakians. Next, Odysseus met his loyal swineherd Eumaeos and son Telemakhos at the Arethoúsa spring; the track-and-path walk from Vathý takes 90 minutes, challenging but with good views. Alalkomenae occupies a hillside 5km (3 miles) west of Vathý, above the road between Fórkynos and the secondary port (and a good pebble beach) of **Píso Aetós**; Heinrich Schliemann excavated here, but most of the finds (now in Vathý's museum) clearly do not date from the Homeric era.

Itháki is almost pinched in two by an isthmus barely wide enough for the main corniche road. The northern half has more lush vegetation and better beaches; below **Léfki** village the secluded pebble bays of **Agios Ioánnis** and **Koutoúpi** grace the west coast. **Stavrós ❽**, 16km (10 miles) from Vathý, is Itháki's second town, with another small museum devoted to finds from local sites with a better claim to being Odysseus' possible home. These are a citadel on **Pelikáta** hill and, more intriguing, an excavation marked as "**School of Homer**" off the road to Exogí. Walls and foundations, a few Mycenaean graves, steps carved into the rock and a vaulted cave-well lie exposed. In size and position, the place feels just right to be the base of a minor chieftain like Odysseus. **Exogí**, the highest village on the island, is seasonally occupied but offers superb views northeast. From Platrithiás village a paved drive goes to **Afáles** bay with excellent sand-and-pebble patches, while another road loops through Agii Saránda and Lahós, partly spared

by the earthquake, en route to **Fríkes**. There are ferries here (to Levkáda) and many yachts, although most visitors continue, past attractive pebble coves, to **Kióni ❾**, Itháki's most upmarket resort, where again various houses survived the quake. At either port, available rooms are scarce during high season.

From Kióni you can walk up the cleared and profusely waymarked old path to Anogí, a three-hour round trip; it's the best hike on the island, with only the last 20 minutes spoilt by the heliport and its access road. In half-deserted **Anogí**, there's a medieval church of **Kímisis tis Theotókou** (Dormition of the Virgin), with heavily retouched Byzantine frescoes and a Venetian belfry. Some 4km (2.5 miles) south, the **Monastery of Katharón** is by contrast a post-quake barracks-like structure, flanked by modern antennae, but the views are unsurpassed.

Kefaloniá (Kefallinía, Cephalonia)

Kefaloniá is the largest and second most mountainous Ionian island,

Stavrós is one of several places in Itháki claiming to be the site of Odysseus' castle, and marks its claim with this bust of the Homeric hero.

Vathý has retained a traditional style.

its population famous for a studied (often creative) eccentricity. It has mixed feelings about being typecast as "Captain Corelli's Island", since political opinions expressed in Louis de Bernières's locally set blockbuster novel are not popular here.

The capital town of **Argostóli** ❿, levelled by the 1953 earthquake, was rebuilt in utilitarian style and has a workaday feel, epitomised by meat and produce markets perched right on the commercial quay near the British-built **Drápano** stone bridge (pedestrian traffic only) across the lagoon. The quay's names honour two islanders: Ioannis Metaxas, 1930s dictator and defier of the Italians, and Andonis Tritsis (1937–92), innovative architect, maverick politician and ultimately mayor of Athens. The heart of town is **Platía Vallianoú**, ringed by hotels and *kafenía*, though trendy cafés have sprouted on the pedestrianised, relatively elegant **Lithóstroto**, beside its smart shops. Specific sights are limited to three museums, of which the **Korgialénios Historical and Folkloric Museum** (Ground floor of Korgialénios library; www.corgialenios.gr; Mon–Sat 9am–2pm; charge) is the most interesting, with pictures of Argostóli before and after the quake, and thorough coverage of traditional daily life. Northwest of town, near the Doric rotunda of **Agios Theodóros lighthouse**, the "sea mills" at **Katavóthres** used to grind grain and generate electricity; salt water pouring down sinkholes here emerges three weeks later near Sámi, but the 1953 disaster reduced the flow to a trickle.

To the east looms **Mount Enos** ⓫ (the ancient Ainos), at 1,628 metres (5,340ft) the highest peak in these islands and still partly covered with native firs (*Abies cephallonica*); two small reserves protect the remaining trees, much reduced by fires and loggers. The inclined south coastal plain at the base of the mountain, **Livathó**, is punctuated by a conical hill bearing the Venetian capital of **Agios Geórgios**, inhabited from Byzantine times until the 17th century. The impressive summit castle (Tue–Sun 8.30am–3pm) has wonderful views. Aristocratic associations linger at certain Livathó villages: pre-quake stone walls enclose vast estates; Lord Byron lived at nearby Metaxáta in 1823; and Keramiés still harbours dilapidated pre-quake mansions and a huge olive mill. The largest beach in the area, with resort amenities, is **Lourdáta**.

On the west shore of Argostóli gulf, reached by frequent ferries used by drivers and pedestrians alike to avoid the tedious journey by road, **Lixoúri** has long been eclipsed by rival Argostóli, but it's a pleasantly sleepy town with views to Zákynthos. Beyond, southwest on the peninsula, lie the busy red-sand beaches of **Mégas Lákkos** and **Xí**; en route you'll see how the fertile, grain-and-grape-planted terrain was heaved and buckled by the force of the quake. Beyond Xí, **Kounópetra** (Rocking Stone) no longer does so since 1953. Northwest of Lixoúri is the long, fine-pebble

Looking out from the Agios Theodóros lighthouse.

beach of **Petáni**, exposed but spectacular, although much the best beach near Lixoúri is the lonely, and facility-less, **Platiá Ammos**, reached by 300 steps from near Theotókou Kipouríon monastery.

Northern Kefaloniá was less damaged by the earthquake, and surviving medieval houses in various states of repair, especially at **Vassilikiádes** and **Mesovoúnia**, serve as poignant reminders of a lost architectural heritage. But the port resort of **Fiskárdo** ⓬ emerged almost unscathed, and ruthlessly exploits the fact despite a lack of beaches. The atmosphere is very pukka, if not precious, and yachts congregate in force, dodging the occasional ferry to Levkáda or Itháki. "Fiskárdo" is a corruption of the name of Norman raider Robert Guiscard, who made Kefaloniá his headquarters, but died here in 1085.

On the west coast, the perfect horse-shoe harbour of **Assos** ⓭ sees only fishing boats and is the better for it; there's good swimming from the isthmus joining this partly preserved village to a pine-covered bluff, with its fine late 16th-century Venetian fort. A bit further south, **Mýrtos** is among the most famous – and over-rated – beaches in the Ionians: coarse-pebbled and downright dangerous if a surf is up.

The water is calmer and the pebbles smaller at **Agía Evfimía**, a fishing village on the east coast; between here and the functional ferry port of **Sámi** lies the **Melissáni cave** ⓮ (daily May–Oct 8am–7pm, Nov–Apr Fri–Sun 10am–4pm; charge), containing an underground lake with its roof partly open to the sky. Nearby, another cave, **Drongaráti** (Apr–Oct daily 9am–8pm; charge) offers multicoloured stalactites and stalagmites, and is the occasional venue for concerts.

Beyond Sámi, a good road threads attractively through vegetated scenery to underrated **Póros**, another ferry/yacht port with a backdrop of green cliffs. From here you loop around the coast to busy **Skála**, with its superb sand-and-gravel beach fringed by pines, and extensive mosaic flooring in a Roman villa (daily 10am–2pm and 5–8pm; free); and then around Cape Moúnda to the all-sand **Kamínia** beach, Kefaloniá's principal turtle-nesting venue.

Zákynthos (Zánte)

Zante, Fior di Levante (flower of the East), said the Venetians, and its central plain – the most fertile in the Ionians – and eastern hills support luxuriant vegetation. The southeastern coasts shelter excellent beaches: some are almost undeveloped, others are home to notoriously unsavoury tourism.

At the once-elegant harbour town of **Zákynthos** ⓯, ferries dock by Platía Solomoú, named for native son Dionýsios Solomós, a 19th-century poet who wrote the words to the Greek national anthem. At the rear of his *platía*, the **Zákynthos Museum of Post-Byzantine Art** (Tue–Sun 8.30am–3pm; charge) features icons rescued from quake-blasted churches, as well as numerous

Kefaloniá blooms.

Peering down over the partly exposed lake of Melissáni cave.

17th–19th-century religious paintings of the Ionian School, founded by Cretan artists fleeing the Ottoman conquest, who met local artists strongly influenced by the Italian Renaissance. At the southern end of the harbour is the church of **Agios Dionýsios** (daily 8am–1pm and 5–10pm), the island's patron saint, designed in its latest incarnation by the archaeologist and Byzantinologist Athanasios Orlandos. The stained glass was donated after the 1953 earthquake by the island's small Jewish community, in gratitude for being hidden from the Nazis by their fellow islanders.

In medieval times people lived above the present town in **Bóhali** district, inside the huge *kástro* (daily summer 8am–8pm, winter 8.30am–3pm; charge), which is mostly Venetian on Byzantine foundations. Here, several tavernas provide superb views.

Unfortunately, most of the 700,000 annual visitors don't stray far from adjacent **Laganás/Kalamáki** ⓰ beach resorts, whose explosive growth since the late 1970s is endangering the survival of loggerhead turtles (see page 145), which have nested here for millennia. Luckily, the tourist tat is easily skirted, and Zákynthos shows its best side in the more remote corners. The **Vasilikós peninsula**, lying beyond forgettable Argási, has the island's best, most scenic beaches, culminating in **Agios Nikólaos** and **Gérakas**, nearest the east cape.

Start a tour of the unspoilt western hill villages from **Kerí** at the far south cape, with its lighthouse; next stop would be **Kilioméno** ⓱, which survived 1953 largely intact. Tourists are coached to **Kambí** to watch the sunset, but **Éxo Hóra** and **Mariés** have more character, with pre-quake churches and wells, vital in this arid region. Still further north, **Anafonítria** village offers an eponymous 14th-century monastery with a daunting gate-keep; plaques recall the local legend that 1578–1622 abbot St Dionýsios forgave and sheltered his brother's murderer here. Nearby, the 16th-century monastery of **Agios Geórgios ton Krimnón** has a round lookout tower in its well-tended courtyard; just beyond is the overlook for **Shipwreck (Navágio) Bay**, the most photographed in the Ionians, where a rusty freighter – driven ashore by the coastguard in the mistaken belief that it was a smugglers' ship – lies half-buried in sand. Boat trips, the only access, visit from **Pórto Vrómi**, below Mariés.

From "Shipwreck", head east through grain fields, and the two **Volímes** villages noted for their honey, textiles and cheese, to reach the east coast near **Makrýs Gialós** pebble beach and the bleak port of **Agios Nikólaos**, with daily summer ferries to Kefaloniá and excursion boats to the **Blue Caves** ⓲ – interconnecting grottoes with spectacular light effects at the right hour.

Back towards town, you wind through **Alykés** (the calmest beach resort), past secluded bays favoured by Greeks, before hitting mass tourism again at **Planós**.

Shipwreck Beach, Zákynthos.

Turtles vs. Tourists

The survival of the loggerhead turtles of Zákynthos is under threat from some of the undesirable effects of mass tourism.

A loggerhead turtle crawls out of the sea onto the moonlit beach of her birthplace, the island of Zákynthos. She has crossed the Mediterranean to return, at last, to this spot. Summoning all her strength, the 90kg (200lb) reptile selects a place in the sand where she digs a nest with her rear flippers. In it she lays about 100 soft eggs, each the size of a ping-pong ball, covers them with sand and returns exhausted to the sea to rest in the shallows. However, the survival of the loggerhead (Caretta caretta) is endangered before she even reaches the beach. It has been estimated that nearly half the females basking in the shallows may be maimed or killed by the propellers of speedboats taking waterskiers and paragliders out to sea. Carelessly discarded litter creates another hazard, as turtles suffocate trying to swallow plastic bags that they mistake for jellyfish, a favourite food of theirs.

For the female turtle, hazards increase when she slips ashore. Disorientated by the glittering lights of hotels and the strange noises coming from the tourists and bars, she may scurry back to the surf-line, uncertain where to deposit her eggs. Those that try to continue their labours may suffer the indignity of ignorant spectators brandishing torches and flashing cameras, frightening the turtles back into the sea where the eggs may be released, never to hatch.

Eggs that are successfully laid are often crushed by thoughtless quad-bikers, horse-riders and motorists who drive across the sand, which also compacts it so that it is impossible for the hatchlings to emerge. Beach umbrellas are unwittingly driven into nests, piercing the eggs. Tamarisk trees, planted to shade sunbathers, pose another problem, as hatchlings become tangled up in the roots. Even sandcastles may create holes that become shallow graves for the young turtles.

Hatching time

Hatching takes place from early August to late September – precisely when most tourists arrive. The 6cm (2.5in) hatchlings may emerge from their hazardous 50-day incubation and, instead of heading instinctively to starlight on the horizon line at sea, frequently wander confused up the beach to hotel and bar lights – an error that brings death from exhaustion or dehydration.

Zákynthos formerly had one of the greatest concentrations of nesting turtles in the Mediterranean. Laganás Bay was a particularly favourite spot but, confused by the combination of boats, lights and noise that tourism has brought, the turtles have abandoned these busy sands. The majority now nest in the more secluded beaches of Sekánia, Gérakas and Dáfni, where there is barely room for the activities of the bewildered reptiles. Fewer than 800 turtles now breed annually on Zákynthos, barely half the number found in the early 1980s.

Protecting the turtles

The Greek Sea Turtle Protection Society (www.archelon.gr), locked in frequent, sometimes violent conflict with unscrupulous developers, succeeded in the 1999 creation of the National Marine Park of Zákynthos (www.nmp-zak.org), encompassing the whole gulf between the capes of Gérakas and Kerí. Three levels of control restrict boating and land access; all affected beaches have dawn-to-dusk curfews. Volunteers are on hand during the season to help inform visitors, and monitor nests.

The National Marine Park of Zákynthos was set up to protect nesting turtles.

KÝTHIRA

Geographically nearer to Crete than to the Ionian group, this is one of Greece's quietest islands. Most visitors are Greeks from Athens – or Greek Australians returning home.

In legend Kýthira, suspended off Cape Maléa in the Lakonian Gulf, was one of the birthplaces of Aphrodite (the other contender is in Cyprus). A bleak plateau slashed by vegetated ravines, the island forms part of a sunken land bridge between the Peloponnese and Crete, from where Venetian refugees arrived in the 17th century.

It has two names (Tsérigo was its Venetian alias); a history of Venetian and British rule, but today governed from Piraeus along with the Argo-Saronics; an architecture that's a hybrid of Cycladic and Venetian; a pronounced Australian flavour, courtesy of remittances and personal visits from emigrants Down Under – and ubiquitous eucalyptus.

Kýthira (also spelled Kýthera and Kíthira) does not put itself out for outsiders. Accommodation is expensive and difficult to secure in summer; good tavernas are thin on the ground. Rough seas, which can play havoc with ferries from Gýthio, Neápoli or Kastélli (Crete), prompted the construction of an all-weather harbour at Diakófti in 1997. Despite all that, Kýthira has become a popular haunt of trendy Greeks, thanks to its appearance in Theo Angelopoulos's 1984 film *Taxídi sta Kýthira* and a more recent television series shot on the island.

Hóra ❶ (also called Kýthira) is one of the finest Aegean island capitals. Imposing, flat-roofed mansions in the lower town date from the 17th to 19th centuries, though the Venetian *kástro* above is of earlier vintage. An elaborate domed cistern system is still intact, while a few rusty cannons guarding a church seem superfluous, given the incredibly steep drop to the sea at **Kapsáli** yacht harbour, where most tourists stay, though the beach is mediocre.

Around the island

Much better beaches lie east of Hóra at **Halkós**, south of **Kálamos** village,

Kapsáli fortress.

and at **Fyrí Ammos**, east of Kálamos, with sea-caves to explore. North of Fyrí Ammos, and easier to get to, more excellent beaches dot the east coast: **Kombonáda**, **Kaladí** with a rock monolith in the surf at one end, and two – **Asprógas** and **Paleópoli** – to either side of Kastrí Point with its Minoan settlement, which was explored by Heinrich Schliemann in 1887.

The beachy strip ends at the fishing anchorage of **Avlémonas** ❷, where seemingly half the island's population comes for weekend lunches at the two fish tavernas. The diminutive octagonal Venetian fort is scarcely more than a gun emplacement. There's a better, 16th-century castle, complete with a Lion of St Mark, at **Káto Hóra**, just outside the attractive village of **Mylopótamos** ❸, with a waterfall and abandoned mill in a wooded canyon. This fortress was not a military stronghold but a civilian pirate refuge, with derelict houses inside.

Some 2.5km (1½ miles) west of Káto Hóra, perched above the surf-lashed west coast, the black-limestone cavern of **Agía Sofía** ❹ (May–Sep Tue–Sun 10am–5pm; charge) is the best of several namesake caves on Kýthira. A 13th-century hermit adorned the entrance with frescoes of Holy Wisdom personified, and three attendant virtues. (Locals insist that Aphrodite slept here, but today the only endemic life is a minute white spider.) About one-sixth of the cave, with marvellous stalactites and stalagmites, is open for visits.

The ghost village of **Paleohóra** ❺ failed the pirate-proof test in 1537, when the notorious Barbarossa sacked it. The ruins, including six frescoed (but locked) churches, cover the summit of a bluff plunging to the confluence of two gorges that unite as **Kakí Langáda**, reaching the sea at a small lake.

Potamós ❻, 2km (1.25 miles) north of the Paleohóra turning, is Kýthira's largest village, notable for a Sunday farmers' market. **Agía Pelagía**, the former ferry port, has come down in the world since **Diakófti** started working. More rewarding is **Karavás** ❼, the northernmost and prettiest of the ravine oasis-villages, which meets the sea at **Platiá Ammos** beach; pebbly **Foúrni** cove lies adjacent.

FACT

So many Kythirans (possibly 60,000) have emigrated to Australia that the post office in Hóra contains a Sydney telephone directory and Australia is informally referred to as "Big Kýthira".

Sailing the waters around Kýthira, which legend links to Aphrodite.

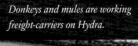
Donkeys and mules are working freight-carriers on Hydra.

ISLANDS OF THE SARONIC GULF

Salamína, Aegina, Póros, Hydra and Spétses.

Mosaic at the Monastery of the Panagía, on Hydra.

The five islands of the Saronic Gulf could be described as "commuter" islands – although that doesn't sound very romantic. As they lie within a short ferry ride (or an even shorter hydrofoil trip) from Piraeus, the temptation exists to treat the islands as an extension of the mainland or, more specifically, suburbs of Athens.

Entrepreneurs have been quick to exploit the islands' proximity. The one-day cruise from Piraeus calling at Aegina, Hydra and Póros remains a popular attraction for tourists visiting Athens (it is rivalled only by Delphi as a day-trip destination), although numbers have been down of late. When the cruise ships mingle with the ferries, the hydrofoils and the catamarans, there is often what resembles a traffic jam on the waters, and foreign visitors temporarily outnumber Greeks.

In spite of all this, the Argo-Saronics are definitely Greek islands, not Athens suburbs – distinctive in character, rich in history and, behind the crowds and the chichi boutiques, remarkably attractive places. Salamína(Salamis), the largest of these islands, is renowned for the epoch-making naval battle in 480 BC, which decided the outcome of the Persian Wars. Aegina (Égina) is home to the beautiful Doric Temple of Aphaea, which is one of the most important antiquities to be found on any Greek island.

Greek worry beads, or komboloi.

Póros and its channel have been immortalised by American author Henry Miller (1891–1980) in *The Colossus of Maroussi*, and forested Spétses (thinly disguised as Phraxos) by John Fowles in his celebrated 1966 novel *The Magus*. Not to be outdone, since the early 1960s Hydra (Ýdra) has attracted artists, filmmakers, well-heeled Athenians, trendy Europeans, movie stars and other international celebrities.

ARGO-SARONIC ISLANDS

These six islands all lie within easy reach of the mainland, and thus are popular destinations. Nevertheless, they are distinctive, rich in history and remarkably attractive.

Low, flat Salamína (ancient Salamis) is invariably overlooked by island-hoppers intent on more glamorousdestinations. It's the largest Saronic Gulf island, but so close to Athens (and so frequently connected from Pérama port) that most Athenians regard it as a commuter dormitory.

Salamína

Salamína is best known for the naval battle in 480 BC in which outnumbered Athenian ships routed Xerxes' Persian fleet, the Greek ships being the "wooden walls" that the Delphic Oracle had predicted would save Athens. Today the island is decidedly workaday, especially the port of Paloúkia, with its naval base; Selínia, 6km (4 miles) southwest, has tavernas and two hotels.

Most islanders live in the busy capital, **Salamína ❶** (or Kouloúri), which has an archaeological and a folk museum, and decent tavernas. The 13th-century **Faneroméni Convent ❷** overlooks the northwest coast, 6km (4 miles) from Salamína; it now houses nuns and has vivid 17th-century frescoes. **Eándio**, a pleasant village on the west coast, has a good hotel. From here you can reach the southeast coast resort of **Peráni** and the small but very pretty harbour of **Peristéria**.

Aegina and Angístri

An hour and a half by ferry from Piraeus, or 45 minutes by hydrofoil, Aegina (Aigina, Egina) has little trouble attracting visitors. Long a favourite Athenian weekend retreat, it remains more popular with them than among foreign tourists or other Greeks. Shaped like an upside-down triangle, Aegina's south is punctuated by the prominent cone of **Mount Oros**, the highest (532 metres/1,745ft) peak in the Argo-Saronic islands, visible on a pollution-free day from the

Main Attractions
Faneroméni Convent
Hristos Kapralos Museum
Temple of Aphaea
Paleohóra churches
Zoödóhou Pigís monastery
Hydra Town
Bouboulina Mansion
Agía Paraskeví beach

Aegina locals.

Acropolis in Athens. The centre and eastern side of the island is mountainous; a gently sloping fertile plain runs down to the northwestern corner where Aegina Town (Egina) partly overlays the ancient capital.

From 1826 until 1828, Aegina served as the first capital of the modern Greek state. Elegant **Aegina Town** ❸, streaked purple with jacaranda-tree flower in late spring, has numerous 19th-century buildings constructed when the country's first president, Ioánnis Kapodístrias (1776–1831), lived and worked here. In Livádi suburb, just north, a plaque marks the house where **Níkos Kazantzákis** lived during the 1940s and 1950s, and wrote his most celebrated book, *Vios ke Politia tou Alexi Zorba* (*Zorba the Greek* in English). The modern harbour, crowded with pleasure craft and fishing-boats, abuts the ancient harbour, now the shallow town beach north of the main quay. Aegina's main produce is pistachio nuts, sold all along the quay. The **Archaeological Museum** (Tue–Sun 8.30am–2.40pm), about 10 minutes'

Fishing boats in Aegina harbour.

walk from the ferry quay, features exquisite Middle Bronze Age pottery with squid or octopus motifs. It stands in the precinct of the ancient Temple of Apollo (built 520–500 BC), of which only a single column – **Kolóna** – remains, a landmark for approaching boats. Continuing 3km (2 miles) north from here brings you to the **Hristos Kapralos Museum** (June–Oct Tue–Sun 10am–2pm and 6–8pm, Nov–May Fri–Sun 10am–2pm; charge), housed in the studio of this prominent sculptor and painter (1909–93), heavily influenced by Henry Moore. There's a replica of his famous *Monument of the Battle of the Pindus*, the original frieze adorning the Greek Parliament building.

Aegina's main attraction is the exceptionally beautiful **Temple of Aphaea** ❹ (Aféa; daily 8am–4.40pm; charge), in the northeast, on a pine-tufted hilltop commanding a splendid view of the gulf. Built around 490 BC in the Doric order, it is the only surviving Greek temple with a second row of small, superimposed columns in the interior of the sanctuary, and

Argo-Saronic Islands map showing the Saronic Gulf, Attikí, Pelopónnisos, and islands including Salamína, Egina (Aegina), Póros, Ýdra, and Spétses.

one of the most completely preserved – wait for any crowds to disperse to enjoy it in solitude. A short distance below lies the beach resort of **Agía Marína**, now perking up after some very lean years, though there are much better tavernas – if not swimming – at quieter **Pórtes**, 8km (5 miles) south.

On the way to the temple you will pass the **Convent of Agios Nektários** (see margin, right); a steady stream of pilgrims approaches his tomb in expectation of miracles. Across the ravine from Agios Nektários is the abandoned medieval **Paleohóra** (Old Town), established after the island was sacked by pirates in the late 9th century, and inhabited until 1827. Some 38 churches and little monasteries remain more or less intact, but only around six – Agios Geórgios Katholikós, Agii Anárgyri, Agía Kyriakí, Kímisi Theotókou and Metamórfosis are usually unlocked – retain frescoes of any merit or in recognisable condition; a helpful map near the site entrance (always open) helps locate them.

The west coast of the island is quite gentle, with much the best, gently shelving beach just south of **Marathónas**, another, much smaller one at shadier **Eginítissa,** and the best – Klíma – beyond Pérdika. **Pérdika ❺** itself is a picturesque inlet with popular tavernas; from its harbour several daily boats cross to uninhabited limestone **Moní** islet, a nature reserve with swimming in pristine waters.

Angístri is the small, pine-covered, low-key island opposite Aegina Town. Like many of the Argo-Saronics, it was resettled by medieval Albanians, but in recent decades was colonised by Germans and Athenians, who bought up houses in the villages of hillside **Metóhi** and coastal **Mýlos**, which bracket the port, sandy beach and main resort of **Skála**. Car-ferries stop at Skála, while hydrofoils call at Mýlos. Tourism is mixed and increasing: young Greek trendies camping on the pebbly beaches (and fuelling a lively nightlife), plus British and Scandinavian package-holiday-makers. A rough path heads south from Skála for pebbly **Halikiáda**, supposedly

FACT

Wonder-working Bishop Nektarios was born Anastasios Kefalas in 1846 in Silívria, Thrace, died in 1920 and was canonised in 1961 – the first modern saint of the Orthodox Church. The church on Aegina (near Paleohóra) honouring him is the largest in all Greece and his 9 November feast day is a major event.

The unique two-layered Temple of Aphaea.

Bell tower.

View from the Póros rooftops across to Galatás.

Greece's oldest naturist beach, while the paved road from Mýlos through the forest passes scenic **Dragonéra** cove en route to the southerly hamlet of **Limenária**.

Póros

Póros is separated from the Peloponnese by a narrow channel, which gives the island its name – *póros* means "ford". As you sail down the 350-metre/yd wide passage from its northwest entrance, **Póros Town ⑥** comes into view, presiding over one of the most protected anchorages in the Aegean, with scores of yachts berthed in a row. From an approaching boat, the sight of the pyramidal, orange-roofed town culminating in a blue-and-white hilltop clock tower is one of the iconic images of the Argo-Saronics. **Galatás** village on the mainland opposite is comparatively dull, but sends constant passenger shuttles (and regular car barge-ferries) across. Póros Town, built on several hills, occupies most of the little sub-islet of **Sferiá**, attached to the bulk of Póros (called Kalávria) by a narrow isthmus cut by a disused canal. Whichever route you choose to climb to the clock tower, you'll probably lose yourself in narrow lanes overhung with vines and flowers. Down on the waterfront, pride of place is given to a busy meat and seafood market similar to Aegina's, and a small but worthwhile **Archaeological Museum** (Tue–Sun 8.30am–2.40pm; charge) with finds from the island and mainland opposite.

Despite mediocre beaches on Kalávria (the best of these are **Monastiríou** in the east and **Megálo Neório** to the west), Póros sees far more (Scandanavian) package tourism than its neighbours, along with Athenian weekenders and second-home owners. The island has never been über-fashionable, but has had a naval connection since 1846 when a cadet-training station was established just beyond the isthmus bridge.

The main inland sights are both on Kalávria. The early 19th-century **monastery of Zoödóhou Pigís ⑦** (Virgin of the Life-Giving Spring), home to four monks, sits on a wooded hillside (20 minutes from town by bus), next to the Argo-Saronics' only natural spring. From here, the paved road winds further inland through the pines to the 6th-century BC **Sanctuary of Poseidon** (unrestricted but much roped off), near the island's summit. It's currently being re-excavated by the Swedish Archaeological School, though there isn't much to see yet beyond foundations – and a superb view.

Hydra

The island of Hydra (or Ydra, the ancient Ydrea, "the well watered") is today mostly a long, barren rock with a few stands of pine. But the postcard-perfect harbour bracketed by grey-stone mansions and Byzantine-tiled vernacular houses is incomparable, attracting the artistic and the fashionable since the 1950s, and many others ever since. It is one of the few

islands declared an Architectural Heritage Reserve, which has helped Hydra retain its original beauty through strict building controls and the banning of most motorised transport – the donkeys and mules you see are working freight-carriers, not just photo opportunities.

The central port-town, also called **Hydra ❽** (Ydra), is a popular destination, packed out during summer and at weekends most of the year. The harbour, girded by a slender breakwater, forms a perfect crescent, its two ends flanked by 19th-century cannons. Overhead, white, tile-roofed houses climbing the slope are accented by massive grey *arhondiká*, mansions built by shipping families who made fortunes in the 18th and 19th centuries. Some of these imposing *arhondiká* are open for visits, for example the gorgeously restored **Lazaros Koundouriotis Museum** (Tue–Sun 9am–4pm; charge), on the western slope, and the **Historical Archives** (daily 9.30am–4pm; charge) on the east quay, also displaying costumes, engravings and nautical paraphernalia. Just back from the quay, with its multiple gift shops aimed at cruise passengers, is a wonderful marketplace and the belfry-studded, 18th-century cathedral of **Kímisis tis Theotókou**, built largely of stone removed from Póros's Poseidon temple.

The higher reaches of the town and the hills beyond, accessed by narrow alleys and steep stairways, remain surprisingly untouched, charming and full of Greek colour. The uniformity of white walls is broken again and again by a century-old doorway, a bright-blue window frame, a flight of striking scarlet steps, or a dark-green garden fence. An hour's walk upwards and inland leads to **Agía Evpraxía Convent** and the **Profítis Ilías Monastery**, while **Zoúrvas Monastery** stands at the extreme eastern tip of Hydra. Island beaches, however, are less impressive. **Mandráki ❾**, northeast of town, has the only all-sand beach. It's more interesting to follow a wide path tracing the coast southwest to the hamlets of **Kamíni** and **Vlyhós**, with its 19th--century stone bridge. There are some good tavernas in both places, and water-taxis to return to town. Better beaches are found in the far southwest at **Bísti** and **Agios Nikólaos**, with boat access only; the hardy can walk an hour and a quarter to **Limnióniza** bay on the southeast-facing shore.

Spétses

Spétses (or Spétsai) is the southwesternmost of the Argo-Saronic Gulf islands. In antiquity it was known as Pityoússa (Piney Island), and despite devastating fires in 1990 and 2001 it is still marginally the most wooded of this island group, and with the best beaches. Tourist development here is far more extensive than on Hydra but less than on Póros or Aegina; building in **Spétses Town ❿** is controlled, though not quite as strictly as on Hydra, and while private cars are banned within town limits, scooters and taxis are not. As with Hydra,

On an island where most motor vehicles are banned, Hydra's mules and donkeys perform all haulage.

though, there are no car ferries serving the island.

Like Hydra, Spétses was one of the main centres of activity during the Greek War of Independence, using its fleet for the Greek cause. It is distinguished for being the first in the archipelago to revolt against Ottoman rule in 1821, and the fortified **Dápia** harbour still bristles with cannons. Although Spétses's fleet declined after that war, with the emergence of Sýros, then Piraeus, as the main seaports, shipbuilding traditions continue, especially in the east end of town at **Baltíza** inlet, where a few boatyards continue to build caiques the old way. The local **museum** (Tue–Sun 8.30am–2.40pm; charge) in the imposing *arhondikó* of Hatzigiannis Mexis, a late 18th-century shipowner, contains painted ship-prows of the revolutionary fleet, and an ossuary with the bones of heroine Laskarina Bouboulina (see box). Passed en route to Baltíza, the **Paleó Limáni** (Old Harbour) still radiates a gentle grace thanks to 18th-century mansions where wealthy Athenian families spend the summer. Above it, the courtyard of **Agios Nikólaos** church has a particularly outstanding pebble mosaic, a highly developed Spetsiot art.

Out of town in the opposite direction (west), in more modest **Kounoupítsa** district, stands the **Anargyríos and Korgialénios College**, a Greek version of an English public school, where John Fowles taught, memorialising institution and island in his 1966 novel *The Magus*. Like the Edwardian waterfront Hotel Poseidonion, it was founded by local benefactor Sotirios Anargyros; the school no longer operates, but is occasionally used for conferences and children's summer programmes.

A paved road circles the island, giving access to several fine beaches. Heading anticlockwise, the first tempting stop is sandy **Zogeriá**. Next is pine-backed **Agía Paraskeví**, the most scenic on Spétses, then **Agía Anargyrí**, the longest, sandiest and most developed. Solitude-seekers will prefer less crowded **Xylokériza** pebble cove to the west.

Fishing boats on Hydra.

NATIONAL HEROINE

The national heroine of the War of Independence, Laskarína Bouboulína was a wealthy Spetsiot who commanded eight of the local fleet's 22 ships after her seafaring husband was killed by corsairs. A colourful figure, she was said to have seduced her lovers at gunpoint (so plain was she reported to be), and ended up being murdered in 1825 by the father of a girl with whom her son had eloped. The now defunct 50-drachma note showed her on her flagship *Agamemnon*, directing the gunnery crew; on land, she organised a successful ruse to deter an Ottoman landing by perching fezes atop asphodels on the shore, to simulate a massed army. Her mansion behind the Dápia (daily Mar–Oct 9.45am–8pm, guided tours only; charge), still owned by her descendants, is now a museum dedicated to her life and works.

Waiting for the water-taxi, Hydra.

THE CYCLADES ISLANDS

Andros, Kéa, Tínos, Kýthnos, Sýros, Mýkonos, Sérifos,
Sífnos, Andíparos, Páros, Náxos, Mílos, Kímolos,
Folégandros, Síkinos, Íos, Amorgós, Santoríni, Anáfi.

Firá, Santoríni.

The 24 inhabited Cyclades evoke visions of sun-drenched hillsides and intimate little coves. The famous white Cubist houses have inspired many modern architects, Le Corbusier among them. The beaches are dazzling, the food fresh, fellow travellers companionable, and seagoing connections allow you to take in more than one "small paradise" on a short holiday.

For many people the Cyclades *are* the Greek islands; other groups are mere distractions from this blue-and-white Aegean essence. The scenic high point is probably dramatic, southernmost Santoríni, created by a volcanic explosion about 3,500 years ago, and there is nothing like it. The spiritual centre remains Apollo's ancient Delos: "Cyclades" means a cycle around Delos.

Ocean's bounty.

There are three basic ferry routes from either Piraeus or Rafína ports: the easternmost takes in bucolic Ándros, religious Tínos and cosmopolitan Mýkonos, sometimes extending to metropolitan Sýros. The latter is also served on the "central" line from Piraeus, continuing to Páros, Náxos, Íos and Santoríni. Another route continues past Náxos to the "Back Islands" like Skhinoússa and Koufonísi before winding up at Amorgós and Anáfi. The westernmost itinerary calls at Kýthnos, Sérifos, Sífnos and Mílos, usually extending to Folégandros and Síkinos. Especially in high season, links are possible between these basic routes. With scant connections to other Cyclades, Kéa attracts Athenian weekenders.

The Cyclades were inhabited as early as 6500 BC. By the third millennium a flourishing culture had emerged, with beautiful crafts and lively commerce, as anyone who visits the Museum of Cycladic Greek Art in Athens will appreciate. This museum is the world's first devoted to Cycladic art, most famous for its marble female figurines. High culture continued through Roman-era decline, and while this may not be evident amid the hedonistic jet-setters of Mýkonos or youthful merrymakers of Íos, one sunset over the Vale of Klíma, the valley in Mílos where the Venus de Milo was discovered, will convince you.

As Greek Nobel laureate poet Odysseas Elytis, wrote in Axion Esti: "Íos, Síkinos, Sérifos, Mílos – each word a swallow to bring you spring in the midst of summer."

THE CYCLADES

From the hectic nightlife of Mýkonos and Íos to the rugged beauty of Mílos and Sérifos or the quiet seclusion of tiny Kímolos and Anáfi, there is something for all tastes on these islands.

Glorious beaches, Bronze Age art, oak groves, gleaming white villages and the archaeological marvels of ancient Delos are just some of the reasons visitors return to the Cyclades again and again.

Andros

The reddish Andros soil makes everything glow sienna at sunset, especially on the heights of the north, settled centuries ago by Orthodox Albanians; their basic stone huts contrast with the whitewash and red tile of other, wealthier villages. Farmland is still divided by painstakingly built drystone walls, the *xirolithiés*, sporting a pattern of triangular slates incorporated into them.

The port town in the northwest, **Gávrio**, also doubles as a serviceable resort, though **Batsí ①** 6km (4 miles) south, is more conventionally picturesque, with even more development and an attractive beach. On the east coast, **Andros Town ②** (Hóra) has more upmarket tourism and a significant contingent of Athenians with weekend homes here. The Goulandrís shipping family established the excellent **Museum of Contemporary Art**, a few steps north of the main square (June–Sep Wed–Mon 10am–2pm, Oct–May Sat–Mon 10am–2pm; charge), featuring works

by top-notch figures like Matisse and Kandinsky, as well as temporary exhibits and an exquisite sculpture garden. The prize exhibit in the **Archaeological Museum** (Tue–Sun 8.30am–2.40pm; charge) is the Hermes of Andros, a 1st-century BC copy of Praxiteles' statue.

Between Batsí and Andros Town extends a long, deep valley, with terraces all the way up its sides towards the island's highest mountain range, which rises to 994 metres (3,261ft). Plane, mulberry and walnut trees are

Main Attractions

Andros, Museum of Contemporary Art
Ermoúpoli townscape
Mýkonos nightlife
Ancient Delos
Andíparos cave
Folégandros Kástro
Hozoviótissa Monastery
Anáfi beaches

Fresco inside the Santoríni Archaeological Museum.

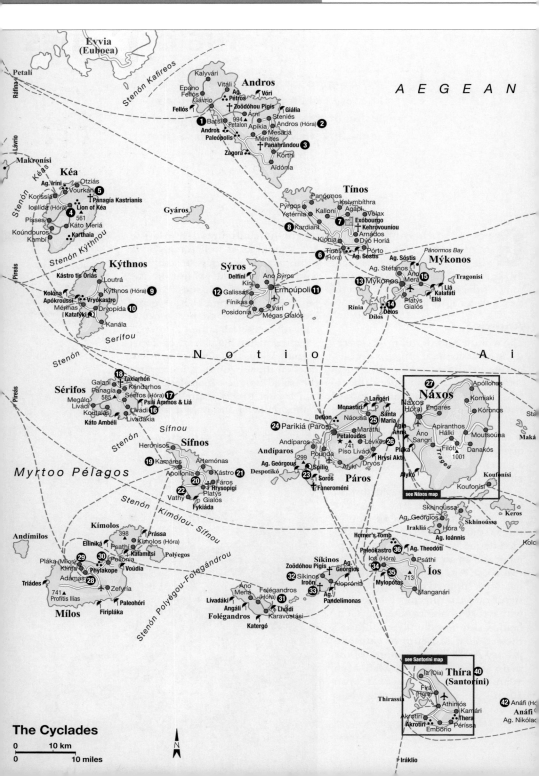

Evvia
(Euboea)

Petali

Rafína

Lávrio

Makronísi

AEGEAN

Stenón Kafíreos

Kalyvári
Vitáli
Epáno
Fellós
Gávrio
Fellós
Ag.
Pétros

Andros

Vóri
✝ Zoödóhou Pigis
Ámi
Apíkia
Steniés
Andros (Hóra) 2
Mesariá
Ménites
Paleópolis
Zágora
✝ Panahrándou 3
Kórthi
Aïdónia

1 Batsí
Andros
994

Giália

Kéas

Kéa

Otziás
Ag. Iríni
Vourkári
✝ Panagía Kastrianís
Korissía
Ioulída (Hóra)
Pisses
Koúndouros
Kambí
Kámbí
Káto Meriá
Karthaía

Lion of Kéa 5
4
561

Gyáros

Tínos

Panórmos
Pyrgos
Ystérnia
Kolymbíthra
Agápi
Kalloní
Vólax
Exóbourgo
✝ Kehrovouníou
Kardianí
Arnádos
Kiónia
Dyó Horiá
Tínos
(Hóra)
Ag. Sóstis
Pórto

7
8
6

Panórmos Bay

Ag. Sóstis

Mýkonos

Ag. Stéfanos
Áno
Merá
Mýkonos
Rínia
Platýs
Gialós
Délos
Dílos

Tragonísi
Liá
Kalafáti
Eliá

13
15
14

Stenón Kýthnou

Stenón

Kástro tis Oriás
Loutrá
Kýthnos (Hóra)
Kolóna
Apókroussi
Mérihas
Katafýki
Dryopída
Kanála

Kýthnos

Vryókastro

9
10

Sýros

Delfíni
Kíni
Áno Sýros
Galissás
Fínikas
Posidonía
Vári
Mégas Gialós
Ermoúpoli

12
11

Serífou

Notio

Ai

Pireás

Stenón

Sérifos

Galaní
Panagía
Megálo
Livádi
Koutalás
Káto Ambéli
Taxiárhon
Kéndarhos
Sérifos (Hóra)
Livádi
Livadákia
585
Psili Ámmos & Liá

18
17
16

Sífnou

Herónisos

Sífnos

Kamáres
Artemónas
Apollonía
Kástro
Faros
Hrysopigí
Platýs
Gialós
Fykiáda
Vathý

Stenón Kímólou-Sífnou

19
21
20
22

Myrtoo Pélagos

Deílion

Náxos

Langéri
Monastíri
Naoúsa
Sánta
Maríma
Petaloúdes
741
Léfkes
Píso Livádi
Pounda
Dryós
Alykí
Atlykó

Parikiá (Páros)
Andíparos
Andíparos
Despotikó
Ag. Geórgous
Spília
Sorós
✝ Faneroméni

Páros

24
25
26
23

299

Náxos map area:

Náxos
(Hóra)
Apóllonas
Komiakí
Kóronos
Engarés
Apíranthos
Háiki
Moutsoúna
Áno
Sangrí
Fílóti
1001
Danakós
Alykó
Koufonísi
Koufonísi

27

Tragéa

see Náxos map

Stá

Maká

Keros

Skhinoússa
Ag. Geórgios
Iraklía
Skhinoússa
Hóra
Ag. Ioánnis

Kolc

Kímolos

Ellinikà
Psáthi
Prássa
Kímolos (Hóra)
Kalamítsi
Pollónia
Voúdia
Polýegos

398

Andímilos

Pláka (Mílos)
Klíma
Adámas
Triádes
741
Profítis Ilías

Mílos

Zefyría
Paleohóri
Firipláka

29
30
28

Phylakópe

Homer's Tomb

Ag. Geórgios
Iraklía

Síkinos

Síkinos
Iroón

Zoödóhou Pigis
Áno
Meriá
Folégandros
(Hóra)
Lívadáki
Angáli
Folégandros
Katergó
Karavostási

Ag.
Pandelímonas

Alopróniá

31
32
33

Ánó
Meriá

Livádi

Ios

Paleókastro
Ios (Hóra)
Psáthi
Mylopótas
713
Manganári

34
35
36

Stenón Polyégou-Folegándrou

Thíra
(Santoríni)

la (Ola)
Fíra
(Hóra)
Athiniós
Kamári
Thera
Périssa
Akrotíri
Embório

40

Thirassía

see Santoríni map

Anáfi (Hó
Anáfi
Ag. Nikólac

42

Iráklio

The Cyclades

0 _____ 10 km
0 _____ 10 miles

N

nourished by a series of springs that flow from the heights, most notably at **Ménites**, with its church of **Panagía Koúmoulos**. Its multi-spouted spring is considered sacred; possibly there was once a big temple to Dionysos sited here. The centre of Andros is good walking country, with some of the 12 waymarked local trails.

The Convent of **Zoödóhou Pigís** (Life-Giving Spring) also claims a sacred site by its eponymous spring. Situated in the hills northeast of Batsí, it is today inhabited part-time by one elderly nun; the most vital and populated (by monks) monastery on the island is that of **Agía Marína**, near Apíkia north of Hóra. Three km (2 miles) east of Gávrio, the purpose of the remarkable, round Hellenistic tower of **Agios Pétros** remains a mystery.

South of the Paleópolis–Hóra road is the most spectacular of Andros's fortified Byzantine monasteries, unreliably open cliffside **Panahrándou ❸** – more than 1,000 years old, it was founded in 961. The round trip on foot lasts about three hours from **Mesariá**, a green valley town with the Byzantine Taxiárhis (Archangel) church.

Paleópolis, the ancient capital, doesn't give much hint of its past, but the Hermes statue in the archaeological museum was discovered here. A bit further south, **Zagorá** promontory is the site of a walled town that flourished in the 8th century BC, Homer's time.

Andros has many fine beaches; the easiest to get to are **Nimborió** north of Hóra, the string of beaches either side of Batsí, and **Giália** (near Steniés, north of Andros Town). Kórthi in the far southeast is popular with windsurfers.

Kéa

During the 19th century there were a million oaks on Kéa, and many still survive. Since ancient times, the island has also been noted for its

Intricately designed stone dovecotes are a feature of Tínos, where the Venetians were the first to embark on the systematic breeding of pigeons.

Journey's end for pilgrims to Tínos – the Panagía Evangelístria.

almonds, though olive trees are curiously lacking. Traces of four ancient cities – Koressia, Ioulis, Karthaia and Poiessa – testify to the island's one-time importance. Kéa (popularly Tziá, in ancient times Keos) has long been popular with Athenians. Regular Kéa-bound boats leave from Lávrio, some 50km (30 miles) from Athens, and land at **Korisía**; perhaps once a week there is a continuation to other Cyclades.

Kéa's main town, **Ioulída** ❹ (Hóra), covers a rounded ridge overlooking the island's northern reach; home to most islanders, it was a spot chosen precisely because it was inaccessible for pirates. Unlike most Cycladic villages, its houses have pitched, tiled roofs. The **Archaeological Museum** (Tue–Sun 8.30am–2.40pm; free) contains abundant finds from the four towns of ancient Keos; the most interesting antiquity is the 6th-century BC **Lion of Kéa**, a 15-minute walk northeast of Hóra. Carved from granite, almost 6 metres (19ft) long, it represents a real lion brought in to eat malicious Nereids.

The scalloped coast has surprisingly few accessible beaches; **Písses**, at the mouth of a fertile valley, **Koúndouros** with Athenians' villas and **Kambí** with a good taverna are among the exceptions. Close to Korissía is the bayside village of **Vourkári** ❺ popular among yachties, and with a notable concentration of fish tavernas. Further around the same bay stands a ruined Minoan palace at **Agía Iríni**. Northeast of Agía Iríni, a paved road leads to **Otziás**, a sandy but exposed bay, and continues to **Panagía Kastrianís** monastery (open June–Sept), focus of a 15 August pilgrimage. Southeast of here, a dirt road leads to excellent **Spathí** beach.

Walkers are well served by a network of numbered trails, intelligently rehabilitated and marked with EU funds. The best are from Ioulída to Otziás, and from Ioulída to ancient Karthaia, with two ruined temples to see.

Tínos

Tínos receives many thousands of visitors annually, mainly Greek Orthodox pilgrims bound for the church of **Panagía Evangelístria** (Annunciation). In 1822, the nun Pelagia dreamt of an icon of the Virgin; it was duly unearthed and the church was built to house it. The icon's healing powers have made **Tínos Town** ❻ (Hóra) the Lourdes of Greece. Women fall to their knees upon arrival, and crawl painfully to the church (the marble steps are carpeted). Healing miracles are said to occur. On the Virgin's feast days – 25 March (Annunciation) and 15 August (Dormition) – thousands of Greeks pour off the boats for the procession of the little icon, which is carried downhill in an ornate baldachin over the kneeling supplicants. The church complex is full of marble, precious votive offerings (especially silver boats), and contains several museums. Like nearby Sýros, the island is, ironically, actually half Catholic in population.

The site of the Temple of Poseidon and Amphitrite at **Kiónia** beach, one of the few ancient sites, is neglected, though the town's **Archaeological Museum** is worth a look (Tue–Sun 8.30am–2.40pm; charge). Among the exhibits are a Roman-era marble sundial from Kiónia that shows the time, the equinoxes and solstices; and a large number of artefacts from excavations at Exómbourgo.

Tínos is renowned for marble work – especially fanlights and bas-relief plaques – and there is still a marble-sculpture school and many active workshops in the village of **Pýrgos**. Tínos's other speciality is Greece's most elaborate dovecotes. There are hundreds of them inland, a tradition started by the Venetians. Their pattern of triangular windows is mimicked over doorways, on fences and in window shapes. It is a pliant symbol, which seems to represent anything from the shape of a sail to the Holy Trinity.

For an insight into Catholicism on Tínos, visit the peak of **Exómbourgo** ❼ 643 metres (2,110ft) high, with a ruined Venetian fortress, and the surrounding villages, which are mostly Catholic. Xinára at its base is the seat of the local Catholic bishop, and there are Catholic monasteries and convents in nearby villages. Tínos was the last island to fall to the Turks, in 1715. **Vólax** village, famous for its basket-weavers, is surrounded by weird, mushroom-shaped, wind-sculpted rocks; the climate up here is cool year-round, and potatoes flourish.

Kardianí ❽ on the Pýrgos-bound road is exceptional among Orthodox villages, a spectacularly set oasis settlement with views across to Sýros. From Ystérnia, a bit beyond, a mostly surviving marble-paved *kalderími* or cobbled path, among the finest of several on the island, leads down to Órmos Ysterníon. Southeast of Exómbourgo, the well-watered, arcaded villages of **Arnádos** and **Dýo Horiá** are equally handsome, and have attracted outsiders looking for second homes. Just above looms the Byzantine **Convent of Kehro-vouníou**, where Pelagía had her vision of the icon.

Easter Sunday mass on Andros.

Local colour.

Galissás beach resort, Sýros.

Kolymbíthra in the north is Tínos's best beach, though **Agios Fokás**, **Agios Sóstis** and **Pórto** on the south coast, closer to the Hóra, are fine, if more commercialised.

Kýthnos

Unfashionable with foreigners, and among the quietest of the Cyclades, Kýthnos appeals mostly to Athenian weekenders of more modest means. Native Kythniots are mainly dairy and livestock farmers, belying the apparent infertility of the dun-coloured, undulating countryside. Elderly and/or unwell visitors frequent the thermal spa at **Loutrá** (the island's medieval name was Thermiá), on the northeast coast, whose 19th-century spa building was designed by Ernst Ziller – though the resort is now making conscious attempts to appeal to a broader spectrum of visitors. About 90 minutes' walk northwest is medieval Kástro tis Oriás, once home to thousands but abandoned by the 1700s.

Mérihas port on the west coast has most of the island's accommodation. In summer, taxi-boats run from Mérihas to **Episkopí**, **Apókroussi** and **Kolóna** beaches, the last a stunning sand-spit tethering **Agios Loukás** islet to the rest of Kýthnos. Near Apókroussi, **Vryókastro** is an ancient 10th-century BC town where a huge hoard of artefacts was uncovered in 2002.

Landlocked **Kýthnos** ❾ (Hóra) 6km (4 miles) northeast of Mérihas, is exquisite. Whereas most Cycladic towns crawl spider-like over local topography, Hóra adheres mostly to a rectangular plan. Wood-beamed arches span narrow streets to join two sides of one house; in the passages underneath, pavements are playfully decorated in whitewash with fish, stylised ships, or flowers. There is a small main square, around which are the better island tavernas (though not much lodging). Fields at the back of town rise gently from the ravine to the south, dotted with farmhouses and tile-roofed chapels.

A stream bed splits into two **Dryopída** ❿ successor to Kástro as medieval capital; the chambered **Katafýki** cave here is linked in legend with the Nereids. The town itself presents,

MINERALS AND MINING

Mílos is, in reality, a far older, cooled-down version of Santoríni – at some point in the distant past a volcano collapsed, leaving a caldera, which became today's huge central bay. Its volcanic mineral wealth has always been extensively mined: in prehistory for obsidian, nowadays for bentonite, perlite, pozzolana, kaolin and china clay. Gaping quarries disfigure the landscape, especially in the east, and the local mining companies still provide employment for a quarter of the islanders. Kímolos has quarries from which Fuller's earth and, to a lesser extent, bentonite, are extracted. The latter has various uses (it even turns up as an ingredient in Nivea cream). Ironically, the chalk (*kimoliá* in Greek) which gave the island its name is no longer extracted locally.

like Ioulída on Kéa, an appealing red-roofed spectacle, especially seen from above.

Sýros

When Sýros was overtaken as Greece's premier port by Piraeus in the late 1800s, it was left, as one writer put it, "a grand but old-fashioned lady who lives on her memories of the good old days and on her half-forgotten glories". This is a shame, for with its excellent inter-island ferry links and low-key but useful facilities, Sýros – still capital of the Cyclades – makes a pleasant and rewarding place to stay. Not so the exceedingly barren islet of Gyáros just northwest, used as an exceptionally cruel prison for political dissidents by the Romans, and again by modern Greece between 1946 and 1974.

Just one large shipyard barely survives at the port-capital, **Ermoúpoli** ⓫ which doesn't help its resort image, but hasn't prevented the elegant neo-classical town from being designated a UNESCO Heritage Site. The congested quay with its scent of roasting octopus doesn't give much away, but head inland and you'll see why the honour was bestowed.

The marble-paved main square, **Platía Miaoúlis**, is lined with imposing buildings, some housing lively bars and cafés, and hosts a buzzing evening *vólta*. The Apollon Theatre, on nearby Platía Vardáka, is modelled after La Scala in Milan; its 1980s renovation is still a point of pride. Beyond the Apollon, the imposing dome and twin belfries of **Agios Nikólaos** mark the **Vapória** quarter, where the wealthiest 19th-century shipowners and merchants built sumptuous mansions with painted ceilings and the like.

Ermoúpoli is dominated by two hills, each capped by a church. On the lower, **Vrontádo**, stands the Greek Orthodox **Church of the Resurrection** (Anástasis). On the higher is **Ano Sýros**, the medieval Catholic quarter – like Tínos, Sýros is approximately half Catholic – dominated by **Agios**

Geórgios cathedral and the 16th-century Capuchin monastery (adjacent is a British World War I cemetery). One of Greece's greatest *rebétika* musicians, Markos Vamvakaris, was born an Ano Sýros Catholic, and the **Vamvakáris Museum** (daily 11am–2pm and 7–10pm; charge), duly honours him. The worthwhile **Industrial Museum**, on the road to Kíni (Mon and Wed–Sun 10am–2pm, Thur–Sun 6–9pm; charge), commemorates the island's now vanished shipping and mining enterprises.

The south of Sýros is gentler and greener than the rugged, empty north and has good beaches, especially near **Galissás** ⓬ a sizeable resort. Further up the west coast, **Kíni** and lonelier **Delfíni** bay offer more good bathing. South of Galissás, **Fínikas** and **Posidonía** – the latter immortalised by Vamvakaris, along with other Syrian locales, by its alternative name, Dellagrázia, in his overplayed standard *Frangosyriani* – are more mainstream resorts. Pythagoras' teacher, Pherekydes, the inventor of the sundial, hailed from here, and several

FACT

Much of Kýthnos's electricity is supplied by a "wind park" just east of Hóra and a "solar park" on the road to Loutrá. However, overall less that 10 percent of Greece's power needs are currently supplied by wind turbines.

Dryopída, the blue domes of its church stark among the red roofs.

Elegant façade on Platía Miaoúlis, with the Anástasi church overhead.

Sérifos Town.

caves bear his name. The southerly loop road continues east through **Mégas Gialós** and **Ahládi** towards **Vári**, the most protected of the local coves.

Mýkonos

Mýkonos represents an emphatic victory of style (and self-promotion) over intrinsic substance. This rocky, tree-less, gale-force windy, dry island, with admittedly excellent, granite-sand beaches and a Cycladic-cliché port town of dazzling beauty, receives close to a million visitors in a good year. They are drawn by a deserved reputation for big-city-standard shopping, sexy nightlife for all orientations and some of the most luxurious accommodation in the islands – all of which makes Mýkonos the most expensive of the Cyclades, rivalled only by Santoríni.

Mýkonos Town ⓭ like the island overall, is one of the world's premier **gay** (male) **resorts**, with legendary clubs, some including live drag shows in their repertoire. Cruise ships are also very much part of the picture,

especially during spring and autumn, with passengers packing out the town for some retail therapy, then horn-blasted back aboard, clutching purchased designer clothing and jewellery.

It is possible to eschew all this and still enjoy Mýkonos. The **Folklore Museum** (Apr–Oct Mon–Sat 4.30–8.30pm; free) and the **Archaeological Museum** (Tue–Sun 9am –2.40pm; charge), at different ends of the quay, are full of interesting objects, including grave stelae and a Hellenistic copy of a 5th-century cult statue of Herakles. And the town is among the most photogenic and most solicitously preserved in the Cyclades, with wooden balconies loaded with flowers, red-domed chapels and irregular whitewashed surfaces. The odd-shaped **Panagía Paraportianí** (Our Lady of the Postern Gate), four chapels lumped into one structure, is probably Greece's most photographed church – and a noted gay cruising area after dark.

The town mascot has long been a **pelican** called Petros. The original one settled on the island in 1955 after being blown off course by a storm. After various adventures, including an alleged kidnapping by a fisherman from Tínos, the original Petros was killed by a car in 1985. His replacement, who still inhabits the quay-side, scattering his pink feathers, was donated in 1986 by a German zoo, although there are now actually three pelicans in residence.

Caiques depart from Mýkonos town for **ancient Delos** ⓮ (modern Dílos), the sacred island that is the hub of the Cyclades (see page 174). Or you could strike inland to **Ano Merá** ⓯ 7km (4 miles) east, the only real village on the island, which is less spoilt by tourism. Its main attraction is **Tourlianí Monastery**, with red domes and an ornate marble belfry. It houses some fine 16th-century Cretan icons and embroidery. Mýkonos is famous, indeed notorious, for its all-night bars and all-day south-coast

transiting between Ibiza and India. Beyond a husk of modern hotels and Athenian second homes is the 1440s-vintage, barely inhabited *kástro*, one of the finest such in the Cyclades, of a type seen elsewhere only at Síkinos and Kímolos: a square compound with just a single arched entrance and a central cistern/chapel.

Andíparos measures only 11km by 5km (7 miles by 3 miles), so there are no daunting distances, especially if you bring a scooter over from Páros. The approaching ferry passes two islets; on one, **Saliangós**, British excavators in 1964 revealed a Neolithic (pre-4000 BC) settlement, including a fat female figurine now in the Parikiá museum. The other islet belongs to the Goulandrís family, they of the museums in Andros and Athens.

Beaches are surprisingly numerous, the better ones on the east and south coasts. **Glýfa** is the closest to the town, and tamarisk-shaded Psaralíki, just beyond, is decent enough, but with your own transport (or the seasonal bus) **Sorós** 9km/5.5miles away on the southeast coast is Andíparos' best

beach, with two tavernas. **Agios Geórgios** in the far south faces the goat-grazed islet of Despotikó.

Páros

Parikiá 24 (also called Páros) is the attractive capital of this heavily visited island. In August, make sure you book ahead, as the cheaper rooms go fast – although in the evening they are empty as their tenants hit the town. Parikiá is as pretty as Mýkonos Town, but less labyrinthine; it has one of the better town beaches in the Cyclades just northeast at Livádia, where tiny children confidently learn to sail at the Nautical Club. The beautiful 6th-century **Ekatondapyliani Church** (Our Lady of a Hundred Doors; open 7am–9pm) retains its Byzantine form, including a side chapel adapted from a 4th-century BC building. By the church is a **Byzantine Museum** (same hours; charge) full of icons, while the prize exhibit at the nearby **Archaeological Museum** (Tue–Sun 9am–3.45pm; charge) is a chunk of the Parian Chronicle, embossed on a marble slab. The ancient **cemetery** is on

Inquisitive goat, Páros.

Gloriously clear waters on Sífnos.

the seafront, while the 13th-century Venetian *kástro* southwest along the water incorporates a Classical watchtower and is otherwise largely built of masonry recycled from a 6th-century BC temple that stood here.

At beautiful **Náousa** 🐵 on the north coast, the little harbour's colourful fishing boats nudge right up against the quayside houses, and the old quarter forms a quasi-kástro. Though the village has become notably fashionable, with upmarket boutiques, accommodation and restaurants, the port still retains its traditional charm. There are half a dozen fine **beaches** around the bay, accessible on foot or by taxi-boat. To the east, protected **Langéri** has heaped dunes, while windsurfers repair to **Sánta María**, facing the straits with Náxos. Otherwise, head northwest to the lighthouse peninsula and monastery of **Ágios Ioánnis Détis**, giving its name to the natural reserve just behind, car-free and criss-crossed with marked hiking trails. Best of the southeast-coast beaches are **Logarás** and **Hrysí Aktí**, both with plenty of

facilities and the latter another mecca for windsurfers.

Unspoilt **Lévkes** 🐵 the Ottoman-era capital, is the largest inland village, with several 17th-century churches, and a lovely lower *platía* flanked by cafés. From Lévkes, walkers can follow a surviving portion of the old marble-paved *kalderími* that used to cross the entire island. Go east to Pródromos and Mármara, with views en route to looming **Náxos** 🐵 across the straits (see pages 188), or north to Kóstos, then west to **Maráthi**, whose ancient tunnel quarries – still active until 1844, now fenced off – supplied the world with some of the finest marble.

Southwest of Parikiá lies the much-visited **Valley of the Butterflies** (Petaloúdes), a walled garden with huge trees. The black-and-yellow butterflies – actually Jersey tiger moths – are colourful and countless in summer (May–Sept daily 9am–8pm; charge). En route, stop in at **Hristoú stou Dássous**, a picturesque 18th-century convent whose church of Agios Arsénios, unusually, is off-limits to men (in Greece it's usually the other way around). South of Petaloúdes lies the workaday fishing port (with beaches and tavernas) of Alykí.

Mílos

Volcanic Mílos is a geologist's paradise. Snaking streams of ancient lava formed much of the island's coastline. The lava dripped into caves and solidified as it hit the sea, thrusting up weird rock formations that take on animal shapes, shadowed purple in the rays of the setting sun. Offshore clusters like the Glaronísia are popular boat excursions. On the map, Mílos resembles a bat in flight; almost all the island's population of just under 5,000 inhabits the northeastern wing; the southwestern wing is ruggedly beautiful.

Modern Miliots have graciously adapted to the thin stream of tourism the island receives, concentrated in **Adámas** 🐵 (Adámanda), the main port, and Pollónia, a smaller harbour

The snug little harbour of Náousa.

in the northeast. The closest of several open-air hot springs is at Kánava beach, 3km (2 miles) east; the water wells up at 50°C (120°F) in the shallows, mixing to a comfortable temperature. Inside **Agía Triáda** church in Adámas, Cretan-style icons dominate. Links have always been strong between Mílos and the "Great Island": Cretan refugees founded Adámas in 1853 (though ancient tombs have been found on the town site), and the island was colonised by Minoans who came to trade obsidian.

Pláka ㉙ (Mílos), the island's attractive capital, 4km (2.5 miles) northwest, has both an **Archaeological Museum** (Tue–Sun 8.30am–2.40pm; charge), whose star is the Minoan "Lady of Phylakope" idol, and a **Folklore Museum** (Tue–Sat 10am–2pm and 6–9pm, Sun 10am–2pm; charge). The latter, set in an old house, offers diverse exhibits from rock specimens and goat horns to samples of local weaving. A climb up the old *kástro*, with its vast rain-collection system and churches of **Panagía Thalássitra** and **Kímisis tis Panagías**, provides splendid views of the well-protected bay and, weather permitting, over many other islands. The escutcheon on Panagía Thalássitra is of the Crispi family, who wrested Mílos from another Venetian family, the Sanudi in 1363.

Southwest of Pláka about 1km (0.5 mile) lies the verdant **Vale of Klíma**, where the ancient Meliots – their "dialogue" with the Athenians immortalised by Thucydides prior to their annihilation in 416 BC – built their city. Excavations undertaken by the British School in Athens in the late 1800s uncovered a Dionysian altar, remains of an ancient gymnasium with a mosaic, and a well-preserved Roman-era theatre. Nearby, a marble plaque marks the spot where a farmer unearthed the Aphrodite of Mílos (Venus de Milo) in 1820. In a feat of robbery approaching that of the appropriation of the Parthenon friezes (though here the French were the villains rather than the British) she was whisked off to Paris, never to return. The statue was probably carved in the 1st century BC of Parian marble, since Mílos lacks suitable stone.

FACT

The Venus de Milo was entrusted to the French Ambassador in Istanbul (she probably lost her arms in transit), to keep her safe from local lime-kiln operators. The Ambassador promptly shipped her off to France, where Louis XVIII put her on display in the Louvre. She has been there ever since.

Exploring the tunnel quarries at Marathi is no longer allowed.

The Cycladic Bronze Age

Numerous artefacts illuminate the Bronze Age culture of the Cycladic islands, shedding light on the way the ancient people lived and died.

Bronze Age Cycladic peoples left behind many beautiful artefacts, most famously their stylised marble sculptures, evidence of an organised and flourishing culture. Settlements and cemeteries excavated on a number of Cycladic islands are generally considered to be the first complex, organised, settled communities in Europe.

The Early Cycladic Bronze Age is thought to have begun close to 3200 BC, and to have lasted until around 2500 BC. The middle Bronze Age in the Cyclades (2500–2000 BC) falls into two general periods, referred to by scholars and archaeologists as Middle and Late Cycladic respectively. These periods increasingly display the influence of the Minoan culture of Crete and the move towards urban settlement. In general, the term "Cycladic culture" refers to the Early Cycladic era, and it is during this period that the individuality of

Cycladic figurine in the Santoríni Archaeological Museum.

the culture of the Cycladic islands is most evident.

Early Cycladic settlements were small, numbering around 50 people, comprising densely packed stone-built housing, usually of only one storey. Accompanying the settlements, outside the residential area, are cemeteries of small cist graves (rectangular graves lined with stone) and chamber-tombs, clustered in family groups; the dead were inhumed in a contracted (foetal) position, along with everyday objects. Much of the evidence we have of how Early Cycladic society functioned comes from these cemeteries.

The often stark differences in grave goods between tombs provides evidence of a stratified society. While some graves contain an extremely rich variety of artefacts, including gold and silver jewellery, others have very little, often only a single marble figure. How these differences between rich and poor were manifest in practice is a matter of conjecture, but many artefacts display a high degree of skill in their manufacture, indicating the presence of skilled craft workers.

Besides hunting, fishing, animal husbandry and agriculture, much trade was carried out from the Cycladic islands, pointing to the existence of a merchant class, presumably among the wealthier members of society. The Cycladic peoples were skilled sailors and had contact with the Greek mainland, Crete, Anatolia and even the distant Danube Basin.

White marble figurines

Of all the items left by these peoples, the marble figurines are perhaps both the most beautiful and enigmatic. Their different typologies are used by scholars to differentiate the various Cycladic eras.. The predominantly female figures are generally around 20cm (8in) in length (a few near life-sized sculptures have been discovered) and are made of white marble. Almost two-dimensional in their execution, they have flattened oval heads and arms folded below schematically rendered breasts; many features would have been painted onto marble (on the face, only the nose is rendered in relief). It is conjectured, from the position of the feet, that the figures were intended to lie horizontally, but there is no conclusive evidence for this, just as there is no firm consensus about their function. Explanations from scholars range from their being apotropaic (intended to ward off evil), to divinities, to ancestors, to symbolic companions for the deceased.

Below ancient Melos lurk the **Christian catacombs** (Tues–Sun 8am–2.40pm; 15-min group tour; charge). Carved into the hillside, they are the earliest evidence of Christian worship in Greece. Hundreds of tombs arranged along three subterranean corridors held as many as 5,000 bodies, all now vanished. Though cheerily lit by tiny electric lanterns, frescoes and religious graffiti are hard to discern, and only the initial 50 metres (164ft) are open to the public. Steps from the catacomb area lead down to the shore and one of the island's most picturesque villages, **Klíma**, with brightly painted boathouses at sea level, carved into the volcanic cliff.

Mílos's best beaches are in the southwest "bat wing", starting with **Paleohóri** – its far end part-naturist, with steam vents in the sand near which eggs can be fried, and hot water bubbling up in the sea – and ending with isolated **Triádes**, facing the sunset. Others hereabouts are easiest (or only) accessible by boat.

Ten kilometres (6 miles) northeast from Adámas lies the rubble of the ancient city of **Phylakope** (Fylakopí; Tues–Sun 8.30am–2.40pm; charge), whose script and art resembled that of the Minoans. It flourished for 1,000 years after 2600 BC. The famous flying-fish fresco from here is now in Athens, but many objects are in the Pláka museum. All around Phylakope are strewn flakes of obsidian, used for sharp tools before bronze became common; visitors came to Mílos for it from 7000 BC onwards. Mílos's polychrome geology is especially impressive here. Next to the site glitters the **Papafrángas ravine**, where precipitous stone steps take you down for an atmospheric swim in a pool connected to the sea by an inlet running under a rock bridge. **Sarakíniko**, futher west, is another inlet framed by wind-sculpted white rock formations.

Pollónia 30 12km (7.5 miles) northeast of Adámas, is a wind-buffeted resort popular with boardsurfers and

scuba-divers. Decent beaches are limited to **Voúdia** (Tría Pigádia), with the island's best hot springs erupting, to an ideal temperature, in a rock formation just offshore, at the far right as you face the sea. Pollónia is also the departure point for several small daily ferries across to Kímolos.

Kímolos

This tiny island – 41 sq km (16 sq miles), with a population of about 700 – is an alluring temptation when seen from Pollónia on Mílos, about a nautical mile across a strait. The boat takes only 20 minutes to cross to **Psathí**, Kímolos's little port. Some ferries to and from Adámas also stop here. **Kímolos** or **Hóra**, the single hilltop town, is a 15-minute walk up from the quay; at its core is a two-gated, 16th-century *kástro*, which, unlike the ones on Sífnos and Síkinos, is mostly uninhabited and derelict. Just outside the *kástro* precinct stands un-whitewashed, well-preserved **Agios Ioánnis Hrysóstomos** church, of the same era.

Kímolos, once a pirates' hideout, today provides a limited refuge from

An ice-cold frappé hits the spot.

The cove at Alogómandra, Mílos.

*Detail of a ruined
kástro doorway on
Síkinos.*

*Poppies and daisies
carpet this field on
Mílos.*

the more crowded islands – there are fewer than 500 tourist beds. Although blessedly undeveloped (the mining and lack of water sees to that), it has half a dozen beaches – going anticlockwise along the south and east shores – **Elliniká**, **Bonátsa**, **Kalamítsi**, **Alykí**, **Skála** and **Prássa**, all within easy walking distance, some with tavernas and a few rooms to let. The northern half of the island is abandoned and inaccessible except on foot; on the eastern shore between Klíma and Prássa, **thermal springs** of varying utility pour into the sea.

Folégandros

The sheer palisades of Folégandros's coast have deterred invaders over the centuries and so lent the islanders security. Despite its tiny size – 32 sq km (12 sq miles) populated by barely 700 people – its role in recent history has not been insignificant: many Greeks were exiled here during both the 1930s Metaxás dictatorship and the 1967–74 junta. Its ancient and early Christian ties with Crete were strong, and many icons of the Cretan School can be found in its churches today.

For such a small island, Folégandros has a fair number of beaches, especially on the less sheer eastern and southern coastlines. The easiest to reach are **Livádi** (with an organised campsite); **Várdia**, by the port; **Angáli**, at the narrow waist of the island on the west shore; naturist **Agios Nikólaos** just beyond; and **Livadáki** in the far southwest. From Livádi hamlet it is possible to walk (strenuously) south to the remote, scenic beach at **Katergó**.

A paved road (and bus service) links **Karavostási**, the port, to the capital, **Folégandros** or **Hóra** ㉛ a magnificently sited medieval town with an inner *kástro* perched above a sheer drop to the sea. The dazzling, wedding-cake church of Kímisis tis Theotókou presides over the town and marks the general direction of the **Hrysospiliá**, the "Golden Cave" in the cliff beyond, now accessible only to technical climbers. Folégandros is now decidedly trendy with both Greeks and foreigners, something reflected in the variety, prices and mixed clientele of the numerous bars, tavernas and lodgings in and around Hóra.

The island's second settlement, **Ano Meriá**, is actually a series of straggly hamlets strung out along the ridge road, comprising stone houses, a few shops and cafés, farms and knoll-top chapels; the bus continues out here regularly to drop walkers at the start of trails to some of the beaches noted previously. Threshing cirques, for processing the barley that is still grown here, are conspicuous as well.

Síkinos

Rocky Síkinos, despite the usual variety of harbour-side lodgings, couldn't be less like its larger neighbour, Ios. Although connected to Piraeus and other Cyclades regularly by ferry, and by caique to Ios and Folégandros in summer, Síkinos (with just over 200 permanent inhabitants) so far seems to have shrugged off tourism. It also escapes mention in the history books for long periods, but there are antiquities and venerable churches to be seen.

The main beaches, **Aloprónia** (also the port), **Dialiskári** and **Agios Geórgios** to the northeast, and **Agios Pandelímonas** to the southwest, face Ios. From Aloprónia harbour there's a high-season-only bus or an hour's hike to **Síkinos Town** ㉜ consisting of conjoined **Hóra** and **Kástro**, with yet another such Venetian defensive complex at its heart. There are few places to stay but several tavernas and *kafenía*, some serving limited-production local wine – Síkinos's former name, Oenoe, alludes to a long history of producing wine (*oinos* in ancient Greek). The half-ruined convent of **Zoödóhou Pigís** (church open in the evening) dominates Kástro to the northeast; nearby, the small chapel of **Panagía Pandohará** was dedicated in 2011 to poet Odysseas Elytis by his lifelong companion Ioulita Iliopoulou.

Síkinos has few obvious diversions other than walking. One destination of note, the **Iroön** ㉝ at **Episkopí**, is an elaborate Roman family temple-tomb, incorporated into a 7th-century church. Hikers can continue down to the coast at Agios Pandelímonas and thence back to Aloprónia.

Ios

A small island with few historic attractions, Ios has drawn the young and footloose since the 1960s. The contemporary influx, who flock here to party by night and hit the beach by day, are a faint echo of their hippie forbears; "family" tourism is now actively promoted, holiday villas sprout north of the harbour, and rough camping is a thing of the past.

The centre of Ios's nightlife shifts constantly among dozens of bars and dance clubs in the tiny capital town, **Hóra** ㉞ (also called **Ios**). By 11pm, the last beach stragglers (a bus runs regularly between the beach and Gialós harbour, via Hóra, to bring them back) have arrived for the night-time revels; once ensconced inside a bar, they could be anywhere in the Mediterranean. Veteran Hellenophile travel writer Michael Haag less charitably

The steep, terraced slopes of Folégandros.

In the village of Langáda, Amorgós, a boy in local costume performs a traditional dance.

One of the numerous tavernas in Hóra, Folégandros.

deemed them "a plague of locusts who pack snack bars, boutiques and discotheques, appreciating nothing, giving nothing, taking everything."

The results of industrial-strength tourism have been twofold: Ios is no longer poor, and traditional life has disappeared, since there are no small, remote villages where people maintain old traditions. Weddings were once four-day feasts for all comers; now, unless they are held in winter, they last an evening, as everyone is too busy tending tourist-related enterprises. However, with all the action concentrated in and around Hóra, it is still possible to find quiet corners and relatively empty beaches.

Ios is not devoid of natural beauty or charm; even the bleary-eyed can see it. **Gialós** port is one of the Aegean's prettiest. The hilltop **Hóra**, capped by a windmill and blue church domes, reached by a long marble stairway from Gialós, appears vaguely Levantine with its palm trees and kasbah-like layout.

The most famous beach is **Mylopótas** ㉟, with organised water sports

and youth-oriented campsites. Alternatives include posher **Manganári Bay** in the south, served by both bus and caique; superior **Agía Theodóti** in the northeast; and **Psathí** in the east. Between them stand the remains of **Paleókastro** ㊱ a Venetian fortress containing the marble-clad ruins of what was the medieval capital. At a lonely spot towards the island's northern tip, beyond Plakotós Cove, is a series of ancient **graves**, one of which the islanders fervently believe is **Homer's**.

Amorgós

Narrow, rugged and mountainous, Amorgós is a haven for walkers, bohemians and connoisseurs of still vibrant island culture, rather than for beachcombers. Before a road was opened between them in the late 1970s, the two port-resorts of Katápola and Egiáli were gateways to two effectively separate islands; ferry schedules still alternate in calling at them. **Katápola** ㊲ is bigger and more commercialised and with fewer beaches, but more convenient to the uphill **Hóra** ㊳ (or Amorgós

Town), accessible by a regular bus service or a well-preserved *kalderími*. Its whitewashed houses and numerous domed and belfried churches cluster around a 13th-century Venetian castle.

Half an hour east of Hóra, clinging limpet-like to a 180-metre (590ft) cliff – French explorer and botanist Joseph Pitton de Tournefort likened it to a "chest of drawers" – the spectacular 11th-century Byzantine **Panagía Hozoviótissa Monastery** ❸❾ (daily 8.30am–1pm and 5–7pm) is home to a revered icon of the Virgin from Palestine, as well as to three hospitable monks who treat visitors to a shot of *rakómelo* (spiced spirit) with *loukoúmi*, and a ground-floor treasury-museum. The 20–21 November festival, despite being subject to dodgy weather, is attended by pilgrims from Athens and across the Cyclades. Below the monastery, **Agía Anna** and **Kambí** beaches are the most famous of several protected south-coast coves.

Southwest from Hóra, **Agios Geórgios Valsamítis**, 4km (2 miles) away, is built atop a sacred spring that had served as an oracle since pagan times, and was only cemented over in the 1950s (though the flow still irrigates lush gardens). Vivid frescoes adorn a sort of gazebo over the *agíasma* inside the church where the water is still audible, and (briefly) accessible for collection.

Because there were reasonable anchorages, three ancient cities thrived here. **Minoa** (just above Katápola) is still being excavated; **Arkesíni**, in the far southwest, comprises a burial site and dwellings on Cape Kastrí, plus the well-preserved Hellenistic fortress at **Agía Triáda**, near modern Arkesíni village. Of ancient **Aigiale** (above modern **Egiáli** and its beaches), very little remains, but the nearby village of **Tholária** (Vaults) takes its name from Roman tombs in the vicinity.

Anáfi

In legend, Apollo conjured up Anáfi to shelter Jason and the Argonauts when the seas grew rough and they risked losing the Golden Fleece; an Apollo shrine was built here in thanksgiving. Divine intervention has never again been reliable. Earthquakes originating

FACT

Locals are convinced that Homer is buried on Ios: he either died here on a voyage from Sámos to Athens, or his mother was born on Ios and the poet chose to return here to die. Either way, he is celebrated by the so-called Omíria cultural events, from May to September.

Inside a Katápola kafeníon, Amorgós.

AMORGÓS WALKS

The best part of the well-marked and well-mapped Amorgian trail system links Egiáli in a triangular route with both Tholária and **Langáda**, handsome villages with excellent tavernas and seaward views. Hardy hikers can strike out beyond Langáda, first past the ancient **Theológos Monastery** with its frescoes of John the Evangelist, and then on a spectacular corniche trail to **Stavrós** church, at the base of **Mount Kríkelos**, the island's highest point, rising to 822 metres (2,696ft). In the week after Easter, the icon of Hozoviótissa goes walkabout (*periforá*); devout pilgrims, some walking barefoot as a penance, follow it back from Egiáli to the monastery for five hours along the ancient trail that was the island's lifeline before the automobile age.

By ferry or by caique, any trip out to the "Back Islands" should include a quiet day on the beach.

Amorgós, a magnet for walkers.

on its volatile neighbour **Santoríni ⓵** (see page 191) usually affected Anáfi with tidal waves and a rain of volcanic debris. Anáfi's appearance has probably not altered much since then: it still looks like a rough boulder heaved up out of the sea and kept in place only by divine benevolence.

However, a different god is involved now: **Zoödóhou Pigís Monastery ⓵** (daily 11am–1pm & 4–6pm) was erected over the old Apollo temple in the island's southeast corner, and incorporates plenty of marble masonry fragments from its predecessor. Above the monastery, with festivities 11 days after Easter and on 7–8 September, perches the smaller **Monastery of Kalamiótissa**, atop a 450-metre (1,480ft) high limestone monolith – claimed to be larger than Gibralter – that is Anáfi's most distinctive feature. A swooping but well-engineered path takes you there in under an hour; some people stay overnight at the top to catch the sunrise.

About 250 people live on the island today, surviving mainly by fishing and subsistence farming. In recent years, though, the economy has been boosted slightly by summer tourists, attracted by Anáfi's peace and quiet, and superb south-facing beaches. The island is no longer a traveller's dead end; there are main-line ferries from Piraeus, which for the foreseeable future will continue on to Crete and certain Dodecanese, then back again.

The south-facing harbour, **Agios Nikólaos**, has few facilities, but the main town, **Hóra ⓶** (or Anáfi Town), a short bus ride or half-hour walk up, offers a wider choice and finer setting. It's a windy place, sharing anti-earthquake vaulted roofs with Santoríni.

The closest of the beaches is palm-tree-adorned **Klisídi**, walkable east from Agios Nikólaos, with reliable food and lodging. From near there, the old path (and a newer road, inland) heads further east to superb **Roúkounas** beach, with dunes, the **Katelímatsa** coves, **Katsoúni** and **Monastíri** beach – all clothing-optional except the last, owing to its proximity to Zoödóhou Pigís. Inland from Roúkounas looms **Kastélli**, site of both ancient Anaphe and a Venetian castle.

The Back Islands or Minor Cyclades

The so-called "**Back Islands**" between Náxos and Amorgós were far more inhabited in antiquity. Now Donoússa, Irakliá, Skhinoússa and Koufonísi have populations of 100 to 200 each, but appreciable summer tourism, especially Athenians. Mains power only arrived during the mid-1980s, and fresh water is scarce on all these islets. They're hardly secret (or cheap) destinations now, with ample facilities including bank ATMs on each one. Getting to them is fairly easy: the somewhat buckety, splashy but reliable small caique *Express Skopelitis* (nicknamed the *skylopník-tis* or "dog-drowner" by the unkind) plies an almost daily schedule among them, leaving Amorgós at dawn and returning from Náxos around 3pm. Several times a week faster, more comfortable Blue Star ferries call from Piraeus as well.

Hilly **Donoússa**, remote from the others due east of Náxos, has good south-facing beaches near **Stavrós** port at **Kédros** and **Livádi**, both with fluffy blonde sand, naturism and free camping. Livádi stretches below **Mersíni**, the only inland hamlet, with a gushing fountain under a plane tree. Ill-advised bulldozing has ruined what was until recently a comprehensive network of cobbled paths.

Koufonísi (technically Áno Koufonísi) is the flattest of the quartet, and the busiest with a Páros-Mýkonos-type clientele, thanks to excellent southeast-facing beaches and a charming main village. The entire south coast looks across to **Káto Koufonísi** (day-trip accessible, with another beach and taverna) and hulking **Kéros** (off-limits), which was a third-millennium BC burial site and source of much of the Cycladic material in Greek museums. Beyond appreciably developed seaside Hóra stretch the beaches: **Fínikas**, **Italída**, **Platiá Poúnda** with sheltering sea caves, and **Porí** with yachts at anchor, all linked by road or pat.

Skhinoússa is far quieter, with most facilities in the hilltop Hóra 1km (0.5 mile) above the port; there are 16 beaches scattered around the island, of which only **Tsigoúri** has amenities. Solitude-seekers prefer nearby **Alygariá** and **Almyrós** in the south, less than half an hour's walk distant from Hóra.

Irakliá (or Iraklía) is the largest of the "Back Islands", and has two proper settlements: the northerly port of **Agios Geórgios**, with all tourist facilities; and smaller **Hóra** (aka Panagía after its main festival date). Compared to its neighbours, Irákliá's beaches are disappointing – Livádi is the best – but it does have an undeniable attraction in the huge **Cave of Agios Ioánnis** in the far south, reached by following one of the 8 marking hiking routes prepared for walkers.

A sunny backstreet.

Hozoviótissa Monastery clings to an Amorgós cliffside.

NÁXOS

Rugged, lofty Náxos offers green valleys and
sweeping sandy beaches along its southwest-facing
coast, as well as superb medieval and ancient
monuments.

*The Portára gateway of
the unfinished temple
of Delian Apollo.*

Rugged, lofty Náxos offers green
valleys, lush even in the height
of summer, and sweeping sandy
beaches along its southwest-facing
coast, as well as superb medieval and
ancient monuments.

Hóra ➊ (Náxos Town) is a labyrinth
of mansions, fortifications, post-Byzantine churches and ancient and medieval
ruins. The **Orthodox Cathedral** to the
northeast marks the Fondána district;
the adjacent residential Boúrgo quarter is full of arched passageways and
narrow lanes. Higher up, within the
gated *kástro*, live Catholic descendants
of the Venetians; look for their coats
of arms over doorways. The former
French Commercial School, built into
the ramparts, briefly educated Nikos
Kazantzakis until his suspicious father
came to rescue him from the Jesuits.
Today it houses the **Archaeological
Museum** (Tue–Sun 8.30am–2.30pm;
charge), with a huge and excellent collection (including Cycladic figurines
and a Hellenistic mosaic).

On **Palátia** islet (connected by a
causeway) to the north of Hóra's ferry

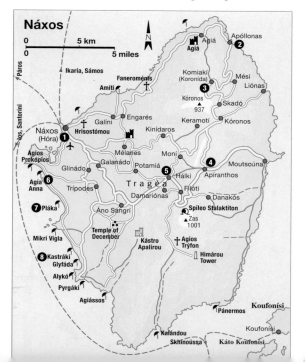

dock, a colossal free-standing marble door frame, the **Portára**, marks the entrance to the **Temple of Delian Apollo** of 540–530 BC. It was never completed, despite the efforts of Lygdamis, Náxos's tyrant. Had it been, it would have been Archaic Greece's largest temple.

The rest of the island rewards exploration by hired car, bus or on foot. Hemmed in by the Cyclades' highest ridges, the interior recalls the wilder parts of the Peloponnese. **Mount Zas** (a corruption of Zeus) is 1,001 metres (3,284ft) high, but not hard to climb for superb views. In the central **Tragéa** region, orchards conceal Byzantine churches and crumbling manors.

On the northern shore of Náxos, at the end of a bus line, sits the little resort of **Apóllonas ❷**. A huge *kouros* (Archaic statue of an idealised youth) lies on the hillside above it, abandoned around 600 BC when the marble cracked. (Two other flawed *kouroi*, smaller but more elaborately worked, repose at Flério, 10km (6 miles) east of Náxos, respectively in a walled garden at Melanés, and up a nearby hillside.)

On the road from Apóllonas to Hóra, handsome **Koronída ❸** (Komiakí), the island's highest village, looks over terraced vineyards, and is home of the local *kítron* liqueur – and of emery miners until nearby deposits became unprofitable. Marble-paved **Apíranthos ❹** (Aperáthou), 20km (12 miles) south, was settled by Cretan refugees in the 17th and 18th centuries, and is the natal village of Manolis Glezos, the leftist activist, later politician, who tore down the Nazi flag from the Parthenon on 30 May 1941.

Filóti, 8km (5 miles) below Apíranthos, is the second-largest settlement; a paved road leads south around Mt Zas to the 20-metre (65ft) Hellenistic **Himárou Tower**. The Tragéa extends west from Filóti to **Hálki ❺**, with several fine churches, including 11th-century **Panagía Protóthronis (rarely open)**. Next door is the 17th-century

Grazia-Barozzi Tower, one of many defensive towers across Náxos.

From Halkí a good road heads north to **Moní**, known for its restaurants with mountain views. Just before the village is the turning for **Panagía Drosianí** (The Dewy Virgin; daily 10am–4pm), built in stages between the 4th and 12th centuries and retaining some of the oldest, albeit battered, frescoes in Greece.

From Ano Sangrí just southwest of the Trageá, a paved road descends 5 km (3 miles) through a beautiful valley to the well-reconstructed **Temple of Demeter** (grounds always unlocked), dating from circa 530 BC).

Some of the Cyclades' best beaches line the southwest coast. The merged resorts of **Agios Prokópios** and **Agía Anna ❻** are the main bases for holidaymakers; the long white sands of **Pláka ❼** just southeast have fewer facilities, and more scantily clad beachcombers, the further you go. **Kastráki ❽** and Glyfáda beyond Mikrí Vígla headland with its kite-boarders, offers more of the same. Once past scenic **Alykó** headland with its coves lie beaches at **Pyrgáki** and **Agiássos**.

Laid-back sightseeing on the ferry to Náxos.

SANTORÍNI

Santoríni's whitewashed villages cling to volcanic cliffs above beaches of black sand. It is an island shaped by geological turmoil, and one of the most dramatic in all of Greece.

Main Attractions
Firá museums
Ancient Thera
Ia
Kamári beach
Pýrgos

Sailing into the bay of Santoríni is one of Greece's great experiences. Broken pieces of a volcano's rim – Santoríni and its attendant islets – trace a multicoloured circle around a deep submerged caldera that, before the cataclysmic volcanic eruption in about 1625 BC, was a hummocky volcanic plateau. The earthquakes, tsunamis and rains of pumice that followed the eruption devastated much of the Aegean, and contributed to the end of Minoan civilisation. The island's long crescent, formed of solidified lava, seems at sunset still to reflect fire from the dormant volcano.

The sensual lines of Cycladic architecture, augmented here with anti-earthquake barrel-vaulting cemented with pozzolana (sandy volcanic ash), are doubly disarming on Santoríni, set against the smoky purple or rusty orange striations of weathered lava in the background. Thera is the island's ancient name, and Thíra the official one in modern times. Both Greeks and foreigners, however, prefer the medieval Santoríni, after Saint Irene, one of three sisters martyred by Diocletian in AD 304.

Only excursion boats put in at **Skála Firás**, 580 steps below Firá (*skála* means both landing stage and staircase in Greek); most seacraft dock at ugly **Athiniós**, 10km (6 miles)

further south. **Firá ❶** (Hóra), the capital, sits high on the rim, its white houses mostly rebuilt in concrete after a devastating earthquake in 1956. The town is largely pedestrianised, its winding cobbled streets terraced into the volcanic cliffs.

Firá has an **Archaeological Museum** (Tue–Sun 9am–3.40pm; charge) and the far better **Museum of Prehistoric Thera** (Tue–Sun 9am–3.40pm; charge), devoted to the Minoan Akrotiri site – star exhibits are original frescoes of cavorting blue

View towards the volcano cone of Néa Kaméni.

On the phone in Firá.

Remains at Thera, on the Mésa Vounó headland.

monkeys, elegant women and Nilotic vegetation proving seafaring contacts with Egypt. The **Megaro Gyzi Museum** (May–Oct Mon–Sat 10am–4pm; charge) occupies the former Catholic archbishopric, spared by the 1956 earthquake, which is stuffed with antiquarian engravings, documents and maps as well as pre-earthquake photographs. The **Lignos Folklore Museum** in Kondohóri suburb (daily 10am–2pm and 4–8pm; charge) completely reproduces a 19th-century cave-house, along with mocked-up workshops for all the vanished rural crafts of the island.

Although packed with more jewellers and chichi boutiques than strictly necessary, Firá can still enchant, especially over a drink at sunset while contemplating the midnight-blue caldera waters with their volcanic islets. Traditionally, Santoríni was said to be the main Greek home of vampires – possibly because corpses failed to decompose completely in the lava soil – and at this witching hour the undead do seem a distinct possibility.

Ancient Thera and Akrotiri

East of Firá, the landscape drops into fertile, level, pumice-rich fields, though in the southeast some non-volcanic mountains shrug themselves up. On one of them, the non-volcanic Mésa Vounó headland, sits ancient **Thera ❷** (Tue–Sun 8.30am–2.45pm), founded during the 9th century BC just uphill from the only freshwater spring on the island, still flowing, and remained inhabited (with a Hellenistic zenith) until medieval times. The best approaches are the fine, if twisting, cobbled paths up from either Kamári or Périssa (see page 193).

In the south, ancient **Akrotiri ❸** (Tues–Sun 8am–4.40pm; charge), a Minoan town preserved in volcanic ash like Pompeii, had comfortable two-storey houses, good plumbing and attractive little squares. Only about 20 percent has been excavated thus far and no bones have been found, which suggests that the inhabitants had some warning of the pending eruption, and fled with their valuables (though leaving other artefacts behind). The beautiful frescoes, pots and furniture found

SANTORÍNI WINERIES

Santoríni is now an AOC domaine and winemaking is the only flourishing traditional trade. For a few euros (or even sometimes free), winery tours allow generous sampling. Boutari, near Megalohóri (www.boutari.gr; tel 22860 81011; tours daily Apr–Oct 10am–5.30pm) is the biggest and most visited, but there are also microwineries like Art Space in Episkopí Goniá (www.artspace-santorini.com, May–Oct), the oldest on the island with a museum inside a long subterranean gallery. Domaine Sigalas at Baxédes near Ia (www.domaine-sigalas.com; daily tastings April–Nov hours vary), has expensive but superior products. Ktima Argyrou (www.estate-argyros.com), also in Episkopí Goniás, does the excellent red Mavrotragano and the distinctive Aidani white. Most Santoríni wineries produce *vinsánto*, a fortified dessert wine.

here are divided between the Museum of Prehistoric Thera, and the National Archaeological Museum in Athens (see page 115).

Ia and the caldera

Santoríni's population swells fivefold in summer from the permanent winter population of about 15,000; while Firá is the most developed tourist centre, many other places offer accommodation and places to eat, although bus services are hopelessly overcrowded. **Ia ➍** (Oía), on the island's northernmost peninsula, is among Greece's most photographed villages, carefully restored since the 1956 earthquake destroyed most of its famous cavehouses. Today, these same cave-houses converted into exclusive accommodation are an Ia speciality. A steep walk down twisting stone steps from the western end of town leads to the tiny twin ports of **Arméni** and **Ammoúdi**. The gentle trail-hike along the caldera's edge from Ia to **Imerovígli** (3km/2 miles north of Firá) allows you to experience the island's tempestuous geology from close up.

The volcano is only dormant, not extinct; besides regular earthquakes, it has produced the two cinder-cones of **Néa** and **Paleá Kaméni** (the Burnt Islets) out in the caldera. Regular boat tours from both Skála Firás and Ammoúdi take you to them, where you can swim to sulphurous hot springs off Paleá, and hike up to a crater on Néa which still emits gas and steam; the last actual eruption was in 1950. Tours and regular small ferries from Ammoúdi continue to **Thirassía**, the only one of Santoríni's satellite islets which is inhabited, with a pace of life still stuck in pre-tourism once the day-trippers have gone – there are tavernas, and rooms to rent, though few beaches.

Coastal resorts and the central plain

After Firá and Ia, the next major resorts are **Kamári ➎** and **Périssa ➏** on the east coast. Both have roasting hot,

black-sand beaches (the one at Périssa is 8km/5 miles long); Kamári is pitched at families, Périssa at the youth market. From ancient Thera (see page 192), between the two, another good path heads west to Santoríni's summit, Profítis Ilías (566 metres/1,860ft), home to multiple antennae and an eponymous 18th-century monastery (rarely open to the public) that is the focus of the island's major 19–20 July festival.

From here, a steep road descends to conical **Pýrgos ➐** village on the central plain, its houses arrayed around a Venetian citadel with several bulbous churches. It contrasts with **Mesariá ➑** further north, which seems to consist only of more church domes, until the approach reveals a warren of dwellings and alleys sunk below ground level. The farmland around and between features yellow grain sheaves, vines twisted into wreaths to protect grapes against the wind, and tiny thick-skinned tomatoes, grown without water for concentrated flavour, then dried. Small caves (*kánaves*), natural or dug out, are used as toolsheds, barns and (formerly) as homes.

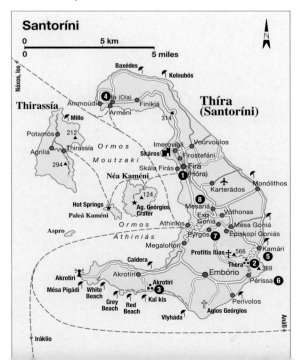

THE SPORADES AND EVVIA

Skiáthos, Skópelos, Alónissos, Skýros and Evvia.

A Skópelos miss.

The Sporades – meaning "sporadic" or "scattered" – is a group of four islands in the northwest Aegean. Evvia, extending along the Greek mainland south of the Sporades, is Greece's second-largest island, after Crete.

Mainlanders have long appreciated Skiáthos's beaches and made annual pilgrimages, though they are now outnumbered by foreigners. In spite of a rich history, Alónissos is the least developed of the Sporades in terms of tourism, while Skópelos falls somewhere in between in terms of beaches and level of development. Skýros, the largest and in certain ways the most interesting of the group, is remote from the others, with a deeply entrenched local culture. Evvia, despite easy access from the mainland, has been mostly unspoilt by tourism. Its diverse landscape and rich history make it almost a microcosm of the whole country.

Hopping between Skiáthos, Skópelos and Alónissos is very easy, but reaching Skýros usually involves a longer trip via Evvia, with only mid-summer connections with its three northern neighbours. Skiáthos alone of the Sporades has an international airport with regular overseas arrivals, mainly from Britain, Italy and Scandinavia, and domestic flights to Athens and Thessaloníki. Skýros Airport also receives planes from Athens and Thessaloníki, scheduled to allow long weekends away. Conventional ferries and catamarans run to the three northerly Sporades from Vólos and Agios Konstandínos on the mainland.

Skiáthos Town bathers.

The islands are what remains of a mountain range that detached itself from the mainland in a geological convulsion and "sank". Prevailing winds and other factors produce reliable winter rainfall and lush vegetation, notably pine forests. Summers can be humid, especially on south-facing shores, but the *meltémi* helps keep a lid on temperatures.

The traditional trade route between the Mediterranean and the Black Sea passed the Sporades. This strategic position has often brought unwanted callers, including invasion fleets and pirates, so medieval remains and major archaeological sites are few.

Restored doorway, Skiáthos Town.

used as a locale by the *Mamma Mia!* film-makers.

Alónissos

On a hill west of **Patitíri ❼**, the port of this rugged island and last call on ferry or catamaran routes, is **Paleá Alónissos ❽** (Hóra), the former capital shattered by an earthquake in March 1965. This compounded the blow the islanders had already suffered when all their grapevines withered and died from phylloxera during the 1950s. Alónissos seems to have been always jinxed: the ancient capital, Ikos, literally disappeared when the ground on which it stood slumped into the sea.

In 1970, Palaeolithic-era evidence was found that could mean that Alónissos was inhabited before any other Aegean island, and it was considered a prize worth fighting over by Philip of Macedon and the Athenians. Its famous **wines** were once shipped all over ancient Greece in amphorae stamped "IKION"; today there is a modest revival of the industry based on phylloxera-resistant vines, though you're more likely to be offered the luscious local apricots or pickled *tzitzírafa* (terebinth) shoots.

A marked, cobbled path links Patitíri and Paleá Alónissos (45 minutes' walk); there is also a bus. By 1977, coercive government policies had forced the total abandonment of Hóra by locals; as at Paleó Klíma on Skópelos, Athenians and foreigners bought up the old ruins and restored them in variable taste. The effect is somewhat twee, and most food and drink is predictably overpriced, but the views west to Skópelos and north as far as Mount Athos are undeniably spectacular.

The way the island has adjusted to its unrealised potential and bad luck is something for which many visitors are grateful. Alónissos remains the least developed of the Sporades, with second-home ownership matching short-term tourism, which tends to be low-key and trendy, with art exhibitions, a yoga school and a homeopathy academy – although there are also two Italian-dominated all-inclusive resorts. Walkers are admirably catered for with an accurate topographic map, numbered and maintained paths, and a walking guide written by resident expat guide Chris Browne.

Usable, accessible beaches are concentrated on the more protected south and southeast coasts. Several are a short distance by path or track from Hóra, but superior ones lie northeast of functional Patitíri, Roussoúm Gialós and Vótsi ports at **Kokkinókastro** (site of ancient Ikos), **Tzortzí Gialós** and **Leftós Gialós**. Improved roads make wheeled access easy (and safer than on Skiáthos or Skópelos); overland journeys have largely replaced summer taxi-boats from Patitíri up the coast as far as **Agios Dimítrios**. **Kalamákia** is an authentic fishing port – nearby waters are rich in marine life – while yachts like to put in at **Stení Vála**.

National Marine Park

Alónissos, as well as half a dozen islets scattered to the east and north, fall

A flock of sheep on Skýros.

WHERE

The Manos Faltaïts
Museum on Skýros
(www.faltaits.gr; daily
10am–noon and
5.30–8pm (summer
6–9pm); charge), in a
mansion north of the
town, is a private
collection presenting the
life of the island through
rare antiques, pottery, a
traditional house
mock-up, documents,
costumes and
photographs.

within the **National Marine Park of the Northern Sporades**, established in 1992 to conserve declining fish stocks and provide sanctuary to seabirds and marine mammals, in particular the severely endangered Mediterranean monk seal, of which fewer than 400 survive worldwide. The park is proving, however, a bane to traditional livelihoods; many local fishermen have been paid a stipend of a few tens of thousands of euros to cease work and smash up (under close supervision) their historic wooden kaïkia.

Two of the islets – **Pipéri** and **Giourá** – are off-limits to all but licensed scientists for conservation reasons. **Skántzoura**, with its empty monastery, is rather out of the way, but seasonal **caique excursions** from Patitíri visit others. The first stop is **Kyrá Panagiá**, which belongs to Megístis Lávras monastery on Mount Athos and itself has a restored 10th-century monastery inhabited by one farmer-monk. With enough passengers to defray fuel costs, peak-season tours extend to northerly **Psathoúra**, with the tallest (26 metres/81ft) lighthouse

A goatman at Skýros Carnival.

in the Aegean (built in 1895, now solar-powered) and a lovely white-sand beach. Olive-covered, only seasonally inhabited **Peristéra**, cradling Alónissos to the east, is the usual final afternoon swim-stop in low season. Passengers are most unlikely to spot seals, but will probably encounter dolphins.

Skýros

The main character in the "goat dance" of **Skýros Carnival**, staged in the four weekends before Lent and with its roots in a pre-Christian pagan festival, is the *géros* (old man) who wears a goat pelt and kid-skin mask, plus tens of kilograms of sheep bells, which he shakes noisily with waist movements. The *géri* are accompanied by their "brides" the *korélles* (maidens), young men in drag. Foreign visitors enjoying the spectacle ought perhaps to know that the third type of figure (the *frángos*), a buffoon dressed in ridiculous clothes and blowing on a *bouroú* or conch shell, represents a foreigner.

Only recently has Skýros shed its near-complete economic dependence on the Greek navy and air force and courted foreign tourism, mostly Italian, French, Dutch and British, although the island has been well known to Greeks for years. The effects of the summer season have not yet eclipsed a vigorous and idiosyncratic local culture, even if the older generation, which faithfully wore the vaguely Cretan island costume, has pretty much died off. Cubist white houses often contain amazing collections of copperware, embroidery and painted ceramics, the last acquired by trade or piracy and serving as a spur to the development of a local pottery industry based in several kiln-workshops at Magaziá beach. Carved wooden furniture passed down though the generations is often too small to be practical, so may be hung on the wall.

Skýros Town ❾ (Hóra) is on the northern half of the island, fanning out on the lee side of a rock plug

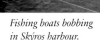

overlooking the east coast. Life in the town is played out all along the meandering main commercial street or *agorá*, which begins near the downhill edge of what is a remarkably workaday place, albeit with picturesque archways and churches.

A left fork in this thoroughfare leads down towards a plaza at the northern edge of town, where a nude bronze male statue representing *Immortal Poetry* (in memory of Rupert Brooke) commands the view. Just below this is a worthwhile **Archaeological Museum** (Tue–Sun 8.30am–3pm; charge), with fine Geometric-era pottery, and the Mános Faltäits Museum (see page 206). The right-hand option wanders up to the *kástro*, the old Byzantine/Venetian castle built atop the ancient acropolis where, in legend, King Lykomedes raised Achilles and later threw Theseus to his death. Sadly, since a 2001 earthquake the *kástro* and the monastery inside are closed for safety reasons.

Long, sandy **Magaziá** beach below Hóra merges seamlessly with the one of **Mólos**, which terminates at **Pouriá** point with sea-weathered, squared-off rocks quarried by the Romans. There are better, if sometimes exposed, beaches in the north at Gyrísmata, **Kareflóu** and **Agios Pétros**, bracketing the airport/air force base, and the site of Bronze Age **Palamári** (Mon–Fri 7.30am–2.30pm; free). The paved loop road continues through pines past other coves with mediocre beaches like Atsítsa, until reaching longer, sandier **Péfkos**. Linariá ⑩, the ferry port, also has accommodation and tavernas, but most visitors will continue on the circuit back towards Hóra, perhaps pausing at **Aspoús**, with a good beach.

At one time Skýros may have been two islands. Today's halves – **Merói** and **Vounó** – join in a noticeably flat valley connecting Kalamítsa Bay with Ahílli fishing port. In contrast to northerly Merói, Vounó (dominated

by Mount Kóhilas) is relatively barren, though strong springs emerge on the northwest flank facing the "divide", and there is enough pasture on the heights for the island's wild ponies, which have been bred here since ancient times. Beaches, except for **Kolymbáda**, are few and compare poorly with those in the north. Most visitors are bound for **Trís Boúkes** ⑪ and the **grave of Rupert Brooke**. Serving as a naval officer in the fleet bound for Gallipoli, the poet died of blood poisoning on a French hospital ship on 23 April 1915 and was buried in the olive grove here.

Roads beyond this point are minimal, and accordingly **boat excursions** from Linariá are popular. They visit **Sarakinó islet** with its sandy inlet and sea-caves in the sheer coastal cliffs extending all the way up to Ahílli, home to seemingly innumerable Eleonora's falcons.

Fishing boats bobbing in Skýros harbour.

The Manos Faltaïts Museum above Skýros Town.

EVVIA

Greece's second-largest island is largely unspoilt by tourism, and little known to foreigners. Although barely separated from the mainland, Evvia has a distinctive character.

Main Attractions

Halkída Kástro
Erétria Museum
"Dragon Houses"
Kárystos
Dimosári Gorge
Límni

The spa town Loutrá Edipsoú.

Halkída, the capital of Evvia (Euboea) is close enough to the mainland for a drawbridge and a newer suspension bridge to arc over. Aristotle is supposed to have been so frustrated by trying to understand the rapid, fluctuating tides in the Evripos channel here that he killed himself by jumping into the roiling waters.

In antiquity Evvia's most prominent cities were Chalcis (modern Halkída) and nearby Eretria (Erétria), which both established colonies across the Mediterranean. Evvia then came under the control of the Athenians, Macedonians, Romans, Byzantines and Ottomans, and became part of Greece in 1830, after the War of Independence.

Halkída ❶ (Hálkis) is now an industrial town, but the **Kástro** district, with a 15th-century **mosque** and ornate **fountain**, plus the Crusader-modified **Church of Agía Paraskeví**, are worth visiting. In the newer district are an **Archaeological Museum** (Tue–Sun 8.30am–3pm; charge) and, lodged in the old prison, a **Folklore Museum** (Wed–Sun 10am–1pm, Wed also 6–8pm; charge), as well as a 19th-century **synagogue** still used by the remaining Jewish Romaniote community. **Erétria ❷** to the south is a crowded, grid-plan summer resort where ro-ro ferries call from Skála Oropoú on the mainland. The small **Archaeological Museum** (Tue–Sun 8.30am–3pm; charge) and adjacent archaeological site with its mosaics are worth a stop.

The road south hugs the coast past the attractive resort of **Amárynthos** until just before **Alivéri**, where it turns inland to a junction at **Lépoura**. The northerly option goes through **Háni Avlonaríou**, with a large 13th-century **Basilica of Agios Dimítrios**, and continues to **Stómio** beach, before threading through **Platána** resort to the nondescript harbour at **Paralía Kýmis** and ferry to Skýros. **Kými** proper, up the hill, is a sizeable town, and start of a mountain road back to Halkída.

Southern Evvia, reached by the other option at Lépoura, is drier and less green. From the main road beyond Almyropótamos, along the slimmest part of the island, there are views down to the sea on either side. Near **Stýra** ❸ are the ruins of three mysterious stone buildings, known locally as "**Dragon Houses**" (*drakóspita*). The most convincing theory is that they are temples built by slaves or immigrants working nearby quarries in the Classical era.

The main town in the south is **Kárystos** ❹, stuck in a 1970s time-warp, with a long beach, scattered Roman ruins and a Venetian tower. On **Mount Ohi** (1,399 metres/4,617ft) just inland there's the medieval **Castello Rosso**, another *drakóspito* and the start of the three-hour traverse through the superb **Dimosári Gorge**.

Northeast of Halkída, **Steni** ❺ on the slopes of **Mount Dírfys** (1,743 metres/5,718ft), is a favourite goal for Athenians seeking clean air and grill restaurants. **Prokópi** ❻, on the main road north, sits on a broad upland purchased by Englishman Edward Noel in the 1830s. On Mount Kandíli to the west,

the family estate of his descendants is now available for holiday lets and hosts special-interest courses. Prokópi was settled after 1923 by refugees from Cappadocia who brought with them the relics of 18th-century Saint John the Russian (actually Ukrainian). They are revered in a 1960s church.

North of Prokópi lie some of Evvia's finest beaches; most renowned (and developed) is **Angáli**. Just uphill is **Agía Anna** ❼, with an excellent **Folklore Museum** (Wed–Sun 10am–1pm, 5–7pm; charge). Continuing along this coast, you pass the beaches of **Paralía Kotsikiás**, **Psaropoúli** and **Elliniká**, the last the smallest and prettiest.

Límni ❽ on the southwest coast is Evvia's beauty spot, a 19th-century port with an interesting **Ethnographic/Archaeological Museum** (Mon–Fri 9am–1pm, Sat 10am–1pm, Sun 10.30am–1pm; charge), and **Agíou Nikoláou Galatáki Convent** in the hills behind, its narthex vividly frescoed. The closest beaches are at **Spiáda** and **Hrónia**, on the way to **Loutrá Edipsoú** ❾, a spa town and ferry port with some Belle Epoque and Art Deco hotels.

FACT

The famous bronze statue of Poseidon (or perhaps Zeus) poised to hurl a trident (or a lightning bolt), in Athens's Archaeological Museum (see page 115), was found in 1928 in the sea off Cape Artemísion in the north.

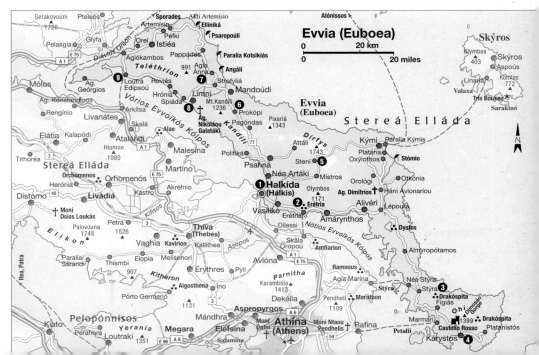

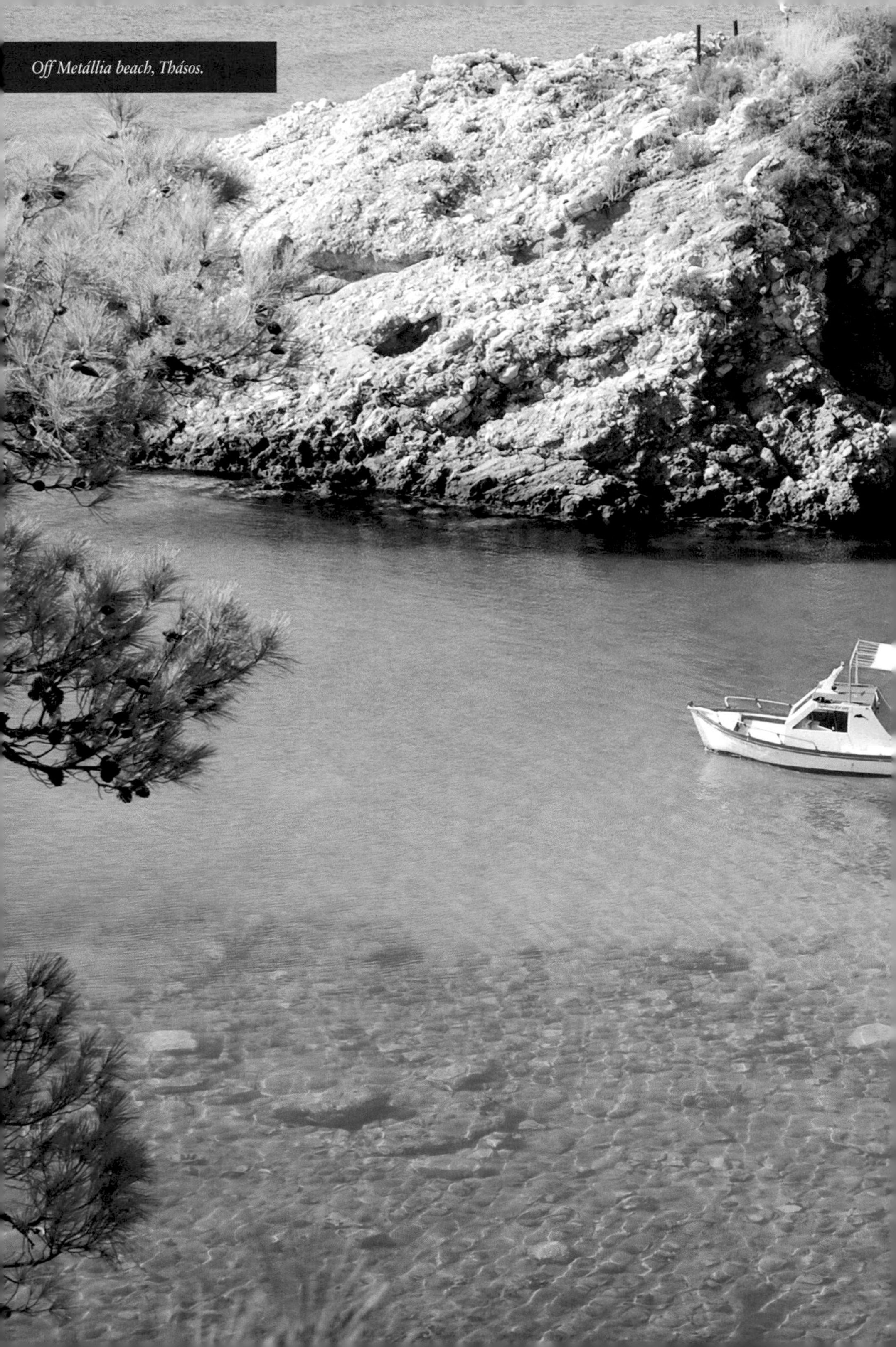

Off Metállia beach, Thásos.

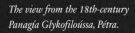
The view from the 18th-century
Panagía Glykofiloússa, Pétra.

THE NORTHEAST AEGEAN

Thásos, Samothráki, Límnos, Ágios Evstrátios, Lésvos,
Psará, Híos, Ikaría, Foúrni, Sámos.

Lésvos pottery.

The northeast Aegean islands have little in common other than a history of medieval Genoese rule. Northerly Thásos, Samothráki, Ágios Evstrátios and Límnos in the north have few connections with the south Aegean; indeed, Thásos belongs to the Macedonian province of Kavála, and Samothráki to Thracian Évros. Greeks' affection for these islands, so convenient for the mainland, exceeds that of foreign tourists. Except for marble-cored Thásos, these isles, as well as Lésvos, are volcanic in origin, with thermal springs, their slopes home to lava-loving oaks.

Lésvos, Híos and Sámos to the southeast were once prominent in antiquity, colonising across the Mediterranean and promoting the arts and sciences, though scant traces of ancient glory remain. All three served as bridges between Asia Minor and peninsular Greece and were joined to Asia Minor until the end of the Ice Ages isolated them. Turkey is still omnipresent on the horizon, less than 2km (1 mile) away across the Mykale Straits at Sámos. Híos, Sámos and Ikaría are rugged limestone and schist (with lots of granite, too, on Ikaría), forested with pine, olive, oak and cypress. Delicate wild flowers, especially on Sámos, heighten their appeal, and numerous small mammals and birds thrive, some (like Lésvos's red squirrel) having migrated over from Anatolia before the rising sea marooned them. Beaches vary from long shores of fist-sized pebbles to sheltered, sandy crescents.

A beach on Sámos.

As ever, transport to, between and on these islands varies with population and level of tourism. Samothráki has a skeletal bus service and overpriced ferries from Alexandroúpoli; Thásos has frequent buses and regular car ferries from Kavála and Keramotí. Límnos and Lésvos have regular flights and sailings from Piraeus, Lávrio and Thessaloníki, plus from each other; Híos is linked daily with Athens and Lésvos, less regularly with Sámos and Ikaría. Ikaría is connected to certain Cycladic islands. Sámos is best connected, with seasonal hydrofoils to all the isles from Pátmos to Kós, plus flights to Rhodes, and receives more international charters than the runner-up, Lésvos.

THÁSOS, SAMOTHRÁKI AND LÍMNOS

Greece's most northerly islands see relatively few foreigners, but they offer more than enough by way of ancient ruins, empty beaches and picturesque villages.

Whether you want to wander through olive groves, laze on sandy beaches or take in some major archaeological sites, you will be happy on these northerly islands.

Thásos

Just 7 nautical miles (12km) from mainland Macedonia, Thásos – always a favourite retreat of northern Greeks – has, since the 1980s, welcomed a cosmopolitan assortment of foreigners. Yet the island seems relatively unspoilt, with package tourism well quarantined. Almost circular, mountainous Thásos is essentially a giant lump of marble, mixed with granite and schist, crumbling into white sand at the island's margins. Lower elevations, covered in olive plantations, remain attractive, but the "Diamond of the North" (*Diamándis tou Vorrá*) had its lustre severely dulled in 1981, 1985, 1989 and 1993 by forest fires, deliberately set by developers wanting cheap building land. Thásos is now three-quarters denuded of its original pine forest, which survives only in the northeast. Elsewhere, only the inland villages and a thin fringe of surrounding vegetation were saved, and while there is regrowth, it is painfully slow – it takes 50 years for a conifer forest to regenerate completely. The bus service around the coastal ring road is quite adequate, although most visitors hire motorbikes or cars (Thásos

is small enough for a long day tour). The east and south coasts have better beaches; the west coast gives access to most inland villages.

Thásos's past glory, fuelled by local gold deposits, is evident at the harbour capital of **Liménas ❶** (Limín, also just Thásos), where substantial remnants of the ancient town have been excavated; choice bits of the ruined acropolis are illuminated by night. The biggest area of the Old City, behind the picturesque fishing harbour that traces the confines of the old commercial port, is the **agora**.

Main Attractions

Acropolis and agora, Thásos
Alykí
Samothráki (Hóra)
Sanctuary of the Great Gods
Mýrina kástro
Evgátis beach
Allied World War I
   cemeteries

Natural seawater pool on Thásos.

EAT

Locally made honey, candied walnuts and tsípouro, the fire-water of northern Greece, are favourite souvenirs of Thásos.

In the nearby **Archaeological Museum** (Tue–Sun 8.30am–2.30 pm; charge), the prize exhibit is a 4-metre (13ft) high Archaic *kouros* carrying a ram.

The first village clockwise from Liménas, slate-roofed **Panagía ②**, is a large, busy place where life revolves around the *platía*, with its plane trees and four-spouted fountain. **Potamiá**, further down the valley, is less architecturally distinguished: visitors come mainly for the sake of the **Polygnotos Vagis Museum** (May–Oct 10am–1pm and 6–8pm; free), featuring the work of the eponymous locally born sculptor. Beyond, the road drops to Potamiá Bay. **Skála Potamiás**, at its south end, is

all lodging and tavernas, with more of that to the north at **Hrysí Ammoudiá**. In between stretches a fine, blond-sand beach. There are even better strands at **Kínyra**, 24km (15 miles) from Liménas, but most tourists schedule a lunch stop at one of the several tavernas of **Alykí ③** hamlet, architecturally preserved thanks to adjacent ruins: an ancient temple and two atmospheric Byzantine basilicas. The local topography of a low spit, sandy to the west, nearly pinching off a headland, is strikingly photogenic. So too is the **Convent of Arhangélou Mihaíl** 5km (3 miles) to the west, high above a barren coast – but mainly from a distance;

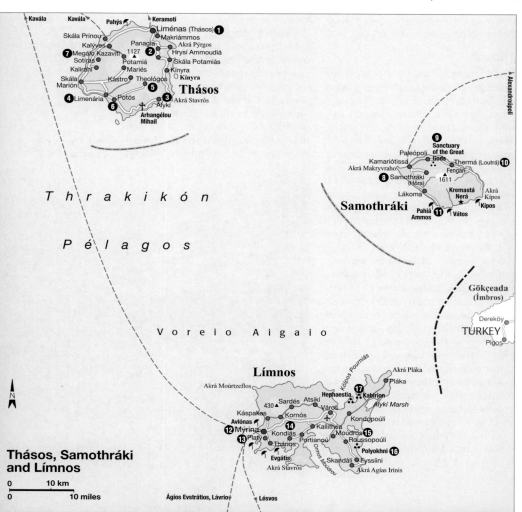

Thásos, Samothráki and Límnos

it has been renovated hideously.

At **Limenária ❹**, now the island's second town, Ottoman-era mansions of departed German mining executives survive. More intriguingly, it's the starting point for a safari to hilltop **Kástro**, the most naturally pirate-proof of the inland villages. Beyond Limenária, there's little to encourage a stop.

Theológos ❺, actually reached from the overdeveloped resort of **Potós ❻**, was the island's Ottoman capital, a linear place where most houses have walled gardens. **Mariés** sits piled up at the top of a wooded valley, just glimpsing the sea. By contrast, **Sotíros** enjoys phenomenal sunsets, best enjoyed from its central taverna under enormous plane trees. Of all the inland settlements, **Megálo Kazavíti ❼** (Megálo Prínos) has the grandest *platía* and the best-preserved traditional houses, snapped up and restored by outsiders. Ground-floor windows still retain iron bars, reminders of pirate days.

Samothráki

Samothráki (Samothrace) raises forbidding granite heights above stony shores and storm-lashed waters, both offering poor natural anchorage. Homer described Poseidon perching atop 1,611-metre (5,285ft) **Mount Fengári**, the Aegean's highest summit, to watch the action of the Trojan War just east. Fengári and its foothills occupy much of the island, with little level terrain except in the far west. Its southwest flank features scattered villages lost amid olive groves varied by the occasional poplar. North-facing slopes are damper, with chestnuts and oaks, plus plane trees along the numerous watercourses. Springs are abundant, and waterfalls even plunge directly to the sea at **Kremastá Nerá** in the south.

Only the northwest of the island has a rudimentary bus service. Tourism is barely developed, and the remaining islanders prefer it that way. In its absence the population has dipped below 3,000, as farming can only support so many. Boats and occasional hydrofoils dock at **Kamariótissa**, the functional port where rental vehicles are in short supply.

Hóra or **Samothráki ❽**, the official capital 5km (3 miles) east of

Byzantine-era tower on Samothráki.

ANCIENT THÁSOS TOUR

Beginning at the **Temple of Dionysos**, a good path permits a rewarding walking tour of the ancient walls and acropolis. First stop is the Hellenistic **theatre** (open only for occasional summer festival performances) that was later remodelled by the Romans to serve as an arena. Continue to the **medieval fortress**, built by a succession of occupiers from the masonry of a temple dedicated to Apollo. Tracing the course of massive 5th-century BC walls brings you to the foundations of a **Temple of Athena**, beyond which a **Shrine of Pan** is visible in badly eroded relief on a rock outcrop. From here a vertiginous "secret" stairway plunges to the **Gate of Parmenon**, the only ancient entry still intact, at the southern edge of town.

Kamariótissa, is more rewarding, nestling almost invisibly in a circular hollow. A cobbled commercial street serpentines past sturdy, basalt-built houses, many now unused. From outdoor seating at the two tavernas on Hóra's large *platía*, you glimpse the sea beyond a crumbled Byzantine-Genoese fort at the edge of town.

Samothráki's other great sight lies 6km (4 miles) from Kamariótissa along the north coast road. From the late Bronze Age until the advent of Christianity, the **Sanctuary of the Great Gods** ❾ was the major religious centre of the Aegean. Local deities of the original Thracian settlers were syncretised with the Olympian gods of later Aeolian colonists, in particular the *Kabiroi*, or divine twins Castor and Pollux, patrons of seafarers (who needed all the help they could get in the habitually rough seas hereabouts).

The **sanctuary ruins** (daily, summer 8am–7.30pm, winter until 3pm; charge) visible today are mostly late Hellenistic, and eerily impressive, if overgrown. Obvious monuments include a partly re-erected Doric temple of the second

initiation; the peculiar round Arsinoe-ion, used for sacrifices; a round theatre area; and the fountain niche where the celebrated Winged Victory of Samothrace, now in the Louvre, was discovered. The 4th-century BC statue of Victory (Athena Nike) was discovered in 1863 by the French diplomat Charles Champoiseau, who immediately sent it to Paris. The Greek government has long demanded its return, but so far has had to settle for a plaster copy. The site **museum** (same hours but closed Mon) contains finds from the Archaic to Byzantine eras.

Some 6km (4 miles) further east, hot springs, cool cascades and a dense canopy of plane trees make the spa hamlet of **Thermá** ❿ (Loutrá) the most popular base on the island, patronised by an uneasy mix of the elderly infirm and young bohemian types, who flock to a late-summer 'ethno-trance' festival which many years is shut down by the authorities. Hot baths come in three temperatures and styles – including outdoor pools under a wooden shelter – while cold-plunge fanatics make for **Gría Váthra** canyon to the east. Thermá is also the base camp for the climb up Mount Fengári, a six-hour round trip.

The villages south of Hóra see few visitors, though they lie astride the route to **Pahiá Ammos** ⓫, the island's only sandy beach. From **Lákoma** village, it's about 8km (5 miles) by road to the beach, where a single seasonal taverna operates. Beyond Pahiá Ammos, you can walk to smaller **Vátos** nudist beach, but you'll need a boat – or to drive clockwise completely around Samothráki – to reach the pebble beach of **Kípi** in the far southeast.

Límnos and Agios Evstrátios

Dominating the approaches to the Dardanelles, Límnos has been occupied since Neolithic times, and always prospered as a trading station and military outpost. The Greek military still controls much of the island's area, including half the airport, belying an otherwise peaceful atmosphere. The

Límnos windwill.

volcanic terrain dwindles to excellent beaches, or produces excellent wine and other products. The surrounding seas yield plenty of fish, thanks to periodic migrations through the Dardanelles.

Most things of interest are found in the port-capital, **Mýrina** ⑫, or a short distance to either side – luckily, since the bus service is appalling and rental vehicles scarce at peak season. Volcanic stone has been well used in the older houses and street cobbles of Mýrina, while Ottoman mansions face the northerly town beach of **Romeïkós Gialós**, with its popular cafés. The southerly beach of **Néa Máditos** abuts the fishing port with its seafood tavernas.

Mýrina's **Archaeological Museum** (Tue–Sun 8.30am–3pm; charge) showcases the island's ancient sites. Public evidence of the Ottoman era is limited to an inscribed fountain and a dilapidated, octagonal dervish hall near the harbour end of the long market street. On the headland above, the *kástro* (always open) offers great sunset views.

The road north from Mýrina passes popular **Rihá Nerá** beach en route to even better **Avlónas**. In the opposite direction lie decent beaches at **Platý** ⑬ and **Thános**, with tiered namesake hillside villages just inland. Southeast from Thános brings you to **Evgátis**, the island's best beach. **Kondiás** ⑭ village just beyond is home to the **Balkan Art Gallery** (Sat–Thur 10am–2pm, 7.30–9.30pm; charge), established by the Bulgarian painter Svetlin Russev.

Two **cemeteries** maintained by the Commonwealth War Graves Commission flank drab **Moúdros** ⑮. During World War I, Moúdros was the principal base for the disastrous Gallipoli campaign. Of roughly 36,000 casualties, 887 are buried outside Moúdros on the way to **Roussopoúli**, while 348 more lie at **Portianoú**, across the bay.

Límnos's major archaeological sites are all in the far east of the island. **Polyokhni** ⑯ (Polyóhni), was a fortified town even older than Troy, destroyed by an earthquake in 2100 BC and never rebuilt. **Hephaestia** (Ifestía) was

Límnos's ancient capital until the Byzantine period. Traces of a temple of Hephaestos (the island's patron deity) and a Roman theatre are visible. Across the bay at **Kabirion** ⑰ (Kavírio) was a sanctuary of the *Kabiroi*. Not much remains except the column stumps.

A sliver of land south of Límnos, **Ágios Evstrátios** (Aï Strátis) is the most desolate spot in the northeast Aegean, especially since a 1968 earthquake devastated the only village. Owing to corruption, reparable dwellings were bulldozed and the surviving inhabitants (22 died) given ugly, prefabricated replacement housing. This, plus 20 surviving old buildings on the left, is what you see when when disembarking ferries stopping here on the Lávrio–Kavála route, or the Límnos-based *kaïki* – together Aï Strátis's lifelines.

There is little arable land aside from the valley behind the sad prefab settlement. There are a couple of taverna-cafés and three pensions for mostly Greek summer tourists, Aï Strátis has gotten popular lately, and you may have company at a few beaches 90 minutes' walk north or south of "town".

FACT

In the Polyokhni ruins, Italian archaeologists discovered a hoard of gold -jewellery from the 3rd millennium BC. It is now on display in Athens.

Límos' ruined kástro overlooks the town.

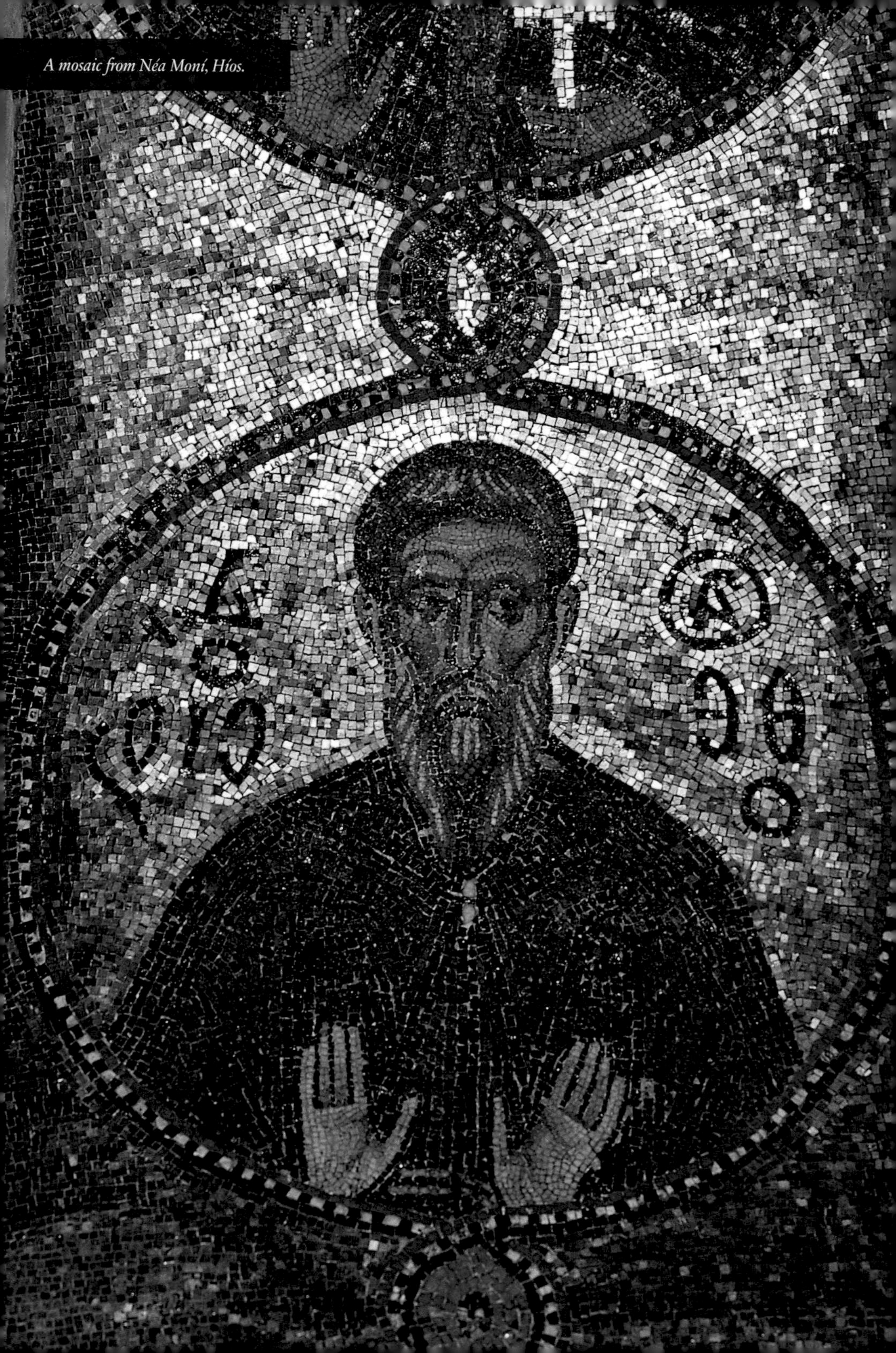

A mosaic from Néa Moní, Híos.

LÉSVOS, HÍOS, IKARÍA, FOÚRNI AND SÁMOS

These were some of ancient Greece's wealthiest islands, although today there are more reminders of their dramatic recent history.

These islands, with their gentle wooded slopes, have long been popular with Greek visitors, who appreciate their relatively untouristed feel and natural advantages.

Lésvos

Greece's third-largest island, measuring 70 by 40km (43 by 25 miles) at its widest, Lésvos is the antithesis of the *nisáki* (cute little islet). Between far-flung villages lie 11 million olive trees producing 45,000 tonnes of oil every year. Shipbuilding, fish-curing, *oúzo*-distilling and livestock-rearing remain important, but no enterprise rivals the olive, especially since it complements the second industry – tourism. Nets to catch this "black gold" are laid out in autumn, as soon as the tourists leave.

Lésvos was a preferred Roman holiday spot, what with its thick southern forests, idyllic orchards and hot springs– the island's thermal baths and spa facilities are still a considerable draw. The Byzantines considered it a humane exile for deposed nobility, while the Genoese Gattilusi clan held court here from 1355 until 1462. To the Ottomans it was the "Garden of the Aegean", their most productive, strictly governed and heavily colonised Aegean island.

Following 18th-century reforms within the empire, a Christian land-owning aristocracy developed, served by a large population of labouring peasants. This quasi-feudal system made Lésvos fertile ground for post-1912 leftist movements, and its habit of returning Communist MPs since the junta fell has earned it the epithet "Red Island" among fellow Greeks. The years after 1912 also saw a vibrant local intelligentsia emerge, but since World War II Lésvos's socio-economic fabric has shrunk considerably with emigration to Athens, Australia and America. However, the founding here in 1987 of the University of the Aegean has helped arrest decline.

Main Attractions

- Theóphilos & Thériade Museums
- Mólyvos
- Sykiás Olýmbon Cave
- Néa Moní
- Armenistís beaches
- Sámos Archaeological Museum
- Kímisis tis Theotókou Church

Taking the shade in Plomári.

Garlic for sale.

Mólyvos surmounted by its medieval castle.

Mytilíni ❶, the capital (its name a popular alias for the entire island), has a revved-up, slightly gritty atmosphere, as befits a port town of almost 30,000. Behind the waterfront, assorted church domes and spires enliven the skyline, while Odós Ermoú one street inland threads through the heart of the bazaar, passing a mosque (ruined) and Turkish baths (well restored) en route. On the headland to the northeast sits the medieval *kástro* (Tue–Sun 8.30am–2.30pm; charge), with constructions from various eras.

Behind the ferry dock is the two-wing **Archaeological Museum** (Tue–Sun 8am–2.40pm; charge); the new gallery a bit uphill features Hellenistic mosaics depicting scenes from Menander's comedies.

Even more noteworthy are two museums at **Variá**, 4km (2.5 miles) south of town. The **Theophilos Museum** (Tues–Sun 10am–4pm; charge) contains more than 60 paintings by locally born Theophilos Hatzimihaïl, Greece's most celebrated Naïve painter. The adjacent **Thériade Museum** (Tue–Sun summer 9am–2pm, 5–8pm, winter 9am–5pm; closed for works until 2015) was founded by another native son who, while an avant-garde art publisher in Paris, assembled this astonishing collection, with works by Chagall, Miró, Picasso, Matisse, Léger and others.

The road running northwest from Mytilíni follows the coast facing Turkey. **Mandamádos ❷**, 37km (23 miles) from Mytilíni, has a surviving pottery industry and, on the outskirts, the enormous **Monastery of the Taxiárhis**, with its much-revered black icon of the Archangel Michael. At **Kápi** the road divides; the northerly fork is wider, better paved and more scenic as it curls across the flanks of **Mount Lepétymnos**, passing by the handsome village of **Sykaminiá ❸**, the birthplace of novelist Stratis Myrivilis, and its photogenic, taverna-crammed port.

You go back down to sea level at **Mólyvos ❹** (officially Míthymna), linchpin of Lésvos tourism and understandably so: the ranks of sturdy tiled houses climbing to the medieval castle are an appealing sight, as is the stone-paved fishing harbour. But its

days as a retreat for bohemian artists and alternative activities are over, with package tourism dominant since the late 1980s. **Pétra ❺**, 5km (3 miles) south, accommodates the overflow behind its long beach; inland looms a rock plug crowned with the **Panagía Glykofiloússa** church. At its foot the 18th-century **Vareltzídena Mansion** (Tue–Sun 8.30am–2.40pm; free) with its extensive murals is well worth a look, as is the frescoed, 16th-century church of **Agios Nikólaos**.

From Pétra, head 17km (11 miles) south to **Kalloní ❻** market town and the turning east for **Agía Paraskeví** with the excellent **Museum of the Olive-Pressing Industry** (Wed–Mon 10am–6pm, closes 5pm winter; charge), in the old communal olive mill.

Alternatively, head west towards more rugged **western Lésvos**, with its lunar volcanic terrain. Stream valleys foster little oases, such as the one around **Perivolís Monastery ❼** (daily 10am–1pm and 5–6pm), 30km (19 miles) from Limónos, decorated with wonderful frescoes. After 10km (6 miles), the **Monastery of Ypsiloú ❽** with its small museum, on top of an extinct volcano, contemplates the abomination of desolation – complete with scattered trunks of the "Petrified Forest", prehistoric sequoias mineralised by volcanic ash.

There are more fossilised trees in and around **Sígri ❾**, 90km (56 miles) from Mytilíni, a sleepy place flanked by good beaches, and very much the end of the line, though most years it's an alternative ferry port. Most people prefer livelier **Skála Eresoú ❿**, 14km (9 miles) south of Ypsiloú, for a beach experience on its 3km (2 miles) of sand. In particular, numerous lesbians come to honour Sappho, who was born here.

Southern Lésvos, between the two gulfs, is carpeted with olive groves and chestnut forests, rolling up to 968-metre (3,176ft) **Mount Olympos**. Back on the coast is **Plomári ⓫**, Lésvos's second town, famous for its *oúzo* industry; the Varvagiánni distillery

lays on tours. Most tourists choose to stay at pebble-beach **Agios Isídoros** 3km (2 miles) east, although **Melínda** 6km (4 miles) west is more scenic. **Vaterá ⓬**, with its 7km (4.5-mile) sand beach, reckoned the best on the island, lies still further west, reached by a different road. En route, you can stop for a soak at the restored **medieval spa** – one of four on the island – outside **Polihnítos**, 45km (28 miles) from Mytilíni. Inland from Plomári, the remarkable hill village of **Agiásos ⓭** nestles in a wooded valley under Ólymbos. Its heart is the major pilgrimage church of **Panagía Vrefokratoússa**, focus of the 15 August festival, Lésvos's biggest.

Híos, Inoússes, Psará

Although Híos (alias Chíos) had been important and prosperous since antiquity, the Middle Ages made the Híos of today. After the Genoese seized control here in 1346, the Giustiniani clan established a cartel, the *maona*, which controlled the highly profitable trade in gum mastic. During their rule, which also saw the introduction of silk

Lésvos claims to produce the finest olive oil in all Greece. The olives are harvested in November and December, and pressed within 24 hours of being picked.

A monastery on Híos.

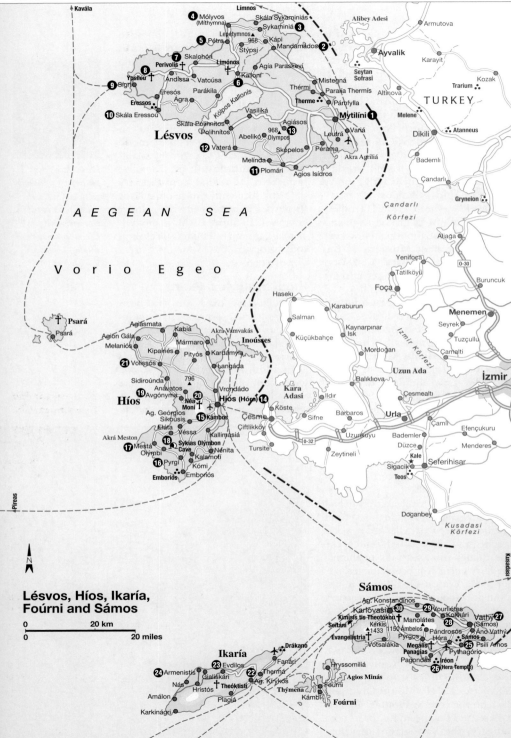

Lésvos, Híos, Ikaría,
Foúrni and Sámos

0   20 km
0   20 miles

and citrus production, Híos became one of the wealthiest and most cultured islands in the Mediterranean.

In 1566 the Ottomans expelled the Genoese, but granted the islanders numerous privileges, so that Híos continued to flourish until March 1822, when poorly armed agitators from Sámos convinced the reluctant Hiots to participate in the independence uprising. Sultan Mahmut II, enraged at this ingratitude, exacted a terrible revenge. A two-month rampage, commanded by Admiral Kara Ali, killed 30,000 islanders, enslaved 45,000 more, and saw all the island's settlements razed, except the mastic-producing villages. Híos had only partly recovered from this outrage when a March 1881 earthquake destroyed much of what remained and killed 4,000 people.

Today Híos and its satellite islet Inoússes are home to some of Greece's wealthiest shipping families. The catastrophic 19th century ensured that **Híos Town** or **Hóra** ⓮ (population 25,000) seems offputtingly modern at first glance. But scratch the ferro-concrete surface and you will find traces of the Genoese and Ottoman years. The most obvious medieval feature is the **kástro**; moated on the landward side, it lacks a seaward rampart, destroyed after the 1881 earthquake.

Just inside the *kástro*'s impressive **Porta Maggiore** stands the **Giustiniani Museum** (Tue–Sun 9am–2.30pm; charge), a continually changing collection of frescoes and icons rescued from rural churches. On a small nearby square is the Turkish cemetery, with the tomb of Kara Ali – the admiral responsible for the 19th-century massacre, blown up along with his flagship by one of Admiral Kanaris's fire-boats in June 1822. The square itself is enlivened by a popular, trendy bar-ouzerí. Still further inside lies the old Muslim and Jewish quarter, with a derelict mosque, hamams (one restored as an exhibit venue) and overhanging houses; Christians had to live outside the walls.

The lively bazaar extends south of central **Platía Vounakíou**, with Aplotariás as its backbone – fascinating alleys between this street and Venizélou culminate in a wonderful

Harvesting resin from the mastic trees, Híos.

THE MANY USES OF MASTIC

The mastic bushes (*Pistacia lentiscus; skhiniá* in Greek) of southern Híos are the unique source of gum mastic. In the past, it was used as a chewing gum to freshen the breath of the sultan's concubines; the Romans had toothpicks made from mastic since it kept their teeth white and prevented tooth decay; the "father of medicine", Hippocrates, praised its therapeutic value for coughs and colds; and lately some alternative medicine practitioners have made even more ambitious claims on its behalf.

The first stage of the mastic production process has remained unchanged since ancient times. In late summer, villagers make incisions in the bark of the trees, which weep resin "tears"; these are carefully scraped off and cleaned of leaves or twigs. Next, the raw "tears" are washed, then baked or sun-dried and re-formed at a processing plant. Up until 2012 when a devastating fire damaged the plantations, 150 tonnes of mastic were produced annually, most of it exported to Middle Eastern countries where it is a culinary spice; this level of production will dip for some time until the plantations recover.

It also appears in Greek *mastíha* liqueur, *tsouréki* bread and the chrism oil (myron) used in the Chrismation (confirmation) ritual of the Orthodox Church. Mastiha Shop (www.mastihashop.gr) is a Greek chain selling products using it, from shower gel to chocolate and nougat.

Donkey taking shade under the olive trees.

An exquisite example of xystá decorations in Pyrgí.

Belle-Epoque meat-and-produce gazebo. Also on Platía Vounakíou, the **Mecidiye Mosque** is now a locked warehouse for lapidary fragments; the **Archaeological Museum** (Tue–Sun 8.30am–3pm), in the south of town, well laid out, is more rewarding.

South of Hóra lies **Kámbos** ⑮, a broad plain of high-walled citrus groves dotted with the imposing sandstone mansions of the medieval aristocracy, set back from narrow, unmarked lanes. Many were destroyed by the earthquake, while a few have been restored as accommodation or restaurants. Irrigation water was originally drawn up by a *manganós* or waterwheel; a few survive in the centre of ornately paved courtyards.

The onward road heads southwest towards southern Híos, with its 20 *mastihohoriá* (mastic villages), built as pirate-proof strongholds by the Genoese during the 14th and 15th centuries. Each village is laid out on a dense, rectangular plan, with narrow passages over-arched by earthquake buttresses, and the backs of the outer houses doubling as the perimeter wall.

Pyrgí ⑯, 21km (13 miles) from Hóra, is one of the best-preserved *mastihohoriá*. A passageway off its central square leads to Byzantine **Agii Apóstoli** Church, decorated with later frescoes. In Pyrgí's back alleys, tomatoes are laboriously strung for drying in September by teams of local women. Some 11km (7 miles) west, **Mestá** ⑰ seems a more sombre, monochrome labyrinth, which retains defensive towers at its corners. Several houses have been restored as accommodation. Such quarters are typically claustrophobic, though, and guests will appreciate the nearby resorts of **Kómi** (a sand beach) and **Emboriós** (volcanic pebbles).

Southeast of Mestá is the mastic village of Olýmbi, after which the road south to the coast leads to the **Sykiás Olýmbon Cave** ⑱ (June–Aug Tue–Sun 10am–8pm, Sept 11am–6pm; charge). Stumbled across as recently as 1985, this 150-million-year-old cavern, a riot of stunning rock formations, is fantastically floodlit.

From Mestá, if you have your own transport the beautiful, deserted west

coast, with its many coves, is accessible via atmospheric **Véssa**, more open and less *kástro*-like than other *mastihohoriá*. Between **Kastélla** and **Elínda bays**, a good road snakes uphill to **Avgónyma** ⓳, a densely clustered village well restored by returned Greek-Americans. Just 4km (2½ miles) north perches almost deserted, crumbling **Anávatos**, well camouflaged against its cliff. In 1822, 400 Hiots leapt from it to their deaths rather than be captured.

Some 5km (3 miles) to the east, **Néa Moní** ⓴ (daily, summer 8am–1pm, 4–8pm, winter 8am–1pm, 4–6pm) constitutes one of the finest surviving examples of mid-Byzantine architecture, founded in 1049 by Emperor Constantine Monomahos IX. It suffered heavily in 1822 and 1881, first with the murder of its monks, plus the pillage of its treasures, and then with the collapse of its dome. Despite the damage, its mosaics of scenes from the life of Christ, which emerged in 2009 from a five-year restoration, are outstanding. The outbuildings have lain in ruins since the events of the 19th century. By the gate, an ossuary displays the bones of the 1822 martyrs, together with generations of monks. The onward road eventually takes you to castle-crowned **Volissós** ㉑ in the northwest. To either side of this half-empty village are the island's finest beaches – and visible scars from several fires since 1981, which have burnt two-thirds of Híos's forests.

Despite provincial appearances, the peaceful, green islet of **Inoússes** (Oinoússes), some 16km (10 miles) north of Híos harbour by regular caique, is actually among the wealthiest territories in Greece, home to the Livanos, Lemos and Pateras shipping families. Appropriately, a marine academy training seamen for Greece's merchant fleet stands at the west end of the quay, with a small private maritime museum in the centre of the single town. Small but decent beaches lie to either side.

The tiny islet of **Psará**, about 30km (19 miles) offshore from Volissós, derives its name from the ancient Greek adjective *psarós* (grey) – and a grey place it is, especially since 1824, when 14,000 Ottoman troops landed

FACT

Psará's other claim to fame is being the birthplace of Ioannis Varvakis, hero of the 2012 film *God Loves Caviar*.

The Muslim cemetery on Híos.

here to avenge continued harassment
of their shipping by Psaran Admiral
Kanaris, who commanded the third-
largest Greek fleet after those of Hydra
and Spétses. Some 27,000 islanders
died – many blowing themselves up
in a ridge-top powder magazine rather
than surrender – and only about 3,000
escaped. The Ottomans burnt any
remaining buildings and vegetation.
Today about 350 inhabitants remain
on melancholy Psará, its bleakness
relieved only by occasional fig trees.
Besides the lone port village, there's
just a monastery in the far north, frequented once a year at its 5 August festival. Six beaches lie northeast of the
port, each better than the one before.
Just a few tourists trickle over from
Híos on the local ferry from Híos
town; long-haul ferries call rarely from
Sígri on Lésvos, Límnos and Kavála.

Ikaría and Foúrni

Narrow, wing-shaped Ikaría is named
after the mythical Ikaros (Icarus), who
supposedly fell into the sea nearby
when his wax wings melted. One of
the least developed large islands in
the Aegean, Ikaría has little to offer
anyone intent on ticking off four-star
sights, but it appeals to those disposed
to an eccentric, slightly Ruritanian
environment. During both the 1930s
Metaxas dictatorship and the 1946–9
Civil War, the island served as a place
of exile, first for opponents of Metaxas
and then hundreds of Communists.
Local people thought the latter were
the most noble, humanitarian folk
they had ever met, and still vote Communist in droves.

Throughout 2012, Ikaría made the
international news with a series of articles with titles like "The Island Where
They Forgot to Die", highlighting the
unusual longevity of the locals and
attributing it to their stress- and pol-
lutant-free lifestyle, plus a healthy, basic
diet. Unfortunately for this thesis, since
then quite a number of the nonagenar-
ians profiled have indeed passed on.

Although little more than a fishing
village, **Agios Kírykos** ㉒ is the capital and main southerly port. Its tourist facilities are geared to the clientele
at the neighbouring spa of **Thermá**.
Beyond that, there is a long beach at
Fanári and an impressive Hellenistic
tower at **Cape Drákano**.

Taxis are far more reliable than
the bus for the spectacular 41km
(25-mile) drive over the 1,000-metre
(3,300ft) Atherás ridge to **Evdilos**
㉓, the north-facing second port and
would-be resort. Another 16km (10
miles) takes you past **Kámbos**, with
its sandy beach and ruined Byzantine
palace, to **Armenistís** ㉔ Only here
do foreign tourists congregate, for the
sake of excellent beaches – **Livádi** and
Mesaktí, just east – though the surf
can be deadly.

Nás, 4km (2.5 miles) west, is named
for the *náos* or temple of Artemis Tav-
ropoleio, on the banks of the river,
which drains to a popular pebble
cove. **Gialiskári**, a fishing port 4km
(2.5 miles) east of Armenistís, is distinguished by its photogenic jetty chapel.

There are few bona fide inland villages, as the proud Ikarians hate to live

Foúrni landscape.

on top of each other, and like to keep plenty of room for orchards between their houses. Above Armenistís are four hamlets lost in pine forest, collectively known as **Ráhes**. At **Hristós**, the largest of these, people cram the café-bars all night long, sleep until noon, and carry their belongings (or store potent local wine) in hairy goatskin bags. The surrounding countryside completes the hobbit-like image, with vertical natural monoliths and troglodytic cottages for livestock made entirely of gigantic granite or slate slabs. One of these formations, inland from Kámbos, shelters the **chapel of Theoskepastí**, just above frescoed **Theóktisti monastery**.

Foúrni, one of several islets southeast of Ikaría, makes a living from its thriving fishing fleet and boatyards. Seafood dinners figure high on the agendas of arriving tourists, who mostly stay in the main – and surprisingly large – port town. A road links this with Agios Ioánnis Hrysóstomos in the south – superior beaches like **Vlyháda**, **Kasídi** and **Vitsiliá** lie nearby – and Hryssomiliá in the far north, the only other habitations. Good beaches within walking distance south of the port include **Kámbi**, just over the ridge, with some tavernas, or the naturist beach of **Aspa** beyond.

Sámos

Sámos, an almost subtropical island with vine terraces, cypress and olive groves, surviving forests of black and Calabrian pine, hillside villages, and beaches of every size and kind, appeals to numerous tourists. Half a dozen wildfires since 1986 – the worst in July 2000 – and development have blighted the eastern half of the island, but impassable gorges, the Aegean's second-highest mountain, and beaches accessible only on foot beckon in the far west.

Natural endowments take precedence here over man-made ones, and Sámos has an identity problem owing to a 15th-century depopulation and

later recolonisation. First settled in the 13th century BC, by the 7th century Sámos was a major maritime power thanks to its innovative triremes (warships), still shown on local wine labels. The island's zenith came under the rule (538–522 BC) of Polykrates, a brilliant but unscrupulous tyrant who dabbled in piracy. Wealth, however it was accumulated, supported a luxurious capital of 60,000, and a court attended by the likes of philosopher-mathematician Pythagoras, the astronomer Aristarhos and the bard Aesop. Decline ensued with Polykrates' death at the hands of the Persians, and the rise of Athens.

Heavily developed **Pythagório** ㉕ occupies the site of Polykrates' capital, three of whose monuments earned Herodotus' highest praise: "I have spoken at greater length of the Samians because of all the Greeks they have achieved the three greatest constructions." From the immense harbour mole constructed by ancient slaves (the first great construction), you can watch Mount Mykale in Turkey majestically change colour at

One column is all that remains of Polykrates' great temple to Hera. He planned it to be the largest temple in Greece, but it was never completed.

The remote chapel at Gialiskári port, Ikaría.

FACT

Pythagório (formerly Tigáni) was renamed as recently as 1955, to honour the great Samian Pythagoras – an irony, since the mathematician exiled himself in disgust at the greed of the tyrant Polykrates.

dusk. The main in-town attraction is the 2010-opened **archaeological museum** (Tue–Sun 9am–3.40pm; charge), where highlights include a huge hoard of Byzantine gold coins found in 1984, and monumental Roman statuary.

The 1,040-metre (3,412ft) **Evpalínio Orygma** (Eupalinos' Tunnel), an aqueduct engineered by Eupalinos of Megara in the 6th century BC through the hillside northwest of town, is the second marvel, and one of the technological wonders of the ancient world. Surveying was so good that two work crews, beginning from either end, met with no vertical error and a horizontal one of less than 1 percent. You can visit the first 150m (Tues–Sun summer 8am–7pm, winter 8.30am–2.40pm; charge) along the catwalk used to remove spoil from the water channel far below.

The ruins of the third construction, the **Hera Temple** (ancient Heraion, Iréon in modern Greek; Tue–Sun summer 8am–8pm; winter 8.30am–3pm; charge), stand 8km (5 miles) west of Pythagório, past coastal Roman baths and the airport. But

Polykrates' grandiose commission was never actually completed, and Byzantine builders later pilfered most of the cut stone.

Vathý or **Sámos Town** , built along a deep inlet on the north coast, has been the capital and main port since 1832. The **Archaeological Museum** (summer Tue–Sun 9am–3.40pm, winter 8am–2.40pm; charge) is one of the best in the provinces, with a rich trove of finds from the Heraion. Given pride of place is a 5-metre (16ft) almost intact *kouros* (male votive statue), the largest ever found. The small-objects collection in a separate wing confirms the Middle Eastern slant of worship and clientele at the temple, with orientalised ivories and locally cast griffin's heads.

Ano Vathý, the large village clinging to the hillside 1.5km (1 mile) southeast, existed for almost two centuries before the harbour settlement. A pleasant stroll will take you through steep cobbled streets separating 300-year-old houses, their overhanging second storeys in lath and plaster more evocative of northern Greece and Anatolia than the central Aegean.

The first stop of note on the north-coast road is **Kokkári** after 12km (7½ miles), a former fishing village now devoted to tourism. The original centre is cradled between twin headlands, and windsurfers zip along off a long, westerly pebble beach. Overhead loom the now much-denuded crags of **Mount Ambelos** (1,150 metres/3,773ft), formerly a favourite of hikers. Paths still go up directly from behind Kokkári, while cars climb a road just past **Avlákia** to **Vourliótes** , a thriving village with several tavernas. A trail (and a separate road from the pleasant coastal town of Agios Konstandínos) continue up to more dramatically set **Manolátes**, where some tavernas stay open in winter.

The coastal highway continues west to **Karlóvasi** , 29km (18 miles) from Vathý; just before it is reached, a side road leads up through Kondakéïka to

Giant kouros in the Archaeological Museum, Vathý.

the **Church of Kímisis tis Theotókou** at Petaloúda, a bit beyond, the oldest (late 12th century) and most vividly frescoed of several painted chapels on the island.

Karlóvasi is a somewhat dishevelled place, sprawling over several districts. **Néo**, the biggest, has ornate mansions, and cavernous, derelict warehouses down by the water at **Ríva**, vestiges of the leather-tanning trade that thrived here before 1970. In one former warehouse, the excellent **Tanning Museum** (**Mousío Vyrsodepsías; Tue–Sat 9am–2pm, summer also 6–9pm; free**) gives a fascinating overview of the vanished industry, including massive machinery in situ. **Meséo** is more villagey, as is **Ano** (or Paleó), lining a vegetated valley behind the sentinel church of Agia Triáda. **Limín**, just below Ano, has the most local tourist facilities, including the ferry port.

West of here beckon some of Sámos's best beaches, including **Potámi**, a sand-and-pebble stretch visited by most of Karlóvasi at weekends. Beyond Potámi, a pair of remote, scenic beaches at **Seïtáni** can only be reached on foot.

Karlóvasi lies roughly halfway round an anticlockwise loop of the island, threading an interior dotted with small villages of tiled, shuttered houses and churches with striped domes. At Agii Theodóri junction 5km (3 miles) south of Karlóvasi, the southwesterly turn takes you past **Ormos Marathókambos** port to **Votsalákia**, Sámos's largest beach resort. More secluded coves lie further west along the road curling around the base of **Mount Kérkis** (1,433 metres/4,700ft), which forms the west end of the island. The refuge of several hundred guerrillas, then Civil War fighters, from 1943 to 1948, it is usually climbed from uninhabited **Evangelístria Convent** on the south slopes – a full day's outing.

The southeasterly choice of route at Agii Theodóri heads for Pythagório. You could schedule stops in **Pýrgos** for a can of local honey, and at the **Monastery of Megális Panagías** (Mon–Sat 10am–1pm, 5.30–8pm), just below Mavratzëï, which has partly cleaned frescoes dating from around 1586, second in merit only to Petaloúda's.

Lounging cat, Sámos.

Fishing boats in Pythagório harbour.

Church in Mandráki, capital of Nísyros.

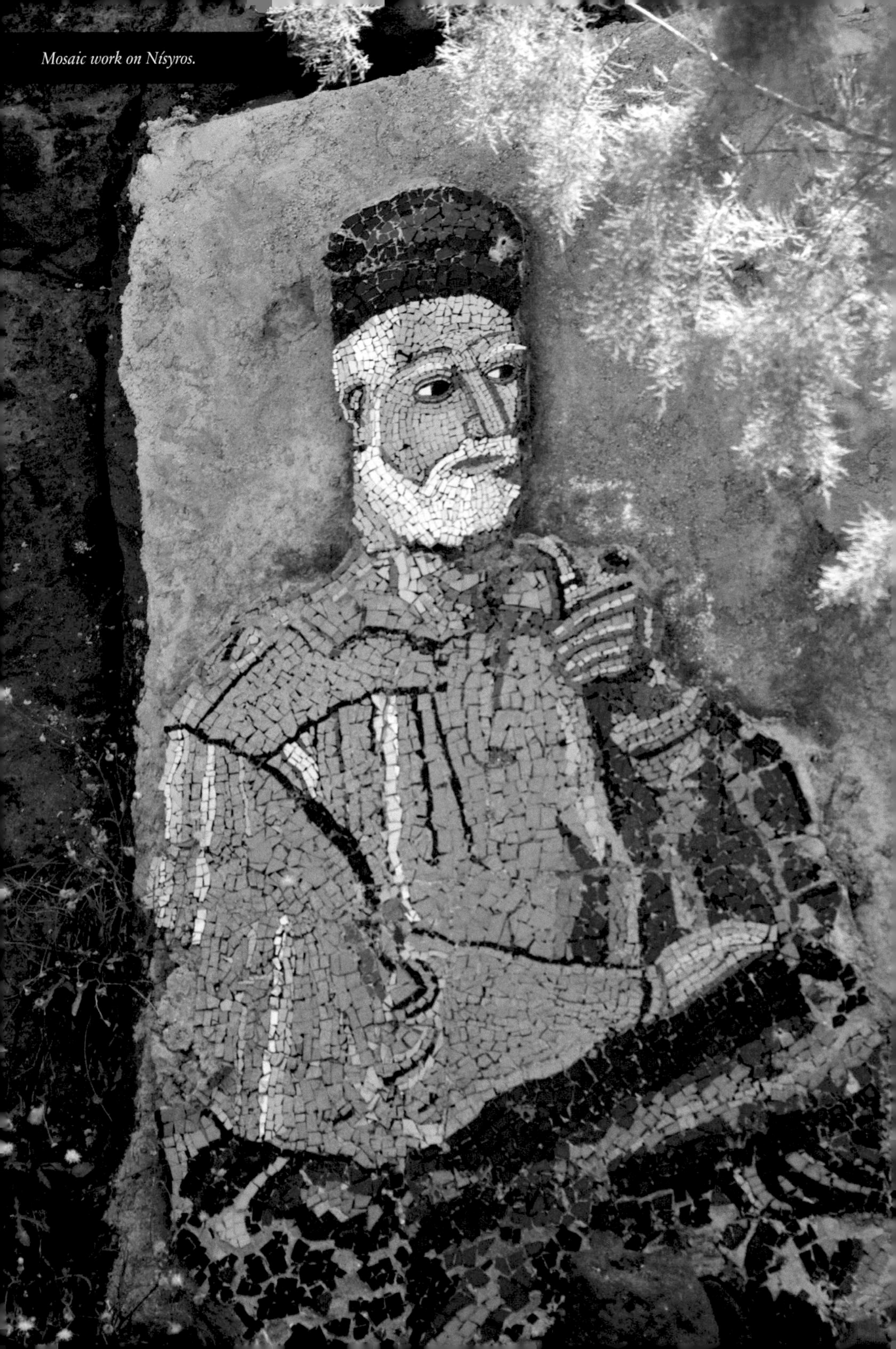

Mosaic work on Nísyros.

THE DODECANESE

Rhodes, Kárpathos, Kásos, Hálki, Kastellórizo, Tílos,
Sými, Nísyros, Kós, Psérimos, Astypálea, Kálymnos,
Télendos, Léros, Lipsí, Pátmos, Arkí, Agathonísi.

Young island-hoppers.

The term "Dodecanese" is relatively new. When these far-flung islands were ruled by the Ottomans, they were known, incongruously, as the southern Sporades. In the early 1900s, in response to the withdrawal by the Young Turks of historic privileges granted by various sultans, 12 islands (*dódeka nisiá* in Greek) jointly protested. Their rebellion failed, but the name stuck – hence the Dodecanese (*Dodekánisos* in Greek). In fact, there have always been many more than 12 islands in this archipelago, depending on how you count: 14, 18 or (including every deserted islet) even 27 islands.

The 18 islands in these chapters are divided into three sections. Rhodes, as the capital and main local transport hub, appears separately. The collective term "Southern Dodecanese" means the islands immediately around Rhodes, most easily reached by a domestic or international flight into that island, followed by a feeder flight or ferry.

Kós harbour.

"Northern Dodecanese" islands, on the other hand, use Kós as the closest touchdown point, though some, such as holy Pátmos, are also easily reached from Sámos in the northeast Aegean. Seasonal catamarans or hydrofoils fill in the gaps between aircraft and conventional boats.

The Dodecanese were Greece's final territorial acquisition in 1948. Before that they were ruled (briefly) by the British; before which there had been a 21-month occupation by the Germans; who had succeeded the Italians on their capitulation in late 1943. The Italians had ruled since 1912 with delusions of recreating the Roman Empire, leaving extravagant architectural follies to mark their passing. They had taken over from the Ottomans, who ousted the Knights Hospitaller of St John in 1523 and administered these islands (except for Rhodes and Kós) with benign neglect. To walk the streets of Kós or Rhodes is to witness a cultural patchwork: a minaret on one corner facing an Italian villa, across an expanse of excavated Hellenistic foundations, overshadowed by the fortifications of the crusading Knights.

RHODES

According to the ancient Greeks, Rhodes was "more beautiful than the sun". Even today's brash resorts cannot dim the appeal of its benign climate, entrancing countryside and fascinating history.

he capital of the Dodecanese and fourth-largest Greek island, Rhodes (Ródos) has been on the package-tour trail since the 1970s. It is one of the most cosmopolitan resorts in Greece, attracting every conceivable nationality in a seasonal repertory lasting from April to November: Italians and Spaniards in August (especially in the Old Town), Germans in spring and autumn out in the countryside, Scandinavians intent on sunshine and cheap booze during early summer, Israelis and Turks on gambling sprees, Brits and Russians seemingly all the time.

But far from the madding crowds in Neohóri (Rhodes New Town) and the serried ranks of umbrellas and sunloungers on the beaches, you can still find a more unspoilt island light years away from the laddish T-shirts and tawdry knick-knacks of the resorts. Frequent bus services run down both coasts from beside the "New Market", but it is worth hiring a car or jeep if you really want to explore deserted beaches, remote monasteries and castles perched above forest.

Patchwork history

The legacy of ancient Greeks, crusading Knights of St John, besieging Ottomans and colonialist Italians forms a fascinating palimpsest in Rhodes Town, from castle turrets to the late

Government House detail.

Classical street plan. There are temple pillars and Byzantine churches, mosques with minarets, plus the twin bronze deer guarding the waters of Mandráki harbour where, supposedly, the Colossus of Rhodes once stood.

This wondrous statue depicting Apollo Helios, the work of local sculptors Kharis and Lakhis, stood over 30 metres (100ft) tall. Legend made it even more impressive by describing it as standing astride the harbour entrance. But to do so it would have to have been more than 10 times its

Main Attractions

Museum of Modern Greek Art
Rodíni Park
Street of the Knights
Ancient Kameiros
Monólithos castle
Thárri monastery
Panagía Church, Líndos

Wannabe ship's cat on Rhodes.

actual size, an impossible engineering feat. Wherever it actually was, the monument stood until it collapsed in an earthquake in 226 BC. The bronze was sold for scrap during the 7th century AD.

Late in the Byzantine era, Rhodes was governed by the Genoese – until the Knights of St John, who had fled Jerusalem via Cyprus, captured the city in 1309, beginning a rule that lasted 213 years, under 19 Grand Masters. They substantially refortified the city, and raided Ottoman shipping. Finally, in 1522, Sultan Süleyman the Magnificent took Rhodes after a six-month siege that pitted 200,000 warriors against 650 knights. The Grand Master and 180 surviving brethren surrendered and, with a number of civilians, were allowed safe conduct to Malta. The Ottomans held the island for 390 years. Churches were converted to mosques, and Christians were banned from living within the city walls.

In 1912, Italy occupied Rhodes while at war with Turkey, and embarked on a massive archaeological re-construction programme. During World War II, when Italy capitulated in 1943, the Germans took over. Rhodes was liberated by the Allies in 1945, and the Greek flag hoisted three years later when the Dodecanese became united with Greece.

These days, the island is still under siege – by tourists. Present-day **Rhodes Town ❶** (Ródos) divides neatly into the various parishes of the New Town (Neohóri), settled by Greeks in Ottoman times, and the Old City. The contrast is marked: fast food, designer clothes and beaches on two sides, versus cobbled streets and a village-like feel.

The New Town

Here, smart shops abound, peddling designer labels at northern European prices and above despite the crisis (except during the August and February sales). Inexpensive umbrellas are big business here, and you can have any logo you like embossed on them. Sit and watch the world go by from one of the expensive, touristy pavement cafés at **Mandráki** port.

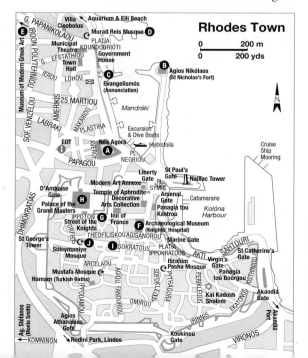

Rhodes Town

0   200 m
0   200 yds

A GRAND PALACE

The **Palace of the Grand Masters** (summer Mon 9am–3.40pm, Tue–Sun 8am–7.40pm, winter Tue–Sun 8am–2.40pm; charge) was almost completely destroyed when a munitions store in the nearby church of St John exploded in 1856, killing 800 people. During 1937–9, it was rebuilt by the Italians as a summer residence for King Victor Emmanuel and Mussolini, neither of whom ever used it. Traipse up the grandiose staircase to view ostentatious upper-floor decorations, including Hellenistic mosaics brought here from Kós. Two adjacent ground-floor galleries are devoted to ancient Rhodes and medieval, pre-Ottoman Rhodes, which, with their coverage of daily life in the Hellenistic city and the role of the Knights' outpost as a trade entrepôt respectively, are jointly the best museums on the island.

Marginally cheaper are the cafés inside the Italian-built **covered market**  (Néa Agorá), whose highlight is a whimsical raised gazebo from which fish was once sold.

Excursion boats leave Mandráki quay by 9am for the island of Sými, usually calling first at Panormítis Monastery, or heading down the east coast to Líndos. But all scheduled services (except for catamarans, leaving from Kolóna) depart from Akandiá harbour, a hot 25-minute walk (or more sensibly, short, expensive taxi-ride) east.

Mandráki, guarded by the lighthouse bastion of **Agios Nikólaos** B, is also an established port of call on the international yachting circuit, with local charters, too. Along the west quay stands a cluster of Italian-built monuments (see page 251), in its time the Foro Italico: they include the provincial administration building with its Gothic arches, the **Church of the Annunciation** C (Evangelismós) next door, with superb 1950s frescoes by neo-Byzantine artist Photis Kontoglou; and across the way the post office, town hall and municipal (originally the Puccini) theatre, all in quick succession.

Opposite the theatre, the **Mosque of Murad Reis** D stands beside one of the island's larger Muslim graveyards. On the other side of this is the **Villa Cleobolus**, where Lawrence Durrell lived from spring 1945 to spring 1947, while working as a British-occupation civil servant. A stroll along popular **Élli beach**, past the **casino** installed in the Italian-era Albergo delle Rose, brings you to Rhodes's northernmost point, with its Italian-built **Aquarium** (daily; summer 9am–8.30pm, winter 9am–4.00pm; charge). Immediately south, on Ekatón Hourmadiés (Hundred Date Palms) square (actually an oval), stands the **Museum of Modern Greek Art** E (Tue–Sat 9am–2pm; charge). Housed in the Nestorídeio Mélathro, this is the most important collection of 20th-century Greek painting outside Athens or Andros. Two annexes (one in the Old Town)

host worthwhile temporary exhibits; one ticket allows entry to all sites.

Inland Neohóri was once the nightlife capital of the Dodecanese, but a change in tourism patterns combined with the ongoing economic slump has cut a huge swathe through the bars – perhaps 20 remain from a 1990s zenith of 200. Surviving establishments tend to line Orfanídou and its perpendicular streets, just in from westerly, wind-buffeted **Psaroupoúla** beach.

Some 2km (1 mile) southwest of Mandráki, **Monte Smith** – more correctly, Agios Stéfanos hill – offers panoramic views over the town and sea on both sides. This was the site of Rhodes's Hellenistic acropolis, with a stadium, a heavily restored *odeion* and evocatively re-erected columns of a Temple of Apollo dating from the 3rd century BC. South of town, en route to Líndos, **Rodíni Park**, set in a canyon, was the home of the ancient rhetoric school and is today a shady, cool streamside retreat with little dams, bridges and – on the clifftop just south – a large fenced reserve for the miniature Rhodian deer, *Dama dama*.

The sublime Aphrodite Bathing wrings out her tresses in Rhodes' Archaeological Museum.

A loophole in the city walls.

The Old Town

The medieval walled town, a Unesco World Heritage Site, with its ramparts and 11 surviving gates, is so well preserved a visitor half expects to bump into a Knight of St John in one of the narrow cobbled streets. Most main streets follow their right-angled ancient predecessors: in the maze-like Ottoman quarters, it's easier to get lost.

Step through the northernmost **Liberty Gate** (Pylí Eleftherías) into **Platía Sýmis** to view the foundations of a Temple of Aphrodite, and the main annexe of the Modern Art Museum. Contiguous **Platía Argyrokástrou** is flanked by the Inn of the Order of Auvergne and the **Decorative Arts Collection** (closed indefinitely), with costumes, ceramics and carved woodwork gathered from across the archipelago. Just opposite stands the Knights' cathedral, **Panagía tou Kástrou**, formerly a Byzantine museum; its collection of icons and frescoes rescued from rural chapels has moved to the Palace of the Grand Masters.

Next stop is the 15th-century **Knights' Hospital** ❺, now the

Archaeological Museum (summer Tue–Sun 8am–6.40pm, Mon 9am–3.40pm; winter Tues–Sun 8am–2.40pm; charge). Among the exhibits in the Hellenistic statuary gallery is the eerily sea-eroded *Aphrodite Adioumene*, Durrell's "Marine Venus", and the more accessible *Aphrodite Bathing*, wringing out her tresses.

From the museum, the **Street of the Knights** ❻ (Odós Ippotón) leads in medieval splendour uphill to the **Palace of the Grand Masters** ❼ (see page 242). Italian-restored, and preserved from commercialisation, the thoroughfare houses more inns of the Knights, as their lodgings were divided by linguistic affinity. The **Inn of France**, emblazoned with the heraldry of several Grand Masters, is the most imposing.

The main commercial thoroughfare is **Sokrátous** ❶, hosting a few jewellers and fur shops but mostly ever-tattier tourist knick-knacks and T-shirt shops. Sokrátous links **Platía Ippokrátous** with its ornate fountain and Kastellanía (medieval "stock exchange") with the pink

Agios Nikólaos guards Mandráki port.

Süleymaniye Mosque ❿ at the top of the hill, recently restored but not yet open to the public. The Old Town still has a sizeable Turkish minority, using the active Ibrahim Pasha and Mustafa mosques on Plátonos and Platía Aríonos respectively, though since the Cyprus crises they deliberately keep a low profile.

Another sporadically functioning Ottoman monument on Platía Aríonos, esteemed by Orthodox and Muslim alike, is the **hamam** (Turkish baths or Dimotiká Loutrá; currently closed for repairs).

The other local minority that dwelt in the Old Town were the Jews, deported to Auschwitz by the Nazis in June 1944. Few returned, and their **synagogue** (15 April–15 Nov Sun–Fri 10am–3pm) on Simíou is essentially maintained as a memorial, although it also contains an excellent museum on the former life of the community and its far-flung diaspora. Surviving **nightlife**, pitched at Greek rather than foreign tourists, comprises a dozen or so of high-decibel, annually changing bars on Miltiádou and its offshoots.

The west coast

Rhodes's west coast is the damper, windier, greener side of the island, with agriculture at least on a par with tourism. Scrappy shingle beaches failed to slow hotel construction at **Ixiá** and **Triánda**, busy resorts that blend into each other and Neohóri. A road leads inland 5km (3 miles) from Triánda to the site of ancient **Ialysos** ❷ (summer Tue–Sat 8am–7pm, Sun 8.30am–2.45pm, winter until 2.45pm; charge), better known today as **Filérimos**, after the Byzantine monastery established here. Of the ancient city, only a Doric fountain and some Hellenistic temple foundations are evident. The restored Gothic **monastery**, with its vaulted chambers, early Christian mosaic floor and rampant bougainvillea is the main attraction.

The **airport** lies between coastal Kremastí and **Paradísi** village, to whose cafés tourists often resort for solace when their homeward flights are delayed (a not uncommon occurrence).

Just past Paradísi, another inland turning leads to a famous Rhodian beauty spot, the **Petaloúdes** ❸

FACT

The magnificent walls of the Old Town date from the 14th century and are up to 12 metres (40ft) thick in places. Sadly, access from beside the Palace of the Grand Masters is no longer permitted.

Rhodes souvenirs.

FACT

At Ialysos, a Via Crucis leads to a giant cross, re-erected in 1995 as a replica of a 1934-vintage Italian one destroyed during the war to prevent Allied airmen from using it as a landmark.

(Butterfly Valley; Apr–Oct daily 8am–dusk; charge). The access road crosses the canyon about halfway along its length. Head upstream or downstream, along paths and over bridges, past the *Liquidambar orientalis* (sweetgum) trees on which Jersey tiger moths roost during summer. Black and yellow when at rest, they flash bright red wing-tops in flight. From the top of the valley, about 6km (4 miles) inland from **Soroní** on the coast road, a dirt track leads to the **Agios Soúlas Monastery,** whose 29–30 July festival features donkey races.

The other big tourist attraction of the west coast, 32km (20 miles) from Mandráki, is Italian-excavated **ancient Kameiros** ❹ (summer Tues–Sun 8am–6.40pm, winter until 2.40pm; charge). While no single monument stands out, it's a remarkably complete Doric townscape, without the usual later accretions. Unusually, there were no fortifications, nor an acropolis on the gently sloping hillside.

Back on the coast again, **Skála Kamírou** ❺ (alias Kámiros Skála) is a small port with touristy fish tavernas, and afternoon ferries for the tiny

island of **Hálki** opposite. **Kritinía** ❻ castle (unlocked) just overhead, one of the Knights' rural garrisons, is today a dilapidated shell but merits a visit for the views out to sea. The chapel has been consolidated in anticipation of becoming a small museum, which has yet to happen.

The interior and far south

Inland from Skála Kamírou, sitting at the base of 1,215-metre (3,986ft) Mount Attávyros, **Embona** ❼ is the centre of the Rhodian wine industry; products of the private Emery and Alexandris wineries are considered the best. Roads looping around the base of the mountain through conifer forests to east and west converge on the attractive village of **Siána**, famous for its honey and *soúma* – a strong, deceptively smooth grape-distillate spirit. Some 4km (2.5 miles) further, flat-roofed **Monólithos** ❽ village gives access to the eponymous **castle** (unlocked) perched on a narrow pinnacle, with a 200-metre (656ft) sheer drop all around and sweeping views west, which makes up for the fact

Archaeological Museum, Rhodes Old Town.

that little remains inside. The road then continues down to the secluded **Foúrni** beaches.

Inland Rhodes is the perfect antidote to the coastal resorts, its rolling hills still partly wooded despite repeated fires started by arsonists since the late 1980s. Spared so far is densely shady **Mount Profítis Ilías** (798 metres/2,618ft), from where an old trail descends to the village of **Sálakos**, near which "Nymph" brand spring water is bottled.

Alternatively, from **Apóllona** on the mountain's south side, a paved road leads through a burnt zone, the result of a 2008 fire, to **Láerma**, and thence to the Byzantine **Thárri Monastery**, reinhabited in 1990 by monks who oversaw the cleaning of its vivid 13th- to 15th-century frescoes. The road continues in round-about fashion via Profýlia and Kiotári to **Asklipió** village, where slightly later frescoes in the church of **Kímisis tís Theotókou** are in better condition, owing to the dry climate. Together these constitute the finest Byzantine art *in situ* on the island.

From Asklipió you return to the southeast coast at **Kiotári**, a post-1995 resort with a number of large hotels, and **Gennádi**, with vast stretches of open gravel beach. Further south, **Plimmýri** has a lovely medieval church and a sandy bay; **Prassonísi** (Leek Island) at Rhodes's southern tip is tethered by a broad, sandy causeway much favoured by windsurfers. The main island coast road loops back to Monólithos via the villages of **Kattaviá** ❾ and **Apolakkiá**, 4km (2½ miles) north of which is the tiny Byzantine chapel of **Agios Geórgios Várdas**, with smudged but most engaging frescoes.

Most inland villages here are moribund, with house owners living in Rhodes Town or overseas. This is especially evident in the old quarter of **Lahaniá** near Plimmýri, though the wonderful square with its taverna and pair of fountains beneath a plane tree remains traditional. From here head northwest to the fine hilltop village of **Mesanagrós**, where a 13th-century chapel hunches amidst the larger foundations of a 5th-century basilica. If you're overtaken by

Monastery icon.

Knights' Castle at Kritinía.

FACT

Skiádi Monastery has a miraculous icon of the Panagía (Blessed Virgin) which supposedly bled when it was stabbed by a heretic in the 15th century.

darkness and can't face the drive back to town, the kindly keepers at **Skiádi Monastery** ⑩ just to the west may invite you to use the (gender-segregated) guest quarters.

The east coast

The east coast, sandier and more sheltered than the west, with a warmer sea, was only developed for tourism after the 1970s, and much of it remains unspoilt. **Koskinoú** is famous for its ornate doorways and intricate pebble-mosaic courtyards. Immediately downhill, **Pigés Kallithéas** ⑪ (daily summer 8am–8pm, winter until 2.40pm; charge), a former spa, is a

splendid orientalised Art Deco folly built by the Italians and complete with domed pavilions and palm trees. One rotunda is home to a small exhibition space and a permanent gallery on the history of the spa, which had its heyday from 1910 to 1940. Below the spa, various rock-girt beaches with supplemented sandy patches are popular, as there are no other swimming spots this close to Rhodes Town with any real character.

Wall-to-wall, multi-storey hotels pitched mainly at families characterise the north end of **Faliráki Bay**. Faliráki proper, to the south, is now but a shadow of its former youthful, boozy

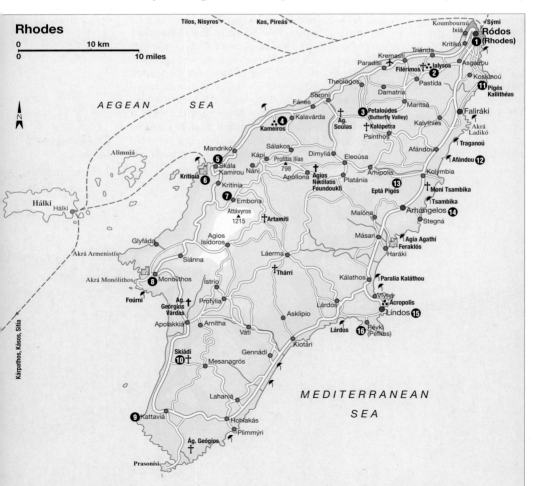

self since a 2003 crime spree prompted a police crackdown, and the more recent economic crisis administered the coup de grâce.

Immediately to the south looms **Cape Ladikó**, where *The Guns of Navarone*, starring Anthony Quinn, was made in 1961. Beyond the cape stretches the long pebble-and-sand beach of **Afándou 12**, scarcely developed except for the 18-hole golf course just inland.

Inland beauty spot

Heading inland from the Italians' model-farm scheme at **Kolýmbia**, you reach the leafy glades of **Eptá Pigés 13** (Seven Springs), one of Rhodes's most popular beauty spots. These springs feed a small reservoir dammed by the Italians to irrigate their Kolýmbia colony. If you do not suffer from claustrophobia you can explore an aqueduct-tunnel leading to the little lake, or you can walk there overland, in the company of peacocks screaming in the trees.

The Greek "approach" to fertility treatment, Tsambíka Monastery, teeters high on the headland just behind Kolýmbia, overlooking a sandy namesake beach to the south. It is believed that the Virgin, to whom the monastery is dedicated, can make women fertile. The tiny, well-restored monastic church is thus a magnet for childless women, who come as barefoot pilgrims to revere an 11th-century icon at the 8 September festival.

Arhángelos 14, 29km (18 miles) from Rhodes Town, is the island's largest village, although its former crafts tradition is now only indicated by some pottery studios on the bypass road. Good beaches are found nearby at **Stegná** and at **Agía Agathí**, the latter reached via the little resort and pebble beach of **Haráki**, overlooked by the crumbled Knights' castle of **Feraklós**. Better than any of these, however, is the 4km (2½-mile)-long,

The big rotunda at Pigés Kallithéas.

Tsambíka Monastery icons.

Líndos and its Knights' castle.

Haráki resort and bay.

undeveloped beach at Kálathos, beyond Haráki.

Líndos

There are regular buses to cover the 56km (35 miles) from Rhodes Town to **Líndos** ⓯, but it's more relaxing to take a boat trip and enjoy the coastal scenery. Huddled beneath yet another Knights' castle, Líndos, with its tiered, flat-roofed houses, appears initially to be the dream Greek village. But the narrow lanes of the hottest spot on Rhodes teem with day-trippers and local overnighters in high season. Medieval captains' mansions have ornate gateways and vast pebble-mosaic courtyards. Near the main square, the Byzantine **Panagía Church** (Mon–Sat 9am–3pm, 6.30–8pm, Sun 9am–3pm) preserves vivid 18th-century frescoes by Gregory of Sými. Donkeys, the Lindian taxi service, haul tourists up the steep gradient to the ancient acropolis inside the Knights' castle, with its Temple of Lindian Athena, Hellenistic stoa, and unbeatable views over 40km (25 miles) of coast.

Late into the night the village throbs to the beat of numerous bars, while by day the sand lining the northerly former port is dense with sunbathers, packed together like sardines in a can. The southern harbour, with a slightly quieter beach, is called St Paul's Bay, in honour of the Apostle who landed here in AD 58.

Líndos dates back to the Bronze Age, thanks to the only protected harbour on the island aside from Rhodes Town. With such barren surroundings, it always lived from the sea (though a spring provides ample water). In the 1960s, this then-remote spot attracted Italian, German and British painters, writers and hippie drop-outs. Past alumni include the newspaper astrologer Patric Walker (1931–95), academic and writer Germaine Greer, American humorist S.J. Perelman and various members of Pink Floyd. But now Líndos's days as an artistic colony are long over, superseded by the era of mass tourism.

Around the limestone headland, **Pévki** ⓰ (Péfkos) is less frenetic than Líndos; it was originally an annexe of the latter but is now a package resort in its own right. Its beaches are small and hidden away. At **Lárdos**, 4km (2½ miles) west, the long, gravelly beach is obvious as you approach, and is encroached upon by large hotels; **Glýstra** beach just beyond is more scenic and protected.

Italian Architecture in the Dodecanese

The Greeks understandably wanted to ignore the Italians' three-decade presence, but now recognise that their architecture had ample merit.

Thirty-one years of Italian rule in the Dodecanese left a significant architectural heritage, which has only recently begun to be appreciated. Many structures were long neglected, apparently a deliberate policy by the Greeks, who would prefer to forget the entire Italian legacy, but since the late 1990s maintenance and repair work has been undertaken. In Lakkí, on Léros in the Northern Dodecanese, buildings along the grand boulevards and landscaped squares have undergone a thorough renovation in recent years (see page 275).

These buildings are often erroneously dubbed "Art Deco"; while some, like Rhodes Aquarium and the stadium, certainly contain elements of that style, most are properly classed as Rationalist, or (on Léros) Streamline Modern. They grew out of various post-World War I European architectural, artistic and political trends, particularly Art Deco's immediate predecessor, Novecento, which originated in a movement born in Milan in 1922. The collectivist ideologies of the time were also influential, as were the paintings of Giorgio di Chirico, the Greek-Italian painter born in Vólos in 1888.

From 1924 to 1936, Italy attempted to combine Rationalist architecture and local vernacular elements, both real and semi-mythical, into a supposed generic "Mediterranean-ness". Every island got at least one specimen in this "protectorate" style, usually the police station, the post office, covered market or governor's mansion, but only on the most populous or strategic Dodecanese islands like Rhodes, Kós, Kálymnos and Léros were plans drawn up for comprehensive urban reordering.

On Rhodes, this meant the creation of a Foro Italico (administrative centre) at Mandráki. The evolving imperatives of Fascism also required a square (in Rhodes, the Piazza dell'Imperio in the Foro Italico) for large-scale assemblies. There were also structures in neo-Crusader style, such as the Cathedral of St John (now Evangelismós).

The period 1936–41 was marked by intensified Fascist ideology and increased reference to the islands' Latin heritage (the Romans and their purported successors, the Knights of St John). This entailed "purification", stripping many public buildings in Rhodes (although not in Kós, where a 1933 earthquake devastated much of the town) of orientalist ornamentation, and replacing it with poros stone cladding to match medieval structures in the Old Town. Added to this was a monumental severity and rigid symmetry – as with the theatre in Rhodes – echoing institutional buildings (especially Fascist Party headquarters) in Italy. Many Old Town buildings from the Knights' era were restored or, in the case of the Palace of the Grand Masters (see page 242), entirely rebuilt.

The rebuilt Palace of the Grand Masters, Rhodes Old Town.

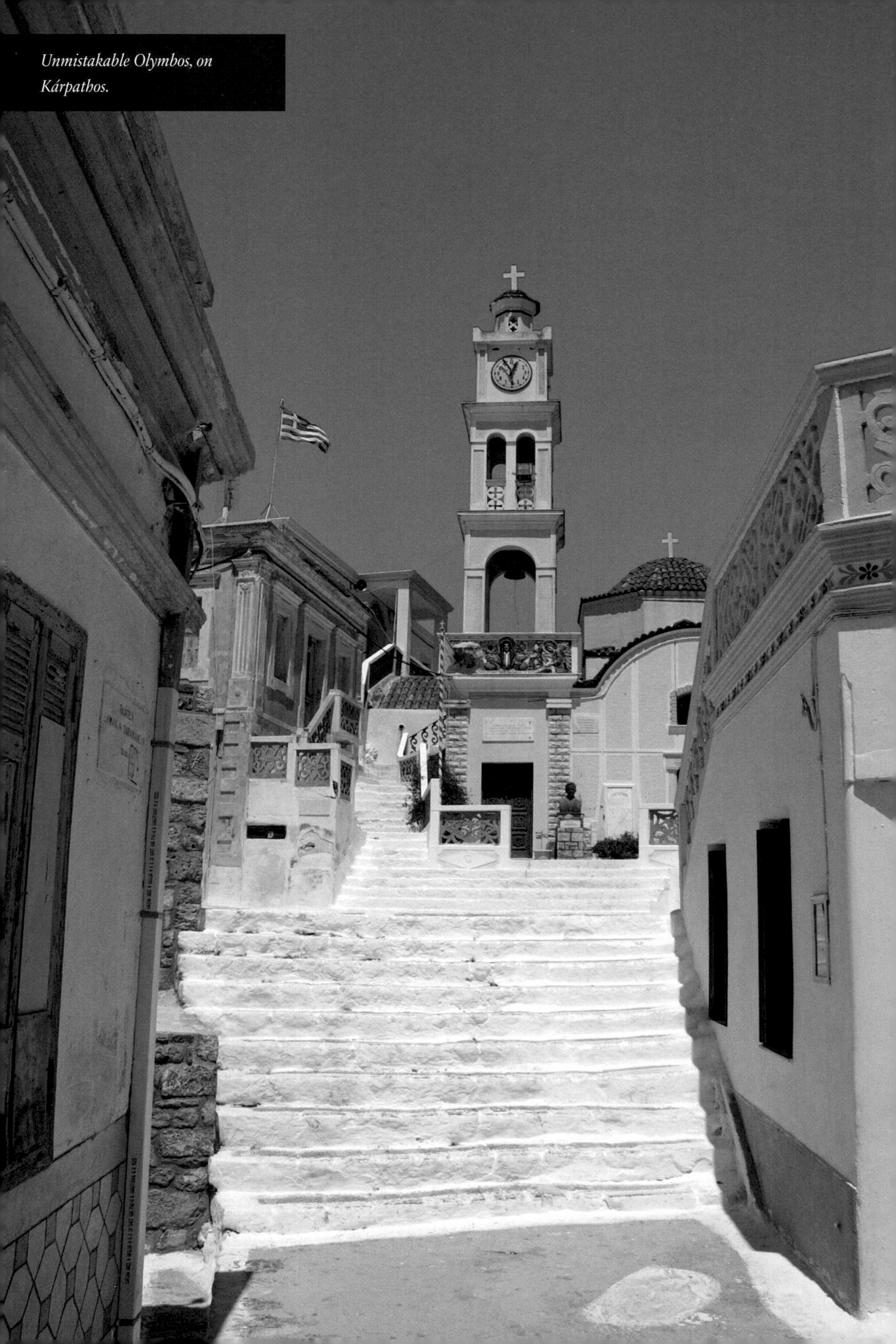

Unmistakable Olymbos, on Kárpathos.

THE SOUTHERN DODECANESE

The farthest from mainland Greece, these islands, which mostly lived in the past from seafaring, have developed an idiosyncratic character, culture and architecture.

The Southern Dodecanese remain among the most tranquil and unspoilt of the islands. The islanders still cling, in places, to traditional customs and live by farming, boat-building and fishing as well as tourism.

Kásos

Kásos is the southernmost and poorest Dodecanese island. Remote and barren, its plight was accentuated by a comprehensive Ottoman massacre in 1824. Before and since Kasiots took to the seas, distinguishing themselves as pilots, and helping to dig the Suez Canal. In six clustered villages on the north flank, many houses lie abandoned: summer sees a homecoming of expatriated Greek-Americans, especially for the major festivals on 17 July (Agía Marína) and 15 August (Dormition of the Virgin).

The capital, **Frý** ❶ (pronounced "Free"), is a bit shabby in parts, but it does have a few tavernas and an attractively enclosed fishing harbour, the **Boúka**, with a narrow entrance. **Emboriós**, down the coast, was the old commercial port, now silted up but still picturesque. The only conventional tourist attractions here are two caves, **Ellinokamára** and **Seláï**, beyond **Agía Marína**, the most attractive inland village.

Except at peak season when a few rental scooters or quad-bikes appear,

you face long, shadeless hikes or expensive taxi rides to get anywhere. The only half-decent beach is **Hélatros**, almost 15km (9 miles) from Frý in the southwest, via **Agios Geórgios Hadión**, one of two rural monasteries. The indolent may take boat excursions to better beaches on the offshore islets of **Makrá** (one big beach) and **Armáthia,** which has five sandy beaches.

Frý has a tiny airstrip with puddle-jumper planes to Rhodes, Kárpathos and Sitía (Crete). Fares are affordable,

A good lobster catch in Livádia, Tílos.

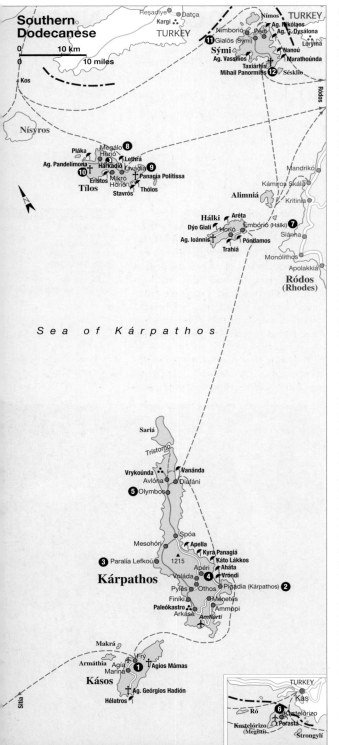

Southern Dodecanese map

and a flight may be your only option when arriving or leaving in heavy seas, when ferries skip the exposed anchorage at Frý.

Kárpathos

Wild, rugged and sparsely populated, Kárpathos just edges out Kós as the second-largest Dodecanese island, marooned in crystalline sea roughly halfway between Rhodes and Crete. With vast expanses of white-sand beaches, usually underused, and craggy cloud-topped mountains soaring to 1,215 metres (3,949ft), it makes up in natural beauty for what it lacks in compelling man-made sights.

Direct seasonal flights serve Kárpathos from overseas; the alternative involves a domestic flight or ferry from Rhodes. The capital and southerly harbour of **Pigádia** ❷ (also known as Kárpathos) has undergone a tourism boom since the 1990s; in any case, the town only dates from the mid-19th century, though photos from the 1950s show an attractive townscape before the eyesore concrete blocks went up. Many families have returned wealthy from America, especially the East Coast, something which has helped fuel the building boom.

Just north of Pigádia, massively sandy **Vróndi** beach, with windsurf boards and kayaks for rent, sweeps past the 5th-century basilica of **Agía Fotiní**. Some 7km (4½ miles) south of town is **Ammopí**, the island's longest established resort, with three coves (two sand, one pebble). Many of Kárpathos's better beaches are served by excursion boat. Among these, on the east coast, are **Kyrá Panagiá** (with the most facilities and turquoise water), or lonelier, more unspoilt **Aháta**, **Káto Lákkos** and especially **Apella,** with a 300-metre/yd-long main cove and a naturist cove a short scramble further on. Several coves in the **Amfiárti** region near the southerly airport are home to world-class windsurfing schools. **Arkása**, on the western shore, is somewhat inexplicably a resort, as the only convenient beach is 1km (½ mile) south at **Agios Nikólaos**; on the headland opposite are remains of the **Paleókastro**, the Mycenaean-Classical acropolis, with the mosaic-floored Byzantine church of **Agía Sofía** at the beginning of the climb. Heading north, the next substantial settlement besides the little port of **Finíki** is **Paralía Lefkoú** ❸ the main rival to Ammopí as a beach base. A remarkable topography of headlands shelters three horseshoe bays of white sand and there are plenty of places at which the visitor can stay and/or eat.

Despite the road network being mostly paved now, exploring Kár-pathos can be challenging. The few filling stations are all near Pigádia, limiting the range of small scoot-ers, and strong winds can blow two--wheelers off the road. Booking a rental car or jeep in advance for pick-up at the airport is the best solution. There are buses and pricey taxis to the less remote mountain villages like **Apéri** ❹, the elegant medieval capi-tal, said to have the highest per capita income in Greece; **Voláda**, with a tiny Venetian citadel; and **Othos**, the highest on the island at 400 metres (1,300ft), famous for its sweet, amber wine from vineyards on the often mist-swirled ridge above.

Although the road there has finally been completely paved, with a bus service mooted, northern Kárpa-thos is still most easily visited via the port of **Diafáni**, served both by local *kaïkia* from Pigádia and most main-line ferries. It makes a peaceful and congenial base, except in August, with coastal walks to good beaches in either direction, but most use it as a stepping-stone to reach **Ólymbos** ❺, the island's most distinctive vil-lage, clinging to a mountainside 600 metres (1,968ft) up. Older Ólymbos houses consist of one divided room built around a central wooden pole, the "pillar of the house", to which are attached embroideries and usually a wedding portrait (and often wedding wreaths) of the owners. On a raised wooden platform behind a carved rail is rolled-up bedding, plus chests of dowry linens and festival clothes.

Neoclassical Gialós, Sými.

FACT

Ólymbos was virtually
cut off from the rest of
Kárpathos for centuries.
A dirt road from the
south was only
completed in 1979;
before that one walked
five hours to Spóa, the
first village with a road.

The rest of the room is crammed with plates, lace, crochet and other souvenirs – a kitsch explosion of fairground colours – gathered by seafaring relatives. Even modern villas often have their front rooms decked out in the same way, a shrine for family photos and icons.

Bread and biscuits are baked in several communal ovens. The flour was formerly ground by the village's several 18th-century windmills, two of which were restored as working museum pieces in the mid-1980s.

Besides the hike between Olymbos and Diafáni, there's the half-day walk via **Avlóna** hamlet to **Vrykoúnda**, where a cave-shrine of St John the Baptist is the focus for a major festival on 29 August. More advanced treks from Avlóna go to Trístomo inlet or back down to Diafáni via **Vanánda** beach.

Kastelórizo

Kastelórizo's official name, Megísti, means "Biggest" – biggest, that is, of a local mini-archipelago, for this is actually one of the smallest inhabited Dodecanese islands. It's also the first point in Europe, coming from the east, and only a few nautical miles away from Kaş in Turkey, where locals go shopping. Before 1900, Kastellórizo had a thriving town of almost 10,000, supported by its schooner fleet. The sale of the fleet to the British, World War I bombardment of French positions here by the Ottomans, and an earthquake in 1926 sent the island into terminal decline, despite its role during the 1930s as a sea-plane halt.

The final nail in the coffin came in July 1944, when a fuel depot exploded, levelling more than half the port. The town had already been looted, and few chose to return after the war, when the population dropped to about 200. The US even tried to persuade Greece to cede Kastelórizo to Turkey in 1964 in exchange for limited hegemony in Cyprus. Recovery from this nadir is due in part to the return of expatriate "Kassies" from Perth and Sydney to build retirement homes, and also to the island's use as the location for the 1991 Oscar-winning film *Mediterraneo*, which spurred a wave of tourists.

ANTHRO-TOURISM

Ólymbos existed in a time-warp for a long time, but sensational journalism by amateur anthropologists – more has been written about the village in publications like Geo than any other in Greece – and thousands of day-trippers annually have together dragged the place into the modern era, and locals are now all too used to visitors. It is preferable to stay the night, when you'll hear the Dorian-influenced local dialect in the tavernas and see the women clomp off at dawn in their high leather boots to the terraces below.

Older women still wear traditional costumes (intricately embroidered jackets, scarves and pinafores) on a daily basis as well as for festivals, although lately a good deal of the embroidery is imported.

A fisherman lays out his nets in Livádia harbour, Tílos.

This limestone island is fringed by sheer cliffs, with no beaches at all. What remains of the red-roofed port town **Kastelórizo ❻** is overseen by a half-ruined, red-stone Crusader castle, which is responsible for the island's Italianate name. The keep houses a small **Archaeological Museum** (Tue–Sun 8.30am–3pm; free) of local finds, including an old lighthouse lens, medieval frescoes and Byzantine pottery, while beyond in the cliff-face is Greece's only Lycian house-type tomb. The quayside mosque, dating from 1755, is now home to the **Historical Collection** (Tue–Sun 8.30am–3pm; free), with a photo archive and ethnographic section.

Also worth seeing once it emerges from restoration, a 45-minute walk from town, is the remote monastery of **Agios Geórgios tou Vounoú** with pebble-mosaic flooring and the frescoed subterranean crypt-chapel of Agios Harálambos. Boats will ferry you to the satellite islet of **Ró**, topped by a Hellenistic fortress, or to the cathedral-like **Blue Grotto of Perastá** on the southwest coast which,

according to local people, rivals its namesake in Capri. The cave is about 45 metres (147ft) long and 28 metres (92ft) high, and the rays of the morning sun create spectacular effects inside. The journey there involves a 90-minute round-trip, plus some time to swim in the deep, glowing waters. Also resident in local waters are two sea turtles, who tend to be found around Psorádia and Agios Geórgios islets or even inside the port. **Agios Geórgios**, with sun-loungers and a snack bar, makes a great day out – taxi-boats from the main port.

Kastelórizo lies 70 nautical miles (114km) from Rhodes, and ferries or catamarans make the long trip only two or three times a week. The tiny airstrip receives almost daily flights from Rhodes, though seats can fill long in advance. The island is now an official port of entry to Greece, and ironically it's more accessible from Kaş, Turkey, which sends daily ferries.

Hálki

Ninety minutes by boat from Skála Kamírou on Rhodes, Hálki (or

Patriotic Karpáthos.

FACT

The most famous ancient Tiliot was the poetess Irinna, whose verses – like Sappho's – have mostly not survived.

Chálki) is pretty, welcoming and very popular, despite being barren, almost beachless and lacking a fresh water supply. **Emborió ❼** (Hálki), the harbour and only settlement, has numerous waterfront tavernas and abundant accommodation in its restored neoclassical mansions, though most of these are block-booked from April to October by tour companies. **Agios Nikólaos** has the highest belfry in the Dodecanese, nearly matched by a free-standing clock tower nearby.

The island's only sandy beach – artificially supplemented – is **Póndamos**, 400 metres/yds west; just overhead, **Horió** village has been deserted since the 1950s but offers spectacular views from its crumbled Knights' fortress. Tarpon Springs Boulevard, built with money from Hálki sponge fishermen who emigrated to Florida, ends at the Monastery of **Agios Ioánnis**, in the west of the island. The monastery has a huge courtyard tree and cells in which to stay the night. There are no other good roads, so pebble coves like **Aréta** and **Dýo Gialí**, on the north shore, or

Trahiá under the castle, are reached only by boat trips or arduous hikes.

Between Hálki and Rhodes, **Alimniá** (aka Alimiá) island has been mostly deserted since World War II, despite having good wells and excellent anchorage. The inhabitants aided the Allies under the very noses of German forces manning submarine pens here. When detected, the islanders were deported to Rhodes and Hálki as punishment, and the few returnees left again in the 1960s. With only another Knights' castle, the derelict village and seasonally grazing sheep to be seen, the island is a very occasional excursion destination from Hálki.

Tílos

Tranquil Tílos has only seen significant tourism since the mid-1980s. It is home to several thousand goats but only about 500 people (the population shrinks to 100 in the winter). Though the island is bare on its limestone heights, neighbouring Nísyros deposited rich lava soil in the lowlands, which with ample groundwater allows the Tiliots to farm, rather than sail as their neighbours do. Indeed, before the 1970s it was the granary of the Dodecanese, with undulating fields of wheat visible from far out to sea. The entire island, and the seas just off it, are notionally a national reserve, but other than a total local hunting ban, little has actually been done. Tílos's late, publicity-seeking mayor, Tasos Aliferis, brought the place to public attention in 2008 by officiating marriages for two Greek same-sex couples; Greek courts invalidated the ceremonies but the couples are pursuing redress as far as the European Court of Human Rights.

The island capital, **Megálo Horió ❽**, is slightly inland, topped by a Knights' castle that incorporates a Classical gateway and stone from the ancient acropolis. It looks south over an orchard-planted plain to red-sand **Eristos** beach, the longest on Tílos. The harbour and main resort

Emborió, Hálki.

of **Livádia** ❾ has a long shingle beach, separated from ample accommodation and eating opportunities by a rigorously pedestrianized, flagstoned walkway. You can also walk on a good path system – assisted by an accurate map and walking guides both human and printed – or go by scooter to the most remote beaches, plus there's a bus service, so boat trips are only offered in summer if there are sufficient numbers (15 passengers minimum). The closest coves are **Lethrá**, **Stavrós** and **Thólos**, with the Knights' castle of Agriosykiá (one of seven on Tílos) en route. Just west of Livádia stands the ghost village of **Mikró Horió**, abandoned in the 1950s. There's another castle here, and a late-hours summer bar in a restored house.

The trans-island road passes another fort and a cave at **Harkadió**, where Pliocene midget elephant bones were found in 1971 and are now kept in a one-room museum in Megálo Horió. Once past Megálo Horió, the road passes the little port of Agios Andónios and Pláka beach before ending at the 15th-century **Monastery of Agíou Pandelímona** ❿ (summer 10am–7pm, winter 10am–4pm), tucked into a spring-fed oasis-ravine. The church has a few frescoes and a fine marble floor. The big island knees-up is here, running for three days from 25 July and including the famous "Dance of the Cup". Almost as important is the 23 August festival at **Panagía Polítissa Monastery** near Livádia, for which special boats are laid on from Rhodes the previous day.

Sými

As you approach Sými on a day-trip boat from Rhodes, flotillas of boats flee the port of **Gialós** ⓫ for remote beaches around the island. The foreign "residents" and overnighters are escaping the daily quota of trippers. Gialós, a legally protected architectural reserve, is a stunning spectacle with its tiers of pastel-coloured houses.

But when the tour boats hoot their arrival, mediocre waterside tavernas gear up to tout for business, and stalls sell imported spices and sponges, plus other knick-knacks. As soon as the trippers leave in mid-afternoon, there is more room to walk on the quay and you will get a stronger drink.

Symiots are famous as boat-builders, and a few wooden boats still take shape at the Haráni yards. Until it was surpassed by Kálymnos after World War II, Sými was also the sponge-diving capital of the Aegean, a role assured by an Ottoman imperial grant of monopoly in the trade. The Nazi German surrender of the Dodecanese to the Allies, which formally ended World War II in Europe, was signed in Les Katerinettes restaurant on 8 May 1945.

Built in a protected gulch and thus stiflingly hot in summer, Gialós is beautiful at night when the bay reflects the lights from the houses above. Popular with the yachting fraternity, and a discerning clientele who book the limited accommodation independently, the notably

An excursion boat from Rhodes approaches Pédi.

The old stone walls of the castle overlooking Horió, Hálki.

expensive "Hydra of the Dodecanese"
has plenty of bars and tavernas scattered about. It is not, however, an
island for the unfit, the elderly or
the very young, who would have to
manage the 357 steps of the **Kalí
Stráta**, the broad stair-street climbing to the upper town of **Horió**. Follow arrows to the worthwhile local
museum (Tue–Sun 8.30am–2.30pm;
charge), which highlights Byzantine
and medieval Sými. Overhead is the
Knights' castle, which was built on
the site of – and using material from
– the ancient acropolis.

The only other significant habitation is the valley of **Pédi** to the
east, where flat land and a few wells
allow vegetable cultivation. On the
south side of the bay here, reached
by a marked trail, lies the naturally
sandy beach of **Agios Nikólaos**, the
only one on Sými. A 2009-built yacht
marina on the north shore accommodates overflow from Gialós. All Sými's
other beaches are pebble; walk across
the island, through the remaining
juniper forest, to **Agios Vassílios** in
the southwest (no facilities), or take

a boat excursion to **Agios Geórgios
Dysálona**, **Nanoú** or **Marathoúnda**
on the east coast –Marathoúnda has
a good taverna if you want to make a
full day of it.

Beyond Haráni, the coastal track
heads north, then west to the bay of
Nimborió, where a Byzantine floor
mosaic and catacombs can be found
just inland. Other notable sacred art is
found at the remote frescoed churches
of **Agios Prokópios**, **Kokkimídis**,
Agía Marína Nerás and **Megálos
Sotíros**, all on or just off the main
road south to the most important
island monastery, **Taxiárhis Mihaíl
Panormítis** ⑫.

The Archangel Michael is the
patron saint of local sailors, and his
feast day (8 November) brings pilgrims here from all over the Aegean.
Even though the monastery was pil-
laged during World War II, the central church with its myriad oil lamps
remains an atmospheric place, set in
the middle of a giant pebble-mosaic
courtyard. Things are tranquil once
the tour boats have gone – it's usually
the first stop coming from Rhodes.

*Excavations on
Karpáthos.*

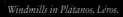

THE NORTHERN DODECANESE

In a country blessed with stunning seascapes, the
Northern Dodecanese have perhaps the most
striking views: between Kálymnos or Nísyros and
their surrounding islets, from the summits of Kos
or Pátmos over half the Aegean.

From the windmills of Astypálea
to the beaches and ancient ruins
of Kós, the spirituality of Pátmos
and the tranquillity of the tiny,
sparsely inhabited isles, the Northern
Dodecanese have something for
everyone.

Astypálea

Bleak, butterfly-shaped Astypálea,
with about 1,500 inhabitants, is geographically closer to the Cyclades
than the Dodecanese; on a clear day
both Amorgós and Anáfi appear
distinctly on the horizon. It belongs
administratively to the Dodecanese,
yet is distinctly Cycladic in architecture and culture, which is hardly surprising since it was in fact (re)settled
from Mýkonos and Tínos during the
15th century.

Ferry connections are still biased
towards the Cyclades and Piraeus
rather than Rhodes, with which the
most reliable link is by air. In high
summer short-term accommodation
fills up, while outsiders have renovated old houses in Hóra as summer
residences. A single stretch of road
linking the main resorts has been
paved, taverna food has improved, and
a bank ATM has been installed, but
further momentous change is unlikely.

Many visitors stay in the principal,
functional port of **Péra Gialós** or
Skála, which dates from the Italian

era. A long stair-street connects Skála
with **Hóra** ❶, the capital, with a
line of derelict windmills trailing
off to the northwest. At the pinnacle
of things sits the tan-walled *kástro*,
the finest example outside of the
Cyclades proper, not a legacy of the
Knights of St John, but a 13th-cen-
tury effort of the Venetian Quirini
clan. Until the late 1940s more than
300 islanders dwelt inside, but now
it is abandoned, except for two fine
churches: **Evangelístria**, supported
by the vaulting of the northwest

Main Attractions

Hóra, Astypálea
Mandráki, Nísyros
Brós Thermá hot springs
Climbing Mount Díkeos
Póthia architecture and
    Archaeological Museum
Agía Kiourá, Léros
Agíou Ioánnou tou
    Theológou Monastery,
    Pátmos

Nísyros landscape.

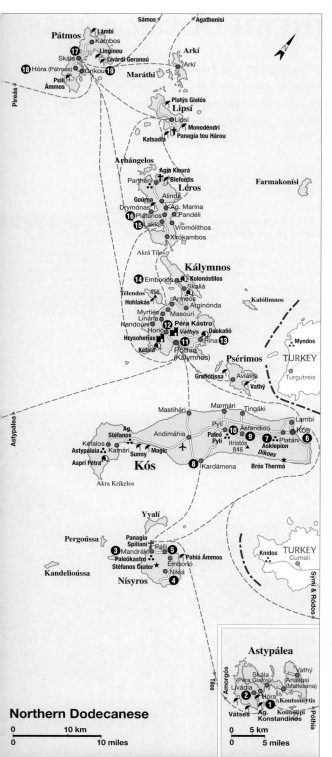

Northern Dodecanese

0   10 km

0   10 miles

Astypálea

0   5 km

0   5 miles

entrance, and **Agios Geórgios** overlooking the sea.

Just west of Hóra's ridge, **Livádia ❷** is the island's second resort, between citrus orchards and a sandy if somewhat scruffy beach. Better beaches, like nudist **Tzanáki**, and taverna-equipped **Agios Konstandínos**, lie further southeast, out on the western "wing". **Kaminákia** and **Vátses** beaches beyond can be reached by the rough onward track or on boat excursions.

The "body" of the butterfly is a long isthmus, just 100 metres/yards across at its narrowest point, by **Stenó** and **Mamoúni** beaches. **Maltezána** (officially Análipsi) to the east has become another resort, more through proximity to the airport than any intrinsic merit. Near Maltezána are the best of Astypálea's many Byzantine church-floor **mosaics**, often covered by protective gravel. A single bus plies regularly between Livádia and Maltezána; otherwise it's a single elusive taxi, or a rented motorbike or car.

Nísyros

In legend Greek Poseidon, pursuing the Titan Polyvotis, tore a rock from nearby Kós and crushed his adversary beneath it. The rock became Nísyros. The groaning of the Titan is still audible beneath the surface of the caldera in Nísyros's most impressive feature, the volcano which forms the heart of the island. Currently dormant, it was last active in 1933, and vulcanism still characterises Nísyros, from black pebbles on the shore to a thermal spa.

Once you're away from its harbour, **Mandráki ❸** proves an attractive capital. Wooden balconies hang cheerfully from tall, white houses ranged around a central communal orchard. Just off this, the 2010-opened, well-labelled **Archaeological Museum** (Tues–Sun 8.30am–2.40pm; charge) does a gallop, over two floors, of every period of Nisyrian history, from Archaic grave goods to Roman stelae and Byzantine painted bowls.

Overhead, a Knights' castle shelters the **monastery of Panagía Spilianí** (*spiliá* means cave), with its appropriately cave-like church, while to the south, the Doric citadel of **Paleókastro** is more impressive.

Mandráki by night is lively, with many tavernas and *kafenía* found, unusually, inland. There are few hotels, as most folk come just for the day from Kós to tour the volcano. In some establishments, you can order *soumáda*, a non-alcoholic drink now made from imported almonds. The island's green interior – from which wild almonds have sadly disappeared – is best appreciated by walking some of the remaining trail system.

The main **Stéfanos** crater, 260 metres (853ft) across, punctuates the nearly lifeless Lakkí plateau, 13km (8 miles) southeast of Mandráki. Tour buses make the trip every morning. With stout shoes, you can visit the caldera floor, braving a rotten-egg stench. Yellow crystals form around hissing steam vents while mud boils out of sight – the voice of Polyvótis. The adjacent Polyvótis crater is smaller

but more dramatic and rarely visited. The Greek power corporation made exploratory geothermal soundings here until 1993, when it departed in the face of islander hostility – though not before destroying the 1,000-year-old *kalderími* (cobbled path or road) back down to Mandráki.

Two scenic villages perch above Lakkí: **Emborió**, almost abandoned and being bought up for restoration by outsiders, and livelier **Nikiá** ❹, with a quirky round *platía*. The Emboriots moved down to the fishing port of **Páli** ❺ after World War II. The biggest sandy beach is 6km (4 miles) around the northeast coast, at **Pahiá Ammos**. West of Páli, the old spa at **Loutrá** (erratic hours; bring a towel; charge) has been restored with EU funds.

Kós

The second-largest Dodecanese in population, Kós is (just) the third-largest in size after Rhodes and Kárpathos. It follows the lead of Rhodes in most things: a sea-transport hub for a gaggle of surrounding islands; a

A hike along the caldera of Nísyros's dormant volcano.

shared history, give or take a few years; a similar Knights' castle guarding the harbour, plus a skyline of palms and minarets; and an agricultural economy displaced by tourism.

However, Kós is much smaller than Rhodes, and much flatter, with only one mountain range, Díkeos, rising to 846 metres (2,775ft) in the southeast. The margin of the island is fringed by excellent beaches, which are most easily accessible by motorbike or even pedal-bike, for which cycle paths are helpfully laid out.

Kós is by no means unspoilt, and visits in midsummer, especially without a reservation, are emphatically not recommended. Yet overdevelopment has its compensations: surprisingly good restaurants scattered across the island, ample water-sports opportunities and a good infrastructure.

Kós Town

Although the Minoans colonised the site of present-day **Kós Town** ❻ during the late Bronze Age and classical eras, the main island city-state was Astypalaia, on the far southwestern

cape of Kéfalos, an ally of Rhodes in the Dorian Hexapolis. Spartan sacking during the Peloponnesian War and a subsequent earthquake (Kós is very susceptible to them) forced the population to relocate to the northern site, a process that had been completed by the mid-4th century BC. According to the geographer Strabo (c.64 BC–AD 24), the new town was a success: "She was not large but inhabited in the best way possible and to the people visiting her by sea pleasant to behold."

Yet another earthquake in 1933 devastated most of Kós Town, except for the Ottoman bazaar of Haluvaziá, but gave Italian archaeologists a perfect excuse to excavate the ancient city comprehensively. Hence much of the town centre is an archaeological park, with the ruins of the Roman *agora*, the eastern excavation, lapping up to the 18th-century Loggia Mosque and the "Plane Tree of Hippocrates", under which the father of medicine is said to have taught. It is not really 2,500 years old, although it probably is one of the oldest trees in Europe, and now

Kós Archaeological Museum exhibit.

THE ASKLEPION

The Asklepion is named after Asklepios, who lived around 1200 BC and, according to legend, was the son of Apollo and Koronis. His cult developed in Kós, and he became revered as the Greek god of healing. Shrines were built to him all over Greece, usually on a spot where there was a natural spring, and people flocked to them from all over the ancient world, hoping for cures for their ailments. The most famous of the Asklepions is this one on Kós, which housed a spa fed by two natural springs. The complex was discovered in 1902 by two archaeologists, the German Dr Hertsok and the Greek Iakovos Zaraftis. It is popularly believed that Hippocrates, after whom the medical Hippocratic oath is named, worked and taught here, but this is unlikely to be true.

dependent on a life-support system of metal scaffolding.

The western digs offer covered mosaics and the *Xystós*, the colonnade of an indoor running track. Just south stand an over-restored *odeion*, which is sometimes used for summer performances, and the **Casa Romana** (closed for works), a restored Roman villa with floor mosaics and murals. The Italian-founded **Archaeological Museum** (closed until 2015) on Platía Elevtherías has a predictable Latin bias in its exhibits, although the star piece, a statue purportedly of the great healer Hippocrates, is in fact Hellenistic. Also on this square is the 18th-century **Defterdar Mosque**, still used by Kós Town's 50 or so Muslim families but not open to the public.

Around the island

Hippocrates himself (*c*.460–370 BC) was born and practised on Kós, but probably died shortly before the establishment of the **Asklepion** ❼ (summer Tue–Fri 8am–7.30pm, Sat–Mon 8am–2.30pm; winter daily 8.30am–2.30pm; charge), an ancient therapeutic centre 4km (2.5 miles) southwest of town. The site is more impressive for its position overlooking the straits towards Turkey than for any surviving structures.

The masonry was thoroughly pilfered by the Knights to build the massive **Nerantziás castle** (Tue–Sun, summer 8am–6pm, winter 8.30am–2.30pm; charge), which, unlike the one at Rhodes, was for strictly military purposes. It's a double fort, the smaller inner one dating from the mid-15th century, and the outer circuit completed in 1514.

Between the Asklepion and Kós Town, pause at **Platáni**, roughly halfway, to eat at one of four excellent Turkish-run tavernas. As on Rhodes, most local Muslims have emigrated to Turkey since the 1960s. There was a small Jewish community here too, wiped out with the Rhodian one in 1944, leaving behind only their marvellous Art Deco **synagogue** by the town *agora*.

The road east of town dead-ends at **Brós Thermá**, enjoyable hot springs that run directly into the sea. West of

Floor mosaic inside Kós's Archaeological Museum.

Rollerblading on the waterfront.

The remains of the Asklepion.

is the island's cheap-and-cheerful resort, with little to recommend it aside from suggestively named bars, dance clubs, and a long, sandy and jam-packed beach. The only cultural diversion is the Knights' castle (always open) near **Andimáhia**, a two-hour walk inland for the energetic.

In the far southwest, facing Nísyros, are more scenic and sheltered **beaches**, with names like "**Sunny**" and "**Magic**", the latter arguably the best. At nearby **Agios Stéfanos**, twin 6th-century basilicas are among several early Christian monuments. The Kéfalos headland beyond saw the earliest habitation of Kós: **Asprí Pétra** cave, home to Neolithic man, and classical **Astypalaia**, birthplace of Hippocrates, of which only the little theatre remains.

town, within easy cycling distance, are the package resorts of **Tingáki** and **Marmári**, ringed by long white beaches, and less frenetic **Mastihári**, with a commuter boat to Kálymnos.

Kardámena ❽ on the south coast, 25km (15 miles) from Kós Town but just 7km (4.5 miles) from the airport,

The appealing villages on the wooded northern slopes of **Mount Díkeos**, collectively known as **Asfendioú** ❾, have retained more traditional character, with whitewashed houses and attractive churches. At **Ziá**, tavernas seem more numerous than permanent inhabitants, and are

especially busy at sunset and later. **Asómati's** vernacular houses are slowly being bought up and restored by foreigners. The surrounding juniper forest provides welcome relief from summer heat; a path from Ziá allows the ascent of **Hristós** peak on Díkeos, with a magnificent 360° view (allow three hours for the round trip in cooler weather).

On the western flank of Mount Díkeos, the Byzantines had their island capital at **Paleó Pylí** ❿ (Old Pylí), today a jumble of ruins – except for the half-intact Arhángelos church, with fine 15th-century frescoes – below a castle at the head of a spring-fed canyon. Modern Pylí, 3km (2 miles) downhill, paradoxically offers something more ancient: the **Harmyleio**, a subterranean Hellenistic family tomb with 12 niches.

Kálymnos

First impressions of Kálymnos, north of Kós, are of an arid, mountainous landmass with a decidedly masculine energy in the main port town of Póthia. This is due to the former dominant industry, sponge-diving, now supplanted by tourism and commercial fishing. But the island's prior mainstay (see page 272) is in ample evidence in the home decor of huge sponges or shell-encrusted amphorae, and the souvenir shops overflowing with smaller sponges.

Póthia ⓫ itself (population 16,000), the second-largest town in the Dodecanese, is noisy, colourful and workaday Greek, its brightly painted houses rising in tiers up the sides of the valley flanks. Mansions and vernacular dwellings with ornate balconies and wrought-iron ornamentation (an island speciality) are particularly evident in the Evangelístria district.

The most dazzling conventional attraction is the 2009-opened **Archaeological Museum** (Tue–Sat 9am–4pm; charge). Stars of the displays from all eras include a huge Hellenistic cult statue of Asklepios, a Roman bronze of a clad woman and an unusual robed, child-sized *kouros* (most were naked). Spare time also for the **Nautical and Folklore Museum** (Mon–Sat 10am–1.30pm; charge for

FACT

Póthia has an orphanage where, until recently, Orthodox priests (the great majority of those who do not live in monasteries are married), would come to choose a bride before they were ordained. A woman without a dowry was reckoned to have little chance of finding a husband outside the Church.

Kós's Castle of the Knights.

Sponge-Diving

Sponge-diving in Kálymnos is now dying out. It has a long history, but in the past it was hard and often dangerous work.

Kálymnos has been a sponge-fishing centre from ancient times, although a combination of fishing restrictions and marine blight have diminished the trade since the 1960s. Sponges come in various grades: the coarser ones for industry, the finer ones for cosmetic and artistic use. Although cheap artificial sponges now dominate the market, many people will still pay extra for the more resilient natural sponge. Sponges were traditionally "cured" in two stages. First the divers trod them underfoot on the deck of the caique to "milk" them of unwanted organic matter; then they strung them together and dropped them back into the sea for a few more days of cleaning.

Sponge-curing can still be observed at a few Póthia factories. Older operations have stone tubs of salt water, others bubbling vats of diluted acid

The first diving apparatus or "machine" – here on display outside a taverna – revolutionised the trade.

which bleach the sponges. This concession to tourist tastes actually weakens the fibres. After this optional process, they are rinsed in salt water again and finally laid out to dry in the factory courtyard.

Over the years sponge-fishers developed various methods of gathering their quarry: spearing them in shallow water; dragging a heavy blade and net along the sea-bottom so that everything – stones and seaweed as well as the odd sponge – was pulled up together; and diving – the most difficult and dangerous method.

Diving methods

In the old days, naked divers used to sink themselves with the heavy *skandalópetra* or "scandal stone" tied to their waists. Holding their breath, they scraped off the sponges fixed to rocks that they had spied from the surface. They could usually get two or three sponges before they had to surface for air –better divers could dive to 40 fathoms. This was before the "machine" was introduced late in the 19th century.

The "machine" (*skáfandro* in Greek), the first diving apparatus, consisted of a rubber suit with a bronze helmet connected to a long rubber hose and a hand-powered air-pump. The diver was let out on a long cable and given enough air-hose for his final depth, where he could stay much longer, thanks to the constant air supply. Too long and too deep, as it turned out. Compressed air delivered to divers at these greater depths bubbled out of solution in their bloodstream as they rose, invariably too rapidly. The results of nitrogen embolism – known as decompression sickness or, more commonly, the "bends" – included deafness, incontinence, paralysis and, all too often, death.

By the 1950s the physiological mechanism was understood and the death and maiming halted, but too late to help hundreds of Kalymnian crewmen. Although the "machine" now seems quaintly antiquated, it was innovative enough for its time to enrich the boat captains and sponge wholesalers, who benefited from the divers' dangerous work.

Ironically, the increased efficiency in sponge-harvesting helped to wind up the industry. The Greek seabed was stripped bare, and Kalymnian boats had to sail increasingly further afield. Over-exploitation of Mediterranean sponge beds was the rule even before a virus devastated them during the late 1980s. Today, sponge-divers are a rare breed: whereas in the old days, huge boats with a crew of 30 would set out in late April for six months of sponge-diving, today perhaps 10 tiny craft with 3 divers aboard make far shorter trips.

Folklore section), with fascinating photos of old Póthia and seafarers' lives, plus poignantly primitive divers' equipment.

To the northwest loom two castles (both open all day; free): **Hrysoherías**, the Knights' stronghold, and the originally Byzantine fort of **Péra Kástro** with several open frescoed churches, standing above the medieval capital of **Horió** ⓬, still the island's second town.

The east coast is harsh and uninhabited except for the green, citrus-planted **Vathýs Valley** extending inland from a deep fjord, which comes as a surprise amid all this greyness as you round a high curve in the approach road. **Plátanos** and **Metóhi** hamlets used to live from their sweet-smelling mandarin and orange orchards, though many of these are now for sale. Yachts patronise a half-dozen tavernas at little **Rína** ⓭ port, from where there are boat trips to the nearby cave of **Daskalió**, a place of Bronze-Age worship, and purportedly of refuge during the Italian era. The limestone strata are riddled with

other, visitable stalactite caves. The best are **Kéfala** in the far southwest, and **Skaliá** and **Kolonóstilos** in the far north.

The great majority of visitors stay at the beach resorts on the gentler west coast, locally referred to as **Brostá** (Forward). Local people and Greek holiday-makers gravitate towards **Kandoúni** and **Linária** beaches, although less developed **Platýs Gialós**, just north, is reckoned among the island's best. Foreign package tourists used to patronise **Melitsáhas**, **Myrtiés** (with the best beach), **Masoúri** and **Armeós**, four contiguous, heavily developed resorts now fallen on hard times. They have to varying degrees reinvented themselves as centres for spring and autumn rock-climbers. Kálymnos is rated one of the top five spots worldwide for the sport.

You could escape any crowds by heading north towards **Argynónda** and **Emboriós** ⓮, the end of the road 19km (12 miles) from Póthia, enjoying a mix of pebble and sand beaches, though bus service beyond Armeós is sparse. In any case, Kálymnos is just

Swapping news after a service in the church forecourt, Póthia.

the right size to explore by scooter or on foot via the surviving path network, and boat excursions are also offered.

Psérimos and Télendos

The cheapest excursion, by daily 9.30am caique from Kálymnos, is to tiny **Psérimos** (population 100). Crowds of day-trippers from Kós flopping on **Avlákia** port's sandy beach can exceed the capacity of Avlákia's few tavernas; if you stay the night, you will find the islanders more receptive. After dark, the only sounds will be the wind rustling through calamus thickets, or the tinkle of goat bells. Alternatives to the main harbour beach – which doubles as the main street – include **Vathý**, just half an hour's walk east, or secluded **Grafiótissa** a similar distance west, 300 metres/yds of fine sand at the base of cliffs.

Seen from Myrtiés or Masoúri at dusk, the bulky islet of **Télendos**, which was split off from Kálymnos by a mid-6th-century AD earthquake, resembles a snail; others claim to see the silhouette of a petrified princess staring out to sea, jilted here by her lover. Regular **caiques** play from Myrtiés (daily 8am–11pm every half-hour in season).

The single waterside hamlet (permanent population 15), also named Télendos, huddles under mammoth **Mount Ráhi** (458 metres/1,502ft). Halfway up the north side of the mount, a long trek away, perches the fortified chapel of **Agios Konstandínos**. Less energetic souls content themselves with the ruined Byzantine monastery of **Agios Vassílios**, at the northern edge of the hamlet, or the Byzantine baths of **Agios Harálambos**. Télendos is more upmarket than Psérimos, and slightly less oriented for day-trippers. Most tavernas are stylish and friendly, and accommodation designed to lure custom over from the main island. Beaches vary in consistency and size; a sandy, tamarisk-shaded one stretches north of "town", while scenic **Hohlakás**, 10 minutes west, has coin-sized pebbles, as do several "pocket" coves (one naturist) beyond the sand beach.

Télendos island, viewed from above Myrtiés.

Léros

Léros, with its half-dozen deeply indented bays, looks like a jigsaw puzzle piece gone astray. The deepest inlet, that of **Lakkí** ⓯ (now the main ferry port), sheltered an important Italian naval base from 1935 onwards, and from here was launched the submarine that torpedoed the Greek battleship *Elli* in Tínos harbour on 15 August 1940.

Today Lakkí seems bizarre, a planned town built during 1935–8 to house the staff of the Italian naval base here, and far too grand for the present population. Its Rationalist/Streamline-Modern buildings (a popular style in the 1930s, Art Deco-influenced, but more practical) have lately been restored, although the landscaped squares and wide boulevards remain spookily empty. The local atmosphere was long weighted by the presence of three hospitals for disabled children and mentally ill adults, though these institutions have been mostly phased out and the facilities turned over in part to the University of the Aegean's nursing faculty.

The rest of the island is more inviting, particularly the fishing port of **Pandéli**, with its waterfront tavernas, just downhill from the capital of **Plátanos** ⓰, draped over a saddle, with a well-preserved Knights' castle containing an excellent ecclesiastical museum (the warden will give an engaging tour). South of both, **Vromólithos** has the best easily accessible and car-free beach on an island not known for good, sandy ones. In most places sharp rock reefs

Lacemaking in the shade – a local lady keeps the old crafts alive.

Vivid colour outlines the steps to this house.

OUR LADY OF DEATH

Near Lipsí's Hohlakoúra Bay, the church of Panagía tou Hárou (Our Lady of Charon) is the focus of a miracle repeated annually since 1943. The church is so named for its icon (now a copy, with the original in the town cathedral) of the Virgin cradling the crucified Christ, the only such in the Greek world. In thanks for a favour granted, a parishioner left a sprig of lilies by the icon; they duly withered, but mysteriously revived on 23 August, the Orthodox day of the Virgin's Assumption into heaven. Each year on that date the icon is processed with suitable ceremony to its old home and then back to the cathedral. Don't try travelling between the islands on this day (called Apódosis Kimíseos in Greek). It's a major holiday and all ferry tickets sell out early.

FACT

Lipsí was the island where, in summer 2002, Alexandros Giotopoulos, the mastermind of the 17 November terrorist group, Europe's longest lasting, was finally unmasked and caught. He had been living here in a villa, under an alias, for many years; Giotopoulos and several other group members were tried on murder and bombing charges, convicted and sentenced to lengthy jail terms by late 2003.

View of Lipsí Town.

must be crossed when getting into the water. **Agia Marína**, beyond Plátanos, is the usual hydrofoil, excursion boat and catamaran harbour and, like Pandéli, offers good tavernas, plus more whimsical Italian architecture.

Alinda, 3km (2 miles) north around the same bay, is the oldest established resort, with a long beach right next to the road – and a poignant Allied War Graves cemetery containing casualties from the five-day Battle of Léros in November 1943, when the Germans ousted an insufficiently supplied British commando force (a small underground museum at Lakkí tells the story, if not very well).

In ancient times Léros was sacred to Artemis, and on a hill next to the airport runway are knee-high remains of the goddess's "temple" –actually an ancient fort. Artemis' reputed virginity lives on in the place name **Parthéni** (*parthenos* is the Greek for virgin), the other side of the airport: an infamous concentration camp during the junta, now a scarcely more cheerful army base, as it was in

Italian times. Things perk up beyond of this, with one of the island's better beaches, **Blefoútis**, plus the unusual chapel of **Agía Kiourá**, decorated by junta-era prisoners with strikingly heterodox religious murals, which the mainstream Church has always loathed – they are legally protected from further erasure.

Other bays tend not to be worth the effort spent getting there. **Goúrna**, in the west, has a long, sandy and gently shelving beach, but it is also a windy and often dirty one. Isolated **Xirókambos** in the south refuses to face the facts of a poor beach as it struggles to be a resort; caiques from Myrtiés on Kálymnos call here in season, but be sure you have onward land transport organised.

Lipsí, Arkí, Maráthi, Agathonísi

The name Lipsí (aka Leipsoí) is supposed to derive from Kalypso, the nymph who held Odysseus in thrall for years. The little island (population around 700) has been transformed by tourism, real-estate development and

regular ferry/catamaran services since the 1980s. The single harbour town (also called Lipsí) has been spruced up, accommodation has multiplied, bulldozer tracks and paved roads creep across the landscape, and scooters are made available to explore them.

An extraordinarily long esplanade links the ferry quay with the village centre, marked by the three-domed cathedral of Agios Ioánnis. Behind this is the main square with tavernas and an **Ecclesiastical Museum** (daily, erratic hours; free) with some amusing exhibits. As befits a dependency of Pátmos, older houses have their windows outlined in bright colours that change periodically. Beaches are scattered across the island. The sandiest are the town beach of **Liendoú**, **Platýs Gialós** in the northwest – with a seasonal taverna – and **Katsadiá**, a double bay in the south, facing Léros, again with a taverna. The most secluded are naturist pebble coves at **Monodéndri** in the southeast, facing scenic islets.

Lipsí appears verdant, but farming is dependent on well water; there is only one spring in the west, at Káto Kímisi. Although tractors and pumps are audible by day, the nights are given over to the sea's lapping, the crowing of errant roosters, or perhaps a snatch of music from one of three bars.

Three more remote islets north of Lipsí are far less developed and can be more quickly reached from Pátmos. The permanent population of **Arkí** is just 40, and falling. There is no real village or fresh water, although a ferry dock has been built and an adjacent sandy beach created. Accommodation and tavernas are adequate in both quality, and quantity – except during mid-summer. **Maráthi**, across a channel, gets some day-trips from Pátmos and Lipsí, for the sake of its long sandy beach. It has just three permanent inhabitants, and an equal number of places to stay and eat.

Agathonísi, off towards Sámos (where shopping is done, children go to school and many islanders live in winter), is more of a going concern with its three hamlets and permanent population of about 85.

Cats are everywhere on Pátmos.

Connections are better too, with a catamaran service dovetailing well with appearances of the small ferry *Nisos Kalymnos*. The islet is much in the news lately as a favourite landing point for illegal immigrants (see page 54), but has a cult following amongst many foreign tourists. Most of them stay at the little port of **Agios Geórgios**, with a convenient beach and several tavernas. More secluded beaches lie around the headland at **Spiliás** and **Gaïdourávlakos**, or in the far east of the island at **Póros** and **Thóli**, the latter with a Byzantine granary just inland.

Pátmos

Pátmos has been inextricably linked to the Bible's Book of Revelation (Apocalypse) ever since tradition placed its authorship here, in AD 95, by John the Evangelist. The volcanic landscape, with strange rock formations and sweeping views, seems suitably apocalyptic. In 1088 the monk Hristodoulos Latrenos founded a monastery here in honour of St John the Theologian (as John the Evangelist is known in

Mosaic adorning the monastery of St John the Theologian.

Greek), which soon became a focus of scholarship and pilgrimage. A Byzantine imperial charter gave the monks tax exemption and the right to engage in sea-trade, concessions respected by the island's later Venetian and Ottoman rulers.

Although Pátmos is no longer ruled by the monks, their presence tempers the rowdier elements found in most holiday resorts. While there is the usual quota of naturist beaches, nightlife is genteel, and the clientele upmarket (including the Aga Khan's extended family, plus various ruling or deposed royal families). Those who elect to stay here appreciate the unique, even spiritual, atmosphere that Pátmos exudes once the day-trippers and cruise-ship patrons have left.

Skála ⓱ is the port and largest village, best appreciated late at night when crickets serenade and yacht-masts are illuminated against a dark sky. By day Skála loses its charm, but all island commerce, whether shops, banks or travel agencies, is based here. Buses leave regularly from the quay for the hilltop **Hóra** ⓲, but a 40-minute

cobbled path short-cutting the road is preferable in cool weather.

Hóra's core, protected by a massive, pirate-proof fortress and visible from a great distance, is the **Agíou Ioánnou tou Theológou Monastery** (Monastery of St John the Theologian; daily 8am–1.30pm, Tue, Thur, Sun also 4–6pm). A photogenic maze of interlinked courtyards, stairways, chapels and passageways, it occupies the site of an ancient Artemis temple. The Treasury (charge) houses the most impressive monastic collection in Greece outside Mount Athos. Among priceless icons and jewellery, the prize exhibit is the edict of Emperor Alexios Komnenos granting the island to Hristodoulos.

Away from the tourist thoroughfares, Hóra is silent, its thick-walled mansions with their pebble courtyards and arcades the preserve of wealthy foreigners who snapped them up in the 1960s. From Platía Lótza in the north there is one of the finest views in the Aegean, taking in at least half a dozen islands on all but the haziest day.

Just over halfway down the path from Hóra to Skála stands the small **Apokálypsis Monastery** (same hours as main monastery), built around the grotto where John had his Revelation. A silver band on the wall marks the spot where John lay his head, while in the ceiling is a great cleft in the rock through which the divine Voice spoke. The courtyard is the usual venue for a sacred music festival in late summer.

Pátmos's remote beaches are surprisingly good, with great seascapes offshore and (usually) excellent tavernas. Buses ply between **Gríkou** ⑲ resort and northerly **Kámbos**, popular with Greek families. The biggest sandy bay is exposed **Psilí Ammos** in the far south, accessible by boat trip or a half-hour walk from the road's end, and favoured by naturists. Beaches north of Skála include (in order) **Melóï**, site of the island campsite; long **Agrioliádi**; **Lingínou**, with a double cove, and popular with nudists; isolated **Livádi Geranoú**, with an islet to swim to; and finally **Lámbi**, which has irresistible, multicoloured volcanic pebbles.

The Agíou Ioánnou toú Theológou Monastery.

Agios Nikólaos.

Koúles fort.

CRETE

Greece's southernmost island – and the largest – is characterised by soaring mountains, a proudly independent people, and unique remains of the first great European civilisation.

Crete (Kríti), claimed by many Greeks to be the most authentic island, is by far the largest. It stretches 256km (159 miles) from east to west and varies between 11 and 56km (7 and 35 miles) in width. A massive mountainous backbone dominates, with peaks stretching skywards to over 2,450 metres (7,958ft) at two points. In the north the mountains slope more gently, producing fertile plains, while in the south they often plunge precipitously into the sea. *Megalónisos* (The Great Island) is what Cretans call their home, meaning great not just in size.

Great can certainly be applied to the Minoan civilisation, the first in Europe and one with which Crete is inextricably entwined. Visitors by the thousand pour through the ruins of Minoan palace complexes, before heading towards one of the scores of excellent beaches. With two international airports, Crete cannot be classified as undiscovered, but by its scale and variety it manages to contain the crowds and to please visitors with widely divergent tastes. While a car is essential for discovering the best of the island, car hire is, unfortunately, comparatively expensive.

Most of Crete's 500,000 inhabitants live along the north coast. The mountains, honeycombed with caves, nurture a proud and ruggedly independent people – among which

there is still a significant separatist movement. Crete also has a particular musical tradition, characterised by *mantinádes* (rhyming couplet songs) and dances such as the spectacular *pentozális*. These are almost invariably accompanied by the *lýra*, the ubiquitous lap-fiddle.

For almost half the year snow lies on the highest peaks, which provide a dramatic backdrop to verdant spring meadows ablaze with flowers. This, as botanists and ornithologists know well, is *the* time to visit. The former

Morosíni fountain.

come to see more than 130 plant species unique to the island, while the latter are thrilled by more than 250 types of birds heading north. These migrants briefly join such rare residents as Bonelli's eagle and Eleonora's falcon. And in spring the island is redolent with sage, savory, thyme, oregano and the endemic *díktamo* (dittany).

Crete, much more than other Greek islands, is a place both for sightseeing and for spending time on the beach. Minoan ruins are the major attractions: as well as the archaeological sites, the Archaeological Museum in the capital, **Iráklio** ❶, houses a unique collection of artefacts from Europe's oldest civilisation. But there are also Greek, Roman, Ottoman and Venetian remains, and literally hundreds of Byzantine churches, many with rare and precious frescoes, usually dating from the 13th to 16th centuries. These paintings often have a distinct Cretan style, recognisable by elongated figures and attention to detail. (Many of the churches are kept locked: enquire at the nearest café for the key.) Dozens of monasteries have

fallen into disuse over the years, but others still function and have treasures as rich as their histories.

Homer's "island of 100 towns" can also be called an island of 100 beaches. Some are simply a place where a boat can behauled ashore, but many are superb stretches of sand, often where nudity is tolerated. The bathing season – especially on the south coast facing the Libyan Sea – is long, stretching from Easter until late autumn.

Iráklio (Heraklion)

The capital of Crete since 1971, greater Iráklio has a population of almost 180,000 and is the fourth-largest city in Greece. Although long exceptionally prosperous from both tourism and agriculture, the economic crisis hit here hard and early, with above-national-average unemployment and often neglected infrastructure. However, it is still a bustling, concrete-laced town, with little appeal outside of the Old Quarter.

Most tourists head for the Minoan ruins of Knossos, but this should be combined (joint ticket available) with

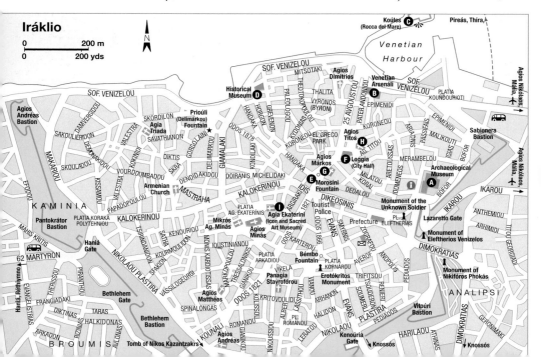

a visit to the outstanding **Archaeological Museum**  (Dec–late May Tues–Sun 8am–2.40pm, Mon 11am–4.40pm; late May–Nov Tues–Sat 8am–7.40pm, Sun 8am–2.40pm, Mon 1–8pm; charge) just off focal, bustling Platía Elevtherías in order fully to comprehend the site and its contents. After a lengthy restoration, the museum will fully re-open in stages through early 2015, with all of its famous treasures – including the Malia bee pendant, the bull-leaping fresco and snake-goddess idols – returning from the temporary "greatest hits" annexe at the back.

Most of Iráklio's other major attractions date from the Venetian era, Crete's most prosperous period in historical times. Flanking the old harbour are the Venetian **Arsenáli**  (covered boathouses) and the restored, nocturnally illuminated **Koúles fortress**  (Tue–Sun 8.30am–2.40pm; charge), whose three reliefs of the Lion of St Mark announce its provenance. A few minutes' walk to the west of the old harbour on Sofoklí Venizélou Street, the **Historical Museum**  (Mon–Sat 9am–5pm; charge; www.

historical-museum.gr) covers Cretan history and ethnography from the Byzantine Empire to the present. Inside are fine icons and fresco fragments, stone relief carvings, documentation of the local Jewish, Muslim and Armenian communities, folk textiles and a re-creation of a traditional Cretan home. Models and prints show how Iráklio has developed, as does an interactive model of the medieval city. Due prominence is given to the struggle for Cretan independence and World War II resistance. Inland, **Platía Venizélou** (also known as Lion or Fountain Square) takes its popular names from the stylish 17th-century **Morosíni Fountain**  and guardian marble lions. Overlooking the square is the Venetian **Loggia**  (city hall) flanked by the churches of **Agios Márkos**  and, set in its own little square, **Agios Títos** ; all three have been heavily restored to repair war damage. Since 1966, when it was returned from St Mark's Basilica in Venice, the skull of St Titus, St Paul's Apostle to Crete and the island's first bishop, has been housed in Agios Títos.

TIP

The Archaeological Museum in Iráklio is best visited in the afternoon, when it is quieter. You can take a break in the garden café – but remember to retain your museum ticket for readmission.

At the Iráklio Archaeological Museum.

The Islands in Film

The islands are proof that a great setting does not necessarily make a great film, although there have been a few memorable ones.

Postcard-worthy beaches, stage-set ports and reliable sunshine suggest ideal film locations. But luminous scenery has not guaranteed quality; many island-shot movies lack coherent plot.

Boy on a Dolphin (1957) starred Alan Ladd, Sophia Loren – and Hydra, the first island on the big screen along with Crete, where the villagers of Kritsá (and Melina Mercouri) graced *He Who Must Die*, Jules Dassin's 1957 adaptation of Nikos Kazantzakis' *Christ Recrucified*. Crete and Kazantzakis, with a Mikis Theodorakis soundtrack, reappeared in Michael Cacoyannis's *Zorba the Greek* (1964), a retelling of Níkos Kazantazákis's novel *Alexis Zorbas*, shot at Pláka and Kókkino Horió, near Haniá. Alan Bates and Anthony Quinn played the leads; Quinn had already starred in 1961's *The Guns of Navarone* (shot at Cape Ladikó on Rhodes (where a bay is named after Quinn), and

Photogenic Santoríni, made for celluloid stardom.

sheer cliffs at Sými's Agios Geórgios Dyssálonas), as the Greek member of a commando team charged with destroying an impregnable German artillery battery. Corfu has also "starred" – in Billy Wilder's Franco-German 1978 drama *Fedora*, and (using the Achilleion Palace, with Roger Moore as James Bond) in 1981's *For Your Eyes Only*. Moore had just played in 1979's *Escape to Athena*, a POW-escape caper set on Rhodes. Rhodes (and briefly, Sými) also figured in *Pascali's Island* (1988), based on Barry Unsworth's novel, with Ben Kingsley as an Ottoman spy and fixer. Luc Besson's *The Big Blue* (1988) was the top grossing French film of the 1980s; loosely based on the lives of two champion free-divers, it had more atmosphere than narrative. The title translates as *To Apérando Galázio* – the name of countless island bars – but the movie also put location Amorgós on the tourism map.

In the Cyclades, trashy *Summer Lovers* (1982) and *Lara Croft Tomb Raider: The Cradle of Life* (2003) both featured Santoríni, while *Shirley Valentine* (1989) showcased Mýkonos beaches and a 40-something, unhappily married woman's (Pauline Collins) affair with a Greek *kamáki* (Tom Conti), the era's stereotypical (now extinct) Romeo. "She's an ex-Shirley Valentine" became universal shorthand for women staying in Greece after the romance that anchored them there ended.

The award for Worst Greek-Shot Film Ever goes to Paul Cox's *Island* (1989), set on Astypálea, with Irene Pappas not redeeming Indo-Euro-Greek nonsense. Things improved with Italian-produced, plotless *Mediterraneo*, filmed on Kastellórizo and winning 1991's Best Foreign Film Oscar; this warm-hearted portrayal of a World War II backwater did for this tiny island what *The Big Blue* had done for Amorgós.

The biggest splashes have since been made by *Captain Corelli's Mandolin* (2001), shot on Kefaloniá (with sets recreating pre-war-and-earthquake places); the virulently anti-resistance politics of Louis de Bernières's eponymous novel incensed many Kefalonians, and filming (with Nicholas Cage and Penélope Cruz) was conditional on excising controversial material; the vapid result sank without trace. No such troubles beset smash hit *Mamma Mia!* (2008), filmed on Skópelos and Skiáthos, with Meryl Streep and Pierce Brosnan. *Fugitive Pieces* (2007), Anne Michaels's best-selling Holocaust novel partly set on Zákynthos (Lésvos, Hydra and Kefaloniá in the film) was pitched as an Important Work, but proved middlebrow in the telling.

Walk south through the noisy "market street", redolent with tantalising smells and jammed with people, but very touristy. Admire the Venetian Bembo Fountain and the adjacent Turkish pumphouse (now a café) at the far end before turning west towards the **Icon and Sacred Art Museum** ❶ (daily 9.30am–3.30pm), inside 15th-century Agía Ekateríni church. Stars of the collection are six icons by 16th-century master Mihaïl Damaskinos, a peer of El Greco.

You may circumambulate the 15th-century city walls which, in their day, were the most formidable in the Mediterranean. The defences stretch for nearly 4km (2½ miles) and in parts are 29 metres (95ft) thick. En route, pause on the Martinengo bastion at the tomb of the great Irákliot author and excommunicated iconoclast Nikos Kazantzakis (1883–1957) to enjoy the views, and to consider his defiant epitaph – "I hope for nothing, I fear nothing, I am free" – reflecting his long fascination with Buddhism. Keen admirers will make for the **Kazantzákis Museum** (summer daily 9am–7pm, winter Sun

10am–3pm; charge) in his natal village of Myrtiá (Ottoman Varvári, 24km/15 miles) due south of Iráklio. Displays illustrate his turbulent personal, literary and political life both in Greece and abroad – he spent long years effectively exiled by the Orthodox Church – with one room entirely devoted to Alexis Zorbas.

The best beaches near Iráklio are at **Ammoudári** (Almyrós), just west of town, and at **Tobroúk** and **Amnisós** to the east. The latter, the ancient port of **Knossos**, has the best sands but lies under the airport flight path.

To Knossos and beyond

Excursions from Iráklio will not only delight Minoan aficionados, but provide opportunities to savour the attractive countryside. The most famous site, of course, is the palace of **Knossos** ❷, a mere 5km (3 miles) southwest of the city centre, and easily reached on a No. 2 urban bus. (For a full exploration of the remains at Knossos, see pages 306.)

At **Arhánes** ❸, 12km (8 miles) south of Knossós, an **Archaeological Museum** (Wed–Mon 8.30am–2.40pm;

Enjoying a drink at Iráklio's market.

The Venetian church of Ágios Títos.

free) has caused a stir with artefacts, apparently of a human sacrifice, recovered from a Minoan temple at **Anemospiliá**, contradicting received notions of Minoan society as uniformly pacifist.

A steep climb from Arhánes leads to the summit of **Mount Gioúhtas** (811 metres/2,660ft), whose profile dominates Iráklio's horizon. At the top are a Minoan peak sanctuary, a 14th-century chapel and caves in which notionally immortal Zeus is supposedly buried. Some 6km (4 miles) south of here, **Houdétsi** village offers the **Museum of Musical Instruments of the World** (summer daily 8am–4pm, winter Sun 10am–3pm; charge), assembled by prominent musician Ross Daly, who lives and conducts workshops locally.

Týlissos ❹, 13km (8 miles) southwest of Iráklio, possesses three well-preserved small palaces, or large villas (daily 8.30am–2.40pm; charge), and is one of the few modern villages to retain its original pre-Hellenic name. Twenty kilometres (13 miles) further west on the same road, the elongated village of **Anógia**, where wool is spun

Detail of the replica procession fresco, South Propylon, Knossós.

and where many homes have looms, is a weaving and embroidery centre. Many local people still wear traditional dress on a regular basis, the men in particular looking like rebels in search of a cause. This is no stage setting: Anógia has a long tradition of resistance and revolt. The village was razed by the Ottomans in 1821 and 1866, and in 1944 the entire male population of the village was killed by German troops.

From Anógia a side road climbs to the magnificent **Nída plateau**, from where it is a 20-minute uphill stroll to the **Idéon Andron** (**Cave of Mount Ida**); this was the nursery, if not the birthplace, of Zeus. Here the god was hidden and guarded by the *Kouretes*, who clashed their weapons to drown the sound of his cries, while the nymph Amalthea fed him goats' milk. Keen hikers might like to push on to the summit of **Mount Ida** ❺ (Psilorítis), at 2,456 metres (7,958ft) the highest point on Crete. The trail, part of the European E4 route, is well marked with red-and-white blazes; allow about seven hours for the round trip.

MINOAN GLORY

The most renowned Minoan ruins – Knossos (Knossós in modern Greek), Phaistos (Festós), Mália and Káto Zákros – date from the Neo-palatial period (1700–1450 BC). Great unfortified palaces, brilliantly decorated, were built; superb pottery and jewellery, used for rituals and personal adornment, were produced. The early palaces of the Proto-palatial period (1900–1700 BC), of which scant remains survive, were almost certainly destroyed by earthquakes, but it's still debatable what ended the Neo-palatial period. In the Post-palatial era (1450–1100 BC) mainland Mycenaeans had supplanted the Minoans and by the Iron Age (after 1100 BC) Dorian city-states had replaced the old palaces. Surviving Minoans (the Eteo-Cretans) retired to the mountains where they maintained their traditions.

East from Iráklio

Return to Iráklio and continue eastwards along the E75 highway for 24km (15 miles) to the notoriously tatty resorts of **Hersónisos** ❻, **Stalída** (Stális) and **Mália** ❼. However, their beaches at least have good sand, though this does make them very popular. Hersónisos features scanty Greek and Roman remains, while close to the beach near Mália is a renowned Minoan site.

The **Malia Palace** (Tue–Sun 8.30am–2.40pm; charge), traditionally associated with King Sarpedon, brother of Minos, is contemporary with that at Knossos. The ruins are not as extensive as those at Knossos or Phaistos but, even without reconstruction, are more readily understood. The remarkable number of store rooms and workrooms, as well as the simpler style of architecture, suggests a country villa more than a palace. Excavations unearthed the Hrysólakkos (Golden Pit) from the Proto-palatial period (1900–1700 BC). The name is derived from the numerous gold artefacts found in this enormous necropolis.

From either Mália or Hersónisos, twisting mountain roads lead up to the **Lasíthi Plateau** ❽, around 840 metres (2,756ft) above sea level and 57km (36 miles) from Iráklio. This fertile upland supports potatoes, cereal crops, apples and pears, but sadly is now depopulated and neglected, with heavy spring rains in many years preventing proper cultivation. **Psyhró** in the plateau's southwest corner is home to the giant **Díkteo Andron** (Diktean Cave; daily, summer 8am–6.40pm , winter 8.30am–2.40 pm; charge), supposedly the birthplace of Zeus. Neaby, **Agios Geórgios village** offers the **Cretan Folklore Museum** (summer daily 9am–4pm; charge) with household, craft and agricultural exhibits.

Descend from Lasíthi via Neápoli to **Agios Nikólaos** ❾, 69km (43 miles) from Iráklio, invariably abbreviated by tourists to "Ag Nik" and once the Saint-Tropez of Crete before the current slump. This tourist paradise, overlooked by the eastern mountains, is magnificently situated on the Gulf of Mirabéllo. Here, and at neighbouring **Eloúnda** ❿ (10km/6 miles away),

Black knitted headscarves (saríkia), pleated, baggy trousers (vrákes) and custom-made, high boots (stivánia) are the traditional dress still worn in many parts of Crete.

Woven goods in Anógia.

A Cretan Myth

The story of the Minotaur is a complicated one that has survived through the centuries and is known all over the Western world.

King Minos, mythical king of Knossos, was the son of Zeus and the Phoenician princess Europa. Zeus, in the form of a bull, had seduced Europa and taken her off to Crete, where Minos and his brothers, Rhadamanthys and Sarpedon, were born. Minos spent nine years in the Diktean Cave with his father learning the arts of kingship, after which he banished his brothers and became sole ruler of Knossos.

Wishing to consolidate his power, Minos asked Poseidon for a sign of approval and the god provided a white bull from the sea to be sacrificed. However, the animal was so beautiful that Minos could not bring himself to kill it, so he sacrificed another in its place. This lack of gratitude enraged Poseidon, who made Pasiphaë, the wife of Minos, fall in love with the bull.

Daedalos, an ingenious member of the court,

built a hollow model of a cow for Pasiphaë in which she could hide while the bull mounted her. The result of this union was a curious child, the half-man, half-bull Minotaur. Minos was, understandably, furious when he found out about Pasiphaë's son and, after taking advice from the Oracle at Delphi, ordered Daedalos to build a huge labyrinth under the court where the Minotaur was to live.

In the meantime the white bull had been taken to the Peloponnese by Herakles as one of his 12 tasks. There it did great damage and Minos' son, Androgeos, set out to hunt it. While out hunting, Androgeos was killed by a jealous Athenian rival. In response, Minos immediately sent his fleet to Athens and after a long war, defeated the Athenians. The Cretan king then demanded a tribute; the sacrifice of seven young men and seven maidens of Athens every year, who were to be delivered to the labyrinth to be killed by the Minotaur.

One year Theseus, son of the Athenian king Aegeus, volunteered for the sacrifice. While on Crete he met and fell in love with Ariadne, the daughter of Minos, who helped Theseus find his way through the labyrinth by providing a ball of thread that he could unravel to mark his way and prevent him getting lost. He entered the maze, killed the Minotaur with his father's sword, and released the surviving captives.

Vase depicting Theseus Slaying the Minotaur, c.540 BC.

Triumphant, he and Ariadne fled by sea, but the story does not have a happy ending. Theseus turned out to be a fickle lover. He soon abandoned Ariadne on Náxos, where she became the consort of the god Dionysos. Theseus was forgetful as well as fickle. He promised his father that if he survived his battle with the Minotaur he would raise a white sail on his ship as he returned home. Unfortunately, this slipped his mind, and when his father saw the ship approaching harbour with no white sail visible he assumed his beloved son was dead. Overcome with grief he drowned himself in the sea which henceforth bore his name (Aegean).

are some of the island's best and most expensive hotels. Unfortunately Agios Nikólaos does lack a decent beach, though there are some passable sands a little way southeast. Restaurants and hotels, bars and cafés cluster around Kitroplatía cove and the small so-called bottomless lake, connected to the now-disused harbour by a canal. Although it is not what most visitors come here for, the town does have a pleasant **Archaeological Museum** (Tue–Sun 8.30am–2.40pm; charge) and a **Folk Museum** (summer Tue–Sun 10am–2pm and 5–7pm; charge).

The nearby island of **Spinalónga** (summer daily 9am–6.45pm, winter by arrangement), an isolated leper colony until 1957 (the last in Europe), with a massive Venetian fortress and poignant memories, is readily reached from Eloúnda or much closer Pláka by boat. The island was immortalised in Victoria Hislop's eponymous novel, and the rather more successful Greek TV series based on it – Greek tourists appear in droves.

Clinging to the hillside 11km (7 miles) from Agios Nikólaos is **Kritsá** , which claims to be "the largest village in Crete". Immediately below Kritsá stands the church of **Panagía Kyrá,** Crete's greatest Byzantine treasure (daily 8.30am–5.30pm; charge). Although many of its frescoes are damaged or still uncleaned, the *Presentation of the Virgin* and *Last Supper* appear in full glory.

Some 3km (2 miles) beyond the church lie the ruins of **ancient Lato** (Lató; unlocked). The pleasure here lies not so much in the fairly extensive remains of a Doric city (although they are worth seeing) but the superb views north towards the Gulf of Mirabéllo and the Sitía mountains.

East of Agios Nikólaos, a motorway is slowly being extended, to bypass some of the sites below en route to Sitía. After 19km (12 miles) on the old road, **Gourniá** ⓬ (Tue–Sun 8.30am–2.40pm; charge) is reached. Spread over a ridge, overlooking the sea, are remains, not of another palace, but of streets and houses of a Minoan town, the best preserved on the island. Especially in spring, when the site is covered with a riot of flowers, even those

There are thousands of irrigation windmills across the Lasíthi Plateau, but none function any longer except as taverna decor, disconnected from their water pumps.

The grand stairway at Phaistos.

bored with old stones will appreciate the site.

From highways new and old, a side road drops to the fishing port-resort of **Móhlos**, with the cleanest swimming on a coast generally beset by tide- and wind-borne debris. The tiny island opposite, which can be readily reached by strong swimmers, bears the same name as the village and has scanty Minoan ruins. Some way beyond is the larger island of **Psíra** where a Minoan town and port are being excavated. (Both islands can be reached by hired boat from Móhlos.)

Sitía and eastern Crete

Sitía ⑬, 70km (43 miles) from Agios Nikólaos, is a laid-back town which, to the delight of (mostly French and Italian) visitors and the chagrin of locals, has not yet hit the big time, something unlikely to happen soon as the project to enlarge the local airport to international status has been suspended indefinitely. Attractions include an inconspicuous Venetian fort, an **Archaeological Museum** (Tue–Sun 8.30am–2.40pm; charge) full of finds

from Zakros, a **Folklore Museum** (Mon–Fri10am–1pm; charge) and a reasonable, in-town beach.

The still-active **Toploú Monastery** (daily 9am–1pm and 2–6pm, winter until 4pm), its tall 16th-century Italianate bell tower beckoning like a mosque's minaret, stands in splendid isolation in the middle of nowhere, 24km (15 miles) beyond Sitía. Its greatest treasure is a minutely detailed 18th-century icon painted by Ioannis Kornaros. The monastery derived its name from a renowned artillery piece (*top* is Turkish for cannon) which formerly guarded it. The monks also had other methods of protecting themselves: observe the machicolation above the monastery gate through which they poured hot oil over their assailants.

The Orthodox Church has long courted controversy by proposing to lease some of Toploú's vast landholdings for a 7,000-bed tourist complex just north on Cape Síderos, complete with golf course. This has outraged environmentalists who point out that there is very little water left for such a development in eastern Crete,

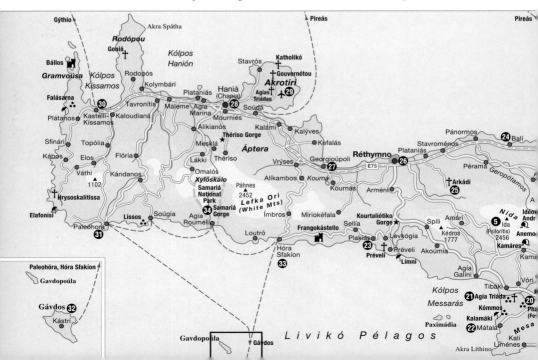

however, economic realities since 2009 mean the project, like the airport expansion, is now shelved.

After a further 9km (6 miles), **Väï** ⑭ is renowned for its myriad palm trees and the large, sandy beach that suggests faraway tropical regions. The inedible-date palm trees (*Phoenix theophrasti*) are not the species associated with desert islands, but are actually native to Crete, Amorgós, Anáfi and southwestern coastal Turkey. The beach here is usually crowded: for a more relaxed time, make for the quieter, mostly palm-free **Ítanos**, 1km (0.5 mile) farther north.

Southwards from Väï is **Palékastro**, which hit the headlines in the 1990s because of the discovery of what may be the largest Minoan town yet – sadly, funds are lacking to uncover it. Nearby beaches, particularly Hióna and Koureménos with its windsurf school, are well worth visiting.

Zákros

Some 20km (12 miles) further on you come to inland **Ano Zákros** and beachside **Káto Zákros**, the latter adjacent to the fourth great Minoan **palace of Zakros** ⑮ (daily, summer 8am–4.40pm, winter 8am–2.40pm). Hikers will prefer to make their way from upper to lower Zákros by walking through the spectacular **Ravine of the Dead**, where caves were used for Minoan burials.

The Neo-palatial period ruins at Zakros, 43km (27 miles) from Sitía, are often waterlogged, partly because Crete is tipping over longitudinally, with its eastern end sinking below and its western end rising above sea level and coastal water-tables. The main site has its customary central courtyard and royal, religious and domestic buildings and workshops radiating outwards; a spring-fed cistern still contains fresh water, inhabited by pond terrapins. Close by are the remains of a Minoan hillside town and a sheltered harbour, ideally situated for trade with the Levant and Egypt.

Unusually, the Zakros dig was originally privately funded. In 1961, prominent Greek archaeologist Nikolaos Platon was asked by the Pomerances, a New York business couple, if any

Lake Voulisméni at Agios Nikólaos was once said to be bottomless, and the home of spirits. Unromantic modern surveyors have found that it is about 70 metres (230ft) deep and fed by an underground river.

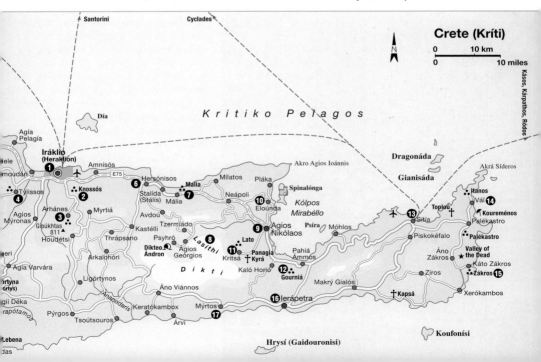

The text of the Law Code of Gortys is written in "ox-plough" fashion, reading left to right along one line, then right to left along the next.

Sitía harbour.

Minoan sites had still to be excavated. Yes, he told them. So what, they asked, was the problem? Money, was the reply. With that, the Pomerances underwrote the dig with no strings attached. Platon died in 1992 at the age of 83, but excavations continue.

Back at Gourniá, a flat road crosses the island's isthmus to **Ierápetra** (35km/22 miles from Agios Nikólaos), the largest town on the south coast (and the most southerly town in all Europe). Despite a small Venetian fort (daily summer 8.30am–7.30pm) and and a small but interesting archaeological "collection" (Tue–Sun 8.30am–3pm) inside a former Koranic school, it's an un-atmospheric supply point for the region's farmers, who have carpeted the coastal plain either side of town with plastic vegetable greenhouses and pretty well put a damper on in-town tourist development.

Fifteen kilometres (9 miles) to the west lies the pretty little beach resort of **Mýrtos** ⓱, with a villagey feel. Eastwards 24km (15 miles) from Ierápetra, past sheltered Agía Fotiá and Ahliá coves, is the more conventional "strip"

resort, and gently shelving beach, of **Makrý Gialós**. From here a minor coastal road leads to the originally 14th-century **Kapsá Monastery**, built snugly into the cliffs at the entrance to a gorge. Encased in a silver casket is the skull of the monk Gerondoyannis, a 19th-century faith healer who, despite not being canonised, is a cult figure.

South from Iráklio

The main road south-southwest from Iráklio, over a lower point in the island's spine, goes via **Agía Varvára**, near which is the **Ómfalos** or "navel stone" supposedly marking the centre of Crete. Just beyond it you will have a breathtaking view of the **Mesará Plain**. Rich soil and a benign climate make this a cornucopia, producing a high percentage of the island's crops.

At the edge of the plain, 40km (25 miles) from Iráklio, is the almost sacred village of **Agii Déka** (Holy Ten), with its heavily restored medieval church, into which are incorporated fragments from the nearby site of Gortys (modern Górtyna). Agii Déka is renowned because in AD 250, during the persecution of the Christians under Emperor Decius, 10 men were executed here for failing to make sacrifice for the ancient gods and the health of the empire, becoming in due course among the most revered of Cretan saints.

After another 1km (½ mile), you reach **Gortys** ⓲ (modern Górtyna; daily summer 8am–6.40pm, winter8am–4.40pm; charge). This was the capital of the Romans who first came to Crete in the 2nd century BC, but weren't in firm possession of the island until 67 BC. Outstanding and upstanding are the Roman *odeion*, the theatre and a triple-naved basilica, although Italian excavations continue. The last is by far the best-preserved early church in Crete, built to house the tomb of St Titus, Crete's first bishop, who died in AD 105. However, the most renowned artefacts are some stone blocks incorporated into the

odeion. About 2,500 years ago more than 17,000 characters were incised on these blocks to produce the Law Code of Gortys, which starkly differentiates the rights of free men and slaves.

Those in search of more ruins, or of health and good swimming, may head south to **Léndas** ⓲ (72km/45 miles from Iráklio). Nearby ancient **Lebena** was the port for Gortys, and its therapeutic springs made it a renowned healing sanctuary with an **Asklepion** (temple to Asklepios, the god of healing). Only traces of this sanctuary – notably a Hellenistic mosaic – remain. In an attempt to equal, if not emulate, the ancients, nude bathing has become popular at **Dytikós**, Léndas's best beach, 15 minutes' walk beyond the headland at the western end of the village.

Phaistos ⓴ (Festós), Crete's second great Minoan site, occupies a magnificent location 16km (10 miles) west of Gortys (daily summer 8am– 6.40pm, winter 8am–4.40pm). Most of the remains date from the Neo-palatial period, although part of the floor plan of the Proto-palatial

palace is discernible. State rooms, religious quarters, workshops, store rooms and functional plumbing can all be identified. An outstanding sight is the Grand Stairway on the west side. Nearby, again on a glorious site with views of the Libyan Sea, are the attractive Minoan ruins of **Agía Triáda** ㉑ (winter 8am–2.40pm, summer 10am–4pm), which was probably a summer villa.

Next, on to **Mátala** ㉒, 70km (43 miles) from Iráklio. This seaside village first gained renown when the sandstone caves in the cliffs around the small, sandy beach – actually ancient tombs – became home to substantial colonies of 1960s and 1970s hippies; Joni Mitchell stopped by too, and her song *Carey* refers explicitly to the place. Today Mátala is a mainstream resort, expensive and often crowded out in season, the cave-dwellers long since evicted and the cliff has become an archaeological site. The main beach is still excellent, but for more seclusion walk half an hour south to "**Red Beach**", although **Kalamáki** beach to the north is much

The 16th-century Venetian fortress on Spinalónga, near Agios Nikólaos, was used as a leper colony until 1957 – the last in Europe.

Káto Zákros bay.

larger and has a Minoan site, Kommos (closed for excavations).

The even larger south-coast resort of **Agía Galíni** lies a bit further west on the Gulf of Mesará, 70km (43 miles) from Iráklio. If Mátala proved too boisterous, then Agía Galíni with its lively, long-hours nightlife, will be far more so. The harbour, with a short quay and a pedestrianised main street jammed with tavernas and bars, is enclosed within steep slopes covered with modest hotels.

West to Réthymno

You are now in western Crete, and Réthymno province; **Plakiás ㉓**, flanked by five beaches and a spectacular mountain backdrop, lies some 40km (25 miles) from the provincial capital, and equally far from Agía Galíni via roundabout roads. The main cultural excursion from Plakiás is to **Préveli Monastery** (13km/8 miles), passing en route the evocative but fenced-off ruins of **Agios Ioánnis Monastery** (also known as Káto Préveli), and a much-photographed arched **bridge**. Préveli itself (daily

The Fortétsa, Réthymno's medieval stronghold.

Apr–May 9am–7pm, June–Oct 9am–1.30pm and 3.30–7pm; charge) has a superb position, and a courtyard fountain with the inscription "Wash your sins, not just your face."

A double bronze statue of a gun-toting monk and a Commonwealth soldier commemorates Préveli's crucial role in sheltering defeated stragglers from the 1941 Battle of Crete; they were evacuated to Egypt by submarine from **Límni** beach below at the mouth of the **Kourtaliótiko Gorge**, which had a local palm forest nearly as large as that at Váï – until it caught fire in 2010. Luckily, natural regeneration is occurring.

West of Plakiás along the coast, the next resort of consequence huddles around the the Venetian **castle of Frangokástello**, overlooking a good sandy beach. On 18 May 1828, 385 freedom fighters from Sfakiá and the mainland, commanded by Epirot warlord Hatzimihalis Daliannis, were killed here by a superior force of Cretan Muslims; the mysterious *drossoulítes* (dewy ones), a sunrise mirage particular to late May, are said to be their ghosts.

Back in Iráklio, the oleander-lined E75 highway runs west towards Réthymno. Some, however, might prefer the more leisurely, picturesque but winding old road. Alternatively, leave the new road 25km (16 miles) along to arrive in **Fódele**, a small village rich in orange trees and locally made embroidery. A restored house here is claimed as the birthplace in 1541 of Domenikos Theotokopoulos, better known as El Greco. Back on the expressway, turn seawards after a further 18km (11 miles) to reach the popular resort of **Balí ㉔**, clustered around three small bays at the foot of a hill.

At **Stavroménos** or **Platanián**, turn southeast for beautifully situated **Arkádi Monastery ㉕** (9am–8pm), 80km (50 miles) from Iráklio or 25km (16 miles) before Réthymno, Crete's most sacred shrine. In 1866, the monastery, sheltering hundreds of rebel fighters and their families, was attacked by Muslim Cretans. Rather than surrender, the abbot ordered that gunpowder stored in the now roofless room in the northwest corner of the courtyard be ignited, thus killing up to 1,500 Muslims and Orthodox. The photogenic, 16th-century rococo church façade survived, and featured prominently on the now-retired 100-drachma note.

Réthymno

Réthymno ㉖, 77km (48 miles) from Iráklio, prides itself on being Crete's intellectual capital – thanks to the internationally respected, 1973-founded university. Réthymno still possesses an intact Old Town with a small and extremely picturesque Venetian harbour guarded by an elegant lighthouse, although most of the medieval walls disappeared early in the 20th century. The only surviving remnant is the Porta Guora, or Great Gate, leading into Four Martyrs Square. The martyrs in question were hanged here in 1824 for apostasising from Islam back to Orthodox Christianity – a capital crime under Ottoman law.

West of the harbour looms the immense **Fortétsa** (daily mid-March–mid-Nov, dawn to dusk; charge), said

Navigating the waters off the coast near Réthymno.

to be the largest Venetian castle ever built. The most intact, and most interesting, structure inside is the **Sultan Ibrahim Mosque** dating from 1647, the largest domed structure in Greece. Réthymno's other monumental attractions – the ornate, still-flowing **Rimóndi Fountain**, the Venetian **loggia** and the **Nerantzés Mosque** –a converted Venetian church – all lie between the harbour and the fortress. Spare time for the **Archeological Museum** (Tues–Sun 8.30am–2.40pm; charge) boasting a fine collection of painted clay sarcophagi, and the **Historical and Folklore Museum** (April–Oct Mon–Sat 9.30am–2.30pm & 6–9pm; charge) with a wealth of rural impedimenta.

Venetian houses with unexpected architectural delights can be found in the narrow streets linking these sights, while Ottoman features in the shape of fountains with calligraphic inscriptions and overhanging enclosed wooden balconies – the famous local *kióskia* – are evidence that Réthymno was almost one-third Muslim before 1923.

Sun-worshippers appreciate Réthymno's wide beach, beginning immediately east of the harbour behind a palm-shaded promenade and stretching for several kilometres past the new town.

Réthymno and Haniá to the west are joined by the E75 and a less used old road. Leave the highway after 23km (14 miles) for **Georgioúpoli** ㉗ at the mouth of the River Almyrós, a pleasant resort with a long beach; 4km (2½ miles) inland is Crete's only freshwater lake, **Kournás**, with tavernas, idyllic swimming and pedaloes or kayaks to rent.

Haniá

Haniá ㉘ (Chania), 59km (37 miles) from Réthymno, one of the oldest continuously inhabited cities in the world, is Crete's second city and was its capital until 1971. Focus of the old town is the double Venetian harbour, whose broad quays are backed by characterful, colourful old buildings, their reflections shimmering in the water. The ambience is of the Levant and this is the place for the *vólta*, the evening stroll.

Cretan goatherds.

The restored 1645-vintage **Mosque of Küçük Hasan** (Yali Tzami), by two years the oldest mosque in Crete, stands at one end of the quay and now hosts art exhibitions; the **Fírkas Bastion** occupies the other end, next to the moderately interesting **Naval Museum** (daily, summer 9am–3.40pm, winter 9am–1.40pm; charge). On the bastion, in December 1913, the King of Greece officially raised the national flag for the first time on Crete. Behind the Naval Museum, inside San Salvatore church at the top of Theotokopoúlou, the well-designed **Byzantine Museum** (Tue–Sun 8.30am–2.40pm) showcases icons, jewellery, coins, a floor mosaic and fresco fragments rescued from country chapels Both Theotokopoúlou and its perpendicular Angélou have splendid examples of domestic Venetian and Ottoman architecture.

The **Archaeological Museum** (April–Oct Tue–Sun 8am–8pm, Mon 2–8pm, Nov–March Tues–Sun 8.30am–3pm), inside a former Franciscan monastery, has a collection strongest on painted Minoan larnakes,

Cretan coins with local motifs, Roman statuettes, and Hellenistic mosaics. Two blocks west, on Kondyláki, **Etz Hayyim Synagogue** (Mon–Fri10am–5pm), is the sole reminder of Haniá's pre-World War II Jewish community of about 350; it has been lovingly restored from its wrecked state, including the *mikveh* or ritual bath, fed by a natural spring.

In the New Town, visit the lofty glass-roofed cruciform **market**, modelled on the Marseilles halles and dating from 1913, still overflowing with vegetables, fruit, fish, meat, herbs and spices, cheese and wine.

Akrotíri

Akrotíri ㉙ (see page 301), a limestone peninsula stretching northeastwards from Haniá to enclose enormous, strategic **Soúda Bay**, is full of interest. First visit the hill of **Profítis Ilías**, where revolutionary Cretans gathered in 1897 to demand union with Greece. Here are the simple graves of Eleftherios Venizelos, born outside Haniá at Mourniés, and his son Sofoklis.

The lighthouse at Haniá, designed like a minaret, dates from 1833 – 40, when Crete was handed over to Egypt as a reward for helping the Turks crush the rebellious Greeks.

Arkádi Monastery can lay claim to a significant past.

AKROTÍRI MONASTERIES

The Akrotíri peninsula has a cluster of historic **monasteries**. The first encountered, 16km (10 miles) from Haniá, is 17th-century **Agías Triádas** (aka Zangarolón; daily 9–7pm; charge), built in Venetian Rococo style, splendid but somewhat commercialised with its keen souvenir sellers. A further 4km (2.5 miles) away and to the north stands **Gouvernétou**, a working monastery not open to the non-Orthodox. From Gouvernétou a rough 40-minute downhill scramble – you need good boots – leads to the abandoned, enchanting and possibly enchanted **Katholikó Monastery**, concealed in a goat-patrolled ravine. Founded in about 1050, this is, if not the oldest, certainly one of the first monastic settlements on Crete.

Other graves, 1,527 of them, are found at the immaculately maintained **Commonwealth Cemetery** near the Soúda shore, where British and Commonwealth troops killed during the 1941 Battle of Crete are buried.

Sandy **Stavrós** cove in the far northwest served as a location for Zorba the Greek (see also page 288).

Southwest from Haniá

From Haniá the westward coast road passes several busy small resorts like **Agía Marína** and **Plataniás** that merge imperceptibly with each other, as well as several thousand Germans buried in the well-tended cemetery at **Máleme**.

Beyond Kolymbári, one emerges at a viewpoint over the broad **bay of Kíssamos**, cradled by the peninsulas of **Gramvoúsa** and **Rodópou**, together resembling rabbit's ears on the map.

A descent to the broad coastal plain brings you to pleasant but characterless **Kastéli-Kissámou** ㉚ (42km/26 miles from Haniá), mostly visited for its ferry connection to the

Peloponnese but also endowed with a superb **Archaeological Museum** (Tue–Sun 8.30am–2.40pm; charge), particularly strong on the Hellenistic and Roman town here – the highlight is the mosaic of the Four Seasons on the villa floor upstairs. The closest memorable beach lies 17km (11 miles) west, via Plátanos village at **Falásarna**, with a small ancient city thrown into the bargain. Boat (or jeep) excursions go from Kastéli to the "Blue Lagoon" and Venetian island fortress at **Bállos**, at the tip of Gramvoúsa.

From Kallergianá just east of Kastéli, a good road leads south through lush countryside. There are chestnut orchards at **Élos** – where the harvest is celebrated with an October Chestnut Festival– while villages like **Topólia**, **Kefáli** and **Váthi** have lovely old chapels with 14th-century frescoes. Beyond Váthi, the route forges through a gorge to the **Hrysoskalítissa** (Golden Stairway) **Convent** (8am–sunset; charge), 39km (25 miles) from Kastélli. The name refers to the legend that one of the 90 steps

Mosque of Küçük Hasan on Haniá's waterfront.

descending from the terrace appears as gold to the extremely pure at heart. Some 5km (3 miles) beyond, the road ends at **Elafonísi**, a small islet sheltering a shallow lagoon and a pale-sand beach of near-tropical beauty; it is a protected zone and thus pretty undeveloped, but it gets hopelessly crowded in season.

A busier road from Tavronítis, near Máleme, leads via **Kándanos**, with more frescoed late Byzantine chapels, to **Paleóhora** ❸ (76km/47 miles from Haniá), a friendly resort with a ruined Venetian castle bracketed by a pebble beach (east) and a long sandy one (west), the latter a favourite with windsurfers. Boats leave at least twice weekly for the islet of **Gávdos** ❸, Europe's southernmost point, now developed touristically but still remaining blissfully calm outside August.

Hóra Sfakíon ❸, 75km (47 miles) via an entirely different road from Haniá, is the "capital" of rugged Sfakiá, celebrated as the one corner of Crete that never fully submitted to Venetian, Ottoman or Nazi rule. Like Préveli, it was a major evacuation point for fleeing Allied soldiers after the Battle of Crete. The current major role of this small, cliff-hanging port is as the local small-ferry terminus, with more services to Gávdos and a daily line west along the roadless coast as far as Paleóhora, stopping en route at the tiny resorts of Loutró, Agía Roúmeli and Soúgia.

But you needn't rely on the boats – west of Hóra Sfakíon is some of the best shoreline trekking in the islands. The path threads "**Sweetwater Beach**" – the closest good one to the town – en route to **Loutró**, pleasant, although again beachless, before traversing **Agios Pávlos beach** with its Byzantine chapel on the way to Agía Rouméli (see page 304) – a long day's hike. Only the most experienced and fit hill-walkers should tackle the next tricky section to enjoyable **Soúgia**, which has a good beach, before the easy final-day section via **ancient Lissos** to Paleóhora. Lissos was known in antiquity for its Asklepion or therapeutic centre, attracting the unwell from far and wide. The Temple of

Haniá harbour in the early morning light.

Octopus hanging out to dry.

Asklepios is in ruins but its mosaic floor can still be seen.

The Samariá Gorge

For most active, first-time visitors, however, the one "must" walk is the spectacular, four-to-six-hour traverse of the **Samariá Gorge** ㉞, at 16km (10 miles) among the longest in Europe. The hike starts with a steep stair-path descent from **Xylóskalo** at 1,200 metres (3,937ft) elevation, at the southern end of the vast **Omalós** plain, itself a 45km (28-mile) tortuous drive from Haniá. Within an hour or so of walking, the path is 600 metres (1,968ft) lower in altitude; some 10km

Wild blooms.

(6½ miles) below the start point, the hamlet of **Samariá**, abandoned in 1962, comes into view.

The going now gets tougher underfoot, albeit with less of a gradient, and involves criss-crossing the riverbed, which usually has water in it. Flash floods can occur in spring and autumn, and patrolling wardens' warnings should be heeded. The gorge progressively narrows and the walls soar straight upwards for 300 to 600 metres (1,000–2,000ft). Soon after passing Aféndis Hristós Chapel, the **Siderespórtes** (Iron Gates) are reached and the gorge, scarcely penetrated by sunlight here, is little more than 3.5 metres (11ft) wide.

The gorge falls within a national park strictly administered by the Haniá Forest Service, which specifically forbids a long list of activities including camping, lighting fires or making loud noises (including singing). Since its creation in 1962, the park has functioned well as a wildlife refuge. You are most unlikely to spot any *krí-krí* (wild ibex), but botanists will be delighted, while ornithologists may glimpse vultures overhead.

You emerge from the narrows at old **Agía Rouméli**, abandoned after World War II, but still face another 2km (1 mile) of hot tramping to reach its modern coastal successor. A cold beer and refreshing swim off the long sand-and-pebble beach are in order, but be aware of the time (and the seat quota) of the last boat out in either direction, or you may find yourself making an unplanned overnight stop here. If you forget the time, or if you decide you would like to overnight anyway, there are two places to stay (see Accommodation, page 334).

The gorge is open 1 May–31 October from dawn to about 4pm (charge), subject to amendments for bad weather. After 4pm you will only be allowed into the first 2km (1 mile) from either end, and the wardens ensure that nobody camps in the gorge.

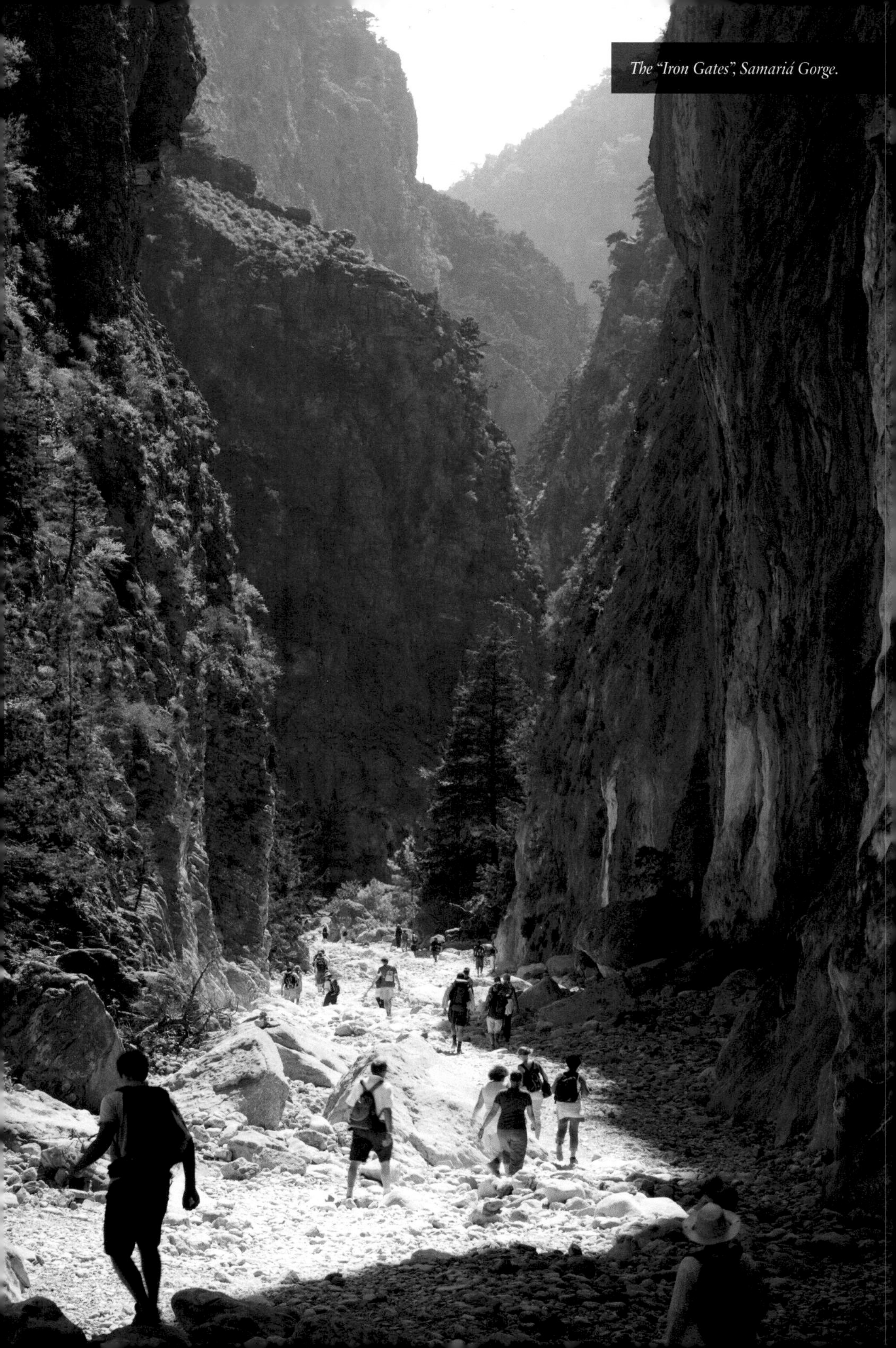

The "Iron Gates", Samariá Gorge.

THE PALACE OF KNOSSÓS

Until 1894, the Minoan civilisation was little more than a myth. Now its capital is one of the largest and best-restored sites in all Greece.

Some visitors to Knossos (modern Greek Knossós) find the concrete reconstructions and repainted frescoes (often extrapolated from very small existing fragments) aid comprehension. But for many, used to other, more recent, ruins that are clearly defensive or overtly religious, the site is mysterious. Can we hope to look back at fragments of a culture from 3,500 years ago and understand its imperatives and subtleties? Hiring a licensed guide – they hang about waiting for custom near the ticket booth – will make a huge difference in your experience of the palace.

In legend, Knossos was the labyrinth of King Minos, where he imprisoned the Minotaur, the human-taurine child of his wife Pasiphaë. In reality, the place was probably not a palace in the modern sense, but perhaps an administrative and economic centre, overseen by spiritual leaders.

Among the 1,300 rooms of the main palace were both the sacred and the commercial: lustral baths for holy ceremonies; storerooms for agricultural produce; workshops for metallurgy and stone-cutting. Nearby are the Royal Villa and the Little Palace.

Try to visit early or late in the day (better still, visit out of season), to avoid the worst of the substantial crowds, and to avoid being swept along by the flow. Look for the subtle architectural delights – light wells to illuminate the larger rooms; hydraulic controls providing water for drinking, bathing and flushing away sewage; drains with parabolic curves at the bends to prevent overflow.

The site is open daily Apr–Sept 8am–7.30pm Oct–Mar 8.30am–3pm (charge).

Minoan fresco at the Iráklio Archeological Museum.

A (replica) fresco depicting the capture of a wild bull decorates the ramparts of the north entrance, leading to the road to Knossós's harbour at Amnisos.

The famous double horns now sitting on the south facade were once regarded as sacred symbols, though perhaps this is an overworking of the bull motif of the site.

The Cup Bearers fresco.

CONTROVERSIAL RESTORATIONS

In 1878 a local merchant, Minos Kalokairinos, uncovered part of Knossos, but the Muslim owners of the land prevented further excavation and even wealthy Heinrich Schliemann got entangled in unproductive negotiations for purchase.

However, once Crete gained autonomy in 1898, the way was open for archaeologist Arthur Evans to purchase the site and begin excavating. He worked here from 1900 until 1931, though by 1903 most of Knossos had been uncovered.

Evans's use of reinforced concrete to reconstruct long-gone timber columns, and his completely speculative upper-storey reconstructions, have received considerable criticism. Moreover, the Minoan frescoes are not only arbitrarily placed, but almost completely modern, painted from scratch by assistants Piet de Jong and the two Emile Gilliéron, father and son. Others have charged that Evans, a fairly typical Victorian chauvinist, manipulated evidence to fit his theory of the thalassocratic Minoans as prehistoric proto-British imperialists. It's also clear that both the restoration and fresco-retouching was heavily influenced by the Art Nouveau and Art Deco styles prevalent at the time.

Sir Arthur Evans, the English archaeologist whose reconstruction of Knossos, a significant quantity of it based on conjecture, was to prove controversial.

Wandering around Knossos – but the scale of the site is most apparent from the air: nearly 2 hectares (5 acres) of palaces ruled a population of perhaps 100,000.

Bull fresco at the Iráklio Archeological Museum.

INSIGHT GUIDES TRAVEL TIPS
GREEK ISLANDS

Transport

Accommodation

Eating Out

Activities

A – Z

Language

Further Reading

TRANSPORT

GETTING THERE AND GETTING AROUND

GETTING THERE

By air

Greece has good air connections with the rest of the world and is served by numerous international airlines. Charter flights to the islands generally operate from early May to late October, even into November to Rhodes and Crete. Unless you are on a multi-stop or round-the-world ticket, e-tickets bought online are the norm. The airlines' own websites can be a good source of discount tickets, matching (or nearly so) prices offered by general consolidator travel sites.

The majority of scheduled airline passengers travelling to Greece make Athens's Elefthérios Venizélos Airport (www.aia.gr) their point of entry, though a number of flights (from the rest of Europe only) arrive at Thessaloníki's Makedonía Airport, which gives easier access to certain north Aegean islands. Scheduled flights (easyJet and other no-frills lines) also go much of the year to Rhodes, Crete (Iráklio or Haniá), Mýkonos, Santoríni and Corfu.

Between Venizélos Airport, central Athens and Piraeus there are various connecting services. Line 3 of the metro (takes you – surprisingly slowly, every half-hour – into town for €8. Alternatively, take the X95 express bus (scarcely slower than the metro) all the way to central Sýndagma Square (Platía Syndagmátos or the X96 express bus to Piraeus port. All express buses depart from outside arrivals, with the same frequency (every 15 minutes) and the same fare (€5 at the time of writing).

A taxi from Venizélos Airport to the centre of Athens will cost about €33–40 depending on time of day or night and your final destination, including airport supplement and per-bag fee. Traffic congestion has improved since the opening of the Attikí Odós (ring road) round northern Athens, but the journey time can still amount to over an hour.

Makedonía Airport is 15 km (9 miles) southeast of Thessaloníki. Regular buses go to the city centre (90 cents, coin-machine-sold tickets, no change given) and take around 35 minutes. Taxis take 15–20 minutes and cost €12–13.

By sea

Most visitors entering Greece by sea do so from Italy. You can catch a boat to Greece from Venice, Ancona and Bari, but the most regular service is from Brindisi.

Daily ferry lines (less frequent in low season) connect Brindisi with the three main western ports: Corfu, Igoumenítsa and Pátra. Corfu is a 6.5-hour trip; Igoumenítsa 8 hours; and Pátra 11 to 14 hours, depending on whether you take a direct boat or one that makes a stop in Igoumenítsa. The "Superfast" ferries between Ancona and Pátra offer an efficient 22-hour crossing.

Igoumenítsa is the ideal port of call for southern Corfu, Paxí or Levkáda, while Pátra is best if you want to head directly to Athens or the southern Ionian islands. Regular buses and trains connect Pátra and Athens (4 hours distant by bus). If you plan to take your car on the boat, you should definitely make reservations well in advance. Otherwise, arriving a few hours before the departure time should suffice, except during peak seasons when booking in advance is essential for seats or berths.

Useful airlines serving Greece from overseas anglophone countries

At the moment, there are only guaranteed direct services to Greece from Great Britain. Services from Eire and North America come and go – Delta and USAir fly in from the American east coast only between May and October – and there has not been non-stop service from Australia for many years.
Aegean Airlines (www.aegeanair. com) Between Athens and London

(Gatwick, Stansted or Heathrow) and Manchester
British Airways (www.ba.com) Between Athens–Heathrow and Thessaloníki–Gatwick
easyJet (www.easyjet.com) Between various UK airports and Athens, Thessaloníki, Rhodes, Corfu, Kefaloniá, Kos, Zákynthos, Haniá, Iráklio
Ryanair (www.ryanair.com) Between

various UK airports and same destinations as easyJet, but not Athens or Iráklio
Qatar Air (www.qatarairways.com) Between Athens and New York
Delta Airlines (www.delta.com) Seasonally between New York and Athens
US Airways (www.usairways.com) Seasonally between Philadelphia and Athens

By land

From Europe

The most direct overland route from northwestern Europe to Greece is a long one: 3,000km (1,900 miles) from London to Athens – a rather arduous and impractical travel option if you are just trying to get to Greece for a brief holiday. The final approach, from Austria onward, will be via either Serbia and FYROM (Former Yugoslav Republic of Macedonia), or Romania and Bulgaria. There's not much to choose between these; the Serbian motorway network is excellent, FYROM's less so. Bulgaria has good motorways either side of Sofia, but approaching the Greek frontier there are still many hazardous under-construction stretches.

It is no longer possible to buy a through train ticket from the UK to Greece, and economically it never made much sense. If, as a railpass holder, you're intent on the journey, consult the ultra-useful rail-travel planning site www.seat61.com. Greece no longer has rail links with any of its land neighbours, so the only feasible route is via Italy, with a final ferry crossing as above.

From Turkey

If you are travelling strictly overland to Greece from Asia you will pass through Istanbul and cross into Greece at the Évros River. Roads are good, and the journey from Istanbul to Thessaloníki

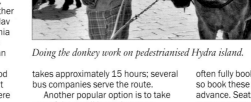

Doing the donkey work on pedestrianised Hydra island.

takes approximately 15 hours; several bus companies serve the route.

Another popular option is to take one of the small boats between western Turkish ports and select Greek islands just opposite. Fares are overpriced for the distance involved, but it is undeniably convenient. The most reliable links are from Çesme to Híos (all year), Bodrum to Kos (the cheapest crossing) and Kuşadası to Sámos (no cars carried).

GETTING AROUND

Public Transport

By air

Flying to or between islands during peak season is considerably more expensive than travelling by boat (up to three times more than a ferry seat, just under double the price of a cabin berth). Fares vary wildly with demand, but as an example the 50–55-minute flight between Athens and Sámos costs anywhere between €65 and €140 one-way in economy class.

Expect at least one of the domestically operating airlines listed in the box below to vanish by the time you read this. In principle, Aegean and Olympic have merged, subject to approval by the EU Commission on Competition in September 2013 (the last attempt at same was disallowed). The best, most current sources of discount tickets on extant Greek airlines are the local travel sites www.myhellas.com, www.travelplanet24.com and www.viva.gr. Foreign credit or debit cards may be viewed with some suspicion, so keep your mobile switched on when booking in case somebody wants to ring you to confirm your identity. Leave plenty of leeway in your domestic flight arrangements if you have to be back in Athens for an international flight. Island flights are

often fully booked over the summer, so book these at least a month in advance. Seats bought from a travel agency or one of the very few walk-in offices for any of the airlines listed below are subject to extra surcharges.

By bus

The KTEL is a syndicate of nationwide bus companies, including the islands, whose buses are affordable and generally punctual, although on the larger islands like Crete and Lésvos frequencies can be sparse because of village depopulation. Buses on the more idiosyncratic rural routes may have a distinctly personal touch, their drivers decorating and treating the coach with great care.

Generally there is only one KTEL station per town; exceptions include Mytilíni, with two terminals, and Iráklio (Crete), with three. On smaller islands, tickets are still sold on the bus by a conductor, but on large islands like Rhodes or Crete you must buy them in advance from ticket booths.

Island buses

On the islands buses may be converted school buses, ultramodern coaches, or even (as on Lipsí) small mini-vans. Some drivers ricochet through mountain roads at death-defying speeds; accidents, however, are rare.

A bus of some description will usually meet arriving ferries (even if a boat is delayed) to transport passengers up the hill to the island's *hóra*, or capital. Bus stops are usually in main squares or by the waterfront in harbours, and vehicles may or may not run to schedule.

Athens city buses and trams

Most of the regular Athens blue-and-white buses are now modern, air-conditioned vehicles, and using them is much less of an ordeal than it used to be. They are still usually overcrowded, and routes can be a

Greek Domestic Airliines

Olympic tel: 801 11 44 444, www.olympicair.com Still possesses the largest route network, including services to obscure islands. 20-kilo baggage allowance

Aegean tel: 801 11 20 000, en.aegeanair.com Cherry-picks the more profitable domestic routes. 20-kilo baggage allowance.

Sky Express tel: 801 11 28 28 88, www.skyexpress.gr Based on Crete, with useful peripheral flights from Iráklio to other islands plus the mainland. Very expensive, though, and 15-kg luggage allowance with no carry-ons allowed in principle.

Astra tel: 2310 489390 www.astra-airlines.gr Based in Thessaloníki, with select routes to many islands.

Minoan tel: 2810 222771, www.minoanair.com Based in Iráklion, duplicating to a large extent Sky Express' route network to nearby islands.

mystery (placards at the stops list only the sequence of subsequent stops). Trolley buses, with an overhead pantograph, are marginally faster, and serve points of tourist interest. Most services run until nearly midnight, a few after that on weekends.

The most useful suburban services for tourists are the orange-and-white KTEL Attica buses going from Mavromatéon 14, by Pédio toú Areos Park, to Rafína and Lávrio (alternative ferry ports for the Cyclades) and Soúnio (for the famous Temple of Poseidon there).

Ticketing can be a trap for the unwary. Plainclothes ticket inspectors will levy fines of 60 times the basic fare for travelling with the wrong ticket, an unvalidated ticket, or no ticket. There are several kinds of tickets: a single journey ticket (€1.20); a 90-minute ticket (€1.40) allowing transfers, which must be re-validated before your last journey; a day pass valid for all urban transport methods (€4, valid 24hr from validation) and a one-week ticket good for seven days from validation. Tickets are only obtainable from a seemingly dwindling network of newsagent kiosks – most can no longer be bothered to sell them – or at booths run by the bus company itself. Athens has a unified fare structure for all means of public transport, so that tickets are completely interchangeable. Note that the express bus ticket into town from the airport is void the minute you leave that bus – no transfer allowed.

Athens metro and tram

The Athens metro system has halved travel times around the city and made a visible reduction in surface traffic. It runs from 5.30am–12.20am Sun–Thur, 5.30am–2.20am Fri–Sat, subject to strikes and staff availability. The stations themselves are palatial and squeaky-clean, with advertising placards kept to a minimum. The

Excursion boats wait in Nísyros harbour.

old ISAP line, in existence since the 1930s, has been refurbished and designated Line 1 (green on maps); it links Piraeus with Kifisiá via the city centre. Line 2 (red) links Ellinikó in the south with Anthoúpoli in the northwest of town. Line 3 (blue) joins Egáleo with the airport at Spáta, via Monastiráki. The main junction stations are Omónia, Sýndagma and Monastiráki.

A single journey on the metro is €1.40 – though it does entitle you to a transfer or two onto above-ground transport within 90 minutes. Alternatively, get a day or week pass from the attended ticket windows (you're encouraged to use the coin-op machines for simple tickets). As on the buses, plainclothes inspectors do a roaring trade in fines levied against fare dodgers.

There are also three tram lines: Néos Kósmos metro station to Agios Kosmás, Glyfáda to Néo Fáliro, and Sýndagma to Glyfáda. Single tickets on this cost €1.20, €1.40 if you want a transfer facility. Daily and weekly cards are valid on these too.

By sea

Ferries

Piraeus is the nerve centre of the Greek ferry network, and the chances are you will pass through it at least once during your stay. In roughly diminishing order of importance, Rafína, Lávrio, Vólos, Thessaloníki, Igoumenítsa, Agios Konstandínos, Kavála, Pátra, Kyllíni and Kalamáta are also useful mainland ports. In high season, especially to the Cyclades and Dodecanese, routes vary from "milk runs" on antiquated boats stopping at five islands en route to your destination, to semi-direct ones on newer craft. There is often little or no price difference, so it is worth comparison-shopping

before buying. It is also advisable not to purchase your ticket too far in advance: only around Easter; from mid-August to early September; and around election times do all classes of tickets actually sell out, but there are frequent changes to schedules which may leave you trying to get a refund if you booked early.

Personalised ticketing for all boats has long been mandatory since 2001; it is no longer possible to purchase tickets on board, though you can upgrade your class of travel. The only exceptions are a few of the ro-ro short-haul ferries (such as Igoumenítsa-Levkímmi, Páros–Andíparos).

When you buy a ticket at Piraeus, get detailed instructions on where your boat is berthed; – the quays are long and convoluted; the staff who take your ticket should also make sure you are on the right boat.

Above all, be flexible when travelling the Greek seas. Apart from schedule changes, a bad stretch of weather can keep you island-bound for as long as the wind blows above Force 7. Strikes too are often called during the summer, and usually last for a few days. Out on the islands in particular, the best way to secure accurate, up-to-the-minute information on the erratic ways of ferries is to contact the Port Authority (*limenarhio*), which monitors the movements of individual boats. Port Authority offices are usually located on the waterfront of each island's principal harbour, away from the cafés. Boats are often very late arriving – to avoid wasting time around the dock, track the real-time progress of your ferry on the live shipping map at www.marinetraffic.com.

If you are travelling by car, especially during high season, you will have to plan much further ahead because during peak season car space is sometimes booked many weeks in advance. The same applies to booking a cabin for an overnight trip during summer – and, from early August to early September, often for just a simple seat.

Gamma class – also known as *touristikí*, deck, or third – is the classic, cheap way to travel the Greek seas. Sadly, open-air deck seating is becoming a thing of the past as older boats are retired, and you may well be forced inside to take up "pullman" seats or occupy the "low class" snack bar.

Catamarans/"high speeds"

Fleets of sleek new "high speed" (*tahyplóö*) ferries or true catamarans, made in France or Scandanavia, are slowly supplanting conventional *(symvatikó)* craft (as a stroll around the quays at Piraeus will confirm). They have some advantages over hydrofoils – they can be even faster, most of them carry lots of cars, and they are permitted to sail in wind conditions of up to Force 8, whereas "dolphins" are confined to port above Force 6.5 or so. The bad news: there may be no cabins (because they mostly finish their runs before midnight), food service is even worse than on the old ferries and there are no exterior decks. The aeroplane-seating salons are ruthlessly air-conditioned and subject to a steady, unavoidable barrage of banal Greek TV on overhead monitors (even in diakikriméni or "distinguished" class). Cars cost roughly the same to convey as on the old-style boats, but seats are priced at hydrofoil levels. Fuel consumption on such craft is horrendous; they only turn a profit when at least three-quarters full, and seem to spend much of their time at half-throttle – or at anchor, except in mid-summer.

Catamarans come in all shapes and sizes, from the 300-car-carrying behemoths of NEL Lines and Hellenic Seaways in the northeast Aegean, Cyclades and central Dodecanese, to the mid-sized ones plying the Argo-Saronic, to the tiny *Sea Star* in the Dodecanese. The useful *Dodekanisos Express* and *Dodekanisos Pride* serve many more of the Dodecanese islands, and can take five cars each.

Hydrofoils

Though catamarans are undoubtedly the wave of the future, there is still some scheduled hydrofoil service to a few islands. Like catamarans, hydrofoils are more than twice as fast as the ferries and about twice as expensive but, as ex-Polish or ex-Russian river craft, are not really designed for the Aegean,

and prone to cancellation in bad weather conditions – their small rear sundecks will be swamped with spray in anything over Force 5.

Hydrofoils (nicknamed *iptaména delfínia* or "flying dolphins" in Greek) connect Piraeus with most of the Argo-Saronic region (Égina, Angístri, Póros, Ýdra and Spétses). In the northeast Aegean, there may still be local, peak-season services between Thásos and the mainland (there weren't in 2013) while in the Dodecanese all the islands between Sámos and Kos, inclusive, are served between mid-May or 1 June and October only.

Port Authority numbers

Piraeus, tel: 21045 11311 or 21041 47800 (recorded outgoing message in Greek only – this is also true of most busy island ports).
The Ionian Islands
Corfu, tel: 26610 32655
Itháki, tel: 26740 32909
Kefaloniá (Argostóli), tel: 26710 22224
Levkáda, tel: 26450 92509
Paxí, tel: 26620 32259
Zákynthos, tel: 26950 28117
The Saronic Gulf Islands
Aegina, tel: 22970 22328
Hydra, tel: 22980 52279
Póros, tel: 22980 22274
Salamína, tel: 467 7277
Spétses, tel: 22980 72245
The Cyclades
Andros, tel: 22820 71213
Íos, tel: 22860 91264
Kéa, tel: 22870 21344
Kýthnos, tel: 22810 21290
Mílos, tel: 22870 22968
Mýkonos, tel: 22890 22218
Náxos, tel: 22850 22300
Páros, tel: 22840 21240
Santoríni, tel: 22860 22239
Sérifos, tel: 22810 51470
Sífnos, tel: 22840 33617
Sýros, tel: 22810 82690
Tínos, tel: 22830 22348
The Sporades

Alónnisos, tel: 24240 65595
Skiáthos, tel: 24270 22017
Skópelos, tel: 24240 22180
Skýros, tel: 22220 93475
The NE Aegean Islands
Foúrni, tel: 22750 51207
Híos, tel: 22710 44433
Ikaría (Agios Kírykos), tel: 22750 22207
Ikaría (Évdilos), tel: 22750 31007
Lésvos (Mytilíni), tel: 22510 24515
Lésvos (Sígri), tel: 22530 54433
Límnos, tel: 22540 22225
Psará, tel: 22720 61252
Sámos (Vathý), tel: 22730 27318
Sámos (Karlóvassi), tel: 22730 30888
Sámos (Pythagório), tel: 22730 61225
Samothráki, tel: 25510 41305
Thásos (Liménas), tel: 25930 22106
Thásos (Prínos), tel: 25930 71290
The Dodecanese Islands
Astypálea, tel: 22420 61208
Hálki, tel: 22460 45220
Kálymnos, tel: 22430 29304
Kárpathos (Pigádia), tel: 22450 22227
Kásos, tel: 22450 41288
Kastellórizo, tel: 22460 49270
Kós, tel: 22420 26594
Léros (Lakki), tel: 22470 22334
Nísyros, tel: 22420 31222
Pátmos, tel: 22470 31231
Rhodes, tel: 22410 22220
Sými, tel: 22460 71205
Tílos, tel: 22460 44350
Crete
Haniá, tel: 28210 98888
Iráklio, tel: 2810 244956
Kastéli-Kissámou, tel: 28220 22024
Réthymno, tel: 28310 22276
Sitía, tel: 28430 27117

Kaïkia and taxi-boats

Apart from conventional ferries, catamarans and hydrofoils, swarms of small kaïkia (caiques) offer seasonal excursions, pitched mostly at day-trippers. Since they are chartered by travel agencies, they are exempt from Ministry of Transport fare controls – as well as from the 30-year-old scrap-the-boat rule that is haphazardly enforced in Greece for scheduled services – and they can be very expensive if used as a one-way ticket from, say, Sámos to Pátmos.

On many islands where there are remote beaches with difficult overland access – most notably Hydra, Itháki, Sými, Hálki, Kálymnos and Pátmos – local "taxi-boats" provide a fairly pricey shuttle service. They are useful, but be aware that they usually run at set hours rather than on demand – check on the return times before you set out.

Ferry/catamaran/hydrofoil timetables

The best schedule resource is the website of the GTP (Greek Travel Pages), www.gtp.gr, which is fairly accurate, with updates at least every few weeks; alternatives include www.openseas.gr (reports only 1 day at a time), and www.goferry.gr.

Alternatively, major tourist information offices (Rhodes, Iráklio, etc) supply a weekly schedule, and most offices hang a timetable in a conspicuous place so that you can look up times even if the branch is

closed. This should, however, not be relied on implicitly – last-minute changes are common. In general, for the most complete, impartial and up-to-date information on each port's sailings the best source is the Port Police (in Piraeus and most other ports), known as the *limenarhío*.

Be aware that when you enquire about ferries at a travel agent, they will sometimes inform you only of the lines with which they are affiliated.

Hiring a boat can be an option.

Private transport

Yacht charter

Chartering a yacht is one of the more exotic ways of island-hopping in Greece. It is by no means cheap, although hiring a boat with a group of friends may not far exceed the price of renting rooms every night for the same number of people.

Depending on your nautical qualifications and your taste for autonomy, you can either take the helm yourself or let a hired crew do so for you. There are thousands of yachts available for charter in Greece, all registered and inspected by the Ministry of the Merchant Marine. For more information, see our feature on sailing. Charter is best arranged in advance from overseas, through reputable agencies like Nautilus (www.nautilusyachting.com), Neilson (www.neilson.co.uk) and Sunsail (www.sunsail.com).

You may also find the following organisation worth consulting before chartering:
The Hellenic Yacht Brokers' Association
Zéa Marína, 185 36 Piraeus; tel: 21045 33134, www.hyba.gr

Taxis

Taxis in Greece, especially in Athens, merit a guidebook to themselves. There are three stages to the experience.

First: getting a taxi. It is almost impossible at certain times of the day in Athens, and probably hardest before the early afternoon meal. When you hail a taxi, try to get in before stating your destination. The drivers are very picky and often won't let you in unless you're going in their direction. If you see an empty taxi, run for it and be aggressive – otherwise you will find that some quick Athenian has beaten you to it.

Second: the ride. Make sure the taxi meter is on "1" when you start out, and not on "2" – that's the double fare, which is only permitted from midnight to 5am, or outside designated city limits. Once inside, you may find yourself with

company. Don't be alarmed. It is traditional practice for drivers to pick up two, three, even four individual passengers, provided they're going roughly in the same direction. In these cases, make a note of the meter count when you get in.

Third: navigating. You need to know exactly where you are headed. There is no equivalent requirement of London's "The Knowledge" for Athens drivers, and many will not even have a street atlas in the cab.

Fourth: paying up. If you have travelled with other passengers, make sure you aren't paying for the part of the trip that took place before you got in. You should pay the difference in meter reading between embarking and alighting, plus the minimum fare (currently €3.20). Otherwise, the meter will tell you the straight price (currently the meter runs from €1.20, not zero), which may be adjusted according to the tariff that should be on a laminated placard clipped to the dashboard. There are extra charges for each piece of luggage in the boot, for leaving or entering an airport or seaport, plus bonuses around Christmas and Easter.

Some drivers will quote you the correct price, but many others will try to rip you off, especially if you're obviously a novice. If the fare you are charged is clearly above the correct price, don't hesitate to argue, in whichever language, until you get it back down to a normal and fair price. Coming out of an airport or seaport waving 50- or 100-euro notes at a driver is asking for trouble – always keep small bills and coins handy.

These rules apply more to Athens than to the islands, although it is still necessary to be pretty assertive in Thessaloníki and on Crete or Rhodes. Shared taxis, Athens-style, are not the norm in the islands, except (oddly) on Kálymnos, where they wait for passengers and only depart when full.

Various radio taxi services exist in Athens and many larger island towns. They can pick you up within a short time of your call to a central booking number, though there are chunky surcharges for this (at least €2).

Cars

Having a car in the rural areas of the Greek islands enables you to reach a lot of otherwise inaccessible corners; however, driving a car in Athens (or any sizeable island town like Iráklio or Rhodes) is unpleasant and confusing. Tempers soon run short as signage, especially warnings of mandatory turning lanes, is practically non-existent or obscured by trees.

Car hire (rental)

Hiring a car in Greece is not always as cheap as you might hope, owing to demand, high insurance premiums and import duties. Prices – from €18 to €40 per day – vary according to the type of car, season and length of rental and should include CDW (collision damage waiver) and VAT at 23 percent. Payment can, and often must, be made with a major credit card. A full home-country driving licence (for EU/EEA residents) or an International Driving Permit (for all others) is required and you must be at least 21 years old.

From overseas, you can book a car in advance through international aggregator websites such as www.comparecarrentals.co.uk, www.skycars.co.uk, www.autoeuroupe.com, www.auto-europe.co.uk, and www.rentalcargroup.com. Only if you're a member of some corporate or other affinity group are you likely to get as good a deal (or better) directly through the websites of major rental chains like Hertz, Avis or Budget.

Driving in Greece

All EU/EEA licences, and licences held by returning diaspora Greeks irrespective of issuing country, are honoured in Greece. Conversely, all other licences – this includes North American and Australian ones – are not valid, as many tourists from those nations attempting to hire cars have discovered to their cost. These motorists must obtain an International Driving Permit before departure (issued by the AAA or CAA in North America on the spot for a nominal cost); the Greek Automobile and Touring Club (ELPA) no longer issues them to foreign nationals in Greece. With the advent of the single European market (EU), insurance Green Cards are no longer required, although you should check with your home insurer about the need for any supplementary premiums – many policies now include pan-European cover anyway.

Greek traffic control and signals are basically the same as in the rest of Continental Europe, although roundabouts are handled bizarrely by French or English standards – in many cases the traffic entering from the slip road, not that already in the circle, has the right of way – watch for "stop" or "yield" signs or invariably faded pavement markings.

Motorway speeds are routinely in excess of the nominal 100–120kph

(62–75mph) limits, and drivers overtake with abandon. On other island roads, posted limits are typically 70–90kph (40–55mph). A red light is often considered not so much an obligation as a suggestion, and oncoming drivers flashing lights at you on one-lane roads means the opposite of what it does in the UK. Here, it means: "I'm coming through" (although often it can mean "Watch out, police control ahead"). Greece has the highest accident rate in Western/ Mediterranean Europe after Portugal, so drive defensively – particularly in August, when Athenians return to their natal islands and apply urban driving habits to backcountry roads.

Greece has a mandatory seatbelt law (€350 fine for non-observance), and children under 10 are not allowed to sit in the front seat. It is an offence to drive without your licence on your person (another draconian €350 fine). Every car must also carry a first-aid kit, reflective warning triangle and 3-litre fire extinguisher (although hire companies tend to skimp on this). Police checkpoints at major (and minor) junctions are frequent, and in addition to the above offences you can be penalised for not having evidence of insurance, paid road tax or registration papers in/on the vehicle. If it's clear you've no fixed residence in Greece, your license may be confiscated and held to ransom at the nearest police station pending payment of the fine (within 10 working days; 50 percent discount on the above quoted fees).

Super and normal unleaded petrol, as well as lead-substitute super and diesel, are readily available throughout Greece, although filling up after dark can be tricky, and lead-substitute super may soon be phased out. Most garages close around 8pm and, although a rota system operates in larger towns, it is often difficult to

Breakdowns

The Greek Automobile Association (ELPA) offers a breakdown service for motorists, which is free to AA/ RAC members (on production of their membership cards). Phone 10400 for assistance nationwide. Some car-hire companies have agreements instead with competitors Hellas Service (dial 1057), Interamerican (dial 1168) or Express Service (dial 1154), but these call centres can be slow to dispatch aid. Preferably, ring a local garage number, especially if this is what the hire company instructs you to do.

ascertain which station is open. Credit cards are widely accepted, but always ask first – card-swiping machines can be mysteriously "broken".

Parking in the larger island towns is uniformly a nightmare; even assuming you find a convenient space, residents-only schemes and pay-and-display systems are the norm. Sometimes tickets are sold from kiosks, sometimes from a machine. When in doubt about a spot, don't park there – fines are typically €70 and upwards.

Road maps

Gone are the days when visitors had to suffer with mendacious or comical maps that seemed based more on wishful thinking (especially projected but unbuilt roads) than the facts on the ground. There are now three commercial Greek companies producing largely accurate maps of the country: Terrain (www.terrainmaps.gr), Emvelia (www.emvelia.gr) and Anavasi (www.anavasi.gr). They can be found country-wide, in tourist-shop racks and better bookshop chains like Newsstand or Papasotiriou. Anavasi (the best by far for Crete, and many other islands) has its own convenient shop in central Athens at Voulís 32, selling some of the other two companies' products as well. Orama is one ubiquitous map publisher whose products are worth avoiding.

Motorcycles, quad-bikes and bicycles

On most Greek islands you will find agencies that hire small motorcycles, various types of scooters, 50cc and above, and even mountain bikes. These give you the freedom to wander where you will, and weekly rates are reasonable.

For any bike of 50cc or over, both helmets and a motorcycle driving licence are theoretically required, and increasingly these rules are enforced. The UK P-type license for scooter-learners is not honoured in Greece. The ill-fitting helmets offered are a bit of a joke, but if you refuse them you may have to sign a waiver absolving the dealer of criminal/civil liability – and police checkpoints can be zealous, levying stiff fines (€175 after discount) on locals and visitors alike. Having only a car license while driving a scooter will get you another, steeper fine. Many rental agencies now refuse to give out scooters to folk without the requisite license, steering them to quad bikes instead – which accounts for their sudden popularity. They are unstable on turns (thus helmets are supplied for riding them too) and arguably the stupidest looking road

conveyance ever devised – they're basically modified tractors – but given the two-wheeler license law you may not have another choice.

Before you set off, make sure the bike – of whichever sort – works by taking it for a test spin down the street. Brakes in particular are often mis-set, lights may need new fuses or bulbs, and spark-plugs get fouled. Otherwise, you may get stuck with a lemon, and be held responsible for its malfunctioning when you return it. Reputable agencies now often furnish you with a phone number for a breakdown pick-up service, or will come retrieve you themselves.

Above all, don't take unnecessary chances, like riding two on a bike designed for one. More than one holiday in Greece has been ruined by a serious scooter accident – hospital casualty wards are wearily familiar with "road rash". It is strongly suggested that where possible you stick to traditional scooters of 50–100cc displacement, with skinny, large-radius ("number 16"), well-treaded tyres. The new, predominant generation of automatic, button-start *mihanákia/ papákia* (as they're called in Greek slang), with their sexy fairings and tiny, fat, no-tread tyres, may look the business but they are unstable and unsafe once off level asphalt. In particular, if you hit a gravel-strewn curve on one of these you will go for a spill, and at the very least lose most of the skin on your hands and knees. In any case, consider buying a pair of biker's gloves – they can be had for around €20. You may feel stupid wearing them in summer, but you'll feel even more stupid with your hands wrapped in gauze for the balance of your holiday.

It's preferable to wear a helmet.

ACCOMMODATION

HOTELS, INNS, RENTED ROOMS AND CAMPSITES

HOW TO CHOOSE

There is a broad range of accommodation in Greece; we list a sample of different categories across the country. On the islands the most affordable lodging are private rented rooms (*enikiazómena domátia*), which are increasingly self-catering studios (if only just a mini-kitchen in the corner) or full-on apartments (*diamerísmata*).

When accommodation-hunting on the spot, local public or private tourist offices can be of help if no rooms are on offer when you disembark.

HOTEL CATEGORIES

The Greek authorities have six categories for hotels, using a star system. Although stars are supposed to accurately reflect the hotel's amenities, a swimming pool or tennis court could rate an establishment as 4-star or 3-star even though in other respects it has indifferent facilities. Also, room numbers can limit a hotel's maximum rating, so you commonly encounter 14-room lesser-starred hotels superior to a 50-room higher-class hotel.

The following general principles apply, however: two-to-five-star hotels all have private bathrooms. Most 1-star hotels have en-suite bathrooms, while the almost extinct no-stars don't.

Four- or five-star hotels must have a bar and at least one restaurant and offer a choice of breakfasts. Two- or three-star should provide a buffet breakfast ("enhanced continental") but classes below that will often offer just a bread roll, jam and coffee.

Multi-starred hotels will have some or all of these facilities: a swimming pool, fitness centre, sauna and/or health spa, "private" beach, conference hall, entertainment programmes for children, 24-hour desk attendance, and "tamed" taxi service. Almost all hotels now offer in-room or lobby wi-fi signal (often charged extra).

TRADITIONAL SETTLEMENTS

Traditional settlements (*paradosiakí ikismí*) have been officially protected as such, with modern constructions banned by law. Buildings in these villages were variably restored as inns under a Tourism Ministry initiative during the 1970s and 1980s, though all are now privatised. Since then, private renovators have opened other, generally higher-quality, inns, rescuing older buildings at risk. Restoration inns exist in the following locations:

Hydra Town (several sponge-captains' mansions, done up as hotels)
Ía, Firá and Imerovígli, Santoríni (interlinked village houses)
Ermoúpoli, Sýros (many Belle Epoque mansions converted to hotels)
Mestá, Híos (several houses, as room-only or suites/apartments)
Avgónyma and **Volissós**, Híos (entire houses, or apartments within)
Kámbos region, Híos (a few restored mansions)
Psará island (a restored prison)
Rhodes Old Town (quality restoration inns in medieval structures)
Haniá, Crete (restoration inns around the Old Harbour)
Réthymno, Crete (restored inns in old-town Venetian buildings)
Gialós and **Horió**, Sými (old houses divided into apartments)
Emborió, Hálki (houses divided into apartments)

Corfu (restored olive mills or manor houses in remote locations)

BOOKING ONLINE

Most of our listings provide a contact website; significant discounts for online booking may be offered, and the high-season price category given only applies from late July to early September, if that; rates usually include breakfast. While web bookings require a credit card deposit, the hotel may not accept credit cards for final payment.

MOUNTAIN REFUGES AND MONASTERIES

The only mountain refuge in the Greek islands is the popular, well-run Kallérgi hut in Crete's White Mountains, near the Gorge of Samariá (elevation 1,680 metres/5,111ft; tel: 28210 33199).

The *xenónes* (guest lodges) of monasteries or convents are intended for Orthodox pilgrims. The only ones used to hosting the heterodox are Skiádi in southern Rhodes, Agíou Ioánni Prodrómou on Hálki, and possibly Goniá on Crete's Rodópou peninsula.

CAMPING

Some visitors to Greece still camp or park a caravan by a secluded beach. While it is illegal to do so, if you are discreet and tidy you will rarely be bothered, especially in peak season when there are often no rooms to be had. Organised campsites are limited to Santoríni, Sífnos, Sýros, Páros, Náxos, Íos, Lésvos and Corfu.

ATHENS

Acropolis House
Kódrou 6–8, metro Sýndagma
Tel: 210 32 22 344
www.acropolishouse.gr
The first neoclassical mansion in Athens to be converted into a pension. The building's listed status prevents some of its well-kept rooms from having en-suite baths, though for the academic clientele that's part of the charm. All rooms have solid wood floors, most have high ceilings (some with murals). Communal fridge and two breakfast rooms. €–€€

Attalos
Athinás 29, metro Monastiráki
Tel: 210 32 12 801
www.attalos.gr
This friendly hotel is good value and retains many of its (1960s) period features, but medium-sized rooms themselves – about half with balconies, costing a tad more – have modern furnishings, double glazing against street noise, parquet floors and pastel/earth tones. Facilities include free wi-fi and a very popular if narrow cramped roof-terrace evening bar. €€

Ava
Lysikrátous 9–11, metro Acropolis
Tel: 210 32 59 000
www.avahotel.gr.
Suite-format hotel, thoroughly overhauled to the highest standards in 2010. Upper units have balconies with courtyard, or oblique Acropolis views. Excellent for families, as their roomier (up to 55 sq metres) units, effectively one-bedroom apartments, comfortably fit four. There are also smaller suites suitable for couples. Breakfast included, Wi-fi throughout, assiduous service. €€€€

Cecil
Athinás 39
Tel: 210 32 17 079
www.cecil.gr
A well-restored 1850s vintage mansion has become a characterful small hotel, right down to its inter-war "cage" lift. The rooms only have ornamental balconies but do offer parquet floors, iron bedsteads, double glazing, free wi-fi and designer-tiled bathrooms. Common areas are limited to a breakfast room with its original wooden floor and painted ceiling, and a street-level café. €€

Fresh
Sofokléous 26, corner Klisthénous, metro Omónia.
Tel: 210 52 48 511
www.freshhotel.gr.
You will either love or hate this startling "design" hotel, with its lollipop colour scheme of panels everywhere from reception to the balconies. Chrome, leather and glass abound, but there is also plenty of oak and walnut. Modern room features include bedside-operated remote control of windows and plasma TV. The rooftop pool-and-bar is a big hit and executive rooms or suites have private Zen rock gardens. €€€

Grande Bretagne
Sýndagma Square
Tel: 210 33 30 000
www.grandebretagne.gr
Perhaps the most famous hotel in Athens, the neoclassical Grande Bretagne dates originally from 1846. A 2004 renovation restored every period detail to its Belle Epoque glory. Highlights of the common areas include the seventh-floor pool-garden, the basement spa (best in town) and the bar with its 18th-century tapestry of Alexander the Great. Rooms are large, typically 35–40 sq metres (375–430 sq ft). Ultra-expensive, of course: never much less than €350 per night. €€€€

Hera
Falírou 9, Makrygiánni
Tel: 210 92 36 682
www.herahotel.gr
The Hera has perhaps the best roof garden in the area, with a heated bar-restaurant for all-year operation. Rooms are on the small side, so it's worth paying extra for three fifth-floor suites with bigger balconies (some fourth-floor rooms also have Acropolis views). The dome-lit atrium-breakfast room, and friendly staff, are further assets. €€€

Marble House
Alley off Anastasíou Zínni 35, metro Syngroú-Fix
Tel: 210 92 28 294
www.marblehouse.gr
This welcoming, family-run pension has an enviably quiet, yet convenient location. All rooms were renovated in 2010, with balconies, mostly en-suite baths, fridges, air con and free Wi-fi. Great value, although breakfast charged extra – book well in advance. €

Phaedra
Herofóndos 16
Tel: 210 32 38 461
www.hotelphaedra.com
At the junction of two usually quiet pedestrian streets, the Phaedra offers the best-value budget accommodation in Pláka. While not all the cheerfully tile-floored rooms are en suite, each has an allocated bathroom, while some

Afternoon tea, Grande Bretagne.

have balconies overlooking a square with a Byzantine church. Breakfast (optional) served in pleasant ground-floor salon. €

Radisson Blu Park
Alexándras 10, metro Viktória
Tel: 210 88 94 500
www.rbathenspark.com
The former Athens Park, dating from 1976, had a remarkable makeover (and rebranding) in 2011 – the Pédion Áreos park opposite has come indoors, as it were, with tree trunks in the foyer, turf-like carpets in three grades of rooms, bicycle decor (and rental), plus light green and russet colours for the soft furnishings. The rooftop, poolside St'Astra Restaurant was always a worthy destination in its own right, now joined by the ground-floor all-day bistro. Free parking (and interconnecting family rooms) are big pluses, as is an indoor gym/sauna and walking distance to the National Archeological Museum. €€€

St George Lycabettus
Kleoménous 2, Kolonáki
Tel: 210 72 90 711
www.sglycabettus.gr
Since its pre-Olympics refit, the St George has styled itself as a boutique hotel, oriented towards business-people. The cool, comfortable rooms and suites are elegant but subdued, while the rooftop pool is a big selling point. Southwest-facing rooms and suites (more expensive) have one of the best views in the city. Basement sauna and gym, two restaurants on-site and free off-street parking. €€€

PRICE CATEGORIES

Price categories are based on the cost of a double room for one night in the high season:
€ = under €70
€€ = €70–120
€€€ = €120–200
€€€€ = over €200

THESSALONÍKI

Bristol
Oplopioú 2, cnr Katoúni
Tel: 23105 06500
www.capsisbristol.gr
One of the city's first boutique hotels, with 16 rooms and four superior suites in an 1870s building near the trendy Ladádika district. On-site Italo-Argentine restaurant also shoehorned into the premises. €€€

Orestias Kastorias
Agnóstou Stratiótou 14
Tel: 23102 76517
www.okhotel.gr
Much the most salubrious and most quietly located budget hotel in town, just a few steps from Agios Dimítrios Basilica. Rooms in this 1920s building, the front-facing ones with balconies, were renovated in 2011 with simple solid-wood furniture and veneer floors; bathrooms have been substantially upgraded. €

Le Palace
Tsimiskí 12
Tel: 23102 57400
www.lepalace.gr
Central hotel in a 1926-vintage building, thoroughly renovated in 2005 in vaguely Parisian style, Le Palace features spacious rooms double-glazed against the street noise. The buffet breakfast is notably generous. €€€

Tobacco Hotel
Agíou Dimitríou 25
Tel: 23105 15002
www.davitel.gr
A tobacco warehouse (as the name would suggest) built in 1922, and renovated in 2004 as a thoroughly modern 4-star hotel with 57 brown-tone rooms furnished in minimalist style. There is a lobby bar and a breakfast lounge, but no restaurant. €€€

Tourist
Mitropóleos 21
Tel: 23102 70501
www.touristhotel.gr
A rambling, Art Deco 3-star hotel dating from 1925 with parquet-floored common areas (including a cheerful breakfast room), a 1920s lift, and en-suite rooms that preserve period details. Very centrally located. It is understandably popular, so advance booking is required at all times. €€

CORFU

There are almost 500 licensed hotels on the island, although many remain in the firm grip of tour operators from May to October, closing in winter. The following are open off-season and/or to independent travellers.

Kérkyra

Bella Venezia
Napoleóndos Zambéli 4, Pórta Remoúnda
Tel: 26610 46500
www.bellaveneziahotel.com
Kérkyra Town's worst-kept secret, and enduringly popular, this 2008-renovated hotel occupies a converted neoclassical former girls' school. The best rooms, with high ceilings and sometimes balconies, are on the first two storeys, though the third-floor suites accommodate families of four. An adequate breakfast is offered in the back-garden conservatory. Stylish lobby bar and helpful staff complete the profile. €€–€€€

Corfu Palace
Dhimokratías 2, north end of Garítsa Bay
Tel: 26610 39485
www.corfupalace.com
The dowager empress of town hotels, a favourite with conference and business folk as well as holiday-makers, this five-star outfit scores for an unbeatable position just 10 minutes' walk from the Listón, and willing staff, as much for its accommodation. Standard rooms are large, with recent soft furnishings and veneer floors, while superior units have better livery and double sinks in the bathrooms; all have sea views over Garítsa Bay. Breakfast is taken indoors or out on the lawn-garden by the salt-water pool. There's also an indoor pool by the small spa, and the island's only casino. €€€€

Grecotel Corfu Imperial
Komméno
Tel: 26610 88400
www.grecotel.gr
Set at the tip of a private peninsula with man-made sandy-cove beaches on the sheltered inland side, this luxurious self-contained resort is considered one of the two or three top lodgings on the island – and thus often booked out. There's a huge seawater swimming pool, shoreline water sports, a choice of restaurants and bars, a tennis club, spa and gym. Rooms are luxuriously furnished and are either in the main block or in bungalows dotted around the pretty grounds with Italianate gardens and olive trees. Open Apr–Oct. €€€€

Konstantinoupolis
Zavitsiánou 11, Old Port
Tel: 26610 48716
www.konstantinoupolis.gr
Renovated building dating from 1862, but still pleasantly old-fashioned, this two-star hotel has both sea and mountain views from the front balconied rooms, which are large – though bathrooms are small and basic, if brightly tiled. Rooms are reached either by a spiral wooden staircase or antique lift, past the more modern mezzanine breakfast area and lounge; free Wi-fi. €€

Kontokali Bay Resort and Spa
Kondókali
Tel: 26610 99000
www.kontokalibay.com
This low-rise bungalow-style resort has most units scattered in clusters through beautiful gardens next to a private sandy beach. Superior standard rooms (redone 2007–08) are like junior suites with their sofas and big balconies, while the garden-view family bungalows were renovated in 2010. Bathrooms have butler sinks and proper shower screens. Facilities are commensurate with a 5-star rating, and include an elevated infinity pool, state-of-the-art freestanding (not basement) spa, tennis courts, water sports at the private port and an imaginative children's club. Open late Apr–Oct. €€€€

Siorra Vittoria
Sofías Pandová 36
Tel: 26610 36300
www.siorravittoria.com
Opened in 2005, this boutique hotel in an 1823-vintage mansion is still in the hands of the same family. Just nine stylish rooms and suites, some interconnecting for families, have beamed ceilings, LCD TVs and tasteful Belle Epoque furnishings. The best unit, with a view of the Néo Froúrio, is the top-floor suite. €€€

Centre-west of Corfu

Casa Lucia
Sgómbou hamlet, at Km 12 of Kérkyra–Paleokastrítsa road

Tel: 26610 91419
www.casa-lucia-corfu.com
A restored olive-mill complex set among lovingly tended gardens with a large pool. Just eight self-catering units ranging from studios to family cottages; all share simple (read, 1980s vintage) but adequate furnishings, and are often occupied by patrons attending the yoga, t'ai chi or massage workshops held here. Peaceful setting at the very centre of the island makes this an excellent touring base. No on-site restaurant per se, but the affiliated Bio-Bistro Lucciola (often with entertainment) is just a few steps away on the main road. Open year round, but Nov–March on weekly or monthly basis. €€–€€€

Fundana Villas
Accessed by side road from Km 17 of Kérkyra–Paleokastrítsa road
Tel: 26630 22532
www.fundanavillas.com
Another 1980s restoration inn, this time converted from a 18th-century manor, with a commanding ridge-top position in the middle of gorgeous nowhere. Units, from double studios to family-sized bungalows or suites, are all different, some with brick-and-flagstone floors or timber beams. Large pool, bar and grill, olive-press museum on site. Active types can follow part of the Corfu Trail, which passes right by. Open Easter–Oct. €€

Levant Hotel
Above Pélekas (fork right at the church), beside "Kaiser's Throne"
Tel: 26610 94230
www.levanthotel.com
1989-built hotel in mock-traditional style, with superb panoramic views both east and west over the island. Rooms are wood-floored, baths marble-trimmed. There's a medium-sized pool and spa tub on a grassy terrace, but with some of the island's best beaches a few kilometres away, you may not use them. Ground-floor common areas comprise wood/marble-floored bar and restaurant,

with the breakfast area outside taking advantage of the view. A popular wedding venue, and overnight stop on the Corfu Trail. Open Apr–Oct. €€

The north of the island
Delfino Blu
Ágios Stéfanos Gýrou
Tel: 26630 51629
www.delfinoblu.gr
This small boutique hotel has a gorgeous setting overlooking one of the best sandy beaches in the area, and is often full, even in spring or autumn. The self-catering apartments and suites, done up in pastel hues, all have sea views, balconies and mod cons. Gourmet restaurant downstairs and excellent pool and beach bars. On-site motor-yacht rental, plus small gym and sauna. Open May–Oct. €€€–€€€€

Kalami Tourist Services
Tel: 26630 91062
www.kalamibay.com
An offshoot of the celebrated Nikolas taverna at Agní Cove, with the same family arranging quality accommodation (studios, apartments, free-standing cottages) on the surrounding hillsides. €€–€€€

Villa de Loulia
Perouládes, 500 metres/yds from beach
Tel: 26630 95394
www.villadeloulia.gr
One of Corfu's few rural restoration inns, this mansion dating from 1803 has been refurbished to provide nine varying rooms, with high-standard furnishings and fittings in excellent taste. The bar, lounge and gourmet restaurant occupy a separate purpose-built structure flanking the large pool. Heating but only fans, no air conditioning. You're paying for the exclusivity – better value out of peak season. Open May–Oct. €€€

The south of the the island
Bella Vista
Benítses centre, 100 metres from beach

Tel: 26610 72087
www.bellavistahotel.gr
Family-run hotel with murals and art-student canvases adorning common areas and pastel-hued rooms respectively, managed by the ebullilent Anthea, with 14 years' experience running an English hotel. Breakfasts, with in-house-baked goodies, are scrumptious and available until 11am. Both the standard-double wing (June–Sept only) and annexe with studios/1-bed apartments were redone in stages between 2003 and 2014. Free air con and Wi-fi. €

Boukari Beach
Boúkari, 4km (2.5 miles) beyond Messongí
Tel: 26620 51791
www.boukaribeach.gr
Two sets of sea-view A-class apartments sleeping up to four, with all amenities including coffee machines and hydromassage showers, just a few paces from the excellent co-managed restaurant. The same family also has a larger, co-managed hotel nearby, last renovated in 2013, with sea views from all rooms and Wi-fi in the lobby. Open Apr–Oct. €€

Marbella Beach
Ágios Ioánnis Peristerón, 2km (1 mile) north of Moraïtika
Tel 26610 71183
www.marbella.gr
Hillside five-star resort over several wings with knockout views to the mainland. Think wood veneer floors, earth-tone soft furnishings, rain showers in stone-clad bathrooms. With 393 units in a vast array of categories (go for the superior doubles with private whirlpool, or suites), it's not intimate, but clever layout ensures privacy. Very family-friendly. Excellent food (especially the breakfasts), reasonable service, a big salt-water pool and a stretch of lido-beach. Only minus, for car-hirers, is limited parking. Open late Apr–mid-Oct. €€€€

THE IONIAN ISLANDS

Itháki
For rooms or villas across the island, contact one of these two travel agencies:
Captain Yiannis
East quay, Vathý
Tel: 26740 33311
www.captainyiannis.com
Delas
Tel: 26740 32104

www.ithaca.com.gr
Polyctor
Tel: 26740 33120
www.ithakiholidays.com
The closest thing to an exclusive "resort" on the island, with just 11 self-catering units set in ample walled grounds with a pool and tennis court. €€

PRICE CATEGORIES

Price categories are based on the cost of a double room for one night in the high season:
€ = under €70
€€ = €70–120
€€€ = €120–200
€€€€ = over €200

Captain's Apartments
Kióni
Tel: 26740 31481
www.captains-apartments.gr
Set up on the hillside towards Ráhi hamlet, with commanding views of Kióni bay, each spacious, air-conditioned studio has a good-sized full kitchen, cable TV and a veranda; there is also a communal garden to relax in. €

Nostos
About 200 metres/yds inland from the quay, Fríkes
Tel: 26740 31644
www.hotelnostos-ithaki.gr
Smallish but upmarket three-star hotel with a large pool, where all rooms look over a field towards the sunrise; renovated in 2007, although the rooms' appointments still don't quite match common areas. €€

Perantzada 1811 Art Hotel
Odysséa Androútsou, Vathý
Tel: 26740 33496
www.perantzadahotel.com
Chic and fairly expensive but by far the loveliest hotel in Vathý, in a renovated 19th-century mansion that survived the 1953 quake. The 19 understated and tasteful rooms (six in a newer wing, are very comfortable. Not on the harbour front itself (and so quieter than some other places), the rooms look out over Vathý's pretty rooftops to the sea. Breakfasts are excellent. €€€

Kefaloniá

Agnantia Apartments
Tselendáta district, Fiskárdo
Tel: 26740 51801–2
www.agnantia.com
Very well maintained and beautifully located (albeit a little way out of Fiskárdo), this apart-hotel stacked up on a hillside makes a lovely place to stay. As well as friendly and efficient service, the units are tasteful and comfortable with a small kitchen area, and most have a balcony with eyefuls of Itháki. Generous buffet breakfast is included. €€€

La Cité
Lixoúri
Tel: 26710 92701
This compact hotel four blocks in from the seafront has been completely renovated with stylish furnishings to add a touch of the French ambience its name suggests. Large swimming pool, well-kept gardens and a quiet but convenient location make it much the best option in town. €€

Emelisse Art Hotel
Émblisi, near Fiskárdo
Tel/fax: 26740 41200
www.emelissehotel.com

Chic "boutique" hotel (member of a small local chain) set in a traditional building. The well designed rooms have luxurious bathrooms and, inevitably, the hotel's infinity pool has a lovely view. For this sort of money, you should expect to be pampered and the service lives up to expectations. €€€€

Ionian Plaza
Platía Vallianoú, Argostóli
Tel: 26710 25581
www.ionianplaza.gr
Excellent-value three-star designer hotel, the better of two similar ones here, with modern bathrooms and balconies overlooking the palm-studded square; the rooms are on the small side, but the bathrooms are well appointed and the staff friendly. Open all year. €€

Kanakis Apartments
Assos
Tel: 26740 51631
www.kanakisapartments.gr
Among the limited accommodation options in picturesque Assos, these comfortable purpose-built studios and maisonettes stand out for their amenities, including a pool. €€

Odysseus Palace
Póros
Tel: 26740 72036
www.odysseuspalace.eu
This modern hotel is a comfortable place to stay in town. Good discounts may be available for the large and airy studios and apartments. Being away from the seafront, the hotel is quieter than most. €€

Panas Hotel
Kilmatsiá Beach, Spartiá
Tel: 26710 69941
www.panas-kefalonia.com
A smallish, very pleasant four-star hotel on Lourdáta Bay, close to a decent beach, accessed through well-kept gardens. The 35 rooms, all with balconies, are fine if a little plain. There are good facilities for children, including their own pool and play area, plus a couple of restaurants and a poolside bar. €€

Regina's
Fiskárdo
Tel/fax: 26740 41125
Most of the smallish but well-maintained rooms in this family-run guesthouse at the back of the village have balconies looking towards the harbour or across the pleasant courtyard. Better value and less cliquey than many establishments here. €

Tara Beach
Skála
Tel: 26710 83341
www.tarabeach.gr

A large but unobstrusive hotel right on the excellent beach. The rooms are furnished to a slightly higher standard than usual (eg faux-antique beds), and if you feel too lazy to walk the few metres to the sea, there is a good pool-with-bar in the lush gardens. €€

Trapezaki Bay Hotel
Trapezáki
Tel: 26710 31501
www.trapezakibayhotel.gr
Perched on the hillside just five minutes' walk from the eponymous beach, this 33-unit hotel run by a returned Greek-American couple, the heart and soul of the place, is only 1999-vintage but has already been renovated once. All the standard amenities, including restaurant, bars and pool, plus allocated parking. Better value in high summer because prices are fixed for the entire season. €€ rooms, €€€ suites

White Rocks Hotel and Bungalows
Platýs Gialós, Argostóli
Tel: 26710 28332–5
www.whiterocks.gr
Large, five-star resort hotel and bungalow complex, 1970s-vintage but well updated, behind the closest of three good local beaches – there's a pool but you won't need it. Obliging staff and decent restaurants complete the picture. €€€

Kýthira

Kýthira has a short season, with much accommodation only open during summer; advance booking is recommended.

Castello Apts
Hóra
Tel: 27360 31869
www.castelloapts-kythera.gr
Lovely tiered group of bright blue and white self-catering studios, with a relaxing garden and great views down to the sea. €

Porto Delfino
Kapsáli
Tel: 27360 31940–1
www.portodelfino.gr
A pleasant bungalow complex with views over the bay, Avgó islet and Hóra. Large infinity pool and spacious common areas; the rooms are plainly furnished but fairly large. €€

Venardos
Agía Pelagía
Tel: 27360 34100
www.venardos-hotels.gr
Large hotel complex with stylishly appointed rooms boasting warm coloured soft furnishings. Facilities include a pool, gym, sauna and spa. €€

Levkáda

Grand Nefeli
Póndi Beach
Tel: 26450 31378
www.grandnefeli.com
This smart beachfront hotel makes a good alternative to staying in nearby, congested Vasilikí; its popular outdoor bar and on-site windsurfing facilities are pluses. €€

Olive Tree/Liodendro
North approach road, Ágios Nikítas
Tel: 26450 97453
www.olivetreelefkada.gr
Halfway up the hill, with oblique sea views from most of the rooms, which have typical pine-and-white-tile decor. Friendly Greek-Canadian proprietors. €€

Ostria
North approach road, Agios Nikítas
Tel: 26450 97483
Email: agnikitasostria@e-lefkas.gr
The 1970s-vintage rooms of this pension can be cell-like, but are enlivened by terracotta floor tiles, dried flowers and wall art. It's the unobstructed balcony views of the Ionian (save for four rooms) and the cool, trendy common areas (including a terrace bar open to all) that make the place a delight. €€

Panorama
Atháni
Tel: 26450 33291
One of the island's true hideouts: simple, clean rooms above an excellent grill-restaurant. There are superb views, and this is as close as you can stay to the stunning beaches of Gialós, Egremní and Pórto Katsíki – although you will still need your own transport to reach them. €

Porto Lygia
Lygiá
Tel: 26450 72000
www.portoligia.gr
Perched on a promontory away from traffic, with a lawn leading down to its own pebble beach, this four-star resort is a good choice for a seaside stay near (but not in) Levkáda Town. Rooms have blue-and-white livery and modern furnishings, although not all of them face the sea. €€

Rouda Bay
Mikrós Gialós (Póros)
Tel: 26450 95634
www.roudabay.gr
Spacious apartments, arranged around a well-tended garden, back on to a fine restaurant where the buffet breakfasts are served, a few paces from the smooth pebble beach. €€

Serenity
500 metres/yds above Atháni
Tel: 6981 853064

www.serenity-th.com
Unusual for Greece, this Israeli-run retreat offers artistically designed suites, a chill-out room, a stunning infinity pool, plus yoga and beauty therapies. €€€

Paxí

Paxos Beach Hotel
Gáïos
Tel: 26620 31211
www.paxosbeachhotel.gr
A hillside bungalow complex from where there is a path leading down through trees to its own small pebble beach about 2km (1 mile) east of town. It's worth getting the higher three ("bungalow suites") of five grades of unit. Closes early Oct. €€€

Planos Holidays
Lákka
Tel: 26620 31744
www.planos.co.uk
One of two booking agencies in this little port, efficiently handling everything from basic studios to luxury villas island-wide.

Zákynthos

Ionian Star Hotel
Alykés
Tel: 26950 83416/83658
www.ionian-star.gr
A smallish and very well-kept hotel, with spotless rooms. Breakfast included at the restaurant that concentrates on Greek food. €

Levantino Studio Apartments
Kamínia beach, Vasilikós
Tel: 26950 35366
www.levantino.gr
Ten quiet and attractive apartments set right behind a beach at the Argási of the Vasilikós peninsula. All have a kitchen and some look out over the garden (which has a bar) and the sea. €€

Nobelos Apartments
Agios Nikólaos
Tel: 26950 27632/31400
www.nobelos.gr
These luxury apartments in the north of the island are eye-wateringly expensive but quite lovely. The four tastefully decorated suites are in a traditional stone-built house, each with an individual character. Along with excellent service, a good breakfast is provided and a secluded bay is close by. €€€€

Palatino
Kolokotróni 10 and Kolyvá, Zákynthos Town
Tel: 26950 27780
www.palatinohotel.gr
The Palatino is one of Zákynthos Town's best-value options, stylish

and well run. The well-maintained rooms, designed principally for business travellers, are decent with all the trimmings. A buffet breakfast is provided, and there is also a full-service restaurant. €€

Pansion Limni
Límni Kerioú
Tel: 26950 48716
www.pansionlimni.com
A disarmingly friendly place in the far southwest, where guests are presented with bottles of homemade wine and olive oil. There is a new, higher-standard annexe, *Porto tis Ostrias*, with some large family apartments, 150 metres/yds inland from the original pension. €

Sirocco Hotel
Kalamáki
Tel: 26950 26083
www.siroccohotel.gr
This is a very acceptable and peaceful option for Kalamáki, and the renovated and stylish standard rooms are reasonably priced, especially out of season; there are also superior rooms and four-person apartments. A large pool is set in an attractive garden, although the beach is not too far away. €€

Villa Katerina
Pórto Róma, Vasilikós
Tel: 26950 35456 (summer)
Tel: 26950 27230 (winter)
www.villakaterina.com
These two quiet buildings, set in pretty gardens, offer studios large and small, as well as two-bedroom apartments. It's within walking distance from Gérakas as well as Pórto Róma beach, and the surrounding area is lovely, making it an excellent and fairly inexpensive choice. €

Windmill/Anemomilos
Korithí, Cape Skinári
Tel: 26950 31132
www.potamitisbros.gr
Two converted windmills sleeping two to four people, along with four spacious rooms in a stone house located at the far north end of the island, and close to the Blue Caves (to which the hotel management offers boat trips). A great get-away-from-it-all option. €€

PRICE CATEGORIES

Price categories are based on the cost of a double room for one night in the high season:
€ = under €70
€€ = €70–120
€€€ = €120–200
€€€€ = over €200

Zante Palace
Tsiliví
Tel: 26950 490490
www.zantepalace.com

This huge hotel sits on the bluff overlooking Tsiliví Bay and Kefaloniá. The studios and one- or two-bedroom apartments are good value, with an

optional breakfast available. If you can't be bothered to walk down to the pleasant beach you can swim in the nicely sited pool. €€

THE SARONIC GULF

Aegina

Brown Hotel
Égina Town
Tel: 22970 22271
www.hotelbrown.gr
Right opposite the southerly town beach, a five-minute walk from the ferry quay, is this converted sponge factory, now a hotel still owned by the original family, whose ancestry was partly English (hence the name). Common areas, rather than the adequate but unexceptional rooms, garner the 3-star rating; the garden bungalows are quieter and desirable. €€

Hippocampus
Pérdika
Tel: 22970 61363
www.hippocampus-hotel-greece.com
Small, Anglo-Greek-run hotel here since 1972, whose rooms – mostly twin-bedded – are on the small side but include some double beds and family quads. There's a roof terrace and lovely courtyard where "enhanced continental" breakfast is taken. €

To Petrino Spiti
Petrítou 5, Égina Town
Tel: 22970 23837
A distinctive three-floored stone house (pétrino spíti) a 10-minute walk from the harbour. There are nine comfortable studios all done out variably– a couple of them in antique style. €

Angístri

Alkyoni
South end of Skála, at clifftop
Tel: 22970 91377
www.alkyoni-agistri.com
Peacefully set hotel with simple but pleasant, flagstone-floored standard doubles on the ground floor and somewhat higher standard family rooms upstairs – just 15 units in total. The terrace restaurant, like the hotel going for over three decades now, is the island's most accomplished eatery, blending traditional Greek dishes with more "oriental" influences. Open all year by arrangement. €

Hydra

Bratsera
200 metres/yds in from centre quay

Hydra Town
Tel: 22980 53971
www.bratserahotel.com
The top comfort and room size available on the island are at this four-star hotel occupying a former sponge factory. Vast common areas (bar, restaurant, conference room and medium-sized pool) serve as a de facto museum of the industry, with photos and artefacts. There are seven grades of rooms and suites to choose from. Open Apr–Oct. €€€

Miranda
Hydra Town
Tel: 22980 52230
www.mirandahotel.gr
Set in a mansion built in 1810, Miranda is another restoration hotel, with 14 differently decorated rooms: some traditional, others Art Deco. The classy atmosphere is enhanced by the in-house art gallery. Breakfast is served in the courtyard garden. Open March–Oct. €€€

Orloff
Tel: 22980 52564
www.orloff.gr
A very comfortable mansion turned boutique hotel with all creature comforts. All rooms (renovated in 2012–13) are individual, in different shapes and sizes. Some look out over the town, others onto the flower-filled courtyard, where a large buffet breakfast is served. Open most of the year. €€€

Pityoussa
Hydra Town, southeast edge
Tel: 22980 52810
www.piteoussa.gr
The best of the mid-range options, Pityoussa's designer units have CD/DVD players, mock-antique furnishings and modernised bathrooms, and most have balconies (or a private courtyard in the case of the "superior"-grade rooms). No breakfast provided, however. €€

Póros

Pavlou
Megálo Neório, Kalávria
Tel: 22980 22734
www.pavlouhotel.gr
Family-friendly hotel with a tennis court and pool, right behind one of Kalávria's better beaches; both the

very acceptable on-site restaurant and the comfortable rooms offer what is probably the best standard on the island. Open Apr–Oct. €€

Saronis
Galatás Trizinías
Tel: 22980 42356
A good solution for avoiding some overpriced lodging on Póros itself – stay here, looking across the narrow strait to the clock tower hill, just a few paces from the foot-passenger ferry. This hotel is basic but cheerful and well-maintained, with a ground-floor cafeteria. €

Sto Roloï
Hatzopoúlou and Karrá 13, Póros Town
Tel: 22980 25808
www.storoloi-poros.gr
Póros's only traditional house restoration complex is located near the prominent hilltop clock tower (rolóï), in a 200-year-old dwelling converted into three apartments. There are two more next door at Anemone House and the Little Tower, plus the more remote Limeri House and Studio, set around a pool. All retain period features such as Belle Epoque tiling, but are furnished with reproduction traditional furnishings. Studios €€, houses €€€

Spétses

Armata Boutique Hotel
Inland from Dápia on pedestrian lane
Tel: 22980 72683
www.armatahotel.gr
A converted mansion hotel, opened in 2004, with 20 very plush rooms, copious breakfast and (unusually for the island) a pool. Open Mar–Oct. €€€

Economou Mansion
Kounoupítsa shore
Tel: 22980 73400
www.spetsesyc.gr/economoumansion.htm
Another restoration inn, occupying

PRICE CATEGORIES

Price categories are based on the cost of a double room for one night in the high season:
€ = under €70
€€ = €70–120
€€€ = €120–200
€€€€ = over €200

part of an 1851-vintage property. The ground floor of the main house has six well-converted rooms retaining ample period features; an outbuilding hosts two luxury sea-view suites. Breakfast is served by the fair-sized pool. €€€

Poseidonion
West of Dápia, on shore
Tel: 22980 74553
www.poseidonion.com
Landmark Edwardian (1914) building which, after years of neglect, reopened in 2009 as the island's top

hotel. Rooms are divided between traditional ones in the original building and less characterful bungalows out back around the pool. Restaurant serves dinner only in summer, though the "Library Bar Brasserie" is open all day. €€€€

THE CYCLADES

Amorgós

Aigialis
Órmos Egiális
Tel: 22850 73393
www.amorgos-aegialis.com
Modern, comfortable hotel built in tiers on the north hillside beyond the bay, with stunning views. Most rooms (in two grades) have been refurbished since 2006; there is a large outdoor pool and a decent restaurant, plus a stunning indoor spa and pool used year-round by local people – a telling accolade. €€€

Pagali Hotel
Langáda
Tel: 22850 73310
www.pagalihotel-amorgos.com
Assorted, large, white-decor rooms and studios fitted with natural-fibre mattresses, in one of the more attractive villages of the island, often booked by special-interest groups. A main advantage is an excellent affiliated restaurant next door. €€

Panorama Studios & Pension
Hóra
Tel: 22850 74016
http://panorama-studios.amorgos.net
A mix of ordinary double rooms and self-catering studios in a commanding position, of a standard one notch up from the normal island decor of cheap pine furniture and white tiles. €€

Anáfi

Apollon Village
Hillside above Klisídi beach
Tel: 22860 28739
www.apollonvillage.com
Top of the heap in all senses for Anáfi, the tiered maisonettes of this small (12-unit) complex are arrayed with a good eye for privacy. Typically Cycladic-style studios have full kitchens, though the restaurants of Klisídi and Ágios Nikólaos are just a short walk away. Open May–Sept. €€

Maroulia Rooms
Hóra
Tel: 22860 61307
Just four simple but well-kept units (two self-catering), with abundant hot water, unobstructed sea views, and a friendly managing family. €

Andíparos

Kouros Village
West end of waterfront, main village
Tel: 222840 61084
www.kouros-village.gr
Family-friendly complex of studios and apartments (up to two-bedroom), plus pool and on-site restaurant, with fine views east. High service level from Greek/Swedish proprietors. Open mid-Apr– mid-Oct. €€

Mantalena
Mid-waterfront, main village
Tel: 22840 61206
www.hotelmantalena.gr
High-standard rooms on the waterfront, with good views of the harbour and across to Páros; the same management also has apartments in the village centre, near the Kástro. €€

Andros

Andros Holiday Hotel
Gávrio
Tel: 22820 71384
www.androsholidayhotel.com
Mainstream resort hotel, overlooking a small private beach just outside town. Attractive, parquet-floored rooms with sea-view terraces, swimming pool, tennis courts and competent restaurant. Open Apr–Oct. €€

Eleni Mansion
Hóra
Tel: 22820 22270
www.archontikoeleni.gr
One of several boutique hotels in the town converted from 19th-century neoclassical mansions, this eight-room outfit has period furnishings and is located on a quieter pedestrian street. €€€

Niki Xenonas
Ándros Hóra
Tel: 2282 029155
Another refurbished mansion on the main pedestrian walkway, elegant and inexpensive. All six rooms have balconies, some facing the main street, some the sea. €€

Paradise Hotel
Hóra outskirts, 800 metres/yds from centre
Tel: 22820 22187
www.paradiseandros.gr

Partly occupying another old mansion, this four-star hotel – twinned with the St George Lycabettus in Athens – is arguably the island's top lodging, with excellent staff. The package comprises on-site art gallery, swimming pool, tennis courts and airy balconied, predominantly white rooms, most of which have sea views. €€€€

St Louis Studios
Hóra outskirts, 700 metres/yds from centre
Tel: 22820 23965
www.saintlouis.gr
Ten immaculately appointed apartments of various capacities in a lush setting, run by a welcoming mother-daughter team. Although units are properly self-catering, breakfast is included. You will need to use taxis, or your own car, however. €

Folégandros

Anemomylos
Hóra
Tel: 22860 41309
www.anemomilosapartments.com
A fully equipped apartment complex built in traditional Cycladic style around a courtyard and pool. Sweeping views from the balconies overhanging the cliff edge. "Green Line" units have only partial views, and thus are cheaper. Open May– Sept. €€€

Castro
Hóra
Tel: 22860 41230
www.hotel-castro.com
A 500-year-old traditional house that is actually part of the ancient kástro walls. Quaint rooms, renovated in 2012, have pebble-mosaic floors, barrel ceilings and spectacular views down sheer cliffs to the sea. €

Polikandia
Hóra, near Poúnda Platía
Tel: 22860 41322
www.polikandia-folegandros.gr
Newish boutique hotel, arrayed around a large pool, with four grades of rooms and suites, plush and rather brightly hued. Other facilities include a communal jacuzzi and a roof terrace. €€€€

Íos

Acropolis
Mylopótas
Tel: 22860 91303
www.hotelacropolis.gr
Tiled rooms with brightly coloured, updated decor (including wall art) and balconies or flagstoned terraces, in a blue-shuttered building overlooking the beach. €€
Íos Palace
Mylopótas
Tel: 22860 92000
www.iospalacehotel.com
Modern hotel near the beach; though notionally four-star, there's a range of rooms and suites for all budgets, with the top grades having unobstructed sea views. On-site spa with a full range of treatments. Open May–Oct. €€–€€€€

Kéa

Porto Kea Suites
Livádi district, Korissía
Tel: 22880 22870
www.portokea-suites.com
Well-designed bungalow hotel, a mix of standard doubles and (large) suites, mimicking local architectural elements with its stone cladding, fronting a pool and its own beach. The top standard on the island. €€€€

Koufonísi

Gitonia tis Irinis
East edge of Hóra
Tel: 22850 71674
www.koufonisia-diakopes.gr
Very charming, traditionally Cycladic bungalow complex, designed by artist-owner Andonis Mavros, with 15 cave-like self-catering units ranging from singles to family quads. €€

Kýthnos

Porto Klaras
Loutrá
Tel: 22810 31276
www.porto-klaras.gr
State-of-the-art mod cons combined with tasteful real and reproduction antique furnishings, colour splashes and white Cycladic niches, in these studios and apartments, set in lovely tiered grounds overlooking the bay. Free Wi-fi. €€

Mílos

Kapetan Tassos
Apollónia
Tel: 22870 41287
www.kapetantassos.gr
Traditional blue-and-white island architecture, offering designer suites with good sea views and nice touches like Wi-fi (often absent in apartments) and complimentary Korres sundries

(the Greek answer to Clarins). Eleven km (7 miles) from Adamás, so you need transport. €€€
Panorama
Klíma
Tel: 22870 21623
www.panorama-milos.com
Small, 1980s-style seafront hotel-taverna, family-run with friendly service. Simple but perfectly adequate rooms with, of course, views. The owner sometimes takes guests fishing. €
Popi's Windmill
Trypití
Tel: 22870 22286
A luxuriously converted windmill with all the amenities for an elegant self-catered stay, plus beautiful views towards Adamás port. Actually two windmills, each with two bedrooms. €€€

Mýkonos

Cavo Tagoo
North of Hóra 500 metres/yds
Tel: 22890 23692
www.cavotagoo.gr
Beautiful furnishings, prize-winning Cycladic architecture, impeccable service, friendly atmosphere, good views, infinity seawater pool. About half the 80 units are "superior" rooms, suites or villas, worth the extra expense for the enhanced views alone. Open May–Sept. €€€€
Harmony
North end of Hóra, overlooking old port
Tel: 22890 28980
www.harmonyhotel.gr
Just 22 units at this self-described boutique hotel in bungalow format, priced by their view; some have bathtubs, others showers, the suites have Jacuzzis. All have small balconies or terrace space, and there are some disabled-accessible rooms. Common facilities include a medium-sized pool, gym and sauna. A bit bland in decor, but a great position and one of the very few lodgings open all year. €€€–€€€€
Matogianni
Matogiánni Street
Tel: 22890 22217
www.matogianni.gr
An excellent mid-range choice, with three floors of designer-minimalism in bright but not outré colour spashes. All rooms have either balconies or a terrace, facing a tiny rear garden or the front terrace where breakfast can be taken – alternatively, it's served in the rather zanier bar. €€€
Philippi
Kalogéra 23, Hóra
Tel: 22890 22294
E-mail: chriko@otenet.gr

The best budget option – by Mýkonos standards, anyway – in town, with good-sized rooms (mostly twin-bedded) sporting white tiles and dark furniture, many looking onto a lovely garden with gourds, citrus trees and ceramic urns. Open Apr–Oct. €€
Semeli
Róhari district, Hóra
Tel: 22890 27466
www.semelihotel.gr
Understated designer hotel with mostly earth-tone palette, exposed stonework and ceiling beams, plus distant sea views for the luckier rooms. Five rooms are near the reception, the rest – standard, superior or suites – surround the exceptionally large pool. Bathrooms, with butler sinks and rain-showers, are naturally lit via translucent panels. The buffet breakfast offers plenty of choice, and the subterranean spa features surprisingly normal prices. Occasional noise from a sports ground just below. Open Feb–Nov. €€€–€€€€

Náxos

Chateau Zevgoli
Kástro, Boúrgos district
Tel: 22850 26123
www.naxostownhotels.com
Just six standard doubles (half with sea view) and two suites, with marble floors throughout in this converted old mansion. The suites, one with private veranda, are the best. Common areas comprise a shady front patio and lounge-breakfast area. There are also two self-catering apartments nearby. Open all year by arrangement. €€
Glaros
Ágios Geórgios beach, Hóra
Tel: 22850 23101
www.hotelglaros.com.
A 2010 renovation made this boutique hotel a top local choice. Overwhelmingly white rooms, most with sea view, score highly for the bathrooms with butler sinks and proper stall showers; size varies, with the biggest suites at the "penthouse" level. €€–€€€
Grotta
Iakóvou Kambanéli 7, Hóra
Tel: 22850 22215
www.hotelgrotta.gr
For many, the best – and best-value – in-town hotel, bar none. Rooms are of boutique standard, done up in light pastel tones, the managing family (especially Nikoletta) is assiduously welcoming, the buffet breakast rich and copious, the views – towards the Kástro, or towards sunsets beyond the Portára and Páros island – cannot be bettered. Easy walk down a path to the town centre, parking nearby. €€

Kavos

Stelída peninsula hillside, Ágios Prokópios
Tel: tel 22850 23355
www.kavos-naxos.com
Hillside oasis of stone-clad cottages in four grades, from studio suites ideal for honeymooners to multi-bedroom bungalows fit for families. Appointment is comfortable rather than luxurious, but pays ample homage to local architectural features. Assiduous service, and a restaurant that's worth dining at (unlike at many multi-star hotels) add up to a superlatively good-value package. Open early May–mid-Oct. €€€

Páros

Astir of Paros

Náoussa, Kolymbíthres beach
Tel: 22840 51986
www.astirofparos.gr
One of Greece's finest de luxe hotels, right on the beach, across the bay from the town. Spacious rooms and suites in five grades, with balconies, and bathrooms lined with Parian marble. There is a large pool, golf course, tennis court and extensive gardens. €€€€

Captain Manolis

Behind National Bank square, Parikiá
Tel: 22840 21244
www.paroswelcome.com
The cheerful rooms here in pastel shades, fitted with laminate flooring plus small balconies, were refurbished in 2012. About the best budget option in the town centre, especially for those planning to hit the local nightlife. Breakfast is offered in the large courtyard. €€

Golden Beach

Hrysí Aktí beach
Tel: 22840 41366
www.goldenbeach.gr
The hotel's lush lawn-garden, fronting the restaurant and bar, extends down to the south end of Páros' longest sandy beach, with wind-surf equipment for hire. The rooms are simple but tastefully done, with marble flooring and some interconnecting units for families. Only some rooms, however, have sea views. It's understandably a popular wedding venue. Open Easter–mid-Oct. €€€

Paros Bay

Delfíni cove, 2km (1 mile) southwest of Parikiá
Tel: 22840 21140
www.parosbay.gr
The closest "resort" hotel to the port, this low-rise, French-run bungalow hotel has 63 quality rooms with LCD televisions and proper shower stalls, a huge salt-water pool, a small spa-and-massage area, an amphitheatre

and the ability to organise events including weddings. Open May–mid-Oct. €€€

Petres

Ágios Andréas district, 1km (0.5 mile) before Náoussa
Tel: 22840 524567
www.petres.gr
Sotiris and Clea, as welcoming hosts as you could hope for, have created an enduringly popular retreat-hotel on this hillside. The 16 rooms plus one suite spread over two wings all have distant sea views – even the ground-floor units; furnishings vary but all share red tile floors and beam-plus-reed ceilings. Common facilities comprise a big pool with adjacent fireplace lounge for spring nights, a tennis court, and a small glassed-in gym with sauna and Jacuzzi. Open Easter/May–7 Oct. €€€

Sofia

Livádia district, Parikiá
Tel: 22840 22085
www.pension-sofia.gr
The USP of this friendly family-run pension is a lush garden-orchard setting, with water features and gazebos where breakfast or a drink may be taken. The 12 rooms, distributed over two wings, punch above their weight with hotel features like makeup mirrors and hair dryers; bathrooms were redone in 2013. Breakfast, with fruit, yogurt, omelette and cafetière coffee options, is well worth the extra charge. You must like cats – there are many, many of them about. €

Santoríni

Afroessa

Imerovígli
Tel: 22860 25362
www.afroessa.com
Most accommodation in Imerovígli glories in stunning views over the caldera to the islets and the sunset, but this 10-unit boutique hotel offers a little bit extra is terms of appurtenances. The obligatory pool next to the bar is the biggest around, swimmable rather than just for a plunge; shower stalls are pebble-mosaic-ed; there are handmade tiles underfoot in the bathrooms. The upper units were old skaftá (dug-out) houses, and one still preserves its original linós (wine press), now glassed over. Helpful, clued-up management a bonus. Open Easter–10 Oct. €€€

Aigialos

Firá
Tel: 22860 25191
www.aigialos.gr
Every house is different in this complex, but all are tastefully

luxurious, quiet and convenient, and have spectacular views, with balconies or terraces overlooking the caldera. Stratoshpheric rates include "American breakfast". €€€€

Chez Sophie

Kamári, south end of resort, behind beach
Tel: 22860 32912
www.chezsophie.gr
Much better than average hotel complex around a small pool – probably not needed given the excellent beach – with willing service and near-boutique standard of appointments in the rooms. Opened in 2008, so minimal wear and tear on facilities. €€

Fanari Villas

Ía
Tel: 22860 71007–8
www.fanarivillas.com
Traditional skaftá (dug-out) cave houses converted into luxury accommodation for up to four people. Pool, breakfast terrace, bar-restaurant, spa and 240 steps down to Ammoúdi Bay. Attentive, friendly service. €€€€

Ikies Traditional Houses

Ía, Perivolás district
Tel: 22860 71311
www.ikies.com
Arguably the best (and most expensive) of several similar complexes in the village, with keen multi-national management and mostly Anglophone clientele. Some of the 11 tiered units – for example the stunning No. 14, for which the rack rate is nearly €1000 – take 4 people, but really only as two couples rather than a family. Open Easter–late Oct. €€€€

Ilioperato

Imerovígli
Tel: 22860 24142
www.ilioperato.com
Right next door to Afroessa near the north end of the village, the Ilioperato is a very honourable fallback choice. The 11 tiered units vary from doubles with a small kitchen area to proper two-bedroom apartments, all furnished in mock-antique style. Bathrooms are spacious, with stall showers. Breakfast is "enhanced" continental, served in the shaded bar. Open 1 Apr–31 Oct. €€€

PRICE CATEGORIES

Price categories are based on the cost of a double room for one night in the high season:

€ = under €70
€€ = €70–120
€€€ = €120–200
€€€€ = over €200

TRANSPORT

ACCOMMODATION

EATING OUT

ACTIVITIES

A – Z

LANGUAGE

Theoxenia
Firá, Ypapandí district
Tel: 22860 22740
www.theoxenia.net
Right on the main cliffside street, this attractive boutique hotel is friendly and efficient, and has all amenities you could wish for, including a spa tub. Upstairs rooms have caldera views. €€€

Sérifos

Indigo Studios
Livádi
Tel: 22810 52538
www.indigostudios.gr
High-standard self-catering units and standard rooms set inland; kitchens aren't really for whipping up full meals, but bathrooms are fine, and breakfast is offered at an affiliated café. €€

Maïstrali
Livádi
Tel: 22810 51220
www.hotelmaistrali.com
Tall, 1970s-vintage hotel, where typically equipped rooms have either sea or Hóra views from their balconies, but what makes the place is the enthusiasm of the proprietor Babis, who will steer you right on your forays around the island. €€

Vaso Stamataki
Livadáki
Tel: 22810 51346
Rambling complex of rooms by the roadside, but most with distant views of the beach, and garden settings. Big balconies, self-catering facilities. Basic, but friendly and walkable from the ferry jetty. €

Sífnos

Alexandros
Platýs Gialós
Tel: 22840 71300
Offering the best value in its class at this beach resort, this hotel – arrayed around a huge pool – comprises unusually large, mock-antique-furnished units ranging from standard doubles to independent cottages that accommodate families. €€€

Artemon
Artemónas
Tel: 22840 31303
www.hotel-artemon.com
Not much to look at from the outside – a 1970s concrete block, in fact – but the rooms, redone in 2004, are perfectly adequate with designer touches, and keenly priced for this island. Rear units overlook fields rolling towards the sea. €€

Elies Resorts
Vathý Bay
Tel: 22840 34000
www.eliesresorts.com
Ultra-luxurious suite-and-villa resort with minimalist ethic; there are some "superior rooms" at the bottom of the scale that are almost affordable. Spa, pool, tennis court and "private" beach complete the profile of a self-contained resort patronised by celebrities Greek and foreign. Open May–Oct. €€€€

Myrto Bungalows
Artemónas
Tel: 22840 31490
www.bungalows-myrto.gr
This bungalow complex of standard rooms and studios at the edge of town is 1980s-built in traditional style, with arches and wood shutters; the landscaped grounds are lovely and the studios take three people at a pinch. €€

Petali Village
Apollonía, Áno Petáli district
Tel: 22840 33024
www.sifnoshotelpetali.com
Genuine three-star standards in a commanding position overlooking all of eastern Sífnos. Five grades of tasteful accommodation, from standard doubles to an apartment hosting four. Pool terrace and roof garden for breakfast. Four-day minimum stay in high season. €€€

Síkinos

Lucas
Aloprónia
Tel: 22860 51076
www.sikinoslucas.gr
Two premises, on opposite sides of the bay, comprising rooms, studios and larger apartments in stereotypical white-and-blue livery, with knockout sea views. The affiliated tavern is your only low-season eating option here. Open Apr–Oct. €

Porto Sikinos
Aloprónia
Tel: 22860 51220
www.portosikinos.gr
The best accommodation on the island: a complex of 18 Cycladic-style buildings right on the beach. Good, if unvarying, breakfast and strong Wi-fi signal. Open May–Sept. €€

Sýros

Dolphin Bay Hotel
Galissás
Tel: 22810 42924
www.dolphin-bay.gr
The largest resort-hotel on the island, four-star and family-friendly with units ranging up to two-bedroom apartments; large swimming pool,

restaurant and beautiful views over the bay. €€–€€€

Faros Village
Azólimnos
Tel: 22810 61661
www.faros-hotel.com
This large beachside hotel is five minutes' drive away from the capital, with all the usual facilities, including two pools and restaurant. All rooms and bungalows have verandas with a sea or garden view. €€€

Omiros
Ermoúpoli
Tel: 22810 24910
www.hotel-omiros.gr
The Omiros is a mid-19th-century neoclassical mansion restored to a high standard. Rooms are furnished in traditional style with views of the lively harbour. €€

Palladion
Stamatíou Proíou 60, Ermoúpoli
Tel: 22810 86400
www.palladion-hotel.com
Very convenient yet quiet hotel, especially if you get a room (some balconied) overlooking the interior courtyard. Rooms have laminate flooring, built-in shelving and modernised baths. Breakfast (included) can be disappointing, though in summer you can choose extra dishes to order. €€

Sea Colours
Ermoúpoli, Vapória district
Book through Teamwork Travel
Tel: 22810 83400
www.teamwork.gr
Ten different sized studios and apartments for up to six, right above their own swimming lidos; one of the quietest spots in town. €€

Tínos

Cavos Studios
Pórto beach
Tel: 22830 24224
www.cavos-tinos.com
Good beachside base in an island short on them; studio bungalows set in vast stoned grounds with rustic touches (niches, beamed balconies) and fully equipped kitchens. Some are semi-detached at ground level, some are in wings. €€

Porto Raphael
Ágios Ióannis district, Pórto
Tel: 22830 23913
www.portoraphael.com
Superbly designed and meticulously managed beachside complex of studios and apartments housing up to six people; the buildings flank a lawn garden rolling down to the sea. No pool, and if it's windy (often the case) you can't really use the adjacent beach. Good breakfast, and on-site

restaurant for other meals; staff are helpful about arranging car hire and/or port transfers, as you are slightly isolated. €€€

Tinion
Hóra
Tel: 22830 22261
www.tinionhotel.gr

Charming old-world hotel in the centre of town, with tiled floors, lace curtains and a large veranda café where breakfast is served. €€

THE SPORADES AND EVVIA

Alónissos

Konstantina's Studios
Hóra (Paleá Alónissos)
Tel: 24240 66165
www.konstantinastudios.gr
High up in the old renovated village, this small, traditionally renovated building houses eight wood-floored studios and one apartment, plus a garden. All have exceptional sea views, flagstone floors and balconies with canvas deckchairs. €€

Milia Bay
Miliá
Tel: 24240 66032
www.milia-bay.gr
Tucked away overlooking tiny Miliá Bay, this quiet retreat consists of 21 ecologically constructed self-catering apartments (sleeping two–six people), all tastefully decorated; in-house restaurant, free Wi-fi in reception. If you don't fancy the short walk to the beach there is a pool, which hosts occasional scuba courses. €€€

Yalis
Vótsi
Tel: 24240 66186
www.yalishotel.gr
Superior suite-hotel on a clifftop with sweeping views (only two of the 20 units don't have them). The biggest suites, all with quality dark-wood furniture, clock in at 45 sq metres (484 sq ft); others are galleried, with a slight step down and roof frame visible overhead. Breakfast, served on airy terrace, has egg-and-bacon options. Free Wi-fi throughout. Open Apr–Oct. €€€

Evvia

Karystion
Kriezótou 2, Kárystos
Tel: 22240 22391
www.karystion.gr
A busy foreigner-friendly hotel in the far south of Évvia, close to the fortress on Kárystos's coastal promenade. Neat, air-conditioned rooms were redone in 2005, and the common areas overlook (and to some extent occupy) part of the shoreline park. There's a good bathing beach immediately to the east. Open Mar–Oct. €€

Mousiko Pandohio
Stení, west entrance to village

Tel: 22280 51202
www.mousikopandoxeio.gr
This is the brainchild of a Greek composer-musician Tassos Ioannides, long resident in Australia. The name means "Musical Lodge", and musical decorative motifs – plus regular weekend acoustic concerts in the lounge – predominate. The rooms vary from standard doubles, some with fireplaces, to quads and suites suitable for families. The attention to detail throughout – with the entire family having participated in the design – is admirable. A one-of-a-kind hotel for the island. €€

Thermae Sylla Spa Wellness Hotel
Loutrá Edipsoú
Tel: 22260 60100
www.thermaesylla.gr
Perhaps Greece's only official anti-stress hotel, this magnificent Belle Epoque edifice at the northern end of the promenade – the most renowned of several such hotels in this resort – is a turn-of-the-century experience brought up to date with beauty and therapy treatments based on the waters of the ancient spa. Spa also open to the public. €€€

Skiáthos

Aegean Suites
Megáli Ammos, 1.5km (1 mile) west of town
Tel: 24270 24069
www.santikoshotels.com
This suite hotel is the adults-only sister to its chain-mate the Skiathos Princess. Not a beachfront position, but it is high enough to avoid road noise and has its own parking. There being just 21 units adds to the exclusive feel. They are all big (55–60 sq metres/592–646 sq ft), with bug screens, Wi-fi and sound systems; "de luxe" ones differ only in having an unobstructed sea view. There is a large pool, small but pleasant gym, a stone-clad breakfast gazebo and a "live cooking" poolside restaurant. Management could be friendlier, though. €€€€

Atrium
Above Agía Paraskeví beach, , 9km (5 miles) from town
Tel: 24270 49345
www.atriumhotel.gr

This four-star resort is tastefully modern without being over the top, with wood tones and white surfaces predominating in the five grades of rooms or suites (which can accommodate four people); the original architect family who designed and built it, still runs it There are two pools, extensive lounges, a restaurant and, of course, free Wi-fi throughout, as well as sweeping sea views south. Breakfast, served by the pool, includes baked goods and traditional egg dishes like strapatsáda. Open May–mid-Oct. €€€€

Mandraki Village
Koukounariés, behind Strofyliá Lake
Tel: 24270 49670
www.mandraki-skiathos.gr
If you're not insistent on staying by the sea, this inland hotel, built in 2007 in broad landscaped grounds, may appeal to you. The junior suites are worth the small price difference over standards for their bigger bathrooms, and there are also family units, all in tasteful pastel colours – although the on-site Elia's restaurant is rather luridly hued. Free Wi-fi throughout. €€€

Skópelos

Adrina Beach/Adrina Resort & Spa
Pánormos
Tel: 24240 23371
www.adrina.gr
This well-designed, four-star hotel complex (39 airy standard rooms and 10 vine-draped bungalows, redone in 2013) occupies a hillside between Pánormos and Miliá, overlooking a wood-decked saltwater pool and private pebble beach with restaurant. Its adjacent stablemate, built in 2011, is the five-star "Resort & Spa" comprising 22 hillside villas accessed by a funicular. These range up to 85 sq metres (915 sq ft), and can fit six

PRICE CATEGORIES

Price categories are based on the cost of a double room for one night in the high season:
€ = under €70
€€ = €70–120
€€€ = €120–200
€€€€ = over €200

easily. Decor here is more minimalist, in grey or beige tones. There's a breakfast/supper restaurant and large infinity pool. The basement spa is appealing. Adrina Beach (May–Sept) €€€, Adrina Resort & Spa (June–Sept) €€€€

Kyr Sotos
Hóra, just in from mid-quay
Tel: 24240 22549
www.skopelos.net/sotos/
A rambling pension in a traditional old house, with 12 wood-floored rooms, all en suite. This is justifiably a favourite budget option on what can be an expensive island for accommodation. The rear units (all with air-conditioning) facing the courtyard are quieter. If you can choose, the best is No. 4, which has a fireplace. €

Madro Travel
Hóra, northwest end ofquay
Tel: 24240 22145, www.madrotravel.com
Handles the best portfolio of self-catering accommodation on the island, from studios in the Hóra to luxurious

villas-with-pool in the surrounding countryside. Wedding party organisation and special activities programmes also offered. €€–€€€

Skopelos Village
Hóra, far east side bay
Tel: 24240 22517
www.skopelosvillage.gr
This is the top accommodation in town, renovated in 2007 – when some of the *Mamma Mia!* film-cast parties took place here – with new units added in 2011. These range from "Sea Breeze" studios up to family apartments that can sleep six people; all have nice touches like Victorian-style taps and rain showers There are two outdoor pools, Wi-fi throughout the complex, a superior restaurant terrace, and a lovely white breakfast buffet salon (included in rates despite notional self-catering layout). Open May–early Oct. €€€

Skýros

Linaria Bay
Linariá, south hillside

Tel: 22220 93274
Very friendly, well-kept rooms, with individual balconies and a common terrace ideal for catching the sunset. A good choice for out-of-season visits when there's little advantage to staying near the beaches. €€

Nefeli – Skyriana Spitia
Hóra
Tel: 22220 91964
www.skyros-nefeli.gr
A mix of standard hotel rooms and a stand-alone group of "traditional Skyrian houses" (actually cosy, two- to three-person studios), this is a well-run complex around a salt-water pool at the village entrance. .€€€

Perigiali
Magaziá
Tel: 22220 92075
www.perigiali.com
Very welcoming secluded mix of studios and well-furnished rooms with phones and heating during winter months, overlooking a large garden where breakfast is offered. €€

THE NORTHEAST AEGEAN

Foúrni

Archipelagos
Overlooking fishing port
Tel: 22750 51250
www.archipelagos.gr
A 2007-built hotel with high-quality fittings for its 18 doubles and suites, a very keen proprietor, and an on-site restaurant operating during summer. €€

Patra's Rooms
Immediately left of the kaïki quay
Tel: 22750 51268
www.fourni-patrasrooms.com
Choose between wood-floored, antique-furnished bedrooms, some with balconies, just above the family sweet shop where you can take breakfast, or 14 superb apartments, some sleeping up to four, in a tiered hillside complex with privacy dictated by the layout but views as expected. Rooms €, apartments €€

Híos

Argentikon Luxury Suites
Kámbos
Tel: 22710 33111
www.argentikon.gr
Much the most opulent of the various Kámbos estates restored as holiday accommodation, the Argentikon reopened in 2005 after a long closure, as one of the most exclusive lodgings in the Mediterranean. The suites are distributed over

five buildings (two dating from the 16th century) and are furnished with valuable antiques. It's a self-contained resort, with full-service restaurant (breakfast typically delivered to one's suite), pool, spa, meeting room and extensive gardens. The estate is deliberately unmarked and unsigned – get directions on booking. €€€€

Chios Rooms
Egéou 110, Híos Town
Tel: 22710 20198
www.chiosrooms.gr
Upstairs rooms with high ceilings and tile-and-wood floors, some en suite, in a lovingly restored building managed by a New Zealand/Greek couple. Best is the penthouse, with a private terrace; others have small balconies. €

Kyma
East end of Evgenías Handrí
Tel: 22710 44500
Email: kyma@chi.forthnet.gr, kkk@otenet.gr
Hotel in a converted neoclassical mansion (plus less attractive modern extension); the best old-wing rooms have large sea-view terraces, although fittings are due for a refurbishment. Pluses are the extremely helpful management and good breakfasts served in the original salon with a painted ceiling. €€

Markos' Place
South hillside, Karfás beach
Tel: 22710 31990 or 69732 39706

www.marcos-place.gr
Inside a disused medieval monastery, Márkos Kostálas has created a uniquely peaceful, leafy environment. Guests are lodged in the former pilgrims' cells; individuals are welcome at several single "cells", as are families (two "tower" rooms sleep four). Minimum stay four days; open Apr–Nov. €

Mavrokordatiko
Kámbos district, 1.5km (1 mile) south of the airport on Mitaráki lane
Tel: 22710 32900
www.mavrokordatiko.com
One of the more affordable restoration projects in the Kámbos, with heated wood-panelled rooms and breakfast (included) served in the courtyard with its *mánganos* (waterwheel). €€

Medieval Castle Suites
Mestá village
Tel: 22710 76345
www.mcsuites.com
No expense has been spared in these high-end apartments located in a central mansion in this listed village. All units have sumptuous baths, mini-kitchens and either a ground-floor patio or roof terrace – the latter a necessity in what can be a claustrophobic environment. Open Easter–Oct. €€

Spitakia
Avgónyma

Tel: 22710 20513–4
www.spitakia.gr
A cluster of small but well-restored houses taking up to five people, near the edge of this stunningly set west-coast village. €€

Volissos Travel
Tel: 22740 21421
www.volissostravel.gr
Six apartments spread over several old village houses restored in the early 1990s. Units, all with period features, accommodate two people or a family of four. Very advantageous offers with hire car included (a necessity if staying here). €–€€

Ikaría

Akti
On a knoll east of the hydrofoil and kaïki quay, Agios Kírykos
Tel: 22750 22694
www.pensionakti.gr
Family-run pension offering a balcony or terrace with stunning views for most rooms and Wi-fi signal through-out. Proprietress Marcia, raised in Ohio, is a mine of local information. An excellent choice if you have an early boat to catch. €

Daidalos
Aremenistís
Tel: 22750 71390
www.daidaloshotel.gr
One of the less "packaged"-feeling hotels in this resort, with decent breakfasts on a shady terrace, rooms appointed with quirky artistic touches and an eyrie-pool above the sea. €€

Erofili Beach
Armenistís
Tel: 22750 71058
www.erofili.gr
Considered the best hotel on the island, though the ample common areas are more impressive than the sea-view rooms. Breakast is served inside, or just outside on a veranda. A small saltwater pool perches dramatically over Livádi beach. €€€

Lésvos

Aphrodite Beach
Eastern end of Vaterá beach
Tel: 22520 61212
www.aphrodite hotel.gr
Owned by an extremely friendly Greek-Canadian family, the blue and white painted units are kept spick and span and have little balconies with sea views. Great food in the attached taverna too. €

Clara
Avláki, 2km (1.5 miles) south of Pétra
Tel: 22530 41532
www.clarahotel.gr
The large, designer-furnished rooms (in grades up to one- and

two-bedroom suites) of this pastel-coloured bungalow complex look north to Pétra and Mólyvos. Particularly renowned for its ample buffet breakfasts relying on local products. Tennis courts and a pool. €€–€€€

Delfinia
1km (0.5 mile) south of Mólyvos
Tel: 22530 71315
www.hoteldelfinia.com
One of the first resort-type hotels erected around Mólyvos, and still one of the best: a mix of standard rooms and bungalows set in 35 hectares (87 acres) of orchard and garden. The rooms could do with a makeover (the bungalows are more updated), but the staff is friendly and willing, and the breakfast (served on an outdoor terrace) is substantial. There is also a castle-view pool and direct access to the best part of Psiriára beach. €€–€€€

Pyrgos
Eleftheríou Venizélou 49, Mytilíni
Tel: 22510 25069
www.pyrgoshotel.gr
The town's premier restoration accommodation in a 1916-vintage mansion, with over-the-top kitsch decor in the common areas. Rooms, most with balconies, are perfectly acceptable, and there are three round units in the tower. "American" breakfast; secure off-street parking. €€€

Sandy Bay
Agios Isídoros
Tel: 22520 32825
www.sandybay.gr
While geared for package tours, this is still much the best hotel in this resort or neighbouring Plomári, set inland and uphill. Well-appointed rooms (although balcony partitions are lacking) set in a pleasant garden laid to lawn around the pool. €€

Vatera Beach
Vaterá
Tel: 22520 61212
www.vaterabeach.gr
A rambling hotel set behind the best beach on the island. Rooms (only a few have sea views) with air-conditioning and minibar, free sunbeds, an in-house restaurant relying on own-grown produce; now being run by the children of the original proprietors. €€

Votsala
Paralía Thermís, 12km (7.5 miles) from Mytilíni
Tel: 22510 71231
www.votsalahotel.com
Especially if you have transport, this makes an attractive alternative to staying in Mytilíni Town proper. This is

a sophisticated beachfront hotel set in gardens, where the erudite owner makes a point of not having TVs in the rooms, or "Greek nights", or a pool, or air-conditioning, or a spa – yet claims to have 60 percent repeat clientele. €€

Límnos

Afrodite Villa
Platý beach
Tel: 22540 23141
www.afroditi-villa.gr
Run by returned South African Greeks who are continually overhauling the various wings and annexes of this complex, this comfortable small hotel has a large pool, sumptuous buffet breakfasts, and hosts occasional barbecue nights. €€

Evgatis Hotel
Evgátis beach
Tel: 22540 51700
Expanded in 2008, this small, modern hotel overlooks the best beach on the island (100 metres/yds across the road), with a decent attached taverna. You will need a car though, as Límnos bus service is almost non-existent. €€

Ifestos
Andróni district, Mýrina
Tel: 22540 24960
An attractive small hotel whose rooms have a mix of seaward and hillside views, balconies, fridges and air-conditioning. €€

Sámos

Amfilissos
Bállos beach, near Órmos Marathókambos
Tel: 22730 31669
www.amfilissos.gr
The hotel itself is nothing extraordinary, but Bállos is a deliciously sleepy place for doing very little except exploring the coast to the southeast and sampling some excellent local tavernas. €€

Arion
1km (0.5 mile) west of Kokkári
Tel: 22370 92020
www.arion-hotel.gr
The best accommodation on Sámos's north coast, a family-friendly, well-designed hotel-wing and bungalow complex on a hillside. Famously good breakfasts. €€€

PRICE CATEGORIES

Price categories are based on the cost of a double room for one night in the high season:
€ = under €70
€€ = €70–120
€€€ = €120–200
€€€€ = over €200

Athena
West beach road, Kokkári
Tel: 22730 92030
Email: h-athena@otenet.gr
The best accommodation available on a walk-in basis at this north-coast resort, with contemporarily appointed rooms distributed over three buildings in carefully tended grounds (including a large pool) right across from the beach. Very clued-up Greek-Canadian proprietor. Open Apr–Oct. €€

Daphne
Platanákia, 1km inland from Ágios Konstandínos
Tel: 22730 83200
www.daphne-hotel.gr
Modern, airy hotel with flagstones underfoot throughout, bathrooms with tubs and marble trim, knockout views (especially from the pool terrace) and fridges in the white-tiled, pastel-tinted rooms. Some package-company allocation, but usually walk-in vacancies. The affiliated restaurant on the shore is Fawlty Towers resurrected – you have been warned. Open early May to late Oct. €€

Doryssa Seaside Resort
Pythagorion, near airport
Tel: 22730 88300
www.doryssa.gr
One of the few actual beachfront resorts on Sámos, with a saltwater pool just in from the sand if the sea is too cold. Choose between the designer-refitted hotel wing or the meticulously constructed fake

"village", no two houses being alike, and incorporating all the various vernacular styles of Greece. An ayurvedic spa is now in place. €€€€

Ino Village
Kalámi district, 1km (0.5 mile) out of Vathý
Tel: 22730 23241
www.inovillagehotel.com
Well-run 3-star hotel with adequate parking, views, a big pool and (unexpectedly) a decent restaurant. The best-value choice for staying in or near the capital. €€

Kerveli Village
Approach to Kérveli beach
Tel: 22730 23631
www.kerveli.pro-samos.com
This is a well-executed, smallish bungalow hotel set among olive trees and cypresses, with superb views across to Turkey and over Kérveli Bay. A good selection of beaches (including the private lido) lie within walking distance, but you'll want to take advantage of in-house car rental. €€

Psili Ammos Apartments
Psilí Ammos (easterly), beyond the right-hand taverna.
Tel: 22730 25140 or 6946 976068
Superior waterside apartments not block-booked by tour companies, with unimpeded views across the straits to Turkish Mount Mykale. A wonderful, secluded retreat. €

Samothráki

Aiolos
Kamariótissa

Tel: 25510 41595
www.hotelaiolos.gr
Samothráki's port and capital is home to a few hotels, including this decent mid-range choice. The rooms are simple but spacious. Some have views overlooking the hills, others look towards the sea. €€

Mariva Bungalows
Loutrá (Thermá)
Tel: 25510 98258
www.mariva.gr
Situated in the island's resort centre, these lovely flower-shrouded bungalows are built on a gentle hillside near the route to the Gría Váthra waterfalls. All units are self-contained, comfortable and reasonably spacious. Hosts summer yoga retreats. €€

Thásos

Kipos Studios
Liménas
Tel: 25930 22469
With a nice flowery garden surrounding its small pool, this place has ground floor doubles and larger apartments on the upper floor. €

Thassos Inn
Panagía village
Tel: 25930 61612
www.thassosinn.gr
Quiet except for the sound of water in runnels all around, this modern building in traditional style has most of its rooms – all with balconies – facing the sea. Free Wi-fi signal. €€

RHODES

Andreas
Omírou 28D, Rhodes Old Town
Tel: 22410 34156
www.hotelandreas.com
At the highest point of the Old Town stands this exquisite little pension with seven comfortable and individual rooms, from galleried doubles to a spectacular tower suite in what was a Turkish mansion. All units are air-conditioned, but some bathrooms are down the hall. New since 2013 is an enormous front patio-garden, the venue for breakfast or drinks; the old terrace bar has arguably the best view in the Old Town. Two-night minimum stay. Open Mar–Nov. €€

Elafos
Profitis Ilías
Tel: 22460 22402
www.elafoshotel.gr
After languishing neglected for decades, this Italian-built period piece from 1929 reopened in 2006

as a boutique hotel. The high-ceilinged units (the three suites are worth the extra charge) have considerable retro charm, and there are great views of sky and forest from the balconies. The à la carte ground-floor café makes a good rest stop if touring – try their homemade carrot-nut cake (evening meals only by arrangement). €–€€

Lindian Village
Near Glýstra Cove, east coast
Tel: 22440 35900,
www.lindianvillage.gr
This ingeniously designed bungalow complex has its own private beach, a small spa/gym, a central "lazy river" bubbling through, several gourmet restaurants and three grades of units (the suites have their own secluded plunge-pools). Although children are accommodated, it is really more of a romantic adults' resort. Open May–Oct. €€€€

Lindos Mare Hotel
Vlýha, east coast
Tel: 22440 31130
www.lindosmare.gr
Situated on a hillside just 2km (1 mile) northwest of Líndos, this tiered hotel (€€€) manages to feel low-key and intimate despite comprising 142 designer units (one-third of them suites). A funicular (or shady walkway) brings you down through lush grounds from the larger of two pools to the beach. There are also two full-service restaurants and a fully equipped spa. Immediately adjacent, the ultra-sleek adults-only **Lindos Blu** €€€€ (tel: 22440 32110, www.lindosblu.gr) is a five-star annexe, with only water features for relief. Unlike its neighbour, its units – in several grades, many with private pools – are often full, thanks in part to exceptional levels of staff service and a repeat clientele. Both open May–Oct.

Marco Polo Mansion
Agíou Fanouríou 42,
Rhodes Old Town
Tel: 22410 25562
www.marcopolomansion.gr
Hardly noticeable off the cobbled thoroughfare, this discreet inn, converted from a rambling old Ottoman mansion, is stunning once inside. All rooms are furnished with antiques from the nearby eponymous gallery, plus natural-fibre, handmade bedding; the garden-side rooms are a bit cheaper (but also less airy). Buffet breakfasts (enhanced continental style, with fruit and muesli) are served in the courtyard which is well, which becomes one of Rhodes' best restaurants after dark. Open Easter–mid-Oct. €€€

Melenos
Líndos, second lane above the north beach, by the school
Tel: 22440 32222
www.melenoslindos.com
Constructed in traditional style, this boutique hotel has taken advantage of the best location in the village. The 12 cedar-wood-trimmed units vary in plan, but all have wooden bed-platforms, big designer baths with glazed Kütahya tiles, and semi-private sea-view patios with mosaics underfoot. Whether it is worth the price tag of up to €800 a night is a personal decision. There is an equally pricey bar-restaurant

sheltering under a fabric marquee with stunning views. €€€€

Niki's
Sofokléous 39, Rhodes Old Town
Tel: 22410 25115
www.nikishotel.gr
An excellent budget hotel, most rooms (last redone in 2006) with balconies, free Wi-fi and air-conditioning. Helpful management and credit-card acceptance. €

Paraktio Apartments
Kiotári
Tel: 22440 47278
www.paraktio.com
Exceptionally well-appointed studios for couples, and galleried four-person apartments with huge seaview terraces, perched on a bluff just above a nice stretch of beach; the units are fully self-catering, but there is a small snack-and-breakfast bar on site. Friendly family management; no package bookings. €€

Rodos Park Suites
Ríga Fereoú 12, New Town
Tel: 22410 24612
www.rodospark.gr
Arguably the best-quality accommodation in the New Town (yet very convenient for the walled city), this boutique hotel offers three grades of rooms or suites with tasteful soft furnishings and sleek modern fittings. Rear units face a quiet hillside and archaeological dig, front ones overlook the fair-sized pool. A highlight is the wood-decked

summer roof-bar, with unrivalled views. The basement spa, free gym/sauna/hammam and two competent on-site restaurants (one poolside) complete the picture. €€€€

Spirit of the Knights
Alexandrídou 14 by Hamza Bey Mosque, Old Town
Tel: 22410 39765
www.rhodesluxuryhotel.com
"Medieval chic" sums up this six-suite, eco-friendly hotel in a painstakingly restored 15th-century manor house on a quiet cul-de-sac. One of the loveliest gardens in the old quarter comes complete with fountain, breakfast tables and jacuzzi. The upstairs suites, many galleried and one with a hamam, all lead off an oriental-style salon with well-stocked library. Pleasant, arcaded bar-lounge downstairs. Felicity and her extended family are keen to please, meeting guests at the designated taxi-drop off point at the D'Amboise Gate. €€€€

Triton Holidays
Plastíra 9, Neohóri
Tel: 22410 21690
www.tritondmc.gr
Full-service agency with a broad portfolio of accommodation not only on Rhodes, but across the Dodecanese, which they can book for you as a bespoke itinerary, at very advantageous prices. All the travel arrangements to get there handled as well. €–€€€

THE SOUTHERN DODECANESE

Hálki
Most accommodation is block-booked by package companies from April to October; here are two exceptions.

Captain's House
North of the church and inland
Tel: 22460 45201
Four-room, en suite pension in a converted mansion with garden bar and ever helpful Christine, your hostess. €

Aïnikolas Hotel
Emborió quay
Tel: 22460 45333
www.ainikolas.com
Occupying the old sponge factory on the south side of the bay, with its own lido, this historic building was gutted and completely rebuilt in 2007–8, and after a false start as the Hiona Art Hotel has been rebranded under new management from summer 2013, and now offers quality accommodation. €€€

Kárpathos
Akrogiali Studios
Potáli Bay, Paralía Lefkoú
Tel/fax: 22450 71178
Just eight spacious units, all with raised bed platforms in traditional Karpathian style and views towards the pebble beach; friendly management and mini-market downstairs for restocking. €

Astro
Ólymbos
Tel: 22450 51421
A good, relatively comfortable en suite guesthouse in this traditional village, kept by the two sisters who manage the Café Restaurant Zefiros, where breakfast is served. €

Atlantis
Pighádia (by the Italian "palace")
Tel: 22450 22777
www.atlantishotelkarpathos.gr
Well-appointed hotel with helpful staff in a quiet setting; easy parking and small pool. Space is held back for

non-package travellers. €€

Glaros
Diafáni
Tel: 22450 51501
www.hotel-glaros.gr
The most comfortable and well-placed lodgings here (although comfort is only relative in northern Kárpathos), 16 tiered studio units on the south hillside, some accommodating families and all with great views north. George and Anna are wonderful hosts. €

Vardes Studios
Amopí beach

Tel/fax: 22450 811111 or 6972 152901
www.hotelvardes.gr
The best standard here among outfits
accepting walk-in trade, with 10
huge studio units overlooking well-
tended gardens some way inland.
Family environment, good breakfasts
available. €

Kásos

Angelica's Traditional Apartments
Frý
Tel: 22450 41268
www.angelicas.gr
A restored family mansion overlooking
Boúka port has been converted into
four, stone- or tile-floored apartments
of varying sizes, from studio to family
suite. Preference given to five-day
minimum stays. €€–€€€

Evita Village
Emboriós
Tel: 22450 41731
www.evita-village.gr
Built in 2007, this impeccable
complex sits on a slight rise
overlooking the sea, and represents
the highest standard on the island
with its large, open-plan studios. €€

Kastelórizo

Karnayo
Platía at west end of the south quay
Tel: 22460 49266
www.karnayo.gr
The best restoration accommodation
on Kastellórizo, designed by an
architect. Rooms, studios and a four-
bed apartment occupy two separate
buildings, with wood-and-stone
interiors. No breakfast provided. €

Kastellorizo
West quay
Tel: 22460 49044
www.kastellorizohotel.gr
This hotel's air-conditioned,
quality-fitted studios or galleried
maisonettes, some with sea view,
offer the best facilities on the island,
featuring mock-antique solid-wood
furnishings, proper shower stalls and
DVD players. Order your breakfast
choices on a checklist the night
beore. Tiny plunge pool, and its own
lido in the bay. Very welcoming hosts.
Open March–late Oct €€

Mediterraneo Pension
North end of the west quay
Tel: 22460 49007

www.mediterraneo-megisti.com
Another architect-executed
refurbishment, this offers simple but
well-appointed rooms with sculpted
baths (non-tiled), mosquito nets and
Asian textiles or other bright colour
splashes. Half facing the sea, the
pièce de resistance is the arcaded
ground-floor, waterside suite. Optional
breakfast includes proprietor Marie's
home-made marmalade, charcuterie,
fruit. €€ rooms, €€€ suite

Sými

Albatros
Gialós marketplace
Tel: 22460 71707
www.albatrosymi.gr
Partial sea views from this
exquisite, small hotel with French
co-management; pleasant second-
floor breakfast salon, and air-con. The
website also gives booking access to
co-managed apartments suitable for
families in various restored houses
around town. €€

Aliki
Haráni quay, Gialós
Tel: 22460 71665
www.hotelaliki.gr
This 1895-vintage mansion right on
the quay was tastefully converted into
one of Sými's most exclusive hotels
during the 1990s. The tasteful rooms
or suites all have wooden floors and
antique furnishings, though be aware
that only some (at a premium price)
have sea views and/or balconies.
Open Apr–Nov. €€€

Les Catherinettes
North quay, Gialós
Tel: 22460 71671
Email: Marina-epe@rho-forthnet.gr
Creaky but spotless en suite pension
above a restaurant of the same name,
in a historic building with painted
ceilings and sea-view balconies in
most rooms. The management also
offers three studios in Haráni, plus a
family apartment. € rooms, €€ studios

Iapetos Village
Gialós, inland from square
Tel: 22460 72777
www.iapetos-village.gr
The best of several fair-sized
bungalow complexes in Gialós. It
comprises maisonettes fitting up to
six and self-catering studios, arrayed
(rather extravagantly for dry Sými)

around a covered pool and luxuriantly
landscaped grounds. Actual room
decor is simple – exposed roof
beams, pale tiles – but adequate. A
generous breakfast is offered by the
pool bar, or you can prepare your own
in the well-equipped kitchens. Open
Apr–Nov. €€€

Symi Visitor Accommodation
Just in from Gialós's west quay
Tel: 22460 71785
www.symivisitor-accommodation.com
Wendy and Adriana offer a wide range
of restored properties, ranging from
simple studios to mansions suitable
for large families. All are serviced
second homes let in their owners'
absence, so they come with fully
equipped kitchens, libraries, music
systems – and unpredictable quirks.
Available Apr–Nov. €€–€€€

Tílos

Blue Sky Apartments
Ferry dock
Tel: 22460 44294
www.tilostravel.co.uk
Nine well-appointed, galleried
apartments for 2 to 3 persons, with
great views of Livádia Bay. €€

Elli Bay
Livádia, start of pedestrian coastal walk
Tel: 22460 44435
www.ellibay.com
Newish, wood-floored apartments
with iron beds and mosquito nets
offer the best standard offered
amongst a cluster of rooms and
studios establishments along the
coastal walk. Rates include breakfast
despite self-catering format. €€

Irini/Ilidi Rock
Livádia
Tel: 22460 44293
www.tilosholidays.gr, www.ilidirock.gr
Long the top hotel on Tilos, just five
minutes' walk from the beach, Irini
(open May–Oct) still wins points for its
beautiful grounds and common areas,
including a large pool, though 1986-
built rooms are due for a makeover.
The same management keeps the
hillside Ilidi Rock Aparthotel (open all
year), which has outstripped its stable
mate with a conference hall, gym,
sauna (but no spa), private beach and
one wing with disabled access; both
studios and four-person apartments
here. € Irina, €€€ Ilidi Rock.

THE NORTHERN DODECANESE

Astypálea

Australia
Skála
Tel: 22430 61855

Rooms and studios upgraded in
2002, with phones, fans and air-
conditioning; there's an excellent
affiliated restaurant below. €€

Kalderimi
East hillside, Livádia
Tel: 22430 59843
www.kalderimi.gr

Eleven variable cottages built in island style, impeccably equipped with air-conditioning, CD players, Wi-fi access and satellite TV, as well as embroidered curtains and some vaulted ceilings. Some units accommodate families. Open Apr–Oct. €€€

Kilindra Studios
Southwest slope of Hóra
Tel/fax: 22430 61131
www.astipalea.com.gr
Mock-traditional units (capacity three) built in 2000 in the shadow of the castle, offering all luxury amenities, including a swimming pool; open Apr–Dec. €€€

Maltezana Beach
Análipsi (Maltezána)
Tel: 22430 61558 (summer); 2105 624823 (winter)
www.maltezanabeach.gr
A state-of-the-art bungalow hotel built in 2003, and the island's largest, with spacious, well-appointed standard rooms and even bigger suites arranged around gardens and a pool. On-site restaurant; open Easter–mid-Sept. €€ standard room, €€€ suites

Venetos Studios
Base of west hillside, Livádia
Tel: 22430 61490
www.venetosstudios.gr
Units in several buildings scattered across an orchard; facilities range from basic studios to four-person cottages. Open May–Sep. €€

Kálymnos and Télendos

Acroyali
Myrtiés, lower road
Tel: 22430 47521 or 6938 913210
www.acroyali.gr
Exceptionally tastefully appointed seaview apartments, with colour splashes offsetting marble flooring, set quietly below the road, each sleeping two adults and two children; you're five steps from the best bit of Myrtiés beach. Unsurprisingly they require booking months in advance. Open May–Oct. €

Oasis
Massoúri
Tel: 22430 47572
This is a reliable two-star hotel choice, with a switched-on owner and staff, small lawn garden plus breakfast terrace, and best views to Télendos from the top floor rooms, all tastefully done up and tile-floored. €

Porto Potha
Tel: 22430 47321
www.telendoshotel.gr
At the very edge of things, but this hotel, a mix of plainly decorated standard doubles and studios, has

a large pool and a friendly managing family. Open Apr–Oct. €

Villa Melina
Evangelístria district, Póthia
Tel: 22430 22682
www.villa-melina.com
The town's top, and top-value, choice: en-suite rooms, refurbished in 2006, in a late 19th-century sponge magnate's mansion, plus an annexe of modern studios behind the pool and gardens. Very good breakfasts served on the patio; a warm welcome assured from Andonis, Themelina and family. €–€€

Kós

Afendoulis
Evrypýlou 1, Kós Town
Tel: 22420 25321
www.afendoulishotel.com
Welcoming, family-run two-star hotel: cheerful en suite rooms with air-conditioning and fridges, most with balconies, plus some cooler basement "caves", much sought after in summer. Proprietors are as helpful hosts as you could hope for – including port transfers with prior arrangement – and Dionysia's breakfasts, served on the front patio, are well worth ordering, up to noon. Free Wi-fi in common areas. Open Apr–late Oct. €

Diamond Deluxe
Néa Alikarnasós, Lámbi
Tel: 22420 48835
www.diamondhotel.gr
The most stylish, 2009-built "wellness and business" hotel in the countryside, with vast common areas including two pools (one for laps, the other irregular), a spa, water features, and a focal bar. Many of the 110 units (often full), in several grades of rooms or suites, give directly onto the bigger pool, though some suites have their own. White-painted, stone-clad mid-category rooms have veneer flooring, computers for internet access, marble-surfaced bathrooms with proper tub/shower screens and Jacuzzi. Open Apr–Oct. €€€€

Fenareti
Mastihári
Tel: 22420 59028
http//:fenareti.kosweb.com
Hillside hotel in the least packaged of Kós's coastal settlements, overlooking the widest part of the beach; rooms and studios in a peaceful garden environment, with kitchen corners and mosquito nets. €

Kos Aktis Art Hotel
Vassiléos Georgíou 7, Kos Town
Tel: 22420 47200,

www.kosaktis.gr
The former Kos Xenia got a designer makeover some years ago, and is now the town's most prestigious address. Both standard doubles and suites, in earth tones, all face the water; bathrooms are lit with light wells and sport butler sinks. Common areas include a gym and very popular beachside restaurant/bar. €€€

Kos Imperial Thalasso
Psalídi
Tel: 22420 58000
www.grecotel.com
One of the premier members of the Grecotel chain, this standard-wing and bungalow hotel with stunning common areas abuts a good beach in landscaped tiers. Individual units are spacious and well-appointed, though not cutting-edge in decor. The thalasso-spa is, of course, the heart of the establishment. Unfortunately, when the wind blows from the northwest, there are whiffs from the nearby sewage plant. €€€

Sonia
Irodótou 9, Kós Town
Tel: 22420 25594
A 2009-renovated small hotel, long a backpackers' haven, overlooking the Hellenistic baths. Rooms are large, wood-floored and en suite. Self-catering kitchen and terrace. Open late Mar–early Nov. €

Léros

Alinda
Alinda beach road
Tel: 22470 23266
www.alindahotel-leros.gr
The first hotel established here, this has well-kept 1970s-vintage rooms (recently refurbished) with a mix of sea and mountain views, plus a respected restaurant downstairs. €

Archontiko Angelou
Alinda, signposted well inland
Tel: 22470 22749
www.hotel-angelou-leros.com
Marvellously atmospheric converted Belle Epoque mansion hiding amid orchards, with the feel of a French country hotel. Victorian bath taps, beamed ceilings, old tile (ground floor) or wood (upstairs) floors and antique furnishings. Two of the eight rooms have balconies; garden bar

PRICE CATEGORIES

Price categories are based on the cost of a double room for one night in the high season:
€ = under €70
€€ = €70–120
€€€ = €120–200
€€€€ = over €200

TRANSPORT

ACCOMMODATION

EATING OUT

ACTIVITIES

A – Z

LANGUAGE

and breakfast area. Open May–Oct. €€€

Crithoni's Paradise
Krithóni, inland
Tel: 22470 25120
www.crithonisparadisehotel.com
Léros's top-rated accommodation, a low-rise complex of four wings with a smallish pool, disabled access and large, well-appointed rooms – though subject (like everywhere on the island) to mosquito invasion. Decent buffet breakfast; very reasonable poolside breakfast. €€

Tony's Beach
Vromólithos beach
Tel: 22470 24742
www.tonysbeach.com
Spacious, 2011-refurbished units set in extensive grounds behind one of the best beaches on the island; access for people with disabilities; ample parking, very quiet. Designer bathrooms, small pool, free Wi-fi. Open mid-May–mid-Oct. €€

Lipsí

Aphrodite
Behind Liendoú beach
Tel: 22470 4100
Built in 1997, this is an attractive studio-bungalow-hotel complex, with large units. It has a small bar near the sandy beach. Open all year in theory. €€

Nefeli
Overlooking Kámbos beach, 700 metres/ yds from the port
Tel: 22470 41120
www.nefelihotels.com
This 2008-built bungalow-hotel complex is Lipsí's most luxurious. Studios and one- and two-bedroom apartments share the same pastel decor; upstairs units are better ventilated. €€ studio, €€€ apartment

Rena's Rooms
Overlooking Liendoú beach
Tel: 22470 41110 or 6979 316512
Email: renas1022@hotmail.com
One of the first, and still one of the best, simple domátia establishments on the island; just five well-kept rooms

on a hilltop (Nos. 3 and 4 overlook the beach). Rena, a font of information (and husband John who runs the best local boat-trips), live upstairs. €

Nísyros

Porfyris
Mandráki centre
Tel: 22420 31376
www.porfyrishotel.gr
The best conventional hotel on the island, whose rooms got a much-needed makeover in 2009 (with another refit set for early 2014) – though breakfasts still need attention. They overlook either orchards and the sea, or the large saltwater pool. Open Apr–Oct. €€

Liotridia
On the shore lane near the windmill, Mandráki
Tel: 22420 31580
Email: liotridia@nisyrosnet.gr
Two comfortable suites in a restored house – one of the few such projects on Nísyros – for up to four people; worth the premium price for sea views and volcanic-stone-and-wood decor. Lively bar downstairs, so noise might be a problem. €€€

Romantzo
Mandráki port
Tel: 22420 31340
www.nisyros-romantzo.gr
The best budget choice on the island, with a mix of rooms and studios, not all of them having bay views – though there is a huge communal terrace. €

Pátmos

Asteri
Skála, Netiá district
Tel: 22470 32465
www.asteripatmos.gr
Great setting on a knoll overlooking the sea to the west, of which the lounge and breakfast salon takes full advantage. Rooms are variably sized; some have air-conditioning or disabled access. Own-grown produce at breakfast, easy parking, free Wi-fi. €€

Blue Bay
Skála, Konsoláto district

Tel: 22470 31165
www.bluebaypatmos.gr
This is the last building on the way out of town towards Gríkou, thus spared the late-night ferry noise that plagues most hotels here. Rooms, with blue soft and quality wood furnishings, also have fridges, balconies (most with bay view), safe and air-conditioning. Under dynamic new management from 2013, with complimentary toiletries and Wi-fi signal. €€

Effie
Skála, Kastélli hillside
Tel: 22470 32500
Bland, blonde-pine-and-tile rooms spread over two hotel wings, but with balconies and air conditioning they're good value and in a quiet setting. €€

Galini
Skála
Tel: 22470 31240
In a quiet cul-de-sac near the ferry quay, this C-class hotel offers B-class standards in furnishings and bathrooms, and excellent value. €€

Porto Scoutari
Hillside above Melöï beach
Tel: 22470 33124
www.portoscoutari.com
The island's top accommodation: enormous rooms and suites, arrayed around the pool, have sea views and air-con, plus antique furnishings and original wall art, all refreshed in 2012. . Elína the proprietor is a font of island knowledge. Excellent pool/sea-view breakfasts. On-site spa, wedding packages available. Open Apr–Oct. rooms €€, suites €€€

Studios Mathios
Sápsila Cove
Tel: 22470 32583
www.mathiosapartments.gr
If you have a car or bike, these bucolically set superior self-catering units make an idyllic base, with their creative furnishing and decor, extensive gardens and a welcoming managing family. The two adjacent coves, however, are not among Pátmos' best for swimming. €€

CRETE

Agía Galíni

Neos Ikaros
Tel: 28320 91447
www.neosikaros.gr
A bit out of the centre, at the foot of a hillside, but still handy for the seafront, this amphitheatrically arrayed, 29-unit hotel has large rooms with pine furniture, blue soft furnishings, air-con and fridge and,

best of all, an inviting pool garden. €€

Agía Rouméli

Tarra Rooms/Hotel Calypso
Tel: 28250 91231
www.agiaroumeli.gr/tarra/index.html
Having hiked the Gorge of Samariá, reward yourself with a beach-side stay rather than pelting off immediately

to Hóra Sfakíon. Two brothers offer either basic rooms, with a taverna downstairs, or a more comfortable nearby hotel. Closed when the gorge is (typically Nov–early Apr). €–€€

Agios Nikólaos

Du Lac
Ikostiogdóis Oktovríou 17
Tel: 28410 22711

www.dulachotel.gr
Right beside Lake Voulisméni in the heart of the action, the excellent-value Du Lac offers a mix of designer rooms and studios (the latter effectively one-bedroom apartments), half of which overlook the water. Convenient ground-floor restaurant and café. €€

Minos Beach Art Hotel
Aktí Ilía Sotírhou, Ammoúdi
Tel: 28410 22345
www.bluegr.com
De luxe coastal resort: mostly bungalows plus a few suites amidst mature gardens, set on a small peninsula studded with specially commissioned contemporary sculpture. A five-star outfit – rack rates for sea view bungalows run from €400–600 for a double – with service standards to match, and a clutch of on-site restaurants. €€€€

St Nicolas Bay Resort Hotel and Villas
Tel: 28410 25041
www.stnicolasbay.gr
On the Nisí peninsula overlooking Mirabéllo Bay 1.5km (about a mile) north of town, the stone-clad St Nicolas Bay offers discreet luxury with an admirable degree of privacy for its suite-sized standard rooms, superior suites with private infinity pools, and a cluster of three- or-four-bedroom villas with a private lido. Sandy coastline is limited to one small cove, but there's a full water sports programme and 10-metre (34ft) sailing boat to charter. A spa, kid's club and several (pricey) à la carte restaurants complete the profile. Open Apr–Oct. €€€€

Elounda Beach
Tel: 28410 63000
www.eloundabeach.gr
One of the most luxurious resorts in Greece, overlooking Mirabello Bay; many of the villas have a private pool and gym, and main-wing rooms are of generous size. Private beach, spa, the usual complement of on-site bars/restaurants, and a high repeat-visit rate amongst the jet-set clientele. €€€€

Elounda Mare
Tel: 28410 68200
www.eloundamare.gr
Stablemate of the co-managed Porto Elounda complex (many facilities are shared), the Elounda Mare strikes a warmer, more intimate note, especially in its bungalows and bungalow-suites with their fireplaces, wood floors and private sea-water pools. Superior suites in the main wing clock an impressive 42–70 sq

metres (452–753 sq ft). The lounge and common areas continue outside as lovely terraced grounds leading down to stone lidos – there's little real beach. Open late Apr–late Oct. €€€€

Anastasia Stathis
Approach road, 5km down from Plátanos village
Tel: 28220 41480
www.stathisanastasia.com
Closest (300 metres/yds distant) quality lodging to the legendary beach here; big, simply decorated pension rooms and self-catering studios. Breakfast on request in the stone-clad salon. €

Anna's House
300 metres/yards across the river bridge, towards Vámos
Tel: 28250 61556
www.annashouse.gr
More accurately Anna's houses, comprising four grades of rooms, apartments and villas, in landscaped grounds around a large pool. Beige-and-brown-accented luxury apartments measure a spacious 60 sq metres (646 sq ft), with butler sinks and properly screened bathtubs. Open 15 March–15 Nov. €€€

All listings are near the Old Harbour and open all year unless stated.

Casa Delfino
Theofánous 7
Tel: 28210 93098
www.casadelfino.com
Honeymoon-calibre suite-format hotel, where designer fittings are juxtaposed with recycled timber. The premises have been renovated by a descendent of the Genoese Delfino family which originally built this mansion. Differing units all have handmade Italian furniture and marble or solid wood flooring. Newer are three suites in an adjacent building, a spa and roof-terrace bar; still the same excellent service. €€€€

Doma
Venizélou 124, Halépa district
Tel: 28210 51772
www.hotel-doma.gr
This converted neoclassical mansion was once the Austro-Hungarian, then the British Consulate. Now it's one of the gems of Crete, neither stuffy nor luxurious but appealing to those who want a low-key yet personal stay recalling the genteel old days. The owner has a prized hat collection and has filled the public

areas with antiques. The top-floor suite is unbeatable, but standard rooms are elegant enough. The dining room serves Cretan specialities for breakfast and pre-booked dinner. Open Apr–Oct. €€–€€€

Porto del Colombo
Theofánous 7, Tophanás
Tel: 28210 70945
www.portodelcolombo.gr
This Venetian mansion had previously served – in the following order – as the Ottoman military command, the French consulate and Eleftherios Venizelos' offices before being restored as a 10-unit boutique hotel, most recently in 2010. Rooms, especially the galleried maisonettes, are large, with carved-wood furniture and coloured tiles plus proper shower stalls in the bathrooms. There are also two-bedroom apartments adjacent. €€–€€€

Theresa
Angélou 8, west side of Old Port
Tel: 28210 92798
www.pensiontheresa.gr
This characterful, budget pension occupies another old mansion in the Tophanás area. Seven en suite, often galleried rooms are accessed by the town's most serpentine wooden staircase; the best are on the first floor. If you arrive and reception is unattended, simply book yourself in. There's a small kitchen, and roof terrace for great views over the harbour. Breakfast is available next door at Café Meltemi, where the Theresa's owner Giorgos Nikitas often sits. Loyal repeat clientele and new word-of-mouth introductions mean advance booking essential in season. €

Vranas Studios
Agíon Déka, corner Kalliníkou Sarpáki, near cathedral
Tel: 28210 58618
www.vranas.gr
Set back a bit from the water, so quieter, and more "modern" than most Old Town restoration projects, but none the worse for it. Tile-floored, wood-ceilinged rooms are spacious and furnished in contemporary manner; although self-catering, breakfast is available in the lounge. €€

PRICE CATEGORIES

Price categories are based on the cost of a double room for one night in the high season:
€ = under €70
€€ = €70–120
€€€ = €120–200
€€€€ = over €200

Ierápetra

Cretan Villa Hotel
Lakerdá 16
Tel: 28420 28522
www.cretan-villa.com
An 18th-century mansion restored as a hotel, the best in the town centre; rooms, arrayed around a pleasant courtyard, are simple but with nice touches like exposed stone pointing. Free Wi-fi zone; friendly owner full of helpful local advice. €

Kakkos Bay
Koutsounári, 9km (6 miles) east of town
Tel: 28420 61241
www.kakkosbay.com
1980s-vintage but very pleasant little resort scattered amidst well-tended gardens, pines and olive trees. Spacious bungalows (preferable to standard ones) resembling Cretan country chapels from outside, with blue-and-white trim and travertine floors inside, acommodating two to three people. The pool with all-day restaurant seems superfluous, since the complex borders one of the calmest sandy coves in the region, sheltered from prevailing winds. Open May–Oct. €€

Iráklio

Galaxy Hotel
Dimokratías 75, south of Platía Eleftherías
Tel: 28102 38812
www.galaxy-hotel.com.gr
The city's top-drawer hotel, with 2008-redone rooms and suites (all the expected comforts), grand public spaces and willing service. Interior-facing units are quieter, and you lose nothing as regards the view. Facilities include a large pool, gym, restaurant and two bars (one at poolside). €€€

Lato
Epimenídou 15
Tel: 2810 228103
www.lato.gr
Iráklio's first self-styled boutique hotel, renovated again in 2012, with the best, balconied rooms or suites facing the Venetian harbour (singles are very small; suites are worth the extra money). Walkable to all attractions yet reasonably quiet at night; summer roof-garden restaurant. Other amenities include a sauna and "mini-gym" plus unbeatable views over the old Venetian harbour. €€€

Lena
Lahaná 10
Tel: 2810 223280
www.lena-hotel.gr
Small (12-room) hotel renovated in 2003 – much of the effort went into the common areas, so rooms are still in two grades: bathless with fan (three rooms) or en suite with air conditioning (the rest). Free Wi-fi access. €

Marin Dream
Doukós Bofór 12
Tel: 2810 300018
wwwmarinhotel.gr
Another boutique hotel with sweeping port views from the spacious front rooms – again, singles are tiny. A good breakfast is provided at the roof restaurant (not otherwise recommended). €€€

Mirabello
Theotokopoúlou 20
Tel: 2810 285052
www.mirabello-hotel.gr
Excellent location makes up in part for the datedness of some of the rooms all of which have balconies. Other facilities comprise communal fridge, free Wi-fi, satellite TV lounge. €

Kastélli-Kissámou

Galini Beach
East end of seafront near sports stadium
Tel: 28220 23288
www.galinibeach.com
Modern but well-executed hotel with Art Deco touches, right behind pebbly Telonío beach. Air-conditioned, spotless rooms and apartments, full (not continental) breakfast served on the terrace. Rooms €, apartments €€.

Káto Zákros

Stella's Traditional Apartments
Tel: 28430 23739
www.stelapts.com
Looking down over the local oasis to the eastern edge of Crete, these comfortable apartments are set in lush terrace-gardens with hammocks. There's spring water on tap and a sense of complete peace. The same family also keep five studios and a villa nearby, and have admirably helped signpost local paths. €€–€€€

Kolymbári

Selini Suites
Rapaniá district
Tel: 28240 83033
www.selinisuites.com
A mix of large studios and one-bed apartments in this beachfront holiday complex pitched at families, with plenty of children's amenities. €€

Loutró

Blue House
Tel: 28250 91127
www.bluehouse.loutro.gr
A mix of seafront, en suite rooms and slightly more expensive upstairs units at this informal *pension*, as well as a very creditable on-site taverna. €

Porto Loutro
Tel: 28250 91433
www.hotelportoloutro.com
The largest hotel in this road-free, beachless settlement, spread over two premises (one five steps from the water). Rooms have beam ceilings, slate floors, marble-trimmed baths. Hospitable Anglo-Greek management. Open Apr–Oct. €€

Makrýgialos

White River Cottages
Aspropótamos district
Tel: 28430 51120
Email: wriver@otenet.gr
The abandoned hamlet of Péfki, comprising 13 traditional stone cottages complete with original fireplaces, has been architect-restored since the 1980s as studio, one-bedroom and two-bedroom apartments around a swimming pool. Excellent local gorge-walking and flora-spotting opportunities, especially in spring or autumn, and you are just inland from some of the most sheltered beaches of southeastern Crete. Open Apr–Oct. €€

Mátala

Eva Marina
Tel: 28290 45125
www.evamarina.com
Blonde-pine furniture and white-tile decor in a small 1980s-vintage hotel, set in lush gardens just 100 metres/yds back from the sea. €

Mýrtos

Big Blue
West edge of town, by Roman cistern
Tel: 28420 51094
www.big-blue.gr
Choose from three grades of lodging at this ecologically run complex with the best views in the resort. Just 10 steps to the beach, with a small terrace garden for breakfast; extremely knowledgeable proprietor. €–€€

Omalós

Exari
Tel: 28210 67180
www.exari.gr
Best of three hotels in this hamlet, aimed at walkers wanting an early start down the Gorge of Samariá; the in-house restaurant relies in part on products of the managing family's cheese factory. The name comes from a famous six-man (*exári* in Greek) local raiding party during one of the 19th-century rebellions against the Ottomans. €

Palékastro

Marina Village
Behind Koureménos beach
Tel: 28430 61284
www.marinavillage.gr
The three small wings of this
1980s-built hotel are idyllically set
in olive groves and orchards, if a bit
hard to find (follow the signs). Rooms
are fair-sized, if a bit nondescript;
common areas include a pool,
tennis court and shady breakfast
gazebo. Snack bar, but no full-service
restaurant. Free Wi-fi. Open 15
April–31 Oct. €€

Paleóhora

Sandy Beach
Tel: 28230 42138
www.sandy-beach.gr
Cosy (12-room) hotel sited, as the
name suggests, behind the town's
main beach, near the castle; with
balconied, spacious sea-view rooms
done up in predominantly dark green
and ochre tones, and a cheerful
ground-floor breakfast salon. €€
Zafiri 2
100 metres/yds back from Pahiá Ammos
(west) beach
Tel: 28230 41811
www.zafiri-studios.com
Studios and apartments on a quiet
lane, with spacious, pleasant bedsit
areas and long, narrow balconies
affording limited sea views, though
bathrooms are dated. The USP is the
vast front lawn-garden where guests
take their breakfast. €€

Plakiás

Just about every rented room, studio
or apartment establishment near the
beach or in the surrounding hamlets
– some 150 of them– can be found,
complete with photos and contact
details, on the community website
www.plakias-filoxenia.gr.

Plataniás

Minoa Palace
West edge of "town"
Tel: 28210 36500
www.minoapalace.gr
This place is well located outside the
tatty main strip just before the river,
although the beach is a short walk
away across the road. The rooms and
suites are up to five-star standard, but
only the superior beachside annexe
have sea views. There are good pools,
a centrepiece basement spa and half
a dozen on-site restaurants and bars,
the main one serving one of the best
hotel buffet breakfasts to be had in
the country. It is family-friendly, so
it seems that the rack rates are not
always levied. €€€

Réthymno

Fortezza
Melissinoú 16
Tel: 28310 55551
www.fortezza.gr
This modern yet stylish hotel on
the north side of the old quarter,
just below the Venetian fortress,
is handy for the town centre and
waterfront, yet quiet. Comfortable,
air-conditioned rooms, renovated in
2011, represent great value; medium-
sized pool in the courtyard. Parking a
few blocks away. €€
Palazzo Vecchio
Melissinoú, corner Iróön Polytehníou
Tel: 28310 35351
www.palazzovecchio.gr
A 15th-century Venetian building
converted into a complex of self-
catering studios and apartments with
warm-toned soft furnishings. Patio
plunge-pool with adjoining bar, but no
restaurant. €€€
Sea Front
Arkadíou 159
Tel: 28310 51981
www.rethymnoatcrete.com
If you want to be on the beach, this
– an old mansion converted into
a pension with 10 well-equipped,
wood-floored, en suite rooms – is the
closest spot, while still convenient to
the centre. The same owners manage
the modern Sea View Apartments
nearby, comprising four studios
and two family units (which don't,
however, have the sea views). €€
Veneto
Epimenídou 4
Tel: 28310 56634
www.veneto.gr
One of the better restoration inns,
occupying a 14th-century Venetian
building in the old quarter, including
an acclaimed in-house restaurant
(half-board rates given). Public areas
– including a large, arcaded courtyard
with three potable springs, where
breakfast is served – somewhat
overshadow the rooms; upper-storey
ones are airier and balconied. €€€

Sitía

Arhontiko
Kondyláki 16
Tel: 28430 28172
An old neoclassical mansion
converted into a basic but
atmospheric pension (only one room
is en suite). There is an orchard-
garden out front. €
El Greco
Arkadíou 13
Tel: 28430 23133
www.elgreco-sitia.gr
Best-value and friendliest hotel in the
town centre, with good views from ·

the higher rooms and a pleasant
lobby. Only down side: tricky street
parking. €
Itanos
Platía Iróön Polytehníou
Tel: 28430 22900
www.itanoshotel.com
Waterfront three-star hotel, with a
roof garden, restaurant and some
disabled-accessible units. Rooms
were redone in 2008. €

Spíli

Heracles
Tel: 28320 22111
Email: heraclespapadakis@hotmail.com
The quietest and best-run of three
extant lodgings in this mountain town,
Heracles has well-kept balconied
rooms with bug-screens; the owner is
a mine of information about the area.
Breakfast included; bicycles available
for rent. €

Vámos

Vamos
Tel: 28250 22190
www.vamosvillage.gr
Restored, stone-built houses
scattered through Vámos Old Town,
just 20 minutes from the sea.
Accommodation ranges from two-
person maisonettes (the majority),
with bedroom and bath upstairs,
lounges with fireplace downstairs,
to houses suitable for up to eight,
with private or shared pool. There's
an affiliated taverna, self-guiding
walks and cooking courses held in an
abandoned olive mill. €€–€€€

Vlátos

Milia Mountain Retreat
Tel: 28210 46774
www.milia.gr
This 'eco-lodge' has rescued a
1945-abandoned village in the hills
of western Crete, off a secondary
road between Kastélli Kissámou
and Paleóhora. Old stone cottages
of different sizes (two–four persons)
have fireplaces for cool nights. An
excellent affiliated taverna serves
up three meals daily, based on local
produce. By day, you can hike through
nearby gorges or take painting
courses; nights are spent gazing at
the stars. €€

PRICE CATEGORIES

Price categories are based on the
cost of a double room for one night
in the high season:
€ = under €70
€€ = €70–120
€€€ = €120–200
€€€€ = over €200

EATING OUT

RECOMMENDED RESTAURANTS, CAFES AND BARS

WHAT TO EAT

There is considerable regional variety in Greek cuisine and sadly, there's also considerable variety in quality.

Vegetarians are not well catered for; most main courses will include fish or meat. Your best bet is combining a selection of *mezédes* (little plates of food and dips, hot or cold), many of which are vegetarian or dairy-based.

WHERE TO EAT

Eating establishments have much the same profile throughout the islands.

However, the classical taverna is by no means the only establishment. You will also find the *estiatório*, the traditional urban restaurant, which ranges from an *(ino)magirío* or tradesman's lunch-hour hangout, with ready-cooked *(magirevtá)* food and bulk wine, up to pricey linen-tablecloth places with bow-tied staff.

The *psistariá* is a barbecue restaurant specialising in lamb, pork or chicken on a spit; a *psarotavérna* specialises in fish and shellfish; while *gyrádhiko* and *souvlatzídiko* stalls purvey *gýros* and *souvláki* respectively, sometimes to a sit-down trade, garnished with salads.

Popular among the intelligentsia are *koultouriárika* restaurants, Greek nouvelle cuisine based on updated traditional recipes; and *ouzerí* (or *mezedopolío*, or *tsipourádika* in the northern islands), where the local tipple accompanies *mezédes*.

Some tavernas, especially in non-touristy areas, may not have menus out, in which case it's wise to establish the price of at least the most expensive main courses.

WHEN TO EAT

For Greeks lunch is taken between 2pm and 3.30pm. The evening meal, between 9pm and 11.30pm, can either be another full meal, or an assortment of *mezédes*.

FISH AND SEAFOOD

Seafood is generally expensive, except for frozen squid. Scaly fish are usually in an iced tray for you to choose from, and your dish is priced by weight (less often by the portion). It is prudent to watch the (uncleaned) fish being weighed, and reiterate the price you are quoted, as "fingers on the scales" and later misunderstandings are not unknown. There is also a great deal of farmed and frozen seafood (often marked on menus only with a "k" or "kat.", for *katapsygméno*, or just an asterisk) lying in ambush for the inexperienced.

ALCOHOLIC DRINKS

Bottled wine at a tavern will cost €12–28 depending on quality and where you are; bulk wine (*hýma*) runs €6–12. Oúzo or *tsípouro* comes usually in 200ml *karafákia*, starting from €6; on Crete, local *rakí* is much cheaper.

COFFEE, CHOCOLATE AND TEA

Whole arabica beans suitable for cafetière or percolator coffee are making steady inroads among locals and tourists fed up with the ubiquitous "Nescafé", which has become the generic term for any instant coffee.

Espresso and cappuccino are becoming nearly as common as in Italy, though not always so expertly made. *Freddoccino*, another resourceful Greek invention, is a cold double cappuccino for the summer months.

Ellenikós kafés is Greek coffee, made from fine-ground robusta beans, boiled and served with the grounds in the cup – the same style as across the Balkans and Middle East. A large cup is a *diplós*. Sugar (lots of it for Greeks) is added at the preparation stage.

Chocolate drinks *(tsokoláta)* can be very good indeed, served cold or hot according to season.

Tea *(tsáï)* is the ragged stepsister of the hot-drinks triad. Quality bulk or bagged tea, whether green or black, is sold in speciality shops, but you'll usually have to make do with teabags of obscure Ceylonese or Madagascan vintage, served either with milk or with lemon *(me lemóni)*. Herbal teas are easy to find in shops, and at more traditional *kafenía*. *Hamomíli* is camomile tea, and *alisfakiá* (sage tea) is found on many of the Dodecanese and Cyclades.

Austerity dining

The ritual of families and friends patronising tavernas twice a week is now suspended, thanks to hard times. Most Greeks, not just students nursing one coffee all evening, have had to learn to be careful with money. It is still considered an honour to snaffle the bill and pay for everyone, but long gone are the days when diners would order more starters towards the end of the meal, destined never to be touched, just to impress.

ATHENS

Avli
Methónis 43, Exárhia
Tel: 210 38 38 167
There is indeed a small *avlí*
(courtyard) here, but most seating
is inside this engaging taverna
doing all the standard oven dishes
and appetizers (plus some creative
recipes like chicken-and-spinach
soufflé) with a deft touch. Open Mon–
Sat lunch and dinner, closed Aug. **€**

Diporto
Sokrátous 9, corner Theátrou, basement;
no sign out
Located at the western edge of
the central market district, *Diporto*
attracts a varied clientele, from
"suits" to market-stallholders. They're
here for the excellent, no-nonsense
grub: grilled or fried fish of the day, a
stew or two, and mountainous salads.
Space is limited, so you're expected
to share tables with strangers. Open
Mon–Sat noon–6pm. **€**

Karavitis
Arktínou 33 and Pafsaníou 4
Tel: 210 72 15 155
Pangráti's last surviving 1920s
taverna, purveying baked casseroles,
a few mezédes or grills, and
inexpensive Mesógia bulk wine.
Large portions somewhat offset high
mains prices. Traditional desserts like
quince or semolina helva; outdoor
seating in a lovely garden across the
street, indoors with the now-empty
wine barrels. Supper only. **€€**

Klimataria
Platía Theátrou 2, central market district
Tel: 210 32 16 629
www.klimataria.gr.
An excellent source of hearty, meat-
based dishes like stir-fry with leeks
or mature lamb with *stamnagáthi*
greens – as the row of *gástres*, the
traditional backcountry stewing
apparatus, tips you off as you enter.
There are vegetarian and fish choices
(like stuffed *thrápsalo*) too, and live
acoustic music Thur–Sun lunch.
Open daily, closed Sun night. **€€**

Kriti (Takís)

Stoa at Veranzérou 5, off Platía Kánningos
Tel: 210 38 26 998
Popular little Cretan stéki (hangout)
serving regional dishes such as
apáki (cured pork), two kinds of
island sausage (prefer the Sfakian),
stamnagáthi greens and marathópita
(fennel pie), along with more usual
titbits like *dákos* salad and of course
Cretan rakí. A bit pricey for the area,
but portions are large. Open Mon–Sat
for lunch (when its popularity can
cause lags in service) and supper. **€€**

Mani-Mani
Falírou 10, Makrygiánni
Tel: 210 92 18 180
www.manimani.com.gr.
Installed on the top floor of a graceful
interwar house, this established
nouvelle-Greek-cuisine restaurant
does (as the name implies) have a
marked Peloponnesian tendency,
what with *sýnglino* (streaky pork) and
talagáni cheese from Messinía on the
menu, but there's a wide variety of
mezédes (try parcels containing cured
meat, goat cheese, Florina peppers,
walnuts in tomato sauce) salads,
pasta dishes and even some seafood
(squid and mussels in shrimp sauce),
as well as creative desserts. Open
Tue–Fri 3pm–midnight, Sat 1pm–
midnight, Sun 1–5.30pm. **€€€**

Nikitas
Agíon Anargýron 19, Psyrrí
Tel: 210 32 52 591
Probably the oldest (1967-founded)
taverna hereabouts, Nikítas purveys
a short but sweet menu, as well as
daily specials like oven-baked cheese
pie. Drink is confined to beer or ouzo,
and there are no sweets. But for good
value you can't beat it, especially
if seated outdoors under the trees
beside Ágii Anárgýri church. Open
Mon–Sat noon–6pm. **€**

Rakoumel
Emmanouíl Benaki 71, Exárhia
Tel: 210 38 00 506
Recently expanded place featuring
Cretan *mezédes* and *rakí* at accessible
prices. The menu (only in Greek)

offers platters like skinny sausages,
gialodádika (greens similar to lamb's
lettuce), and *paximádia* (dark rusks)
rather than bread. Very much a local
bohemian hangout; summer tables
out on the sidewalk. Open Mon–Sat
3pm–midnight; occasionally Sun. **€€**

Santorineos
Doriéon 8, Petrálona, metro Petrálona
Tel: 210 34 51 629
Cult taverna installed in an old
refugee compound and barrel-making
workshop from 1926; seating is in
small rooms or the lovely courtyard.
There's a limited menu of Santoríni
specialities, mostly pork-based (fish
dishes only by pre-order), washed
down by excellent island bulk wine,
thus the extra tag of "*krasotavérna*"
(wine tavern). If some of the dishes
are only three-and-a-half stars, the
atmosphere, service and low prices
merit four to five. Dinner only, Mon–
Sat, also Sun lunch in summer. **€**

Steki tou Ilia
Eptahálkou 5, Thissio
Tel: 210 34 58 052
Thessaloníkis 7, Thissío
Tel: 210 34 22 407
The two branches (150 metres/yds
apart and never open at the same
time) of this enterprise fill with locals
here for the house speciality: a big
platter of grilled succulent lamb chops
(or lamb's liver for the daring). Starters
like fáva, tzatzíki and hórta are more
than competent, service is quick, and
barrelled wine is reasonable. Take a
table in No. 5's garden, or sit indoors
under the wine barrels. Open Tue–Sat
supper only, Sun lunch. **€€**

Zahari kai Alati
Valtetsíou 47, Exárhia
Tel: 210 38 01 253
Self-described "bistrot bar" that
delivers on both fronts: superb, rich
mezédes platters served in a high,
glass-ceilinged atrium, plus a loft
bar with cozy rooms up the long
stairways. Friendly and buzzing, and
worth the slightly higher-than-average
prices for the area. **€€**

THESSALONÍKI

**Angelopoulos (To Meteora Vima tis
Garidas)**
Modiano Market, stalls 58–60, entry at
Vasileos Irakliou 31
Tel 2310 279867
Currently the best ouzerí/tsipourádiko
here, stressing seafood like fried
loútsi (baby barracuda), sardines;

good veggie/dairy mezédes including
khytipití, decent bulk wine. Mon–Sat
lunch/dinner. **€**

Apo Dhyo Horia
Vyronos 7, Platía Navarínou
Tel: 2310 269204.
Tiny spot with maybe 10 tables inside
(including the loft) and a few outdoors

PRICE CATEGORIES

**Prices indicated are for a meal per
person with modest intake of wine
or beer, rakí or tsípouro.**
€ = under 17 euros
€€ = 17–25 euros
€€€ = 25–34 euros
€€€€ = over 34 euros

in summer, but food to die for – both Cretan and Pondian (Black Sea coast) platters. Tuck into Cretan *kaltsoúnia*, Pondian kavourmás, outstanding pickled and baked vegetables (including aubergine stuffed with grated carrot), very spicy sausages, and powerful Cretan raki. **€**

Loxias
Isávron 5
tel 2310 233925.
Bohemian snack-café, a literati hangout (viz photos of authors near entrance), with windows onto Platía

Navarínou Roman ruins; it's okay to have just drinks (there's decent barrel beer) but their food is excellent – enormous heaps of of lamb sausages, mountainous salads, and various desserts. **€**

Toumbourlika
Kalapotháki 11
Tel: 2310 282174
Yet another of the city's famous *ouzerís*, hidden away in a narrow street off Platía Dimokratías, this consists of a couple of small, cosy rooms with a few outside tables. It

specialises in fish *mezédes*. Some live music at weekends. **€€**

Yedi
I. Paparéska 13, Kástra
Tel: 2310 246495
www.yenti.gr
High up next to the Yedi Küle former prison (thus the name), this laid-back and friendly *ouzerí* serves up large portions of *mezédes* from a daily changing menu. Choice of *oúzo*, *tsípouro* or house wine. Dinner only; live music several nights weekly.
€–€€

CORFU

Kérkyra Town

La Famiglia
Maniarízi and Arlióti 30, Campiello district
Tel: 26610 30270
Greek/Italian-run bistro specialising in salads, pasta, lasagne and Italian puddings. Excellent value and efficient service; limited seating both indoors and out, so reservations always mandatory. Open evenings only, Mon–Sat. **€€€**

Mouragia
Arseníou 15, north quay
Tel: 26610 33815
A good mix of seafood such as flash-fried *atherína* (sand smelt) and Corfiot specialities such as *sofríto* and *pastitsáda*, plus competent starters at this seaside ouzerí – though views to the sea, and Vídos islet, are over the road. Open Apr–Nov noon–12.30am. **€€**

Hryssomallis (Babis)
Nikifórou Theotókou 6
Tel: 26610 30342
The sign says zythopsitopolío ("beer-hall-grill"), but it's actually the last traditional oven-cooked food place in the Old Town: stews, *hórta*, *moussakás*, stuffed cabbage leaves, lentil soup and so forth, accompanied by smooth but potent red wine. From the outside tables on the street you can just see the Listón. The Durrells ate here during their 1930s stay; the restaurant has been around even longer. Open daily noon–10.30pm. **€**

Theotoki Family (Kerkyraïki Paradosiaki Taverna)
Alkiviádi Dári 69, Garítsa Bay
By far the best of half a dozen tavernas with tables out in the eucalyptus park here. A full range of *magirevtá* dishes and grills, plus some seafood, at very reasonable prices. Service can be leisurely, even by Corfu standards. Open lunch and dinner. **€**

Tsipouradiko
Prosaléndou 8–10, behind the Efetío

(Appeals Court), Spiliá
Tel: 26610 82240.
Tsípouro is popular on the mainland (but also many islands), accompanied here by such platters as grilled mushrooms, courgette pie, *tiganiá* (pork stir-fry), little fishes, and eggplant specialities. There is also decent bulk wine. The place is always packed with students and the bohemian set thanks to the warm atmosphere and friendly prices. Smoking allowed in the upstairs loft, or outside in the summer courtyard. Large groups must reserve, or be prepared for a long wait. Open Mon–Sat 8pm–1am. **€**

Around the Island

Alonaki Bay
Paralía Alonáki, near Korissíon Lagoon
Tel: 26610 75872
Good country recipes, strong on vegetables and seafood at shady tables on a terrace overlooking the sea. Their version of *biánko*, with *kéfalos* (grey mullet) hygienically raised in the lagoon and garnished with marsh samphire (*Salicornia europaea*), is to die for. Locals, and free-range chickens underfoot, usually outnumber tourists here – a good endorsement. If you can't tear yourself away from this lovely spot, they have inexpensive rooms to rent upstairs as well. Open Apr–Oct daily lunch and dinner. **€€**

Bacchus/Vakhos
Mesongí, south end of beach
Tel: 26610 75301
With a setting that can't be bettered, this waterside fish taverna prides itself on sourcing (mostly) local, fresh ingredients, like baby kalamári, large prawns, perfectly fried koutsomoúra and naturally coloured (not hot pink) taramosaláta. Open May–Oct daily lunch and dinner. **€€€**

Boukari Beach
Boúkari, 4km (2.5 miles) beyond Mesongí, 600 metres/yds before the jetty

Tel: 26620 51791
www.boukaribeach.gr
The best of the seafood tavernas at this seashore hamlet, in an idyllic setting with spectacular views up Corfu's east coast. Typical offerings might include mussels as a starter, heaping salads, succulent octopus (maybe as *bourdéto*) and a range of patently fresh scaly fish at fair prices. The Vlahopoulos family are accomplished hosts, and also have accommodation. Open Easter–Oct lunch and dinner. **€€–€€€**

Etrusco
Just outside Káto Korakiána village, on the Dassiá road
Tel: 26610 93342
www.etrusco.gr
Top-calibre nouvelle Italian cooking purveyed by father, son and spouses, served at a carefully restored country manor with its own farm for organic sourcing. Specialities like *timpano parpadellas* (pasta with duck and truffles), octopus carpaccio or lamb in kumquat sauce, and a 200-label wine list, don't come cheap, but this has been ranked one of the best five Greek tavernas outside of Athens. Early booking essential. Open Apr–Oct, dinner only. **€€€€**

Fagopotion
Ágios Stéfanos Sinión
Tel: 26630 82020.
The most accomplished of the several waterside tavernas here, *Fagopotion* has since 2008 established an enviable reputation for its traditional recipes, fresh (not farmed) fish caught around the Diapóndia islets and fair prices (given the posh location). Signature dishes include fluffy, non-greasy three-cheese *saganáki*, succulent, pork-based *bekrí mezé*, baby squid in late spring, rabbit stew, chard-based *tsigarélli* and melt-in-the-mouth octopus (it's blanched prior to grilling). Kosta's rosé bulk wine is

interesting. Open Easter–Oct daily for lunch and dinner, Nov–Easter Fri–Sat dinner, Sun lunch. €€–€€€

Foros
Paleá Períthia
Tel: 6955 950459.
One of the first tavernas in this once-deserted Venetian village, working out of a former café on the original square, and still one of the best – Rick Stein has called in approvingly. The emphasis here is on grills, but you can have a very enjoyable *mezédes*-only meal – sausages, *kremydópita* (onion turnover), stuffed peppers – while downing *tsípouro* or bulk wine. Save room for their famous *karydópita* (walnut cake) with ice cream. Open May–Oct daily, Nov–Apr weekends only. €

Klimataria tou Bellou
Main square, Benítses
Tel: 26610 71201
www.klimataria-restaurant.gr
Cult seafood taverna known for purveying only fresh items, and for

assiduous service from father-and-son team Nikos and Kostas. Fish is sold by portion or by weight, and includes some innovative dishes like sardine *bourdéto*; starters like leek salad and steamed mussels are commendable too. Good Neméa bulk white wine. Blink and you'll miss the mere eight tables outside, so reservations are highly advisable (though there's more seating inside). Open summer Mon–Sat dinner only, Sun lunch; winter Fri–Sun, but closed 1 Dec–15 Jan. €€–€€€

Kouloura
Kouloúra Cove
Tel: 26630 91253
Fairly priced seafood or fish, large selection of *mezédes* and salads, plus unusually elaborate pies at this taverna overlooking one of the most photogenic anchorages on Corfu. Open Apr–Oct daily all day; reservations needed at peak season.

Little Italy
Kassiopí, opposite Grivas supermarket

Tel: 26630 81749
Jolly trattoria in an old stone house run by Italian brothers; fare includes salmon in pastry parcels, pizza, pastas smothered in made-from-scratch sauces. *Limoncello* digestif on the house may follow. Reservations suggested. €€

Nikolas
Agní cove, south end
Tel: 26630 91243
www.agnibay.com
This taverna is the oldest one here, built as a family home and *café* in 1892. Today, Perikles and relatives serve Corfiot specialities like eggplant-and-cheese *bourékia* and lamb *kapamá*, along with their own wines (the bulk red is excellent). Service usually copes well with typical crowds. Tear yourself away from the picturesque view to browse the old photos and maps lining the walls inside. Open May–Oct daily lunch and dinner; may open winter weekends. €–€€

THE IONIAN ISLANDS

Itháki

Calypso
Kióni
Tel: 26740 31066
Specialities here include onion pie and artichoke soufflé with ham and cheese; not too inflated price-wise considering that yachts tie up nearby. Remarkably full Greek beer list. €€

Kohili
Around east quay, Vathý
Tel: 26740 33565
By far the best of all the harbour-side tavernas in the capital, specialising in traditional oven-baked main courses such as *kléftiko* and *yiouvétsi*, as well as some pasta dishes. €–€€

Nikos
Inland near the National Bank, Vathý
Tel: 26740 33039
A good all-rounder, with grills, a few *magirevtá* dishes daily, and fish; inexpensive bulk wine. Tourists go 8–9pm, then locals hold forth until closing time. €€

Paliocaravo
Around east quay, Vathý
Tel: 26740 32573
This well-established favourite with locals and visitors alike offers a fine range of *mezédes*, salads, meat and fish dishes, which can all be washed down with their light, refreshing bulk wine. €€

Rementzo
Fríkes
Tel: 26740 31719

This taverna features local recipes like *savóro* (cold fish in raisin and rosemary sauce) and chunky *astakomakaronáda* (lobster on pasta), and supports local producers, such as the suppliers of their bulk wine and sticky sweets. Portions on the small side, but so are prices. Open Apr–Oct all day. €

Ulysses
Fríkes
Tel: 26740 31733
Dine on reasonably priced fish and succulent meat dishes like rabbit *stifádo* or lamb *kléftiko*, whilst watching the gentle activity in the harbour. €€

Kefaloniá

Akrogiali
Lixoúri quay, towards south end
Tel: 26710 92613
An enduring, budget-priced institution, with largely local clientele. Tasty food with a stress on oven-casserole dishes (including *giouvétsi*, *kreatópita* and great *hórta*), but also fish and grills in the evening, plus excellent bulk wine. €

Arhondiko
Rizospastón 5, Argostóli
Tel: 26710 27213
Meatballs in roquefort sauce are an example of the unusual fare that is on offer inside this small but classy restaurant or on the even tinier patio. €–€€

Blue Sea (Spyros')
Káto Katélios
Tel: 26710 81353
Its speciality is pricey but clearly fresh and superbly grilled fish from the little anchorage adjacent. The bill can creep up if you add *mezédes* and bottled wine. €€–€€€

Foki
At the head of Fóki Bay
This is a very pleasant taverna, friendly and just opposite the beach. It serves simple but tasty food – *fáva*, *souvláki* and salads – and lovely *milópita* (apple pie). Much better, and far cheaper, than anything to be found in Fiskárdo. €€

Kyani Akti
Andóni Trítsi 1, far end of the quay, Argostóli
Tel: 26710 26680
A superb, if pricey, *psarotavérna* whose wood deck juts out over the water. The speciality is fresh fish and seafood, often with unusual items like the delicious *dáktylia* – "fingers" (razor clams in mustard sauce). There is also a range of *mezédes* and

PRICE CATEGORIES

Prices indicated are for a meal per person with modest intake of wine or beer, rakí or tsípouro.
€ = under 17 euros
€€ = 17–25 euros
€€€ = 25–34 euros
€€€€ = over 34 euros

salads, and some tasty house wine. **€€€**

Nirides
Asos, the far end of the harbour
Tel: 26740 51467
This little *estiatório* in a great spot overlooking the harbour has the usual range of salads and a few grilled and oven dishes, as well as fresh fish by the kilo. It is all well cooked – especially the fried peppers with cheese and *melitzánes imám*. **€€**

Odysseas
Agía Ieroúsalim Cove, 4km (2.5 miles) from Mánganos village
Tel: 6937 714 982
A hidden gem tucked behind this tiny, little-visited northern beach. Delicious home-style recipes like their own olive bread, and lamb stew made with free-range meat and organic vegetables. The proprietors also sell their own preserves. **€€**

Paparazzi
Lavránga 2, SW corner of main square, Argostóli
Tel: 26720 22631
Run by Italians who intend to teach the locals what real Italian food is: trattoria dishes, pasta and theatrical pizzas kneaded and twirled before your eyes. Very reasonable for the quality, with a few tables outside; open all year lunch and dinner. **€€**

Patsouras
Vergotí Kalypsoús, Argostóli
Tel: 26710 24440
Long-established *magirevtá* specialist in a new, swish location off the cenral square. Good rib-sticking food with especially tasty *bámies* (okra), a few grills, big portions and a velvety red house wine. Open all year. **€€**

Pevko
Andipáta Erísou, by the turn for Dafnoúdi beach
Tel: 26740 41360

Appetisers.

A serious contender for the best place to eat on the island, with seating outside under a huge pine tree. A mouthwatering selection of *mezédes*, oven-cooked dishes and some grilled meat and fish. Particularly good are the tomato, mint and *féta keftédes*, the *gígandes* (butter beans) and aubergine with garlic. **€€**

Romantza (Fotis Family)
Póros
Tel: 26740 72294
This *estiatório* is in a charming position, built into the headland at the end of the harbour. You eat on a first-storey balcony looking over the sea to Itháki. The focus of the menu is on a large range of fresh fish (priced by weight), but there are also good *mezédes* and salads. **€€**

Xouras
Petáni
Tel: 26710 97128
The location halfway along the best beach on the Lixoúri peninsula is ideal, and the Greek-American lady owner offers a warm welcome along with a good assortment of meat, fish and veggie dishes, washed down with decent bulk wine. **€**

Kýthira

Platanos
Mylopótamos
Tel: 27360 33397
Venerable former village *kafenío*, now a tavern, in an old building on the platía; *magirevtá* for lunch, grills in the evening. **€**

Sotiris
Avlémonas
Tel: 27360 33922
The better of two seafood tavernas here, doing perfectly cooked fresh fish. Often closed weekdays. **€€**

Levkáda

T'Agnandio
West hillside, Agios Nikítas
Tel: 26450 97383
Tucked away up a lane with sweeping views, one of the friendliest, least expensive home-style tavernas on the west coast. The stress is on *magirevtá* and fresh seafood such as *garídes* from the Amvrákikos Gulf. Creditable barrel wine; dinner only low season. **€€**

Palia Apothiki
Sývota
Tel: 26450 31895
A favourite among yachters, this lovingly converted 1710-vintage warehouse is the place to enjoy fare such as giant prawns wrapped in bacon. Good bulk wine. **€€–€€€**

Pantazis
Nikiána
Tel: 26450 71211

Appealingly set at the far end of the yacht harbour, this locally patronised taverna does fresh seafood at very reasonable prices – though salad trimmings could sometimes be fresher. *Magirevtá* in high-season evenings; open all day. **€€**

(Ta) Platania
Central platía, Karyá
Seating under the giant plane trees of the name, and fresh wholesome grills, salads and beers at budget prices. Tables for two other eateries share the square. **€**

Regantos
Dimárhou Verrióti 17, Levkáda Town
Tel: 26450 22855
Dinner-only taverna with a good balance of grills (especially spit-roasted chicken), oven food and fish; inexpensive and colourful. Sometimes hosts live *kantádes* sessions. Feb–Nov daily, supper only. **€**

Sapfo
On the beach, Agios Nikítas
Tel: 26450 97497
Innovative, deftly executed recipes such as seafood lasagne and cheese-and-courgette pie, decent bulk wine; not overpriced for the quality and arguably the best view in the resort. **€€**

Paxí

Alexandros
Platía Edward Kennedy, Lákka
Tel: 26620 30045
The most authentic *nisiótiko* cooking and most atmospheric setting in town; own-produced grilled meat (especially suckling pig) and chicken, specialities like rabbit *sofríto* and mushroom pie, and a few seafood dishes – but avoid the barrel wine. **€€**

Lilas
Magaziá
Tel: 26620 31102
Inexpensive little meat grill with good bulk wine in an ex-grocery shop at the centre of the island. Usually live accordion or stringed music at weekends. **€**

Vassilis
Longós quay
Tel: 26620 31587
Now often known as Kostakis after the son who's taken it over, this has grown from a grilled-fish specialist to an all-round taverna with imaginative recipes for *magirevtá*, like stuffed mushrooms and peppers, baked meat dishes and various oven pies. **€€**

Zákynthos

Akrotiri Taverna
Akrotíri, 4km (2.5 miles) north of Zákynthos Town
Tel: 26950 45712
A pleasant summer-only taverna,

going since 1958, with a large garden. Grilled meats are a speciality here, but they also bring round large trays of very tempting *mezédes* from which you pick and choose. The house wine is very acceptable. €€

Alitzerini
Entrance to Kilioméno
Tel: 26950 48552
Housed in one of the few surviving 17th-century Venetian village houses, this little *inomagerío* offers hearty, meat-based country cooking and its own wine; *kantádes* some evenings. Dinner only: June–Aug daily, Sept–May Fri–Sun. Reservations essential. €€

Fanari tou Keriou
1.5km (1 mile) beyond Kerí village
Tel: 26950 43384/69726 76302
Watch the moon rise over the Myzíthres sea-stacks below the Kerí cliffs. The food's on the expensive side, but portions are a fair size and quality is high – try the daily-made *galaktoboúreko* or vegetable-stuffed *pansétta*, redolent of nutmeg. Reservations essential. €€–€€€

Kakia Rahi
Pigadakia
Tel: 26950 63670
Set by a tiny stream in a leafy village

a few kilometres inland from Alykés, this taverna serves far more authentic island food, both baked and grilled, in its rambling courtyard than you would find in the resort itself. €–€€

Kalas
Kambí
By far the best taverna in Kambí, Kalas is set in a pretty garden, shaded by large trees, and serves up all the usual favourites (*fáva*, *loukánika*, *horiátiki* and *patátes*), all tasty and freshly cooked. Good bulk wine as well. €

Komis
Bastoúni tou Agíou, Zákynthos Town
Tel: 26950 26915
A lovely *psarotavérna* tucked into a rather unlikely spot behind the Port Authority building. The emphasis is on pricey but fresh and inventive fish and seafood dishes; but there is a good list of *mezédes*, decent wine and tempting desserts. €€€

Malanos
Agíou Athanasíou 38, Kípi district, Zákynthos Town
Tel: 26950 45936
Deservedly popular and inexpensive all-year shrine of *magirevtá*: mince-rich *yiouvarlákia* and *fasolákia yiahní*

are typical offerings. Unusually good bread as well as the expected barrel wine. Often hosts live *kantades*. €–€€

Mikrinisi Kokkínou
1km (0.5 mile) beyond Makrýs Gialós
Tel: 26950 31566
Standard, but reasonable, taverna food – *horiátiki, kalamarákia, souvláki* and other such offerings – but the situation is lovely, on the edge of a headland overlooking a tiny harbour. €

Porto Limnionas
Pórto Limniónas, below Agios Léon
Location can count for a lot. The food here is relatively expensive, standard taverna fare, but it is served on a promontory overlooking an idyllic rocky bay and facing west to the sunset. €€

Roulis
Kypséli Beach, near Drossiá
Tel: 26950 61628
Popular with islanders, Roulis gets very fresh fish – one of its main attractions – but also does the usual salads and vegetables well. The house wine is drinkable, and the generally fresh ingredients make it worth the detour from the main coast road. €€

THE SARONIC GULF

Aegina

Agora (Geladakis)
Behind fish market, Égina Town
Tel: 22970 27308
One of the oldest (founded c.1960) seafood outfits here, offering good value without airs and graces – you'll likely have to wait for a table. Summer seating on the cobbles outside, winter tables inside. Bulk wine or *oúzo* for refreshment. €

Deka
Perdika waterfront
Tel: 22970 61231
About the best-value, longest-running eatery here, with fare such as exceptional taramosalata, crunchy little shrimp, and succulent green beans, fair prices for scaly fish; opens at 6am to serve as the fishermen's café. €€

Ostria
Marathónas shore lane
Tel 22970 27677
The most southerly but one tavern in the line here, with tables on the sand and yes often a south wind (ostriá) for cooling. Small prices for somewhat small portions of seafood (such as the tasty local fish katsoúles); service can be distracted. €€

Angístri

Parnassos
Metóhi hamlet
Tel: 22970 91339
Besides the usual grills and *mezédes*, this friendly, rustically decorated spot, with Kyría Katína at the helm, serves its own-made cheese, a few dishes of the day and good bulk wine. €

Hydra

Gitoniko (Manolis and Christina)
Hydra Town
Tel: 22980 53615
Popular with locals and foreigners alike, To Gitoniko offers discreet rooftop dining as well as indoor seating downstairs. Lunch-hour *magirevtá* run out quickly, by 2pm; in the evening there are also grills, especially fish. Good-value dishes range from simple island vegetarian fare to signature dishes like veal in quince or red wine sauce. Excellent *hýma* wine. €€

Kondylenia
Kamíni
Tel: 22980 53520
The poshest tavern, with the best view, at this Hydriot suburb; select *magirevtá* and seafood (including good grilled cuttlefish on occasion) is the bill of fare. €€€

Koutouki tis Agoras
Rear of market hall, Hydra Town
The most genuine of the island's various *ouzerís*, with rickety tables and unpredictable hours. It's usually got going by early evening, though, with well-priced meat and seafood titbits. €

Póros

Karavolos
Póros Town
Tel: 22980 26158
Meaning a type of snail in Greek, Karavolos is a very popular backstreet taverna. Yes, the restaurant does serve snails, accompanied by a rich sauce, and there's a selection of ready-made *magirevtá* dishes as well as grills. Dine indoors or on a leafy patio. Reservations recommended. €€

PRICE CATEGORIES

Prices indicated are for a meal per person with modest intake of wine or beer, rakí or tsípouro.

€ = under 17 euros
€€ = 17–25 euros
€€€ = 25–34 euros
€€€€ = over 34 euros

Mezedokamomata
Galatás quay
Tel: 22980 43085
It's well worth taking the passenger shuttle across from Póros, then walking 150 metres/yds north, for the accurately described *mezedokamómata* (*mezédes* feats) served here: *stamnagáthi* greens, beets, *tyrokafterí*, grills and bulk wine. A very sweet family who run the place and frontal view of Póros are extra bonuses. Open all year. **€**

Platanos
Póros Town
Tel: 22980 24249
High up in the backstreets under a plane tree (*plátanos*), the speciality here is grills ranging from regular steaks to *kokorétsi*, mixed offal on a long skewer. The atmosphere is relaxed; evening is the best time to enjoy this place. **€**

Exedra (Tou Siora)
Old Harbour
Tel: 22980 73497
High-quality *magirevtá* like *mousakás* and vegetarian *laderá*, as well as some fish dishes, are the stock-in-trade here. Outdoor quayside seating, and a very small price premium considering the quality, compared to neighbouring establishments. **€€€**

Liotrivi
Old Harbour
Tel: 22980 72269

Another fish tavern inside an old olive press (*liotrívi*), with a very attractive location near the old boatyards. Mainly Greek clientele enjoy all kinds of variations on fish and other seafood. Best for evening dining. **€€€**

Patralis
Kounoupítsa waterfront
Tel: 22980 75380
Going since 1935, this is the most upmarket, white-tablecloth venue away from the Dápia, with excellent service. Their *psári à la Spetsióta* (fish in ratatouille sauce) is made with fresh fish, not frozen as in many other places. The bulk wine is satisfactory, and baked-apple dessert rounds off the experience. Open all year. **€€€**

THE CYCLADES

Parea
Platía Kaḍri, Hóra
Tel: 22820 23721
Stone-clad, full-service restaurant doing all the Greek standards – especially meat dishes – with big eyefuls of Parapórti beach out the window. The most keenly priced bulk wine on the island. **€**

Hyma
Hóra, main commercial street
Tel: 6974 786376
Excellent, genuine *ouzerí* in an ex-grocery store, where miracles are worked over a small camp stove. Strong points are salads and seafood dishes, plus a few meat casseroles. *Hýma* (in bulk) is your wine. Open all year, off-season by arrangement. **€**

Limani tis Kyra Katinas
Órmos Egiális
Tel: 22850 73269
Strong contender for best all-round eatery on the island; strengths are seafood, pulses, vegetable casseroles and local cheese. Very reasonably priced for the quality. Open from just before Easter–mid-Oct. **€**

Nikos
Langáda
Tel: 22850 73310
Polished taverna specialising in platters like beets with greens, dips, goat-based dishes, fish and some *magirevtá*. Not cheap for Amorgós, but the quality is high, with seating on perhaps the island's loveliest vine-shaded terrace. **€€**

Santouraki
Tholária village
Tel: 22850 73054

In a village with at least three decent eateries, this stands out for its good *mezédes*, own-reared meat grills and elevated terrace. Open most of the year. **€**

Liotrivi
Hóra
Tel: 22860 61209
Best in show up here, especially for fish; a few vegetable dishes and dips as well, along with Santoríni bulk wine. Sit on the small, popular terrace or in the vaulted interior. Open May–Oct, the longest season of any taverna in the village. **€€**

Roukounas (Tis Papadias)
Just in from Roúkounas beach
Tel: 22860 61206
Going since 1990, and a reliable source of *magirevtá* like *briám* – a more elaborate dish than you'll generally get at a beachside taverna. **€**

Anargyros
Harbourfront
Tel: 22840 61204
The islet's most venerable taverna – it starred in the 1960 movie *Mantalena* – is also a dab hand at traditional dishes like *pastítsio* (a succulent brick laden with béchamel sauce) and thick *fáva* served with onions and lemon. Open April–Oct. **€**

Karnagio
Loutró cove
Tel: 22850 71694
Exceedingly popular quayside *ouzerí*, so reservations mandatory in season; the menu offers a full line of *píttes*,

flashed-fried fish, grilled meat and *rakí* from Náxos; pity, though, about the supermarket bulk wine. **€€**

Melissa
Hóra centre
Tel: 22850 71678
The best taverna in the village, open (unusually) for lunch too, good for *magirevtá* and fish; psychedelic chair-colour scheme offsets somewhat glum service. **€**

Fisherman (Giorgos & Marina)
Áno Méra square
Tel: 22890 71405
www.giorgosmarina.com
The platía of Mýkonos' second village is ringed by tavernas, some surprisingly expensive; this is one of the cheaper and friendlier, open all year as well. They do *móstra* (the local version of Cretan *dákos*) and a preponderance of meat dishes despite the name. **€€**

Madoupas
Harbourfront, Hóra
Tel: 22890 22224
This combination bar, café and *magirío* accomplishes the miracle of hearty Greek fare at almost normal prices – their *revytháda* is excellent, made with split rather than whole chickpeas, the bread wholegrain, the *gávros* crisp and fresh, all in generous portions. A local institution, open all year. **€–€€**

Ma'ereio
Kalogéra 16, Hóra
Tel: 22890 28825
"Mykonian/homestyle tastes' is the motto of this hole-in-the-wall, very popular with locals who come to scoff on *loúza* (Cycladic ham), mushrooms,

fluffy *keftédes* and wholemeal bread; a bit more outlay nets you *psaronéfri* (pork medallions) and the like. The bulk white wine will be a bit too fruity/sweet for some. Open all year. **€€€–€€€€**

Tasos
Paránga beach
Tel: 22890 23002
www.tasostavernamykonos.gr
A superior beach taverna with a deserved cult following. The bread comes with little mini-dip ramekins, "roast eggplant" is more like baba ghanouj on the half-shell with tomato, parsley and garlic, the fried shrimps palpably fresh, the bulk wine decent (though the bottled list is reasonable for Mýkonos). Portions are generous, service efficient and friendly. Open April–late Oct. **€€€**

Náxos

Axiotissa
18th km of road Hóra–Alykó, approaching Glyfáda
Tel: 22850 75107
Arguably the top organic/vegetarian eatery on the island, with locally sourced ingredients. Dishes run the gamut from rocket and *xinomyzíthra* salad, chilli-and-onion sauteed Portobello mushrooms, eggplant with almonds, Armenian sausage and goat or rabbit dishes, accompanied by rosé bulk wine from Moní or a select Greek wine list. Booking mandatory in season. Open weekends only spring and autumn. **€€**

Metaxy Mas
Hóra, Paleá Agorá
Tel: 22850 26425
www.metaximas-naxos.gr
The best-value eatery in the old town, popular with both locals and visitors for its huge portions of local cheese, *hórta*, some seafood and several dishes of the day; summer seating in the lane. Open daily 1pm–late. **€**

Platsa
Kóronos centre
Tel: 22850 51243
The ebullient Matina is heart and soul of one of the best tavernas in Náxos' inland villages, with dishes of the day for lunch and strong *rakí* and candied, organic quince to finish off. Seating is on multiple, arcaded mini-courtyards (*plátses* in local dialect) festooned with plants. Open most of the year. **€**

Sto Ladoharto
Quay, Hóra
Tel: 22850 22178
Carnivores repair to these upstairs premises, with great views of the harbour, for strictly grilled-meat platters plus a few salads and starters. The decor is mock-1950s

grocery-shop: legacy canned goods, strung-up peppers, bagged dry goods. Open all year. **€–€€**

Páros

Anna
Dryós, through road
Tel: 22840 41015
It's worth tearing yourself away from nearby beaches to lunch at this beacon of *magiireftá*, with dishes like *angináres a la políta* (artichoke hearts with carrots and dill), stuffed squash and *katsíki lemonáto*, complemented by their own bulk wine. Secluded upstairs patio seating, or inside a cheery salon at street level. Open late Mar–early Nov. **€€**

Apoplous
South quay, Alykí
Tel: 22840 91935
www.apoplous.gr
Reckoned the best of several in a line here at Páros' most authentic fishing port, Apoplous features Sífnos-style lamb-in-clay-pot, *goúna* (sun-dried mackerel), *paximadokoúloura* (the Parian versian of *dákos*) and lots of fresh seafood. Tipple is either decent bulk wine or a reasonable bottled list. Open Feb–15 Dec. **€€–€€€**

Koukoutsi
Back of National Bank square, Parikiá
Tel: 6978 408504
Equal parts café, bar and *ouzerí*, this bohemian joint is always packed for the sake of reasonable drinks – especially strong bulk *rakí* – excellent platters, and the buzz. Just two or three tables inside, eight or nine more popular ones outside. Open 9am until whenever. **€–€€**

Lemoni
Seafront, about 200 metres/yds beyond windmill, Parikiá
Tel: 6984 474111
Only opened in 2012, but already causing a sensation for its creative cooking at decidedly normal prices. Some of the fusions – *revytháda* with *taramosaláta*, beets with pear-and-yogurt sauce – are a bit outré, but a salad of spinach, rocket, pomegranate seeds, walnuts, raisins, soft cheese and tomatini hits the spot. Mains – mostly meat and poultry, but also such as *atherína* in sesame crust – are solid, as are desserts like mousse, cheesecake or carrot cake. Strictly Greek wine list. Service is jolly and efficient. **€€**

Moskhonas
Old port quay, Náoussa
Tel: 22840 51623
The least expensive, most down-to-earth of several waterfront options in a rather twee setting. Presentation

and fare is basic and sustaining rather than elegant, but the family has their own boat and it is popular. Fare might include *f(r)yssa*, giant autumn sardines of breeding size. Open most of the year. **€€**

Santoríni

Anemomylos
Ía,Perivolás district
Tel: 22860 71410
Forego the crowds, the caldera view and the expense along Ía's main pedestrian street and head here instead for honest *magireftá* (like the best local *moussakás*) prepared by a chef with years of experience cooking on ships. And yes, there is a partial view north toward Baxédes beach. Open Apr–Oct. **€€**

Anogi
Imerovígli, central square
Tel: 22860 21285
Again, diners are rewarded for passing on a caldera view at this ever-popular taverna (reservations mandatory in season) with creative Greek recipes like shrimp *moussakás*, *bekrí mezé* mixing two meats, stuffed *biftéki* and a full range of desserts. The wine list highlights microwineries from across Greece. Service is necessarily brisk, given the pressure on tables, but friendly. Open daily 2pm–midnight. **€€€**

Mas
Éxo Goniá, 100 metres/yds down steps from top church
Tel: 22860 31323
www.santorini-metaximas.gr
The proprietor hails from Haniá, so there's a Cretan flair to the menu here: Sfakian *píttes*, *apáki* (lean cured pork), *stamnagáthi* greens, the tumbler of *rakí* that comes with your generous local bread basket stocked with local soft cheese. There are also local dishes like *fáva* and white eggplant, and the bulgur wheat topped with lamb in yogurt sauce is stellar. Seating is either on outdoor terraces looking to Anáfi, or inside the vaulted old converted house. Open 1pm until late, all year. **€€**

Psaraki
Vlyháda
Tel: 22860 82783
Quite possibly the best seafood/

PRICE CATEGORIES

Prices indicated are for a meal per person with modest intake of wine or beer, rakí or tsipouro.
€ = under 17 euros
€€ = 17–25 euros
€€€ = 25–34 euros
€€€€ = over 34 euros

mezédes taverna for the money on Santoríni, with views over the island's main fishing/yacht harbour to the Hristianá islets. Savour *gígandes* beans in lemon sauce, white eggplant salad, or *lakérda* (bonito) done perfectly medium rare – and save room for desserts like pear poached in *asýrtiko* wine. Sticking to *mezédes*, dishes of the day and the Karamelengos bulk wine will land you in the lower price category. Open daily Apr–Oct. **€€–€€€**

Selene
Pýrgos Village
Tel: 22860 22249
www.selene.gr
The upstairs restaurant, run by a chef famous for his revival of local cuisine (and cooking courses), represents a major outlay. The downstairs "Café-Winebar-Delicatessen",with similar sweeping views, will do for most people, having an equally wide-ranging menu encompassing "local" salad with cheese, squid sautéed with greens, eggplant salad with octopus carpaccio, and a battery of desserts including chocolate mousse doused in rose-geranium sauce or cappuccino pudding. Bulk wine is "easy drinking"; staff could stand to be a bit jollier. Café open daily noon–11pm. **€€€–€€€€**

Sérifos

Fagopoti (Nikoulias)
Avlomónas beach
Tel: 22810 52595

Much the best taverna for the money in the Livádi area, with generously proportioned *biftéki*, expertly butterflied sardines, chunky *tyrokafterí* or eggplant salad, and island wine by the kilo, served with a smile. **€**

Petros
Hóra
Tel: 22810 51302
Of the handful of tavernas up here, this works the longest season, and is open at lunch. Stresses *magireftá*, including bean dishes, eggplant in the oven and stews, plus island bulk wine. **€**

Sífnos

Tou Apostoli to Koutouki
Apollonía, Stenó district
Tel: 22840 33186
Upscale eatery that's a good place to try the clay-pot, meat-based casseroles that the island is known for. **€€**

Leonidas
Kástro
Tel: 22840 31153
Basic-appearing but very accomplished shrine of magirevtá such as revytháda, moussakás, rabbit stew and grilled mastéllo cheese, with views to match the impressive food. **€**

Sýros

Apano Hora
Áno Sýros
Tel: 22810 80565
By day a popular kafenío thanks to its terrace, after dark this becomes an ouzerí, often with live acoustic music at

weekends. Titbits may include carrot-and-cheese turnovers, local sausages and a dish of the day or two. You will have to fight for a terrace table. **€€**

Iliovassilema
Galissás beach
Tel: 22810 43325
Much the best taverna in this resort, with creative renditions of local dishes, like fennel pie and crunchy *atherína*. Open May–early Oct. **€€**

Kyma
Fínikas, mid-beach
Tel: 22801 43526
One of several tavernas here, Kyma stands out for good value in a resort and a long operating season. Signature dishes include thick, fiery *kopanistí*, *hórta*, and of course the local sausages. **€€**

Lilis
Áno Sýros
Tel: 22810 88087
Huge place, with a very popular outdoor terrace, where the emphasis is on meat dishes and salads. There's often live rebétika music at weekends; rebétika great, Markos Vamvakaris, was born in this village and played in the basement annexe in 1955. **€€**

Oinopnevmata
Emmanouíl Roïdi 9, Ermoúpoli
Tel: 22810 82616
The most low-key and reasonable of the places along "Taverna Row" east of Platía Miaoúli, with local sausages, coiled cheese pie, a version of fennel pie, and probably panna cotta dessert on the house. **€€**

THE SPORADES AND ÉVVIA

Alónissos

Elaionas
Leftós Gialós beach
Tel: 24240 66066
The better of two decent tavernas here, with unusual platters like *tzitzírafa*, *ftéri* (fern shoots), *xynógalos*, other chunky dips, marinated tuna, and eight varieties of *píttes* prepared by three generations of ladies toiling in the kitchen. Outdoor seating in a gravel courtyard under the olives of the restaurant's namesake. The affiliated, adjacent beach-bar has a "light" snack menu, so spend the whole day here. Open May–Sept. **€€**

Peri Orexeos
By the bus stop, Paleá Alónissos
Tel: 24240 66421
The only normally priced quality outfit in the old Hóra, its menu ranging from burgers to fusion snacks to tweaked Greek dishes such as beets with

manoúri cheese, aubergine grilled with garlic/tahini, or *pansétta* (spare ribs) in honey-thyme sauce. Portions are on the big side. During summer tables are set up in the little park opposite. **€€**

Votsalo
Rousoúm Gialós
Tel: 24240 65106
The most consistently good of the three tavernas on this cove, with the charcoal grill lit even at midday. Very keenly priced scaly fish by the kilo, a few magirevtá of the day, and easy-drinking Zítsa bulk wine. **€€**

Evvia

Apanemo
Shoreline at Fanári district, Halkída
Tel: 22210 22614
Halkída is famous for its seafood, especially shellfish like *gialisterés* and *petrosolínes*, so there's no excuse for tolerating the hit-and-miss performance of certain midtown

outfits. This seafood taverna has one of the best settings, easiest parking and some of the best food – on the pricey side but worth it. **€€–€€€**

Pyrofani (Livaditis)
Límni, northwest end of quay
Tel: 22270 31640
Slightly bumped-up prices for average-sized portions at this seafood-strong *ouzerí* are justified by the quality, plus nice touches such as sweet-cabbage marinade as a side dish, and big salads. Stick to their *oúzo*, as the bulk wine is not a strong point. **€€**

PRICE CATEGORIES

Prices indicated are for a meal per person with modest intake of wine or beer, rakí or tsípouro.

€ = under 17 euros
€€ = 17–25 euros
€€€ = 25–34 euros
€€€€ = over 34 euros

Smbanios
Opposite ferry dock, Loutrá Edipsoú
Tel: 22260 23111
About the only "normal", and normally priced, taverna in town. Their speciality is grilled sardines, and the bulk rosé wine (a rarity) is good, as are the usual *mezédes*. Pleasant decor includes old photos of the resort. **€**

Alexandros
Old Town, 2 blocks in from fishing port
Tel: 24270 22431
Good grills (especially the lamb chops or diced liver) and oven dishes, beet salad with yogurt and garlic or stuffed squash as starters, and home-made crème caramel or panna cotta for dessert served at tables under the mulberry trees. Usually acoustic music on *bouzoúki* and guitar. Open May–Sept dinner only. **€€**

Amfiliki
South edge of town by clinic
Tel: 24270 22839
Good smells wafting out of the kitchen up front are the clue that you've arrived. Out back, limited seating – about 40 places – with unlimited views of Mégas Gialós Bay, best at twilight (*amfilyki* is the ancient Greek for that). The food lives up to the setting, especially seafood specials like *bráska kipouroú* (monkfish in spicy tomato sauce) or *psári Amfiliki* (fish fillet with capers, courgettes and peppers). Starters include seafood salad, fish croquettes and baby squid in spring. Leave room for dessert. A fireplace roars during the cooler months, but the place shuts Nov–10 Feb. **€€€**

Bakaliko
Airport road, 300 metres/yds past yacht marina
Tel:24270 24024
Best of several eateriesin a row of tavernas plus a bar or two.The decor is a take on a traditional Greek grocer's (*bakáliko*), the fare an unusual twist

to traditional recipes, especially fish dishes, and the seating poised over the water. Open all year. **€€–€€€**

In Hóra (the main harbour), the west quay is the place to eat and where locals go.

Klimataria
Right next to Dimarhío (Town Hall)
Tel: 24240 22273
The best place for reasonable (for Skópelos) fish by weight, plus a few cooked dishes like piperonáti (eggplant, cheese and pepper hotpot), stuffed squash blossoms without the usual heavy batter and other competent *mezédes* – locals conspicuously in attendance. **€**

(Ta) Kymata
Far north end of quay, Hóra
Tel: 24240 22381
About the oldest taverna here, run by an engaging family and renowned for its elaborate *magirevtá* such as lamb and vegetables in *phyllo* triangles or *katsíki* (goat) *lemonáto*. Also, good aubergine salad and real beets with greens attached. Dishes may run out partway through the evening as they cook only daily small batches. **€–€€**

Limnonari (Vangelis)
First taverna, Limnonári beach
Tel: 24240 22242
Better-than-average beachside outfit where palpably homemade *melitsanosaláta* or imaginative salads precede unusual dishes like *vlíta* with feta cheese, garlic and chilli, or *gávros* in tomato-wine sauce. Service can suffer owing to its popularity. **€**

Pavlos
Agnóndas port
Tel: 24240 22409
Reliable fish specialist with fair prices for by-kilo fish or portions of *goúnes* (sun dried mackerel), also unusual *mezédes* like *tzitzírafa* (wild terebinth sprouts) and *krítama* (rock samphire). Good bulk wine from Apostolakis, a local Thessalian vintner. Add waterside seating under trees, and

Pavlos is easily the best of three choices here. Open Mar–Oct. **€€**

Stella
Just above Glyfonéri beach
Tel: 24240 23143
Kyria Stella (and her garden opposite) are the heart and soul of this 1980s time capsule, with a light touch frying up big portions of stuffed biftéki, squid, tzatziki, chips and courgettes. She lets inexpensive rooms too. **€**

Istories tou Barba
Magaziá/Mólos beach boundary
Tel: 22220 91453
Excellent, creative cuisine focusing on seafood at friendly prices guarantees a crush here much of the time, especially given the loveliest sea-view terrace on the island. Oddly, Cretan music preferred for their soundtrack. **€€**

Lambros
Aspoús, through road
Tel: 22220 91388
Efficient, polite service, a pleasant interior or the terrace in fine weather, grilled fish, chops and al dente vegetables all make this a natural all-year favourite for locals and visitors. **€**

Maïstros
Linariá
Tel: 22220 93431
Behind a plane tree on what passes for the central square here, this friendly taverna-ouzerí does an excellent job of *mezédes*, seafood titbits and local meat platters, washed down by bulk Skyros rosé. Not just for lunch before a departing ferry, but good enough to make a detour here for dinner. **€**

Perasma
Start of airport slip road
Tel: 22220 92911
The airport staff and seemingly half the air force personnel on the island eat here, knowing a good thing when they see it: succulent own-raised meat and cheese, at reasonable prices, plus island wine. Seating outdoors or in, according to weather. **€**

THE NORTHEAST AEGEAN

Kali Kardia
Top end of high street, Foúrni town
Tel: 22750 51217
When you tire of overpriced seafood on the front, head inland here for a solid meat feed, including *kokorétsi* (innard roulade) and *kondosoúvli* straight from the spit turning outside. The meat is all from neighbouring Sámos, proudly proclaims the owner. **€**

Fabrika
Volissós,
lower platía
Tel: 22740 22045
www.chiosfabrika.gr
As the name suggests, this taverna is installed in a former olive/flour mill, with the machinery left *in situ*. Ingredients for their salads, eggplant-based dishes and beets

are all grown by the management, while chops, *kondosoúvli* and *kokorétsi* are also locally sourced. Excellent bulk wine from the nearby Ariousios winery. Open most of the year, with seating indoors or out on the flagstone terrace. **€**

Hotzas
Georgíou Kondýli 3, Híos Town
Tel: 22710 42787
Oldest and (unreliably) the best

Alfresco dining in Ermoupoli, Syros.

taverna in the city. Fare varies seasonally, but expect a mix of vegetarian dishes, sausages and fish. Open all year, dinner only (not Sun). **€**

Ikhthyoskala
Tel: 22710 42114
Desperately unromantic setting by the fish plant, but tables are right on the water and the food is to die for: fiery *kopanistí*, fresh *koukiá* beans in lemon sauce, *fáva, radíkio, koutsomoúra* done to perfection, sundried grilled *savrídi* fish. Open dinner only. **€€**

Kapileio
Central Thymianá
Tel: 22710 32453
Tuck into top-notch seafood like butterflied *skorpiós*, and all the usual vegetarian *mezédes* plus every local *oúzo*, in the lovely walled garden out back. **€€**

Mylarakia
Tambákika district, by Híos Town Hospital
Tel: 22710 41412
All eight brands of Hiot *oúzo* available at friendly prices to accompany starters, seafood and some meat dishes. Unbeatably romantic setting on a terrace looking out to the three mills of the name. Dinner year round; lunch on occasion. **€€**

Passas
Langáda harbour
Tel: 22710 74218
Locals come to this east-coast port especially for a seafood meal; this outfit, with seating under eucalypts, is the most professional of several here, with a mix of fishy (and meaty) standards. **€€**

Tavernaki tou Tassou
Stávrou Livanoú 8, Bella Vista district, Híos Town
Tel: 22710 27542
Superb all-rounder with creative salads, better-than-average bean dishes, good chips, *dolmádes*, snails and a strong line in seafood. Open lunch and dinner most of the year, sea-view garden seating in summer. **€€**

Ikaría

Arodou
Xylosýrtis, 5km west of Ágios Kírykos
Tel: 22750 22700
If you have transport, give all the port eateries a miss and head out to this superb tavern next to the church on the shoreline. So far, mainly Greeks go – it's been featured in a number of national publications. Open daily lunch and dinner, closed Mon off-season. **€€**

Kalypso
Fýtema, 2km (1 mile) west of Évdilos
Tel: 22750 31387
Basic but friendly shoreline place with excellent, reasonably priced, own-grown vegetable dishes and fresh fish. Open daily May–Oct, otherwise by arrangement. **€**

Kelaris (tis Eleftherías)
Gialiskári
Tel: 22750 71227
The best of a trio of tavernas here for *magirevtá* and the freshest fish locally. **€€**

Mandouvala
Karavóstamo
Tel: 22750 61204
An enchanting setting in this little-visited port, with a terrace almost swamped by the surf, and food nearly as good as the setting: all the usual *ouzerí* suspects plus Ikarian suspects like *soúfiko* (the local ratatouille). The name, in case you were wondering, comes from a popular song of the 1960s. Open May–Oct daily. **€**

Paskhalia
Armenistís
Tel: 22750 71226
Reliable source of fish grills and dishes of the day, as well as full breakfasts, served ideally on the little terrace overlooking the port. The first tavern to open here (May), the last to close (sometime in October). **€€**

Thea
Nás
Tel: 22750 71491

Returned Ohio-Ikarian lady oversees the best *magirevtá* this end of the island, with lots of vegetarian dishes like *soufikó* (the Ikarian ratatouille) and squash-stuffed turnovers. Daily dinner June–Sept, lunch also midsummer, weekends in winter too. **€**

Lésvos

Anemoessa
Skála Sykaminiás, closest to the harbour chapel
Tel: 22530 55360
Tops for fresh fish, and good *mezédes* like stuffed squash blossoms. Open all year (weekends only Nov–Apr). **€€**

Balouhanas
Géra Gulf seafront, Pérama
Tel: 22510 51948
Seafood *ouzerí* with wood-kiosk seating overhanging the water. Interesting *mezédes* and home-made desserts (like *gioúzleme*) too. **€€**

Captain's Table
Fishing harbour, Mólyvos
Tel: 22530 71241
As the name suggests, a strong line in seafood but also meat and vegetable specialities, such as their "Ukrainian" aubergine dip, and excellent own-label wine (both white and red). Open May–late Oct, dinner only. **€€**

Ermis
Kornárou 2, corner Ermoú, Mytilíni Town
Tel: 22510 26232
The best and most atmospheric *ouzerí* of a cluster in Páno Skála district, with two centuries of claimed operation and indoor/outdoor seating. Special strengths: sardines, sausages, Smyrna-style meatballs. Open daily except Sun eve. **€**

Iy Eftalou
By Eftaloú thermal baths, 4km (2.5 miles) from Mólyvos
Tel: 22530 71049
Well-executed, reasonably priced grills (fish on par with meat), *magirevtá* and salads. Seating under the trees or inside by the fireplace according to season. Only black spot is the sometimes glum service. Open Apr–Oct. **€€**

Taverna tou Panaï
Agios Isídoros, north edge of village
Tel: 22520 31920
Plainly presented but tasty food: vegetarian *mezédes*, grills, cheese and so on. Mostly Greek clientele. **€–€€**

(To) Petri
Petrí village, in the hills above Pétra/ Mólyvos
Tel: 22530 41239
Friendly, family-run taverna serving salubrious *magirevtá* and a few grills; unbeatable terrace seating. Open May–mid-Oct. **€–€€**

Women's Agricultural Tourism Co-op

Central platía, Pétra
Tel: 22530 41238
Upstairs restaurant with lots of simple grills – including seafood – *mezédes* and rather fewer *magirevtá*. Indoor and (weather permitting) outdoor terrace seating. Open May–Oct. €

Límnos

Glaropoula
Néa Koútali
Tel: 22540 92325
This is *the* place in southern Límnos for a seafood blowout, with bay views from the terrace. Reasonably priced, simple presentation. €€

Hristos
Platía of Tsimándria
Tel: 22540 51278
Very cheap, very cheerful, with a tranquil location. From amongst grills and a few *magirevtá*, tick your choices off on the menu-bill combo. €

Man-Tella
Sardés centre
Tel: 22540 61349
Cult taverna doubling as the central *kafenío* (thus open all year) of this highest hill village on Límnos. Big portions off a meat-strong menu; good service, indoor/outdoor seating by season. €€

Mouragio
Kótsinas port
Tel: 22540 41065
The better of two seafood tavernas here, worth the slight price premium in terms of execution and service. €€

Sozos
Main square, Platý
Tel: 22540 25085
Though Sozos himself is gone, this is still the best and oldest *tsipourádiko* grill here, with steamed mussels, chops and *orektiká* all supervised by his daughter. Usually there's a wait for a table. €

Tzitzifies
Rihá Nerá beach
Tel: 22540 23756
A proper taverna at Mýrina town's north beach, with tables on the sand. Good *ímam baïldí*, dips and baked dishes. €–€€

Sámos

Artemis (Kopanas)
Kefalopoúlou 4, near old ferry dock, Vathý
Tel: 22730 23639
For some years now the best taverna in town, with good *hórta* and *fáva*, excellent seafood platters like steamed skate-wing with *skordaliá*, plus standard meat mains. The smooth red bulk wine from Manolátes won't leave you hung over. Open

daily lunch and dinner except Sun night. €€

Delfini
Avlákia
Tel: 22730 94279
Tables are right at water level in this tiny, Greeks-only resort, giving the best view on the north coast. Come here for fresh fish platters, large veggie starters, and Kyría Alexándra, the colourful proprietress. The bulk wine isn't good – choose a bottle instead. Open Mar–Oct. €

Glaros
Iréon seafront
Tel: 22730 95457
A friendly family originally from nearby Agathoníssi runs this basic, popular terrace taverna with heaping portions of scaly fish or cephalopods and superior starters like *hórta*, *dolmádes* and squash rissoles. Watching the full moon rise over Turkey in August is a favourite activity and you'll wait for a table then. €€

Kallisti
Manolátes
Tel: 22730 94661
All three central Manolátes tavernas are excellent, but *Kallisti* is the favourite thanks to the lovely Magda, heart and soul of the place, dishing out hearty stews (lamb-, goat- or pork-based) and starters like non-greasy spinach pie. Very quaffable bulk wine – beware as the road down to the coast is tricky. Daily lunch and dinner in season, weekends only otherwise. €

Kryfi Folia
Platanákia district of Kérveli
Tel: 22730 25905 or 6937 219315
Near the east tip of Sámos in an isolated olive grove, this recently revamped taverna under new ownership has kept the previous menu featuring competent starters and grilled seafood. Open Easter–early Oct. €

Loukoulos
Above Fournáki beach, west end Votsalákia resort
Tel: 22730 37147
In what's otherwise a very touristy spot, Loukoulos is genuinely characterful, reasonable and devoted to quality *magirevtá*. Best in the evenings, as the terrace is unshaded and many dishes aren't ready until then. Open June–Sept. €€

Pera Vrysi
Approach to Vourliótes village
Tel: 22730 93277
There are main courses, but the strength here is imaginative *mezédes* like spinach-cheese croquettes, sweet pumpkin turnovers, and chicken livers in bacon. Excellent bulk wine, and don't order bottled water –

you're next to one of the best springs on the island. Open all day Mar–Oct, some weekends in winter. €

Psarades
Agios Nikólaos Kondakeïkon
Tel: 22730 32489
Long reckoned the best fish taverna on the island, at surprisingly reasonable prices, plus the usual *orektiká*. In season you have to book. Open Easter–Oct. €€

Psili Ammos
Psilí Ammos
Tel: 22730 28301
The taverna on the far right as you face the water and the most consistent one in the area, though fare's restricted to seafood, meat grills and salad. Booking advised for large parties. Open daily Easter–Oct, weekends winter. €–€€

Tarsanas
Little lane 100 metres/yds in from west beach, Kokkári
Tel: 22730 92337
The stock-in-trade at this 1970s throwback are thick-crust pizzas and perhaps two casserole dishes of the day – like the best *moussakás* in town – at bargain prices. Catch the sea breeze at seating in the lane, or at much-sought-after tables down by the beach. Open May–Oct dinner only. €

Samothráki

1900
Hóra
Tel: 25510 41222
With superb views from its vine-shaded terrace, this welcoming spot is the island's best taverna, serving up the likes of stuffed goat and a range of vegetable dishes. €–€€

To Perivoli T'Ouranou
Near Thermá
Tel: 25510 98313
Boasting a lush green setting on the road to Gría Váthra, this highly seasonal taverna offers a good range of *mezédes*, tender grills and often hosts live music. €€

Thásos

Glaros
South end of the beach, Alykí hamlet
Tel: 25930 31547
Oldest, least expensive and most authentic of several tavernas here.

TRANSPORT ACCOMMODATION EATING OUT ACTIVITIES A – Z LANGUAGE

Usually has a modest breed of local fresh fish. Open late May–Sept. €€

Opos Palia
Under the central tree, Sotíros village
Tel: 6979 635703
It's no accident the owner chose to call this place "Like the old (days)" because he creates wonderful dishes from simple traditional recipes such as *bekrí mezé*. €€

(ly) Pigi
Central platía, Liménas
Tel: 25930 22941
Old stand-by dishing out dependable *magirevtá* next to the spring of the name; best at dinner. €

Simi
East waterfront, Liménas
Tel: 25930 22517
Despite the touristy cadre, this makes

a decent fist of fish and *mezédes*. Seating, weather permitting, under trees on a raised terrace. €€

Syrtaki
East waterfront, Liménas
Tel: 6955 304897
Plenty of locals as well as tourists flock here for the excellent fresh fish, ample salads and very palatable barrelled wine. €€

RHODES

Rhodes Town

Koukos
Nikifórou Mandilará 20–26, Neohóri
Tel: 22410 73022
From beginnings as a young peoples' coffee-bar and takeaway bakery, *Koukos* has evolved into one of the few genuine, and most popular, *mezedopolía* in the new town. It's worth showing up just for the multilevel, Tardis-like interior, effectively a private folklore museum, though on fine days everyone is out on the terraces. The fare – seafood probably a better bet than meat – is decent. Open daily most of the day into the evening. €

Marco Polo Café
Agíou Fanouríou 42, Old Town
Tel: 22410 25562
The *Marco Polo Mansion* courtyard hosts the Old Town's most creative cooking. Platters change seasonally but might include cuttlefish on a bed of courgette mousse, *mylokópi* (sea perch) fillet in caper sauce, subtly flavoured pilaf with lamb and raisins, or pork medallions with soft *manoúri* cheese, fig and red peppercorn sauce. Decadent desserts, like chocolate frozen with strawberries, white-chocolate mousse or *kaltsoúnia* (sweet-cheese turnovers). Co-proprietor Spyros is a wine fanatic, so sample his cellar if the bulk wine fails to appeal. Open

mid-May to mid-Oct supper only; last orders 11pm. €€€

Meltemi
Platía Koundourióti 8, Élli beach
Tel: 22410 30480
Classy and surprisingly well-priced-for-the-location ouzerí offering such delights as crayfish nuggets, octopus croquettes, grilled red peppers in balsamic vinegar, chunky hummus and superb roast aubergine with beans and onions. There is a pleasant winter salon with old engravings inside. Open all day. €€

Mezes
Aktí Kanári 9, Psaropoúla
Tel: 22410 27962
The interior, with rust-coloured paint trim and solid wood surfaces throughout, may not have the quirky charm of Koukos, but the food here is arguably better and more generously served. Tuck into starters like superior chickpea stew, breaded mastéllo cheese from Híos, oyster mushrooms or lahmatzoún (Armenian pizza); meat and seafood mains are even bigger. Live music some Saturdays. Open daily noon–12.30am. €€

Sea Star
Sofokléous 24
Tel: 22410 22117
This relatively inexpensive yet quality seafood outlet offers a limited menu of scaly fish (the seared June tuna is

ace), shellfish and starters like kápari (pickled caper shoots), chunky grilled eggplant salad and koliós pastós (salt-cured mackerel). Seating is indoors during the cooler months (not open midwinter), otherwise outside on the little square. €€–€€€

Steno
Agíon Anargýron 29, 400 metres/yds southwest of Old Town
Tel: 22410 35914
Welcoming ouzerí with indoor/outdoor seating according to season, attracting a mix of locals, expats and some savvy tourists. The menu encompasses chunky sausages, pitaroúdia (courgette-based croquettes), hórta, pulses, stuffed squash flowers, green beans with garlic, and simple seafood platters. Daily, dinner only. €

Around Rhodes Island

Gatto Bianco
Líndos, 100 metres/yds into village from Agios Pávlos parking
Tel: 2240 31612
Indisputably the island's best Italian diner. Besides own-made pasta, wood-oven pizza, seafood and a limited line of desserts (panna cotta, tiramisu), killer dishes include fresh-salmon (or beef) carpaccio, eggplant parmigiana Naples style (with mince) and calzone ripieno with salami, mozzarella and Cretan myzíthra cheese. Prices seem on the big side, but so are the portions. Sit either on the ground-level, pebble-mosaic patio, or after dark up on the roof terrace with eyefuls of Lindos acropolis. Open dinner May–early Nov; lunch also spring/autumn. €€€€

Mavrikos
Líndos
Tel: 22440 31232
This family-run restaurant, going since 1933, is rated among Rhodes' best for its extensive menu of creative oven-cooked dishes and seafood (with less prominent meat dishes). Gígandes in carob

Tempting pastries in an Ionian confectioners (zaharoplastío).

syrup, sweet marinated sardines, or beetroot in goat-cheese sauce precede mains like cured tuna with grilled fennel, lamb-liver chunks sautéed with chillies, or pork belly slabs in grape molasses. Excellent (and expensive) Greek wine list. Open Apr–Nov. €€€€

Perigiali
By fishing anchorage, Stegná
Tel: 22440 23444
Locals throng the shady patio at weekends for the sake of excellent seafood like *soupiá* in its own ink, savoury, hand-cut round chips, home-made *yaprákia* (stuffed vine leaves) and salads sufficient for two (the "Perigiáli" has caper greens and grilled aubergine) washed down by good bulk wine. The travertine-marble-clad bathrooms are certainly unique on Rhodes. €€

Pigi Fasouli
Psínthos outskirts
Tel: 22410 50071
Vegetable starters here include chunky aubergine salad and beets with their greens, or expertly fried vegetable slices with skordaliá; mains comprise goat in various guises, a few meat-based casserole dishes, or simply grilled lamb chops. You have to ask if you want to try the owner's own, off-menu bulk wine. The outside terrace overlooks the shady oasis and spring (pigí) here. Open Apr–Oct 9am–10pm, Nov–Mar weekends only. €€

Platanos
Lower platía, Lahaniá village
Tel: 22440 46027
Arguably the most exquisite setting on the island, with outdoor tables between two gushing Ottoman

fountains under the plane tree of the restaurant's name. *Mezédes* (*dolmádes, húmmus, kopanistí*) are top-drawer and inexpensive, as are meat entrées, but fish is as pricey as elsewhere. Open all year, weekends only winter. €–€€

Plimiri Beach
By Zoödóhou Piyís church, Plimýri Bay
Tel: 22440 46003
This ever-popular, very welcoming fish taverna is well placed for lunch on a tour around the island. Presentation (and to some extent prices) are 1980s-style, with excellent chips and a few starters accompanying a wide selection of fresh fish – pick yours from the display. They do wonders with ordinarily overlooked species like *kéfalos* (grey mullet) and *drákena* (weever). Open Apr–Oct noon until late. €€

THE SOUTHERN DODECANESE

Hálki

Paradosiako Piato tis Lefkosias
Emborió quay
Tel: 6946 978151
For years, wherever Lefkosia Peraki was cooking was the top eatery on Hálki, and her recipes have even been featured on the BBC. Since 2009, she's had her own restaurant, featuring elaborate baked dishes, grills, laboriously concocted orektiká and own-sourced ingredients – which means everything from her own livestock and olive oil to home-baked bread. Open Apr–Oct. €€

Kárpathos

L'Angolo-Gorgona
South end of quay, Diafáni
Tel: 22450 51509
A versatile café-restaurant run by Genoese Gabriella, with offerings blending Greek-style salads and seafood with real Italian-standard coffees, lovely desserts and limoncello liqueur. Does breakfast too. Open all day April–Oct. €€

Dramoundana
Mesohóri
Remarkably reasonably priced for Kárpathos, this features local caper greens, village sausages and marinated *ménoules* (a sort of large sardine). €

Ellinikon
One block inland from quay, Pigádia
Tel: 22450 23932
A *mezedopolío* that caters all year to a local clientele with hot and cold *orektiká*, meat and good desserts. €€

Orea Karpathos
Southeast end of main quay, Pigádia
Tel: 22450 22501
The best all-round taverna in the port, with palatable local bulk wine, *trahanádes* soup and great spinach pie. The locals treat it as an *ouzerí*, so it's fine to order just a few *orektiká* to accompany a *karafáki* (small pitcher) or a *katroútso* (250ml) of Óthos wine. €

Pine Tree
Ádia, 7km (4 miles) north of Finíki
Tel: 6977 369948
Sustaining, reasonable rural taverna with country fare like lentils and *htapodomakaronáda* (octopus in pasta), washed down by sweet Óthos wine. Sea-view terrace under trees of the same name. €

Kastelórizo

Alexandra's
West end of quay
Tel: 22460 49029
Probably the best food in the port: sample such delights as octopus or courgette croquettes, grilled halloumi cheese, and *soupiórizo* (cuttlefish and rice) spiced up with ouzo, chilli and parsley rather than the usual cuttlefish ink. Open lunch and dinner during the warmer months. €€€

Billy's
Mid-quay
Tel: 22460 49224
One of the cheaper (relatively!) choices on the island, doing up squid, local baby shrimp and few meat grills and vegie starters including bean dishes. Popular, so expect to wait for a table. Both

quayside and indoor seating allow year-round operation. €€

Paragadi
Quay, near ferry dock
Tel: 22460 49396
Despite the off-putting picture menus, a solid choice with a full range of seaood and meat dishes. Rather tellingly, the Turkish ferry crews (and other Turks) often choose to dine here. Open Apr–Nov. €€

Sými

Dimitris
South quay near ferry dock, Gialós
Tel: 22460 72207
Excellent, family-run, seafood-strong *ouzerí* with exotic items such as *hohlióalo* (sea snails), *foúskes* (mock oysters), *spinóalo* (pinna-shell flesh) and the indigenous miniature shrimps, as well as more usual platters. Open for lunch and supper. €€

Georgios
Top of Kalí Stráta, Horió
Tel: 22460 71984
An island institution: Greek nouvelle cuisine (variable in quality) in large, non-nouvelle portions, served in the pebbled courtyard. Informal live music some nights. €€

PRICE CATEGORIES

Prices indicated are for a meal per person with modest intake of wine or beer, rakí or tsípouro.
€ = under 17 euros
€€ = 17–25 euros
€€€ = 25–34 euros
€€€€ = over 34 euros

Marathounda
Marathoúnda Cove
Tel: 22460 71425
The beach here isn't among the island's best, but folk come here for the sake of the taverna, with fish at or below town prices, good *mezédes* and decent service. Watch out for the mooching goats and wasps, though. Open late May–mid-Sept. €€

Mythos Mezé
South quay, Gialós
Tel: 22460 71488
Dinner-only venue on the roof of the former summer cinema, serving some of the more imaginative cooking on the island. Ignore the menu and let chef Stavros deliver a Frenchified medley which may well include salad, seafood starters, or meat followed by home-made desserts. Open late May–Oct. €€€

Syllogos
Just south of Platía Syllógou, Horió
Tel: 22460 72138
Cavernous place with indoor/outdoor seating, great for taverna standards like *skordaliá*, *arní lemonáto*, fried

fish and aubergine *imám*. The Rhodian bulk wine is good – but food portion sizes could be more generous. Open Apr–Nov. €€

Tílos

Delfini
Agios Andónios port, near Megálo Horió
Tel: 22460 44252
The most reliable waterside taverna in the west of Tílos, with affordable seafood right off the adjacent boats, goat-based dishes, and enchanting seating under the quayside tamarisks. Open May–Oct, lunch and dinner. €–€€

Kastro
Megálo Horió
Tel: 22460 44116
The managing family can be a bit dour, but it's worth putting up with them for their excellent own-raised meat (signature dishes are *katsíki kokkinistó or lemonáto*), goat's cheese and *dolmádes*, served at the best view-terrace on the island. Open lunch and dinner most of the year. €

Kritikos
Near start of pedestrianised seafront, Livádia
Tel: 22460 44077
Portions are on the small side, but the food – goat with aubergine, keftédes, hórta croquettes – is very tasty despite recourse to tinned, cubed vegetables (as many tavernas here unfortunately do). Open May–Oct lunch and dinner. €€

Nikos & Maria
Main road, by police station
Tel: 22460 44148
The pride and joy here is a wood-fired oven, used for pizzas and much else such as kléftiko. Food is made in small batches, so much of the wide-ranging menu can be "off"; service has its longeurs. Open May–Oct lunch and dinner. €€

Omonia (Mihalis')
Just above the harbour square, Livádia
Tel: 22460 44287
Sit under the trees strung with fairy lights and enjoy the closest thing on the island to an authentic *ouzerí* by night; filling breakfasts in the morning. €

THE NORTHERN DODECANESE

Agathonísi and Maráthi

Georgios
Agios Geórgios, east quay
Tel: 22470 29101
A good mix of seafood, salads and a few *magirevtá*; also about the only establishment of the trio here to open reliably at midday, thanks to the shady courtyard. €

Piratis
Southeast end of Maráthi beach
Tel: 22470 31580
The most welcoming of three establishments here, with simple fish and free-range goat served up by piratically garbed Mihalis Kavouras, at attractive prices and to the accompaniment of Greek music. Open all day according to Mihalis's whim. €

Astypálea

Australia
Just inland from the head of the bay, Skála
Tel: 22430 61275
Kyría María presides over the oldest and most wholesome taverna here, with fresh seafood, own-grown veggies and island wine. Open Apr–Nov. €€

Gerani
In the stream bed just behind Livádia beach
Tel: 22430 61484

The most consistently good and consistently open (May–Oct) taverna here, renowned for its excellent *magirevtá*. They also have lovely studios to rent next door. €

Maïstrali (Tou Penindara)
Head of the harbour, Skála
Tel: 22430 61691
The best spot for a local lobster banquet, or less extravagantly a scaly-fish meal or *magirevtá* from a broad menu. Open all year for dinner, lunch as per demand. €€€

Kálymnos and Télendos

Barba Stathis (Tassia's)
Start of path to Hohlakás beach, Télendos
Tel: 22430 47953
Warm little taverna doing just a few magirevtá daily, at bargain prices compared to the waterfront. Better at night, when the grill is lit and the seafront is not so tempting. €

Giorgos Mamouzelos
Linária quay
Tel: 22430 47809
The only seaside taverna between Kandoúni and Platýs Gialós inclusive worth patronising, featuring such delights as swordfish with a side of impeccable medallion chips, or stuffed peppers with balsamic vinegar. You'll have to wait for a table or reserve one, and put up with

sometimes peculiar service. Open May–Oct dinner mainly. €€€

Kafenes
Platía Hristoú, opposite municipal "palace", Póthia
Tel: 22430 28727
Going since 1950, this hole-in-the-wall purveys generous seafood platters like crunchy *maridáki* fish, great local cheese and mountainous salads, for example the "green"one with purslane, rocket, sun-dried tomato and lots of cheese. Throw in reasonable prices and it's easy to see why you may have to wait for a table. Open all year; lovely interior for winter. €

Kafouli (Tou Mihali)
Télendos waterfront
Tel: 22430 47363
Currently the best seaside spot here, with generous octopus portions, a few daily magirevtá such as mince-rich moussakás, and draught beer in chilled steins. The proprietor can be a bit unctuous for some tastes, though. Open May–Oct daily. €€

Pandelis
Behind Olympic Hotel, Agios Nikólaos district
Tel: 22430 51508
The menu only cites the ubiquitous Kalymnian *mermizéli* salad (like Cretan *dákos*) and a few grills, indifferent mezédes or *magirevtá*;

you have to ask for scaly fish (keenly priced and perfectly grilled), and fresh shellfish such as *kalógnomes* (ark shell), *strídia* (round oysters) and *foúskes* (a bizarre marine invertebrate gathered by sponge divers as a sideline). €€€
Tsopanakos
Armeós
Tel: 22430 47929
This family taverna specialises in meat and cheese from local flocks, the speciality being *mourí* (goat or lamb in a clay pot). With indoor/outdoor seating. €€

Kós

Ambavris
Ambávris hamlet, 800 metres/yds south of Kós Town
Tel: 22420 25696
Ignore the perfunctory English-language menu in favour of the constantly changing *mezédes pikilía* or house medley – six platters can encompass such delights as *pihtí* (brawn), stuffed squash blossoms, *fáva* dip, and *loukánika*. Courtyard seating. Open May–Oct dinner only. €€–€€€
Ambeli
1km (0.5 mile) east of Tingáki resort
Tel: 22420 69682
The best policy here is to avoid the mains and order a variety of the excellent starters, such as *pinigoúri* (cracked wheat), *bekrí mezé* (pork chunks in spicy pepper sauce), brawn, medallion chips and *yaprákia* (the local *dolmádes*). Plates are deceptively large, so beware over-ordering. Solid Greek wine list, and iced beer steins. Seating indoors and out beside the vineyard; open May–Oct daily lunch and dinner, winter Fri–Sat dinner, Sun lunch. €€
Hasan
Central junction, Platáni village
Tel: 22420 20230
There have always been several ethnically Turkish-run establishment clustered here, dishing out Anatolian-style *mezédes* and kebabs. The newest (opened May 2012), and currently about the best, is this one, without *mezédes* but a creditable Adana kebab, generous okra stew and (no religious taboos here) a wide-ranging drinks list. Afterwards, finish off with an Anatolian ice cream, at **Zaharoplastio Paradosi** across the way. €€
Koako
Vasiléos Georgíou 8, Kos Town
Tel: 22420 25645
An old favourite in a classy environment, doing all the standards well and generously – in particular

hórta, little fish and less successful mushroom fritters – along with bulk wine (the rosé is fine). Open most of the year. €€
Makis
One lane in from front, Mastihári
Tel: 22420 51592
Long reckoned to serve the best – and best-priced – grilled fish by weight on the island, and an excellent spot to wait for the ro-ro ferry to Kálymnos. No *magirevtá*, a few salads and dips, and oblique sea views at best mean relatively few tourists. €€–€€€
Mavromatis
Start of Psalídi strip, 2km (1 mile) from Kos Town centre
Tel: 22420 22433
A well-established seaside eatery with its own beach loungers, and ace dishes like grilled mackerel and a rocket-parmesan salad that isn't (as elsewhere) mostly lettuce. But tourist tastes mean that you do have to specifically ask proprietor/maître d', Manolis, for real, hand-cut chips and not frozen ones. Open much of year, lunch and dinner. €–€€
Oromedon
Ziá approach road
Tel: 22420 69983
One of the few tavernas here that doesn't need to rely on picture-menus and other gimmicks thanks to the prime view from its roof terrace, and the good, local food. Open Mar–Nov. €€
Palea Pigi
Pylí village
Tel: 22420 41510
Inexpensive and basic (*loukánika*, fried vegetables, *biftékia*, marinated sardines, *bakaliáros* with mashed potatoes, beets) but impeccable fare at this taverna hidden away under a giant icus, beside the giant cistern fountain with lion-headed spouts amidst a bird-filled oasis. Open lunch and dinner, may close Dec–Mar. €
Pote tin Kyriaki
Pissándrou 9, Kós Town
Tel: 22420 48460
Going since 1997, Kos' only genuine *mezedopolío* has signature platters like *marathópita* (fennel pie), *kavourdistí* (pork fry up) and assorted seafood at friendly prices, complemented by proprietress Stamatia's very strong bulk *rakí*, and a soundtrack of Greek music for Greeks, not tourists. Open summer Mon–Sat dinner only, winter Fri–Sat. €

Léros

Dimitris O Karaflas
Spiliá district, on road between Pandélli

and Vromólithos
Tel: 22470 25626
Some of the heartiest food on the island, and the best view of Vromólithos. Stars include the chunky, herby Lerian sausages, potato salad or *maridákia*. Moderate prices for large portions. Open lunch and dinner. €€
Mylos Ouzeri
Out by the sea-marooned windmill, Agía Marína
Tel: 22470 24894
The most romantic setting on the island, whether for lunch or dinner. Specialities include *garidopílafo* (shrimp rice), octopus croquettes, baked four-cheese casserole and *kolokythokeftédes* (courgette patties). Ouzo is exorbitantly priced. The adjacent, affiliated roof bar is the haunt of local gilded youth. Open late Mar–late Oct; reservations mandatory July–Aug, when Turkish yachties crowd the place. €€€
Sotos
Drymónas anchorage
Tel: 22470 24546
It's worth the trek out here for the solely seasonal, fresh, local seafood proudly featured: scaly fish, good grilled octopus, and shellfish like oysters, mussels, scallops and sea urchins. Keep the (potentially considerable) bill down with palatable bulk wine. Open Apr–Oct. €€€–€€€€
Tou Mihali Pandéli
Plaza where one-way system goes inland
Tel: 22470 25800
Give the uniformly touristy beachside tavernas a miss in favour of this characterful spot doing only reasonable fish, salads and copious amounts of drink at bargain prices. Presentation is basic but hygienic. €€

Lipsí

Dilaila
Katsadiá, left-hand bay
Tel: 22470 41041
Incongruously classy in its rural surroundings, where good herbal smells announce the most creative cooking in the region. This season's platters might include octopus carpaccio with red mulberries, tuna tartare, or squash and carrot salad,

PRICE CATEGORIES

Prices indicated are for a meal per person with modest intake of wine or beer, rakí or tsípouro.

€ = under 17 euros
€€ = 17–25 euros
€€€ = 25–34 euros
€€€€ = over 34 euros

with unvarying favourite banoffee pie for dessert. The adjacent after-hours bar sometimes hosts live music. Open mid-May–mid-Oct. **€€–€€€** .

Giannis
Mid-quay, port town
Tel: 22470 41395
Excellent all-rounder, with meat and seafood grills but plenty of salads and *laderá* dishes for vegetarians too. The only taverna open for lunch as well as dinner all season long (early May–early Oct). **€€**

Nísyros

Apyria (Triandafyllos)
Emborió village centre
Tel: 22420 31377
The former *kafenío* of this all-but-abandoned village has been transformed into the best meat taverna on island – *gouronópoulo* on the spit during summer, otherwise just a few *mezédes* like beets or skordaliá and select meat platters like *pansétta* daily, accompanied by decent bulk wine.. Indoor/outdoor seating; open all year (weekends only winter). **€**

Balkoni tou Emboriou
Emborió village plaza
Tel: 22420 31607
Always packed in season for the sake of their keftédes, beets with greens, caper greens, cheese dishes and (by night) grills – and for the amazing view over the volcanic zone from said balkóni. Open May–Oct, lunch and usually dinner. **€**

Barcareto Margarita
Levkandió district, Mandráki
Tel: 22420 31842
Despite the name, chef Davide Sacco is very much in charge here, with a large repertoire of Venetian dishes, especially seafood, and Italian wine to

go with it. Unique in the Dodecanese, let alone to Nísyros. Open May–Oct dinner only. **€€–€€€**

Limenari
Eponymous cove west of Páli
Tel: 22420 31023
This secluded tavern has a big share of the local market thanks to fair prices and portions for caper-topped salads, fish, a few dishes of the day like *papoutsáki*, and made-to-order *tyrokafterí* (which takes a while to arrive). Occupies a lovely spot in terraced valley above the bay. Islanders and army conscripts go all year, always a good sign. **€**

Pátmos

Benetos
Sápsila cove, 2km (1 mile) southeast of Skála
Tel: 22470 33089
This eatery has a reputation as one of the best spots on the island for Mediterranean/Pacific Rim fusion cuisine, with a stress on seafood. A three-course meal might include bean and salmon croustade, *astakomakaronáda* (lobster pasta) and lemon sorbet. Open June–early Oct, dinner only except Mon; must reserve in summer for rigid seating times. **€€€€**

Ktima Petra
Pétra beach, south of Gríkou
Tel: 22470 33207
Hands down the best beach taverna on the island. Chunky *melitzanosaláta*, lush rocket salad, *dolmádes*, brown bread and pork *giovétsi* are typical of lunchtime offerings, with excellent *retsína* from Thebes; at sunset the grill is lit, and still later the place becomes a full-on bar. Open May–7 Oct; lunch only low season. **€€**

Lambi
Lámbi beach, north end of island
Tel: 22470 31490
Another reliable beach taverna, going since 1958; food presentation is fairly simple, emphasising grilled fish. Open Easter–Oct 10. **€–€€**

Livadi Geranou
Above eponymous beach
Tel: 6972 497426
Doesn't look like much, but this taverna has a cult following for the sake of its coarse-cut *hórta*, roast goat, *keftédes* and seafood dishes – plus views over the entire island. **€**

Panagos
Upper Kámbos
Tel: 22470 31570
A beacon of magirevtá for the whole island. The autumn menu might feature baked *palamídi* (north Aegean tuna), chickpea hotpot, good bulk wine, and yogurt dessert on the house. Holds a museum's worth of old photos inside. **€€**

Trehandiri
Main lane to Hókhlakas, Skála
Tel: 22470 34080
Opened in 2012 and already a contender for most popular *ouzerí* in town, overtaking other old favourites like Ostria and Hiliomodi. No sea view – no view at all, in fact – but honest portions of starters and all manner of seafood. Open most of the year. **€**

Tsipouradiko
Konsoláto anchorage, Skála
Tel: 22470 32803
Another recent entrant on the restaurant scene, purveying mainly vegie starters, seafood and a well-priced drinks list. With tables both outside on the hard sand and indoors, it works all year (dinner only), often with live music. **€€**

CRETE

Agios Nikólaos

Avli
Príngipa Georgíou 12
Tel: 28410 82479
All the usual *ouzerí* standards, as well as desserts like lemon mousse. Polite service and a vine-shaded courtyard (*avlí* in Greek) setting are big pluses, as is wine from their own vineyard in the Sitía mountains. Open April–Oct daily. **€€**

Chrisofyllis
Aktí Papá Pangálou,
Kitroplatía cove
Tel: 28410 22705
Creative *ouzerí* with platters like *sfoungáta* (onion-sausage soufflé),

eggplant with *graviéra* cheese and beets in yogurt-walnut sauce. A minimalist interior sports old photos (some are for sale). Open daily, noon until late. **€€–€€€**

Argyroúpoli

O Kipos tis Arkoudenas
On road towards Episkopí
Tel: 28310 61607
Lamb and pork specialists, serving up good food below the trees of its rear garden. This is a better option than the cluster of tavernas at the famous springs in the village. **€**

Arkalohóri

Manioros
Central village junction
Tel: 28910 22394
You'll almost certainly pass through this large village en route between Iráklio and the south coast, and this strategically placed rakádiko is ideal for a snack of rakí and mezédes (all the standards). Much of the appeal, though, is in the long narrow premises, completely crammed with old photos, folk sayings and mantinádes lyrics. Your host, Marinos, may grab his mandolin and play in the evenings. **€**

Frangokástello

Kali Kardia
Tel: 28250 92123
Old-fashioned taverna where the best tack is to eat what the proprietors are eating: perhaps a fry-up of the very fresh local fish and wild-picked greens such as *stífnos*, washed down with good *hýma* wine. €

Haniá

Ask the locals where they eat away from the two Venetian harbours and they'll recommend Aktí Papanikolí, just west of the walls at Néa Hóra, with its many seafront tavernas, or Halépa seafront east of the walls. We list a few reasonably priced choices in the Old Town.

Halkina
Aktí Tombazi 29–30, old harbour
Tel: 28210 41570
Tucked inconspicuously between the tourist traps of the two Venetian ports is this *rakádiko*, well attended for titbits like eggplant roulade, *marathópita* (fennel pie) and *apáki*. Oddly, their bulk wine is preferable to their *raki*. Open daily, 1pm until late. €–€€

Kalamoti
Venizélou 142, Halépa district
Tel: 28210 59198
A favourite seaside hangout of locals, thanks to sizeable casserole dishes (these can sell out at lunch), vegetarian platters and seafood. Try *dolmádes*, *myzíthra* cheese or grilled *soupiá* (cuttlefish), accompanied by the decent local *retsína* (pine-resin-flavoured wine). €€

Ouzythino
Aktí Papanikolí 6, Neahóra
Tel: 28210 73315
With summer tables set out on the fishing-port jetty, this is a popular taverna here, thanks to heaping helpings of marinated anchovies, Sfakian sausages, courgette patties and cheese-stuffed peppers. The name means "ouzo-beer-wine" – all present and correct, as well as *raki*. Open daily, lunch and dinner. €€

Tamam
Zambeliou 49, Evraïkí district
Tel: 28210 96080
This former hamam (Turkish bath) built in 1645 contains one of the best, most atmospheric restaurants in town. It's predictably stuffy inside in summer, with outside tables at a premium (bookings taken). The fare is Cretan, plus Mediterranean/Middle Eastern specialities like Iranian pilaf and lots else for vegetarians. Success has prompted the opening of an annexe opposite, with modern decor. Open daily, lunch and dinner. €€–€€€

Seafood platter with calamari and prawns.

Ierápetra

Levante
Stratigoú Samail 38
Tel: 28420 80585
The most reliable of the tavernas behind the seafront, with castle views, going since the 1930s. Homestyle dishes like milk-based *xýgalo*, stuffed cabbage leaves, *papoutsáki* and *omathiés* – rice-and-offal sausage. €€–€€

Iráklio

Giakoumis
Fotíou Theodosáki, off Evans
Tel: 2810 284039
Classic marketplace taverna, in several contiguous premises in this alley. It specialises in succulent lamb chops, crispy potatoes, seasonal salads and equally good rosé or white bulk wine from the local Lyrarakis vintners; service can be distracted, however. Open Mon–Sat lunch and dinner.

Ippokambos
Sofoklí Venizélou
Tel: 2810 280240
Highly regarded *ouzerí* by the Venetian harbour. Excellent *mezédes* (including snails), reasonably priced seafood and winning service. It gets busy, so go early; no reservations taken. Open Apr–Nov Mon–Sat for lunch and dinner. €€

Karnagio
Mínoös 3, corner shore road, Tálos district
Tel: 2810 280090
A local favourite, tops for seafood like grilled cuttlefish or octopus, and rich risotto. Both scaly fish and shellfish are affordable, and squirmingly fresh; the house-label bottled wine is also excellent. Daily, lunch and dinner. €€–€€€

Paradosiako
Vourváhon 9
Tel: 2810 342927
Secluded, no-nonsense taverna with courtyard seating and intriguing *objet trouvé* interior, reached by a pedestrian passage; grills, *mezédes* and a few dishes of the day are the stock in trade. Open Mon–Sat 2pm–midnight. €€

Syllogos Erasitehnon Alieon (Amateur Fishermen's Club)
Tel: 2810 223812
Despite the name, this seafood *ouzerí* in an ex-cold-storage plant near the harbour is open to all, with parking out front. By city standards, the scaly fish and shellfish are eminently affordable, perhaps reflecting the unglamourous surroundings. €€ .

Kournás (Lake)

Lygaria
Shoreline
Tel: 28250 61695
At the far end of the "strip" here, *Lygaria* eschews (for the most part) picture-menus, relying instead on its excellent *apáki*, *stífno* greens, stuffed squash blossoms and chunky house *melitsanosaláta* to draw customers. Open all year (weekends only winter). €–€€

Móhlos

Kohylia
East quay
Tel: 28430 94432
A reliable choice amongst several establishments here, also the oldest (founded 1902). Expect fresh artichokes in spring, stews, and daily casseroles like stuffed vegetables or *moussakás*. A pleasant interior allows cool-season operation. Respectful, non-pushy service. Open Feb–Nov, lunch and dinner. €€

PRICE CATEGORIES

Prices indicated are for a meal per person with modest intake of wine or beer, raki or tsípouro.
€ = under 17 euros
€€ = 17–25 euros
€€€ = 25–34 euros
€€€€ = over 34 euros

Nída Plateau (above Anógia)

Nida
Tel: 28340 31141
At the base of Psiloritis, Crete's highest mountain, this country taverna serves hearty meat- and chicken-based oven dishes and grills. Open daily Apr–Oct; weekends otherwise. €

Palékastro

Angistri (Nikolas O Psaras)
Village centre, Angathiás
Tel: 28430 61598
Some of the cheapest, and freshest, fish in the region here, straight from Nikolas' boat. His son and daughter grill and serve respectively. A few cooked dishes as well, plus superb views from the terrace by day.
€€–€€€

Paleohóra

Caravella
Harbour quay
Tel: 28230 41131
The top local seafood restaurant, with bulk wine from nearby Kastélli Kissámou. High-standard apartments upstairs as well. €€€
The Third Eye
Some 50 metres/yds inland from west beach, south end
Tel: 28230 42223
A remarkable vegetarian restaurant, with an extensive Asian/Indian menu plus a range of desserts. Breakfast also offered; occasional concerts by night. Open all day from before Easter to end Oct. €€

Plakiás area

Ifigeneia
Angouselianá village, west outskirts, 10km (6 miles) inland
Tel: 28320 51362
A shrine of traditional Cretan delicacies like volví skordaláta (pickled wild hyacinth bulbs), stamnagáthi, apáki and boiled goat with gamopílafo (white sticky rice). Open nightly all year; booking suggested. €

Pláka

Haroupia
Tel: 28410 42510
Something of an oddity in a seafood-mad resort, this very competent, Greek-patronised ouzerí straddling the through road does simpler, sustaining fare – apáki, mushrooms, dolmádes and rakí. €–€€

Réthymno

Dyo Rou
Pánou Koronéou 28t
Tel: 6936 500892

This self-proclaimed inomagiríon (wine-and-cook-shop) in a quiet part of the old quarter proves a winner for stamnagáthi, keftédes and imám-style eggplant, served with bulk wine or the locally brewed organic beer. Portions aren't huge – the emphasis is on quality. The interior constitutes a quasi-museum displaying black-and-whites of old Réthymno and shadow-puppet figures. Open lunch and dinner. €
Rakodikeio
Vernádou 7, opposite Nerantzés Mosque
Tel: 6945 774407
This exquisite little ouzerí, a big hit with Réthymno's student contingent, offers creatively tweaked dishes like pork fried with saffron and oúzo, Hánia-style píta, or beet salad with yogurt and walnuts. Tables on the pedestrian alley or inside by season. Open mid-summer for dinner only, otherwise 2pm until very late. €€
Veneto
Epimenídou 4
Tel: 28310 56634
Expensive, old-world diner of the eponymous restoration hotel. Its fusion dishes include salmon millefeuille with avocado and myzíthra sauce, and stuffed lamb. Notably well-stocked wine cellar. Open most of the year. €€€€

Sitía

Balkoni/Balcony
Foundalídou 19
Tel: 28430 25084
www.balcony-restaurant.com
Widely travelled owner-chef Tonya Karandinou's menu juxtaposes nouvelle Cretan fare (rabbit with walnuts and rosemary, snails in goat-cheese sauce) with creative salads, and Mexican or Asian dishes – a legacy of her time running restaurants in Laguna Beach and London. Pricey wine list. Open dinner only April–Oct.
€€€€
Sergiani
Karamanlí 38 (beachfront)
Tel: 28430 24092
Properly flash-fried atherína (sand smelt), vegetarian turnovers and copious salads constitute some of the staples at this unusually good beachside taverna. €–€€

Soúgia

Anchorage
Main access road (Papadérou Street)
Tel: 28230 51487
www.taverna-anchorage.com
Forego sea views in favour of a vine-shaded courtyard and decent renditions of angináres me koukiá (artichoke hearts with broad beans),

wild hórta, stewed rabbit, and tsigaristó. Open daily Easter–Oct, noon–11pm. €€
Kyma (Paterakis)
On the seafront
Tel: 28230 51688
Kyma's gravel-terrace tables are usually packed, for good reason – big portions of good-value fare like own-made taramosaláta and marathópita, with friendly service. Sadly, the seafood is often frozen, but there's quaffable bulk wine. Open daily late Apr–late Oct noon–11pm. €€

Stavrós, Akrotíri Peninsula

Zorbas
Behind the giant eucalyptus, near bus stop
Tel: 28210 39402
Generally, we run a mile from tavernas so named, but this one's the real deal – the most locally attended of several on this sandy cove, where the disastrous log-transport scene of Zorba the Greek was filmed. There's a good range of seafood, cheeses, lamb dishes and vegetable casseroles in big portions. €
Vóri
Alekos
Behind Agía Pelagía church
Tel: 28920 91094
After visiting nearby Phaistos and Agía Triáda palaces, head for this secluded village taverna. The attractive setting – a courtyard with tables and cushioned bench seating, an interior with fireplace – is matched by the food: hearty portions of deftly executed recipes. A wood-burning oven bakes goat or kid dishes (ordered in advance). Open daily lunch and dinner.
€–€€

Zákros (Káto)

Kato Zakros Bay (aka Platanakis)
Waterfront
Tel: 28430 26887
Tellingly, this taverna at one of eastern Crete's remotest bays gets the most local clientele, for the sake of the homegrown vegetables and home-bred poultry, fair prices and decent quality. Open April–Oct all day. €€

PRICE CATEGORIES

Prices indicated are for a meal per person with modest intake of wine or beer, rakí or tsípouro.
€ = under 17 euros
€€ = 17–25 euros
€€€ = 25–34 euros
€€€€ = over 34 euros

ACTIVITIES

THE ARTS, RELIGIOUS FESTIVALS, NIGHTLIFE AND SHOPPING

THE ARTS

Music and dance

Thanks to Greece's geographical position and the vast number of cultures that have called it home, there is astonishing regional variety in island folk musics. Crete has one of the more vital traditions, characterised by the *lýra* (three-string spike fiddle) and *laoúto* (mandolin-like lute). In the Dodecanese, these are often joined by either *tsamboúna*, a goatskin bagpipe, *violí* (western violin) or *sandoúri*, the hammer dulcimer popularised in the islands by refugees from Asia Minor. Lésvos has a tradition of brass bands, imported apparently from the Asia Minor mainland opposite.

Nisiótika is the general name for Aegean island music; that of the Ionians doesn't really count, being heavily Italian-influenced – especially in its vocal styles *kantádes* and *arékia*

Children's activities

Despite the general child-friendliness of modern Greek culture, there are few activities or facilities specifically aimed at children – certainly nothing in the order of Paris's Disneyland. There are water parks on Crete, Aegina, Corfu and Rhodes, and the growing number of all-inclusive resorts (on islands like Crete, Kós and Corfu) always have child-centred "animation" (entertainment) programmes. Also, any multi-starred hotel is likely to have a separate childrens' pool and (unsupervised) playground.

– and Western in scale.

Contemporary sounds include original compositions or derivations of traditional material. From the islands, worth special mention are the group Haínides and the earlier work of Loudovíkos ton Anogíon, both originally from Crete.

Each archipelago (and sometimes each island within it) has its own particular folk dances. These range from the basic *stá tría* – three steps to one side, followed by a kick (growing gradually faster and faster) – to a frenzied combination of complicated footwork, jumps, slaps and kicks. Troupes, dressed in traditional Greek costume, are most likely to be performing on public holidays (you may also see them on television, or the artificial surrounds of hotel- or taverna-sponsored "Greek Nights").

Quality music venues in the islands often take advantage of pre-existing historic monuments – good examples are ancient amphitheatres or *odeia* on Thásos, Kós and Sámos; castle moats and baileys, as in the Théatro Táfros on Rhodes, the Paleó Froúrio on Corfu or (with spectacular, distracting views) Mólyvos Castle on Lésvos. Corfu's opera house was, sadly, destroyed during World War II but the opera house in Ermoúpoli, Sýros has been well restored, as has Rhodes's Italian-built municipal theatre, Corfu's Ionian Academy auditorium and Iráklio's Níkos Kazantzákis open-air theatre. Unlike in the west, churches are rarely used, the sterling exception being St George's on Corfu.

Island cultural events

The economic crisis has reduced the scope and length (if not the existence) of many events, but there's still a pretty full calendar between late spring and autumn. These are the most likely survivors, with a long track record behind them.

July Music Festival on the island of Itháki (Ithaca).
July–August Corfu Festival: Jazz, Brass bands, local choirs, invited foreign guests.
July–August Thásos Festival, mostly in Liménas ancient theatre.
July–August Rhodes Cultural Festival, with wine festival end August in Rodíni park.
July–August Ippokrateia Festival, Kós.
Aug–Sept Réthymno Renaissance Fair of cultural activities.
July–September Lato Cultural Festival, Agios Nikólaos, Crete.
July–September Sými Festival; mixed classical and Greek pop performances.
July–September Iráklio Festival – concerts, theatre, opera and dance by world-class acts.
August Levkáda International Folklore Festival, with overseas groups.
September Sacred music festival on Pátmos.
September Santoríni Classical Music Festival.
September Paxos International Music Festival; a week or so of chamber music concerts.

RELIGIOUS FESTIVALS

(* denotes that this is also a legal holiday, with everything closed.)
1 January *Feast of Agios Vasílios* (St Basil).
6 January* *Agía Theofánia, Tá Fóta/ Epiphany*: Blessing of the waters – at any island, youths dive for the honour

of retrieving a crucifix cast into the port by the local bishop or priest.

February–March Carnival season for three weeks before Lent: all over Greece. Some islands with celebrations of special interest are Zákynthos, Corfu, Híos (Mestá, Olýmbi), Lésvos (Agiássos), Agía Anna (Évvia), Kefaloniá, Kárpathos, Iráklio, Réthymno and (best of all) Skýros. Depending on the place, expect masqueing, more or less obscene songs, floats, pranks, food-fights, and people rapping each other on the head with squeaky plastic hammers.

Tsiknopémpti or **"Roast-Smell" Thursday** The last day, 52 before Easter, on which the devout may consume meat. All grill-type tavernas are booked up days in advance for a final binge.

"Clean" Monday* Beginning of the fast for Lent – last day of cheese-eating, four days after *Tsiknopémpti*. Picnics in the countryside and kite-flying, all over Greece.

25 March* *Evangelismós/Feast of the Annunciation/National Day*: military parades in all main towns, pilgrimage to Tínos.

Easter Weekend* *Good Friday, Holy Saturday* and *Easter Sunday* are celebrated throughout Greece. The date usually, but not always, precedes or follows Western Easter by one to four weeks; for the exact date in any given year, consult http://5ko.free.fr/en/easter.php

23 April *Feast of St George*: celebrated especially in Kaliópi (Límnos), Asigonía (near Haniá) and Pylí (Kós). If Easter occurs later, George is honoured on Easter Monday.

1 May* *Workers' Day*: picnics in the countryside all over Greece; also usually demonstrations by disaffected labour in larger towns.

May/June *Agion Pnévma*/Pentecost Monday*, 50 days after Easter. The resulting three-day weekend (*triímero*) is the excuse for the first proper excursion to the holiday islands and the start of the "season".

17 July* *Agía Marína*. A big festival in rural areas, as she is (in one aspect) a major protector of crops. In many parts of Greece, especially where refugee communities from the Black Sea are to be found, it's considered bad luck to swim on this day as the saint in a malevolent guise always claims a victim.

19–20 July *Profítis Ilías*/Prophet Elijah. Almost every island has at least one summit in his honour, where there will be gathering, feasting and music (if only from cranked-up car sound systems) outside the saint's chapel or monastery.

6 August* *Metamórfosis toú Sotíros*/ Transfiguration of the Saviour. Mega food-fight with flour, squid ink, etc on Hálki; big commemoration in Pythagório, Sámos, where Christ is said to have aided the victorious Greek fleet in the 1824 battle of the Mykáli Straits.

15 August* *Kímisi tís Theotókou*/ *Dormition of the Virgin*: festivals all over the islands, especially Páros, Agiássos and Ólymbos (Kárpathos). Major pilgrimage to Tínos. In Orthodox theology, the "Assumption" into Heaven takes place eight days later, on 23 August.

29 August *Apokefálisis toú Prodrómou*/Beheading of John the Baptist. Pilgrimage festivals at Vrykoúnda on Kárpathos, and remote Agíou Ioánnou Monastery on Crete's Rodópou peninsula.

8 September *Yénnisis tís Panagías*/ Birth of the Virgin. The second-biggest Marian festival after 15 August; notable observances at Tsambíkas Monastery on Rhodes, where childless women crawl up the steps on hands and knees in supplication for conception, and on Spétses, where the day is also the anniversary

Indoor *ouzerís* and *kafenía*, or at least those with a conservatory, operate through the winter; some of the island's tavernas and bars keep their doors open too, though often only from Friday night to Sunday noon. But if the owner has something better or more profitable to do, like tend a farm or go fishing on an unseasonably mild night, the establishment will remain closed even if it's notionally supposed to be open. Outdoor cinemas, dance clubs and music venues perforce close down, and cultural edification retreats indoors: many islands have a weekly cinematheque showing quality films, and a few tavernas equipped with small wooden stages host live music (often *laïká* or *rebétiko*) at weekends.

of a naval victory over the Ottomans in 1822.

23–24 September *Agios Ioánnis Theológos*/St John the Divine. Special celebrations outside Nikiá, Nísyros, and on Pátmos at the saint's monastery, with special liturgies.

26 October *Agios Dimítrios*/St Demetrios. The name-day of possibly a fifth of the male population, and traditionally the first day new wine was ready to drink.

28 October* *Ohi (No) Day*: anniversary of Greek leader Metaxas's supposed one-word response to Italy's ultimatum in 1940, prior to Greece's unexpected defeat of the Italian invasion force. Military parades in major cities.

8 November *Tón Taxiarhón Mihaïl ke Gavriíl*/Archangels Michael and Gabriel. Of the many rites at churches and monasteries dedicated to them, the grandest are at Panormítis on Sými – effectively extending that island's tourist season until then – and at the monastery outside Mandamádos, Lésvos.

Christmas season All over Greece. In a dwindling number of places, children sing *kálenda* (carols) from door to door for a small gratuity; mostly nowadays an excuse for Western-style commercialism and an outbreak of plastic inflatable Santas on chimneys, balcony railings, etc. Both 25 December and 26 December are legal holidays; the latter is not "Boxing Day" as in Britain, but *Sýnaxis tís Panagías*, the "Gathering of the Virgin's Entourage".

Taverna in the backstreets of Skiathos town.

31 December *Paramoní tis Protohroniás*/New Year's Eve. Many Greeks play cards for money on this occasion, and cut the *vasilópitta* pie with its lucky coin hidden in it. Special celebration in the town of Híos.

NIGHTLIFE

Metropolitan nightlife in Greece (on the islands, this means mainly Iráklio, Haniá, Réthymno plus the larger island capitals like Rhodes and Kérkya towns and the major foreign-dominated resorts) takes the form of barákia, theme bars with a recorded soundtrack, most likely trance, house or ambient; live music venues (most likely Greek *laïká*, or a watered-down version of *rebétika* or even Greek rock); dance clubs with a proper *písta* or floor; and musical tavernas where inflated food prices reflect the live entertainment.

Barákia won't have a cover charge, and in these tough times may offer extended "happy hours" or permanently cheap drink prices (eg €3–4 for a large beer, €5 for single shots); generally, however, you should expect stiff, Northern European tariffs for cocktails (€7 and up). Music clubs typically levy a cover charge (which may include the first drink), whilst live venues cost a minimum of €12–15 to get in.

A big current trend is the all-day beach bar (likely continuing after dark), which won't charge a cover per se but may ask stiff fees for sun loungers. In return you get a soundtrack, possibly a small dance floor and probably ancillary activities such as beach volleyball.

For many older Greeks, however, the **taverna** remains the most popular site for a night out spent eating, drinking and, sometimes, singing and dancing. In general, it's childless Greeks under 30 or

Advert in Skiathos town.

younger who frequent the bars and clubs.

In Athens, the weekly *Athinórama* (in Greek) has an extensive listing of all venues and events; a useful website (albeit in Greek only) is www.clickatlife.gr. For Thessaloníki, fairly comprehensive events websites (some with parent print magazines) include www.aboutthessaloniki.gr and www.cityportal.gr.

During the summer (late June–early September) many Athens and Thessaloníki clubs and music halls close down, with musicians of all stripes touring the countryside and islands, performing for the seasonal festivals.

Casinos

For a more sophisticated – and potentially more expensive – night out, there are casinos in Corfu, Rhodes and Ermoúpoli (Sýros).

Cinema

Going to the movies in Greece during the main tourist season is a special pleasure not to be missed, because nearly all the cinemas operating during summer (the others shut down unless they have air-conditioning) are open-air cinemas. In town centres these are to be found tucked among apartment buildings; in other areas perhaps perched on a sea-side promontory under the stars, or out at the edge of town amongst the fields.

Rising real-estate values are having an attritional effect, but particularly good cinemas survive in Kós Town, in Paleóhora (Crete), Mytiliní (Sámos), in and around Égina Town, in Parikiá (Páros), outside Náxos town, in Firá (Santoríni), in Póthia (Kálymnos), in Híos Town, in Mytiliní Town and Mólyvos on Lésvos, in Skiáthos Town and Levkáda Town (plus, of course, many in Athens).

Tickets, at €7–8, are slightly cheaper than at indoor cinemas and soundtracks are in the original language (with Greek subtitles). On smaller islands there may be only one film showing, at around 9.15pm, while elsewhere there will be two screenings, at 9 and 11pm. There is always a 15-minute *diálemma*, or intermission, about halfway through the feature. The season of operation for outdoor cinemas is dictated by however long it's comfortable enough to sit still outdoors for two hours after nightfall – typically, late May to mid-September.

Shopping

Greece is generally not a retail-therapy paradise – clothes, despite often being imported from the far East or Central Europe, are often eye-wateringly priced, and only become affordable during the August sales. Shoes are still made locally, however, and with careful fitting can be worthwhile bargains. All the international chain labels are represented, plus there's a local menswear entity called Glou which can be of interest. The best-value purchases are jewellery, often made to ancient Greek themes, and foodstuffs – not just the ubiquitous honey, olive oil and olives – impossible to obtain overseas. Mind the strictures of your home destination, however: flights bound for the US are likely to have checked baggage thoroughly combed on arrival.

A – Z

A HANDY SUMMARY
OF PRACTICAL INFORMATION

A

Admission charges

Most archaeological sites and museums, public or private, have admission charges varying from €2 for minor affairs up to €12 for five-star attractions. Occasionally (as in Athens and Rhodes) you can get a joint ticket covering several sites and museums at an advantageous price. From November to March, most state-run sites give free admission to EU nationals on Sunday; Monday or Tuesday are typical closure days. Students with valid ID get one-third to one-half off entry fees, as do certified teachers, archaeology students and people aged 60 or over. On summer full moon evenings, always August but sometimes in July or September too, major archaeological sites like the Parthenon, Lindos or the Heraion have free admission for all until about 1.30am – magical. Ask locally, as not all sites have the staff to participate in this programme.

B

Budgeting for your trip

Greece is no longer by any stretch of the imagination an inexpensive country. Travelling as one of a couple in high season, you should allow a minimum of €30 for a share of accommodation (budget €40–50 each in the biggest cities and name resorts), €15–20 for your half of a sit-down meal, €6–10 daily for site/museum admissions, and €13–17 for your share of the cheapest, smallest rental car – before petrol costs, which have risen steeply in recent years owing to excise taxes. As elsewhere, most things are more expensive for people travelling alone; single-room accommodation often costs almost as much as double.

Business travellers

Business travellers are well catered for; most good-standard hotels now have some sort of "business person's corner" with a computer terminal and printer, as well as Wi-fi signal for laptops (in the common areas if not in all the rooms). The same hotels tend to have multiple conference/event rooms as well as lounges suitable for semi-formal meetings.

C

Children

Children are adored in Greece, and many families are still highly superstitious about their welfare – don't be surprised to see toddlers with amulets pinned to their clothes to ward off the evil eye. So expect your own kids to be the centre of attention. Children are given quite a bit of leeway in Greece and treated very indulgently. They are allowed to stay up late and are routinely taken out to eat in tavernas. You may have to politely put your foot down when shop owners offer free sweets or strangers are over-indulgent towards your own children.

Climate

In general, the north coast of each island is subject to more summer-time gales and cooler temperatures than the protected south coast; be sure to check on a map exactly where a holiday resort is before making a final booking. Many travellers underestimate the differences in climate between individual island chains.

The green, cool Ionian islands, for instance, are prone to rainy spells from mid-September through to the end of May. By contrast, Rhodes and Crete's southern coast can offer swimming for the hardy as late as mid-December. If planning to visit any of the islands from mid-September through to the end of April, a good rule to follow is this: the further south the island is geographically, the better the sunshine rate will be.

On the whole, islands are ill-equipped for visitors during the winter months. Heating can be basic or non-existent, boats are infrequent, tinned food may be all that is available on the smaller islands and amenities are scarce. The tourist season is officially "over" in late October, although it extends into

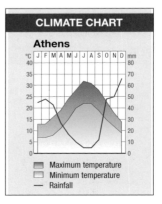

CLIMATE CHART

Athens

- ◼ Maximum temperature
- ☐ Minimum temperature
- — Rainfall

November on Rhodes and Crete, but ends early September on northern islands like Thásos or Límnos.

In general, late spring (late Apr–end June) and autumn (Sept–Oct) are the best times to visit. During these periods, you will find mild to warm temperatures, sunny days and fewer tourists. Throughout July and August, Greece is at its most hot and sticky, and most crowded. Still, millions of tourists seem to prefer the heat and the company.

What to wear

If you visit Greece during the summer months, you will want to bring lightweight, casual clothing. Add a pullover or shell jacket to this and you will be prepared for the occasional cool night breezes, or conditions on open boat decks. Lightweight shoes and sandals are ideal in the summer, but you will also need a pair of comfortable walking shoes that have already been broken in. If you plan to do any rigorous hiking on the islands bring sturdy, over-the-ankle boots with a good tread; leather will be more comfortable in summer temperatures than high-tech synthetic materials. If you visit Greece during the winter months, which can be surprisingly cold, bring the same kind of clothes you would wear during spring in the northern part of the United States or Central Europe.

Crime and safety

Sadly, Greece is no longer the crime-free haven of yesteryear. Locking cars and houses is now the norm everywhere, even in the deep countryside where people until recently used to leave a set of keys dangling from the front door.

Central Athens in particular has become hazardous at times. Cars with valuables exposed (or even not) are routinely broken into in such neighbourhoods as Exárhia, Gázi and Keramikós; the thieves, often apparently drug addicts, will steal almost anything irrespective of value, even old CDs or raggedy items of clothing.

Organised gangs of pickpockets and bag-snatchers frequent the metro lines and stations most popular with tourists, in particular Line 3 from the airport, Line 1 from Piraeus, Monastiráki plus Sýndagma stations, and the X95 bus-stop area at Sýndagma. They usually work in teams, and may be plausibly well dressed. If you are surrounded and pushed up against the carriage wall,

Cold frappés with an unobstructed seaview.

or forced to squeeze past them to retrieve your luggage from the rack in the airport-route cars, your wallet, camera or other valuables are about to be (or have been) lifted. Anything in the outside pocket of a daypack or backpack is essentially forfeit. Your cards will be used to obtain cash advances within minutes at exchange booths that are clearly in cahoots with the thieves. Nothing substantive is being done about the problem other than recorded announcements in the cars telling you to be aware. If you are new in town, and heavily laden, it's probably worth getting off the metro one station before (Evangelismós) or after (Akrópoli) the central ones and walking back to the centre, or getting an onwards taxi.

Young single females should be alert to the possibility of drugged drinks as a prelude to rape attempts in popular, rowdy beach resorts. Be suspicious of men who offer to bring you cocktails, whose preparation you cannot witness. The perpetrators, it must be said, are as (or more) likely to be other foreigners as Greeks. Use common sense when arranging rides afterwards back to your accommodation.

Because of tightened security considerations it is unwise to leave luggage unattended anywhere except perhaps in a hotel lobby, under the gaze of the desk staff. However, belongings inadvertently left behind in a café will still usually be put aside for you to collect.

Customs regulations

Currency restrictions

There are no limits on the amount of euros visitors can import or export. There are no restrictions on travellers' cheques, but cash sums of more than €10,000 or its equivalent should be declared on entry.

Duty-free goods

For travellers arriving from non-EU countries, allowances for duty-free goods brought into Greece are:
Tobacco 200 cigarettes, or 100 cigarillos, or 50 cigars, or 250g of tobacco.
Alcohol 1 litre of spirits or liqueurs over 22 percent volume, or 2 litres of fortified, sparkling or still wine.
Perfume 60cc of perfume, plus 250cc of eau de toilette.

Non-EU residents can claim back Value Added Tax on any items costing over €120, provided they export the item within 90 days of purchase. Tax-free forms are available at a very few tourist shops and department stores. Keep the receipt and form. Make your claim at the customs area of the airport when departing.

Duty-paid goods

In theory, there are no official limitations to the amount of duty-paid goods that can be moved between EU states. However, cigarettes and most spirits are still slightly cheaper in Greece than in Britain and Ireland,

TRANSPORT · ACCOMMODATION · EATING OUT · ACTIVITIES · A – Z · LANGUAGE

so don't stuff your luggage with such articles.

If you buy goods in Greece for which you pay tax, there are no restrictions on the amounts you can take home. EU law has set "guidance levels", however, as follows:
Tobacco 3,200 cigarettes, or 400 cigarillos, or 200 cigars or 3kg of tobacco.
Spirits 10 litres
Fortified wine/wine 90 litres
Beer 110 litres

If you exceed these amounts you must be able to prove the goods are for personal use.

Importing cars

EU-registered cars are no longer stamped into your passport on entry to the country (if you arrive by ferry, keep the tickets as this is considered proof of date of entry). They can circulate freely for up to six months, and are exempt from road tax as long as this has been paid in the home country – however, you are not allowed to sell the vehicle. Non-EU/EEA nationals will find that a bizarre litany of rules apply to importing cars, chief among them that you must re-export the car when you depart, or have it sealed by Customs in an off-road facility of your choosing.

Cars detected circulating after the initial six-month period without valid road tax are liable to seizure by customs/tax undercover agents, and are auctioned off if an enormous import duty is not paid.

D

Disabled travellers

Despite nudging from the EU, Greece has some way to go before becoming fully compliant with regulations on facilities for disabled people.

Athens, with lifts in the metro, "kneeling" buses on many routes, recorded announcements of upcoming stops on the metro plus some buses, and ramps (when not blocked by illegally parked cars) at kerbsides, is furthest ahead. The new Thessaloníki metro should also be EU-compliant regarding facilities for the disabled.

Elsewhere, amenities can be poor – there are few or no sound pips for the sight-impaired at pedestrian crossings, and it is common to see the wheelchair-bound tooling down the middle of the asphalt rather than

risking the obstacle course of a typical pedestrian pavement.

Few hotels in the provinces are disabled-friendly, though things are improving slowly, and some are setting aside a few rooms with wide doors and safety handles in the bath.

E

Embassies and consulates

Foreign embassies in Athens

All embassies are open from Monday to Friday only, usually from 8am until 2pm, except for their own national holidays (as well as, usually, Greek ones).
Australia Corner Kifissías and Alexándras avenues, Level 6, Thon Building, Ambelókipi; tel: 210 87 04 000. www.greece.embassy.gov.au/athn/home.html.
Canada Gennadíou 4, Kolonáki, (Evangelismós metro); tel: 72 73 400.
Ireland Vassiléos Konstandínou 7 (by National Gardens); tel: 72 32 771.
South Africa Kifissiás 60, Maroússi; tel: 210 61 06 645.
UK Ploutárhou 1, Kolonáki (Evangelismós metro); tel: 72 72 600, http://ukingreece.fco.gov.uk/en. Consulates: Corfu, 1st floor 18 Mantzarou Street, Kérkyra Town; tel 26610 23457
Crete, Candia Tower, 17 Thalitá Street, Platía Agíou Dimitríou, Iráklio ; tel 2810 224012
US Vasilísis Sofías 91, Ambelókipi (Mégaro Mousikís metro); tel: 72 12 951, http://athens.usembassy.gov.

Emergencies

The following numbers work country wide:
Police: 100
Ambulance: 166
Fire brigade, urban: 199
Forest fire reporting: 191
For less urgent medical problems, hotel staff will give you details of the nearest hospital or English-speaking doctor.

Entry requirements

Citizens of EU nations and EEA countries have unlimited visitation rights to Greece; your passport will not be stamped on entry or exit. With a valid passport, citizens of the US, Canada, Australia and New Zealand can stay in the country for up to three months (cumulative) within

any 180-day period, with no visa necessary. Over-stayers are fined very heavily on exit, to the tune of several hundred euros. To stay longer, you must obtain a permit from the nearest Aliens' Bureau or foreigners' division of the local police station; however, this is lately proving nearly impossible (and very expensive) to do. Citizens of all non-EU/EEA countries should contact the nearest Greek Embassy or Consulate about current visa and permitted length-of-stay requirements.

Etiquette

The Greeks are at heart a very traditional nation, protective of their families and traditions. So to avoid giving offence it is essential to follow their codes of conduct.

Local people rarely drink to excess, so drunken and/or lewd behaviour is treated with at best bewilderment, at worse severe distaste (or criminal prosecution, as many young louts on Rhodes, Zákynthos, Corfu and Crete have learnt to their cost).

Nude bathing is legal at only a few beaches (such as on the island of Mýkonos), but it is deeply offensive to many Greeks. Even topless sunbathing is sometimes frowned upon,,so watch out for signs forbidding it on beaches. The main rule of thumb is this: if it is a secluded beach and/or a beach that has become a commonly accepted locale for nude bathing, you probably won't offend anyone. Despite assorted scandals and embarrassing espousal of retrograde issues in recent years, the Greek Orthodox Church still commands residual respect in Greece (more in the countryside), so keep any unfavourable comments about the clergy or even Greek civil servants to yourself.

Greek authorities take the unauthorised use of drugs very seriously indeed; this is not the country in which to carry cannabis, let alone anything stronger.

Dress codes

The Greeks will not expect you, as a tourist, to dress as they do, but scuffed shoes, ripped jeans (except in alternative clubs) can be considered offensive by Greek elders.

In certain places and regions, you will encounter explicit requirements or conventions concerning the way you dress. To enter a church, men must wear long trousers, and women dresses with sleeves. Often skirts or wraps will be provided at the church entrance if you do not have them. Not complying with this code will be taken as insulting irreverence.

Some specific areas have their own dress codes. On Mýkonos, for example, male and female tourists alike will shock no one by wearing shorts or a swimsuit in most public places. But dressing in this way would be severely alienating in a mountain village in Crete, or in any other area that is less accustomed to tourists. And while shorts may be uniform male summer apparel at island resorts, when visiting Athens you will notice that *nobody* wears shorts in town, even in roasting temperatures. The best approach is to observe what other people are wearing and dress accordingly.

In general, both Greeks and tourists dine in casual dress. You will only need formal dress if you plan to go to fancy establishments, casinos, formal affairs and so on.

G

Gay and lesbian travellers

Greek society has long been ambivalent about gayness, at least outside the predictable arenas of the arts, theatre and music industry. Homosexuality is legal at the age of 17, and bisexual activity not uncommon among younger men, but few couples (male or female) will express affection in public. Mýkonos, which is the exception to this, is famous as a gay mecca, and Skála Eresoú on Lésvos (where the poetess Sappho was born) serves the same role for lesbians. Most larger islands have at least one partly gay naturist beach. But elsewhere in Greece single-sex couples are liable to be regarded as odd, although usually as welcome as any other tourists. If discreet, you will attract no attention asking for a double room and will find most people tolerant.

H

Health and medical care

There are few serious diseases in Greece, apart from those that you can contract in the rest of Europe or the United States. Citizens of the US, Canada and the EU do not need any vaccinations to enter the country.

The most common health problems encountered by tourists involve too much sun, too much alcohol, or sensitivity to unaccustomed food. Drink plenty of water, as dehydration can be a problem in the heat.

Drinking Water

People carrying a large plastic bottle of mineral water is a common sight in Greece, but it is not the best way of keeping hydrated, as sunlight releases toxic chemicals from the plastic into the water, and the spent bottles contribute enormously to Greece's litter problem. Buy a sturdy, porcelain-lined canteen and fill it from the cool-water supply of bars and restaurants you've patronised; nobody will begrudge you this. Although unfiltered tap water is generally safe to drink, it may be brackish, and having a private water supply is much handier. On the mainland and larger islands, certain springs are particularly esteemed by the locals – queues of cars, and people with jerry-cans, tip you off. If you do want bottled water, it can be bought almost anywhere that sells food, even in beach cafés and tavernas, though more conventionally at kiosks and minimarkets. A large bottle should not cost more than about 70 cents, often less.

Drugs and medicines

Greek pharmacies stock most over-the-counter drugs, and pharmacists are well trained. The Greeks themselves are enthusiastic hypochondriacs and potion-poppers, and all manner of homeopathic or herbal remedies and premium-ingredient dietary supplements are available. Many formulas that would be obtainable only on prescription elsewhere, if at all, are freely obtainable in Greece – though you may have to try half a dozen pharmacies before finding stock, especially on the smaller islands.

Essential drugs, made locally under licence, are price-controlled, with uniform rates all over the country – eg a tube of 1 percent hydrocortisone cream costs about €4 – but discretional sundries and anything imported can be expensive (eg a packet of four water-resistant French-made bandages for €3.50). If you want to be absolutely sure, pack a supply of your favourite remedies to last the trip.

Medical treatment

For minor ailments your best port of call is a pharmacy. Greek chemists usually speak good English and are well trained and helpful, and pharmacies stock a good range of medicines (including contraceptives) as well as bandages and dressings for minor wounds.

Certain pharmacies are open outside of normal shop hours and at weekends, on a rotating basis. You can find out which are open either by looking at the bilingual (Greek/English) card posted in pharmacy windows or by consulting a local newspaper. In big cities, and major tourist resorts such as Crete or Rhodes, one or two pharmacies will be open 24 hours a day.

There are English-speaking GPs in all the bigger towns and resorts, and their rates are usually reasonable. Ask your hotel or tourist office for details.

Treatment for broken bones and similar mishaps is given free of charge in the state-run Greek hospitals – go straight to the casualty/emergency ward (*epígon peristatiká* in Greek). If an UK/EU/EEA resident, bring your European Health Insurance Card, obtainable in the UK online at www.ehic.org. Be aware that holders of such cards are only entitled to free treatment in the casualty ward, and at the few still-functioning agrotiká iatría (remote rural clinics). If you make the mistake of attending a hospital's outpatient clinic, you'll pay full whack for everything at private rates, and charges are eye-watering. For more serious problems you should have private medical insurance. If you have a serious injury or illness, you are better off travelling home for treatment if you can. Greek public hospitals lag behind Northern Europe and the US in both their hygiene and standard of care; the Greeks bring food and bedding when visiting sick relatives, and must bribe nurses and doctors for anything beyond the bare minimum in care. All these conditions have been severely exacerbated by the ongoing crisis, with health-care provision very hard hit.

Animal hazards

Nearly half the stray dogs in rural areas carry echinococcosis (treatable by surgery only) or kala-azar disease (leishmaniasis), a protozoan blood disease spread by sandfleas. So beware of befriending importunate pooches.

Mosquitoes can be a nuisance in some areas of Greece, but topical repellents are readily available in pharmacies. For safeguarding rooms, accommodation proprietors often supply a plug-in electric pad, which vaporises smokeless, odourless rectangular tablets. If you see them by the bed, it's a good bet they will be needed; refills can be found in any supermarket.

On the islands, poisonous baby pit vipers and scorpions are a problem in spring and summer. They will not strike you unless disturbed, but do not put your hands or feet in places (such as holes in drystone walls) that you haven't checked first. When swimming in the sea, beware of jellyfish, whose sting is not toxic but can cause swelling and hurt for days. A good over-the-counter remedy for this is called Fenistil.

At rocky shorelines, it is worth wearing plastic or trekking sandals to avoid sea urchins (those little black underwater pincushions that can embed their sharp, tiny and brittle spines into unwary feet). A local Greek remedy is to douse the wound with olive oil and then gently massage the foot until the spines pop out, but this rarely works unless you're willing to perform minor surgery with pen-knife and sewing needle – which should be done, as spine fragments tend to go septic.

Insurance

The benefits of medical insurance coverage for private treatment are noted above. You will have to pay for private treatment up front, so you must keep receipts for any bills or medicines you pay for to make a claim. If you plan to hire a motor scooter in Greece, or engage in any adventure sport, make sure your travel insurance policy covers such activities and note official license requirements for eg scooter hire.

I

Internet

Greece has become thoroughly "wired" in recent years, with bars, cafés, hotels (sometimes only the common areas) and even many tavernas offering a Wi-fi signal. Much of the time it is free, or free for the price of a coffee, drink or meal, but usually password protected. Speeds are apt to be moderate rather than blistering – especially in rural areas. With the prevalence of tablet devices and full-sized laptops, internet cafés per se are heading towards extinction. Should you have to use one, assume a maximum of €4 an hour, with 15- or 30-minute increments usually available. Hotel internet charges can be ruinous so avoid using the service unless you know the charges beforehand.

L

Left luggage

Hotels Most hotels in Greece are willing to store locked suitcases for up to a week if you want to make any short excursions. This is usually a free service, provided you've stayed a night or two, but the hotel will accept no responsibility in the highly unlikely event of theft.

Commercial offices On the islands there are left-luggage offices in many harbour towns. For a small charge space can be hired by the hour, day, week or longer. Although contents will probably be safe, take small valuables with you.

English-language editions of Greek newspapers are available online.

M

Media

Print and web-based media

Many kiosks throughout Athens and major island resorts receive British newspapers, either late the same afternoon or sometime the next day. The English online edition (www.ekathimerini.com) of centre-right Greek newspaper Kathimerini is the best source of Greek news, albeit heavily abridged from the parent publication. The English online version of Eleftherotypia newspaper (www.enetenglish.gr) and greekreporter.com are also well worth a look. Odyssey (www.odyssey.gr) is a glossy, bi-monthly magazine created by and for the wealthy Greek diaspora, somewhat more interesting than the usual airline in-flight mag.

Radio and TV

Ellinikí Radiofonía was the Greek state-owned radio, divided into three different "programmes". However, ER was shut down abruptly by the government in June 2013, and as of writing a promised successor had not materialised. Try the excellent private station Kanali 1, out of Piraeus (FM 90.4) or there is a plethora of private stations broadcast locally from just about every island or provincial town, no matter how tiny.

The BBC World Service no longer beams directly on short-wave to Greece, but has agreements for rebroadcast of select programmes with the following local stations: Skaï (100.4 FM) and Antenna (102.7 FM).

Until the June 2013 forced shutdown, there were three state-owned and operated television channels (ET1 and NET in Athens, ET3 in Thessaloníki); several private television channels (Antenna, Net, Mega, Star, Skaï (no relation to Rupert Murdoch's Sky) and Alpha) continue to operate. Often they transmit foreign movies and programmes with Greek subtitles rather than being dubbed. Several cable and satellite channels, including Sky and CNN, are also available in the better hotels.

Money

The Greek currency is the euro (*evró* in Greek), which comes in coins of 1, 2, 5, 10, 20 and 50 cents *(leptá)*, plus 1 and 2 euro, as well as notes of 5, 10, 20, 50, 100, 200 and 500 euros (the last two denominations are rarely seen; they, and 100-euro notes, are the most likely to be counterfeit and thus may be treated with extreme suspicion).

All banks and most hotels buy foreign currency at the official rate of exchange fixed by the Bank of Greece. Exchange rates go up or down daily. To find the current rate, check displays in bank windows, or go online at www.oanda.com.

Travellers' cheques are now well and truly obsolete; take instead a prepaid cash-card which can be used in any ATM. It's also worth carrying a limited sum of low-denomination banknotes in US dollars or sterling, which are much more rapidly negotiable at travel agencies and exchange bureaux.

Credit/debit cards

Many of the better-established hotels, restaurants and shops accept major credit cards, as do all airline and ferry-company websites, plus the domestic Greek travel websites www.myhellas.com and www.travelplanet24.com. Many travel agencies and websites, however, will add a surcharge (typically 3%) to credit-card purchases of tickets. The average low-star hotel or taverna does not, however, take cards, or only accepts details as a booking deposit, so enquire before ordering if that is how you intend to pay. You will find that most brands of card are accepted by the numerous autoteller machines (ATMs), upon entry of your PIN number. Most debit and all credit cards, however, will charge a surcharge to do so, the latter's can often amount to over five percent of the transaction value, so debit cards are usually the best option to avoid high charges. This caveat aside, you will find that this is the most convenient and least expensive way of getting funds, and most machines operate around the clock.

O

Opening hours

All banks are open 8am–2.30pm Monday to Thursday, and 8am–2pm on Friday. But since ATMs are now ubiquitous – even the smaller islands will have at least one – few travellers will see the inside of a bank nowadays.

The schedule for business and shop hours is more complicated, varying according to the type of business and the day of the week.

The main thing to remember is that businesses generally open at 8.30 or 9am and close on Monday, Wednesday and Saturday at 2.30pm. On Tuesday, Thursday and Friday most businesses close at 2pm and reopen in the afternoon from 5pm to 8.30pm (winter), 5.30 or 6pm to 9pm (summer).

Supermarkets, both large and small, are the only shops guaranteed to be open all day (Mon–Fri 8.30am– 9pm, Sat 8.30am–8pm). Especially on resort islands, there will be at least one open short hours on Sunday too (typically 10am–4pm).

"Greek time"

Beware Greek schedules. You will soon learn that schedules are very flexible in Greece (both in business and personal affairs). To avoid disappointment, allow ample time when shopping and doing business. That way, you may also enter into the Greek spirit of negotiation, in which a good chat can be as important as the matter of business itself.

Although shops and businesses generally operate during the hours indicated above, there is no real guarantee that when you want to book a ferry or buy a gift, the relevant office or shop will actually be open.

Siesta (mikró ýpno in Greek) is observed throughout Greece, and even in Athens the majority of people retire behind closed doors between the hours of 3pm and 5.30pm. Shops and businesses also close, and it is usually impossible to get much done until late afternoon or early evening. To avoid frustration and disappointment, shop and book things between 10am and 1pm Monday to Friday.

Since 1994 Athens and the largest towns have experimented with "continual" (synéhies) hours during the winter to bring the country more in line with the EU, but this seems to be discretionary rather than obligatory, with some stores observing the hours and others adhering to traditional schedules – which can be rather confusing. So far it has not caught on across the rest of the country.

Tourist shops throughout the country usually trade well into the evening in summer. But butchers and fishmongers are not allowed to open on summer evenings (although a few disregard the law), and pharmacies (except for those on rota duty) are never open in the evenings or on Saturday morning.

P

Photography

Although Greece is a photographer's paradise, taking photographs at will is not recommended. Cameras are permitted in museums, but to be used without tripod or flash. You may have to pay a fee to use your camcorder at archaeological sites. Watch out for signs showing a bellows camera with a red "X" through it, and do not point your camera at anything in or near airports – most of which double as military bases.

Memory chips for most digital cameras are widely available; photo shops will also happily print from chips, or empty their contents onto a CD for a nominal fee (assume €5).

Postal services

Most local post offices are open weekdays from 7.30am until 2pm. However, the main post offices in central Athens (near Eólou near Omónia Square and on Sýndagma Square at the corner of Mitropóleos Street) are open longer hours on weekdays, as well as having short schedules on Saturday and Sunday. Rhodes Neohóri post office also has evening and Saturday hours.

Postal rates are subject to fairly frequent change; currently a postcard or lightweight letter costs 78 cents to any overseas destination. Stamps are available from the post office or from many kiosks (períptera), authorised stationers and hotels, which may charge a 10–15 percent commission, and may not know the latest international postal rates. Outbound speeds are reasonable – as little as three days to northern Europe, a week or so to North America.

If you want to send a parcel from Greece, do not to wrap it until a post office clerk has inspected it, unless it is going to another EU country, in which case you can present it sealed. Major post offices stock various sizes of cardboard boxes for sale in which you can pack your material. They also sell twine, but you had best bring your own tape and scissors.

Letters from abroad can be sent Post Restante to any post office, which will hold it for a month. Take your passport or other convincing ID when you go to pick up mail.

R

Religious services

Most major towns and island resort areas with significant foreign patronage or a large expat community – most notably Rhodes, Sámos, Corfu, Náxos, Crete and Santoríni – have at least one church dedicated to the Catholic, Anglican or other Protestant (eg Swedish Lutheran) rites, or an agreement for part-time use of an Orthodox premises. There are effectively functioning Catholic parishes on Rhodes, Crete, Corfu, Sýros and Tínos, where foreigners are welcome. Etz Hayyim synagogue in Haniá, Crete, welcomes foreign worshippers. Placards posted on the churches themselves, or handouts at the local tourist office, give current information on service schedules (which may be anything from once a month to two or three times weekly).

S

Student travellers

In addition to the museum and archaeological site discounts (see Admission Charges), students and young people under 26, with the appropriate documentation, are eligible for discounted fares and youth passes on OSE (the Greek train network) and on some shipping lines, including those operating to and from Italy.

T

Telecommunications

Foreign mobile owners will find themselves well catered for, with thorough coverage and reciprocal agreements for most UK-based services. North American users will have to bring a tri-band phone to be able to use it in Greece. In the wake of caps on intra-EU call charges, receiving calls within Greece is affordable if you have an foreign-but-EU-based number, but the costs of calling out adds up quickly. If you're staying for any amount of time, you will find it better to buy a pay-as-you-go SIM card from one of the three Greek providers (Vodaphone, Cosmote, Wind). As an anti-terrorism strategy

to keep you from using your phone to set off bombs remotely, you will have to register your identity upon purchase.

For local calls, including to Greek mobile phones, buy an OTE (Greek telecoms) phone card from a kiosk and use a (usually noisy) street-corner booth. Cards come in 100-unit, 500-unit and 1,000-unit denominations; the Hronokarta series is slightly better value.

Calls from hotel rooms typically have a minimum 200–300 percent surcharge on top of the standard rates – to be avoided for anything other than brief local calls.

For overseas calls, almost everyone avoids the truly outrageous OTE rates by buying a code-card, where you scratch to reveal a 12-digit code (or a machine-generated slip with the code printed on it), then ring an 807-prefixed number to enter said code then the number you want. It may all sound a bit of a hassle, but savings can amount to about 70 percent. If you have a laptop, it is worth bringing a Skype headset along to take advantage of Wi-fi zones for calling abroad.

Greece has one of the highest per-capita mobile-phone usage rates in the world, and a mobile is an essential fashion accessory for any self-respecting Greek as well as a means of communication.

Calls within the EU now have capped rates, but beware calling non-EU destinations such as Turkey.

Time zone

Greece is two hours ahead of GMT and, like the rest of Europe, observes Daylight Saving Time from 3am on the last Sunday in March until 3am on the last Sunday in October.

Tipping

Menu prices at most cafés, restaurants and *tavernas* include a service charge, but it is still customary to leave an extra 5–10 percent on the table for the waiting staff. Taxi drivers are not tipped per se but may "round up" fares to the nearest half-euro. Hotel porters should be given a euro or so per bag.

Toilets

Public conveniences, often subterranean ones in parks or plazas, or perched on a harbour jetty, are of variable cleanliness and

rarely have any paper. Most people just buy a drink in a café and use their facilities. In busy areas, some cafés may post signs reading "Toilets for customers only". Elsewhere, establishments are a bit more lenient about those caught short just popping in.

Tourist information

Tourist offices

If you would like tourist information about Greece during your trip, visit the nearest Greek National Tourist Organisation – GNTO, or EOT in Greek. They provide information on public transport, as well as leaflets and details about sites and museums. There are several regional GNTO offices on the islands. The information booth in Athens can be found at the base of Dionysíou Areopagítou, at the edge of the Pláka district.

On many of the islands there are municipal tourist information centres open from June to September. These are usually prominently sited near the centre of the main town, and provide all the local information you might need. Some can even help with finding accommodation.

Tourist police

The Greek Tourist Police are a branch of the local police, found in many large island towns; on the most heavily visited ones, for example Rhodes, they have a separate premises. Each tourist policeman should speak at least one foreign language well. They should be your first port of call in the event of a serious incident involving rogue hoteliers or restauranteurs, and should also be consulted if you are the victim of a serious crime such as assault or robbery, if the regular police seem to be dragging their feet.

Greek National Tourist Organisation offices overseas

Greek National Tourism Organisation, worldwide (www. visitgreece.gr):
Australia: 37–49 Pitt Street, Sydney, NSW; PO Box R203 Royal Exchange, NSW 2000; tel: (2) 9241 1663.
UK and Ireland: 4 Conduit Street, London W1R 0DJ; tel: (020) 7495 9300.
US & Canada: 305 East 47th Street, New York, NY 10017; tel: (212) 421 5777.

Tour operators

Mass-market bucket-and-spade holidays are easy to find on the web.

Otherwise, here are a few suggestions for something unusual: Quality packages and bespoke itineraries on the islands:

GIC the Villa Collection
Tel 020 8232 9780
gicthevillacollection.com.
Excellent portfolio of luxury villas for rent in the Ionian Islands (except Zakynthos), Crete and the Sporades.

Hidden Greece
Tel: 020 87584707
www.hidden-greece.co.uk
Tailor-made specialists to many small, overlooked islands.

Peter Sommer Travels
Tel 01600 888220
www.petersommer.com
Upscale, academic-led, small group tours with a focus on archaeology, both on land or by small schooner, taking in Crete, the Dodecanese and select Cyclades during spring or autumn.

Sunvil
Tel: 020 87584758
www.sunvil.co.uk
Top-quality hotels and apartments, especially strong in the Sporades, Ionian Islands, Límnos, Sámos, Cyclades and Dodecanese.

Swim-between-the-Cyclades holidays
US: tel: 1-877 455-SWIM, UK: tel: 01273 739713
www.swimtrek.com.
For swimming fans.

Travel à la Carte
UK tel: 020 72869055
www.travelalacarte.co.uk.
Villas and apartments on Kefaloniá, Paxí, Itháki, Corfu and Sými.

Sail-and-walk mixed tours
Explore Worldwide, UK
Tel: 0845 013 1537
www.explore.co.uk

Hellenic Adventures, Minneapolis, USA
Tel: 1-800 851 6349
www.hellenicadventures.com

Walking holidays
Exodus, London UK
Tel: 020 8675 5550
www.exodus.co.uk
Jonathan's Tours, France
Tel: 00 33 5 61 04 64 47

Weights and Measures

Greece is completely metric. The only exception is that land is measured and sold by the strémma (1,000 sq metres/10,764 sq ft).

www.jonathanstours.com
Ramblers' Holidays
Tel: 01707 331133
www.ramblersholidays.co.uk
Wildlife tours on Crete and Lésvos
The Travelling Naturalist, UK: tel: 01305 267994, www.naturalist.co.uk
Naturetrek, UK: tel: 01962 733051, www.naturetrek.co.uk
Writing workshops/holistic holidays
Astra, US tel: 1303 321-5403, www.astragreece.com
Skyros Centre, UK; tel: 01983 865666; www.skyros.com
Yoga Plus, UK: tel: 01273 276175; www.yogaplus.co.uk

Websites

Greek weather forecasts are available at:
www.meteo.gr
www.meteorologia.gr
www.poseidon.hcmr.gr
Windsurfers in particular should consult the Greek pages of:
www.windguru.cz
Reviews and sales of books on all aspects of Greece can be found at:
www.hellenicbookservice.com
Buying ferry tickets online and don't just want individual company sites?
www.ticket.gr
www.goferry.gr
For reliable destination information and links have a look at:
www.greecetravel.com
The Ministry of Culture site has impressive coverage of most of the country's museums, archeological sites and remote monuments on:
www.odysseus.culture.gr
Who's on strike in Greece this week/month? Find out at:
www.apergia.gr
Want to buy CDs of Greek music? Go to:
www.xilouris.gr
All the Greek reptiles and amphibians (surprisingly compelling) are at:
www.herpetofauna.gr
All the naturist beaches – which usually happen to be the best ones – are on:
www.barefoot.info/greekgde.html

W

What to bring

Adaptors

220V AC is the standard household electric current throughout Greece. Shavers and hairdryers from North America that are not dual-voltage should be left at home in favour of versatile travel models – they can be bought in Greece if necessary. Otherwise, buy a transformer before you leave home. Greek plugs are the standard round, two-pin European continental type, different from those in North America and the UK; plug adaptors for American appliances are easy to find in Greece, three-to-two-pin adaptors for UK appliances much less so, so these are best purchased before departure in the UK.

Sun protection

A hat, sunscreen and sunglasses are essential for protection from the midday sun, but if you fail to bring them, sunscreens of up to SPF50 are widely available in pharmacies and cosmetics shops, and sunhats and sunglasses can be found everywhere.

Toiletries

Most international brands are widely available, except on the smallest islands. Feminine hygiene products are more likely to be sold in supermarkets than in pharmacies.

Torch/Flashlight

Pack one, as walking home from island tavernas can be tricky if there's no moon. If you forget, Maglites or similar are sold widely.

Universal plug

Greek basins often aren't equipped with plugs, so if you want water in your sink a universal plug is essential.

Women travellers

Lone female visitors may very occasionally be targeted for attention by predatory Greek males, especially around beach bars and after-hours discos, but in general machismo is no longer any more a problem than elsewhere in southern Europe. Inexorable changes in Greek culture mean that Greek women have much more sexual freedom than previously, especially in the cities, so Northern European tourists are no longer such a novelty. There is now little controversy about Greek women spending time with their male counterparts, up to and including cohabiting before (or instead of) marriage.

However, in remote areas, many Greeks are still highly traditional and may find it hard to understand why you are travelling alone. You are unlikely to feel comfortable in all-male drinking cafés.

LANGUAGE

UNDERSTANDING THE LANGUAGE

THE GREEK LANGUAGE

Modern Greek is the outcome of gradual evolution undergone by the Greek language since the classical period (5th–4th centuries BC). The language is still relatively close to ancient Greek: it uses the same alphabet and some of the same vocabulary, though the grammar – other than the retention of the three genders – is considerably streamlined and is less complicated. Many people speak English, some very well, but even just a few words in their native language will always be appreciated.

Pronunciation Tips

Most of the sounds of Greek are reasonably straightforward to pronounce for English-speakers. There are only six vowel sounds: *a*, *e*, *i*, *o*, *u* and *y* are consistently pronounced as shown in the table below. The letter **s** is usually

Political banner in Mytilini, Lesvos.

pronounced "s", but "z" before an *m* or *g*. The sound represented here as **th** is always pronounced as in "thin", not "that"; the first sound in "that" is represented by **d**.

The only difficult sounds are **h**, which is pronounced like the "ch" in Scottish "loch" (we render this as **kh** after "s" so that you don't generate "sh"), and **g** before *a* or *o*, which has no equivalent in English – it's somewhere between the "y" in "yet" and the "g" in "get".

The position of the stress in words is of critical importance, as homonyms abound, and Greeks will often fail to understand you if you don't stress the right syllable (compare *psýllos*, "flea" with *psilós*, "tall"). In this guide, stress is marked by a simple accent mark (´) except for single-syllable words which are, however, still stressed. Greek uses the diaresis (¨) over vowels, which may or may not have the primary stress as well, to mark them off as the second letter of a dipthong.

Greek word order is flexible, so you may often hear phrases in a different order from the one in which they are given here. Like the French, the Greeks use the plural of the second person when addressing someone politely.

We have used the polite (formal) form throughout this language section, except where an expression is specified as "informal".

COMMUNICATION

Good morning *kaliméra*
Good evening *kalispéra*
Good night *kaliníhta*
Hello/Goodbye *giásas* **(informal:)** *giásou*
Pleased to meet you *hárika polý*
Yes *ne*
No *óhi*
Thank you *evharistó*
You're welcome *parakaló*
Please *parakaló*
Okay/All right *endáxi*
Excuse me (to get attention) *Me synhoríte*
Excuse me (to ask someone to get out of the way) *sygnómi*
How are you? *Ti kánete?* **(informal:)** *Ti kánis?*
Fine, and you? *Kalá, esís?* **(informal:)** *Kalá, esí?*
Cheers/Your health! *Yiámas!* **(when drinking)**
Could you help me? *Boríte na me voithísete?*
Can you show me... *Boríte na mou díxete...*
I want... *Thélo...*
I don't know *Den xéro*
I don't understand *Den katálava*
Do you speak English? *Xérete angliká?*
Can you please speak more slowly? *Parakaló, miláte pió sigá*
Please say that again *Parakaló, xanapésteto*

Please write it down for me *Na mou to grápste, parakaló*
Here *edó*
There *ekí*
What? *ti?*
When? *póte?*
Why? *giatí?*
Where? *pou?*
How? *pos?*

TELEPHONE CALLS

the telephone *to tiléfono*
phone card *tilekárta*
May I use the phone please? *Boró na tilefoníso, parakaló?*
Hello (on the phone) *Embrós/Oríste*
My name is... *Légome...*
Could I speak to... *Boró na milíso me...*
Wait a moment *Periménete mía stigmí*
I didn't hear *Den ákousa*

IN THE HOTEL

Do you have a vacant room? *Éhete domátio?*
I've booked a a room *Ého kratísi éna domátio*
I'd like... *Tha íthela...*
a single/ double room *éna monóklino/díklino*
double bed *dipló kreváti*
a room with a bathtub/shower *éna domátio me baniéra/dous*
One night *éna vrádi*
Two nights *dýo vradiá*
How much is it? *Póso káni?*
It's expensive *Íne akrivó*
Do you have a room with a sea view? *Éhete domátio me théa pros ti thálassa?*
Is there a balcony? *Éhi balkóni?*
Is the room heated/air-conditioned? *Éhi thérmansi/klimatismó to domátio?*
Is breakfast included? *Mazí me to proinó?*
Can I see the room please? *Boró na do to domátio, parakaló?*
The room is too... *To domátio íne polý...*
hot/cold/small *zestó/krýo/mikró*
It's too noisy *Éhi polý thóryvo*
Could you show me another room, please? *Boríte na mou díxete éna állo domátio, parakaló?*
I'll take it *Tha to páro*
Can I have the bill, please? *Na mou kánete to logariasmó, parakaló?*
dining room *trapezaría*
key *klidí*
towel *petséta*
sheet *sendóni*
blanket *kouvérta*

Numbers

1 *énas/mía/éna (masc/fem/neut)*
2 *dýo*
3 *tris/tría*
4 *tésseres/téssera*
5 *pénde*
6 *éxi*
7 *eftá*
8 *októ*
9 *ennéa*
10 *déka*
11 *éndeka*
12 *dódeka*
13 *dekatrís/dekatría*
14 *dekatésseres/dekatéssera*
15 *dekapénde*
16 *dekaéxi*
17 *dekaeftá*
18 *dekaoktó*
19 *dekaennéa*
20 *íkosi*
30 *triánda*
40 *saránda*
50 *penínda*
60 *exínda*
70 *evdomínda*
80 *ogdónda*
90 *enenínda*
100 *ekató*
200 *dyakósia*
300 *trakósies/trakósa*
400 *tetrakósies/tetrakósa*
500 *pendakósa*
1,000 *hílies/hília*
2,000 *dýo hiliádes*
1 million *éna ekatomírio*

pillow *maxilári*
soap *sapoúni*
hot water *zestó neró*
toilet paper *hartí toualéttas*

AT A BAR OR CAFÉ

bar/café *bar/kafenío (or kafetéria)*
patisserie *zaharoplastío*
I'd like... *Tha íthela...*
a coffee *éna kafé*
Greek coffee *ellinikó kafé*
filter coffee *gallikó kafé/kafé fíltro*
instant coffee *neskafé (or nes)*
cappuccino *kapoutsíno*
white (with milk) *me gála*
black (without milk) *horís gála*
with sugar *me záhari*
without sugar *horís záhari*
a cup of tea *éna tsáï*
tea with lemon *éna tsái me lemóni*
orange/lemon soda *mía portokaláda/lemonáda*
fresh orange juice *éna hymó portokáli*
a glass/bottle of water *éna potíri/boukáli neró*
with ice cubes *me pagáki*
an ouzo/brandy *éna oúzo/koniák*

a beer (draught) *mía býra (varelísio)*
an ice-cream *éna pagotó*
a pastry, cake *mía pásta*
oriental pastries *baklavá/kataïfi*

IN A RESTAURANT

Have you got a table for... *Éhete trapézi giá...*
There are (four) of us *Ímaste (tésseres)*
I'm a vegetarian *Íme hortofágos*
Can we see the menu? *Boroúme na doúme ton katálogo?*
We would like to order *Théloume na parangíloume*
Have you got (bulk) wine by the carafe? *Éhete krasí hýma?*
a litre/half-litre *éna kiló/misó kilo*
of white/red wine *áspro/kókkino krasí*
Would you like anything else? *Thélete típot' állo?*
No, thank you *Óhi, evharistó*
glass *potíri*
knife/fork/spoon *mahéri/piroúni/koutáli*
plate *piáto*
napkin *hartopetséta*
Where is the toilet? *Pou íne i toualétta?*
The bill, please *To logariasmó, parakaló*

FOOD

Mezédes/Orektiká

taramosaláta **fish-roe dip**
tzatzíki **yoghurt-garlic-cucumber dip**
melitzanosaláta **aubergine purée**
loukánika **sausages**
tyropitákia **cheese pies (small)**
antsoúgies **anchovies**

Wilhelm Dörpfeld sign, Lefkada town.

eliés **olives**
dolmádes, giaprákia **vine leaves**
stuffed with rice
kopanistí **tangy fermented cheese**
dip
saganáki **fried cheese**
tyrokafterí **soft cheese seasoned**
with hot peppers
fáva **puréed yellow split peas**
piperiés florínis **red sweet pickled**
peppers

Meat Dishes

kréas **any meat**
arní **lamb**
hirinó **pork**
kotópoulo **chicken**
moskhári **veal, beef**
psitó **roast or grilled**
sto foúrno **roast**
sta kárvouna **grilled**
soúvlas **on the spit**
souvláki **brochettes on skewers**
kokinistó **stewed in tomato sauce**
krasáto **stewed in wine sauce**
lemonáto **stewed in lemon sauce**
avgolémono **egg-lemon sauce**
tiganitó **fried**
kapnistó **smoked**
brizóla **(pork or veal) chop**
païdákia **lamb chops**
sykóti **liver**
kymás **mince**
biftéki **small burger (without bun)**
keftédes **meatballs**
soutzoukákia **rissoles baked in red**
sauce
giouvarlákia **mince-and-rice balls in**
egg-lemon sauce
makarónia **spaghetti**
piláfi **rice**
me kymá **with minced meat**

me sáltsa **with tomato sauce**
pastítsio **macaroni "pie" with**
minced meat
gýros me pítta **doner kebab**

Seafood

frésko **fresh**
katapsygméno **frozen**
psári **fish**
ostrakoidí **shellfish**
glóssa **sole**
xifías **swordfish**
galéos **small shark**
koliós **mackerel**
barboúnia **red mullet**
sardélles **sardines**
gávros **fresh anchovy**
marídes **picarel**
mýdia **mussels**
strídia **oysters**
kydónia **cockles**
kalamarákia **small squid**
thrápsala **large deep-water squid**
soupiés **cuttlefish**
htapódi **octopus**
garídes **prawns**
astakós **lobster**

Vegetables

angináres **artichokes**
arakádes, pizélia **peas**
domátes **tomatoes**
fakés **brown lentils**
fasólia/fasoláda **stewed white beans**
fasolákia (fréska) **green (runner)**
beans
hórta **various greens**
karóta **carrot**
kolokythákia **courgettes**
kounoupídi **cauliflower**
koukiá **broad beans**

kremídi **onion**
frésko kremídi **spring onion**
láhano **cabbage**
maroúli **lettuce**
melitzánes **aubergines**
pantzária **beetroots**
patátes (tiganités/sto foúrno)
potatoes (fried/roasted)
radíkia **chicory leaves**
revíthia **chickpeas, garbanzos**
skórdo **garlic**
spanáki **spinach**
spanakópitta **spinach pie**
vlíta **notchweed, vlyte**
gígandes **stewed butter beans**
domátes gemistés **stuffed tomatoes**
piperiés gemistés **stuffed peppers**
saláta **salad**
domatosaláta **tomato salad**
angourodomáta **tomato and**
cucumber salad
horiátiki **Greek "peasant" salad**

Fruit

míla **apples**
veríkoka **apricots**
banánes **bananas**
kerásia **cherries**
sýka **figs**
stafýlia **grapes**
lemónia **lemons**
pepónia **melons**
portokália **oranges**
rodákina **peaches**
ahládia **pears**
fráoules **strawberries**
karpoúzi **watermelon**

Basic Foods

psomí **bread**
aláti **salt**

Our Transliteration System

In Greece, most town and village names on road signs, as well as most street names, are written in Greek and the Roman alphabets. There's no universally accepted system of transliteration into Roman, and in any case the Greek authorities are gradually replacing old signs with new ones that use a slightly different system. This means you will have to get used to seeing different spellings of the same place on maps, signs and in this book.

To the right is the transliteration scheme we have used in this book: beside each Greek letter or pair of letters is the Roman letter(s) we have used. Next to that is a rough approximation of the sound in an English word.

A	A	a	far
B	B	v	vote
Γ	Γ	g/y	got except before "e" or "i", when it is nearer to yacht, but rougher
Δ	Δ	d	then
E	E	e	egg
Z	Z	z	zoo
H	H	i	ski
Θ	Θ	th	thin
I	I	i	ski
K	K	k	kiss
Λ	Λ	l	long
M	M	m	man
N	N	n	no
Ξ	Ξ	x	taxi
O	O	o	road
Π	Π	p	pen
P	P	r	room
Σ	Σ/Σ	s	set or charisma

T	T	t	tea
Y	Y	y	mildly
Φ	Φ	f	fish
X	X	h	loch
Ψ	Ψ	ps	maps
Ω	Ω	o	road
AI	AI (ai)	e	hay
AY	AY (au)	av/af	have/raffle
EI	EI (ei)	i	ski
EY	EY (eu)	ev/ef	ever/left
OI	OI (oi)	i	ski
OY	OY (ou)	ou	tourist
ΓΓ	ΓΓ (gg)	ng	long
ΓΚ	ΓΚ (gk)	ng	long
ΓΞ	ΓΞ (gx)	nx	anxious
ΜΠ	ΜΠ (mp)	b	beg
		or mb	limber
NT	NT (nt)	d	dog
		or nd	under
TZ	TZ (tz)	tz	fads

pipéri **pepper**
ládi **oil**
xýdi **vinegar**
moustárda **mustard**
voútyro **butter**
tyrí **cheese**
avgá (tiganitá) **(fried) eggs**
omelétta **omelette**
marmeláda **jam, marmelade**
rýzi **rice**
giaoúrti **yoghurt**
méli **honey**
záhari **sugar**

Desserts

galaktoboúriko **custard pastry**
karydópitta **walnut pie**
halvás **semolina-based dry confection**
katlitsoúnia **sweet-cheese-and-cinnamon-filled pastry**
ravaní **semolina and syrup cake**

ALCOHOLIC DRINKS

býra **beer**
krasí **wine**
áspro **white wine**
kokkinélli, rosé **rosé wine**
mávro **red wine**
me to kiló **wine by the kilo**
hýma **bulk, from the barrel**
(aerioúho) neró **(sparkling, fizzy) water**
retsína **resin-flavoured wine**
oúzo **aniseed-flavoured grape-pressing distillate**
rakí, tsikoudiá **Cretan distilled spirit from vintage crushings, unflavoured**
tsípouro **Sporades/north Aegean version of rakí**

SIGHTSEEING

information pliroforíes
open/closed anihtó/klistó
Is it possible to see... Boroúme na dhoúme...
the church/archaeological site? tin eklisía/ta arhéa?
Where can I find the custodian/key? Pou boró na vro to fýlaka/klidí?

AT THE SHOPS

shop magazí/katástima
What time do you open/close? Ti óra anígete/klínete?
Are you being served? Exiperitíste?
What would you like? Oríste/ti thélete?
I'm just looking Aplós kitázo
How much is it? Póso kostízi?

Do you take credit cards? Déheste pistotikés kártes?
I'd like... Tha íthela...
this one aftó
that one ekíno
Have you got...? Éhete...?
size (for clothes) número
Can I try it on? Boró na to dokimáso?
It's too expensive Íne polý akrivó
Don't you have anything cheaper? Den éhete típota pió ftinó?
Please write it down for me To gráfete parakaló?
It's too small/ big Íne pára polý mikró/megálo
No thank you, I don't like it Óhi evharistó, den m'arési
I'll take it Tha to páro
I don't want it Den to thélo
This is faulty; can I have a replacement? Avtó éhi éna elátoma; boró na to aláxo?
Can I have a refund? Boró na páro píso ta leftá?
a kilo éna kiló
half a kilo misó kilo
a quarter (kilo) éna tétarto
two kilos dýo kilá
100 grams ekató grammária
200 grams diakósia grammária
more perisótero
less ligótero
a little lígo
very little polý lígo
with/without me/horís
That's enough ftáni
That's all tipot'álo

TRAVELLING

airport aerodrómio
boarding card kárta epivívasis
boat plío/karávi
bus leoforío
bus station stathmós leoforíon
bus stop stási
catamaran katamarán
coach púlman
ferry feribót
first/second class próti/défteri thési
flight ptísi
hydrofoil iptámeno delfíni
motorway ethnikí odós
port limáni
return ticket isitírio me epistrofí
single ticket apló isitírio
taxi taxí

PUBLIC TRANSPORT

Can you help me, please? Boríte na me voithísete, parakaló?
Where can I buy tickets? Pou na kópso isitírio?
At the counter sto tamío
Does it stop at...? Káni stási sto...?

Emergencies

Help! Voíthia!
Stop! Stamatíste!
I've had an accident Íha éna atíhima
Call a doctor Fonáxte éna giatró
Call an ambulance Fonáxte éna asthenofóro
Call the police Fonáxte tin astinomía
Call the fire brigade Fonáxte tous pyrosvéstes
Where's the telephone? Pou íne to tiléfono?
Where's the nearest hospital? Pou íne to pio kondinó nosokomío?
I would like to report a theft Égine mia klopí

You need to change at... Tha prépi n'aláxete sto...
When is the next train/bus/ferry to...? Póte févgi to tréno/leoforío/feribót gia...?
How long does the journey take? Pósi óra káni to taxídi?
What time will we arrive? Ti óra tha ftásoume?
How much is the fare? Póso stihízi to isitírio?
Next stop please Káne mía stási, parakaló
Can you tell me where to get off? Tha mou píte pou na katévo?
Should I get off here? Edó na katévo?

AT THE AIRPORT

I'd like to book a seat to... Tha íthela na kratíso mia thési gia...
When is the next flight to... Póte íne i epómeni ptísi giá...
Are there any seats available? Ypárhoun thésis?
Can I take this with me? Boró na to páro avtó mazí mou?
My suitcase has got lost Háthike i valítsa mou
The flight has been delayed I ptísi éhi kathistérisi
The flight has been cancelled I ptísi mateóthike

DIRECTIONS

right/left dexiá/aristerá
Take the first/second right Párte ton próto/déftero drómo dexiá
Turn right/left Strípste dexiá/aristerá
Go straight on Tha páte ísia/efthía
after the traffic lights metá ta fanária
Is it near/far away? Íne kondá/makriá?

Notices

ΤΟΥΑΛΕΤΕΣ toilets
ΑΝΔΡΩΝ gentlemen
ΓΥΝΑΙΚΩΝ ladies
ΑΝΟΙΚΤΟ open
ΚΛΕΙΣΤΟ closed
ΕΙΣΟΔΟΣ entrance
ΕΞΟΔΟΣ exit
ΑΠΑΓΟΡΕΥΤΑΙ ΕΙΣΟΔΟΣ no entry
ΕΙΣΙΤΗΡΙΑ tickets
ΑΠΑΓΟΡΕΥΤΑΙ ΤΟ ΚΑΠΝΙΣΜΑ
no smoking
ΠΛΗΡΟΦΟΡΙΕΣ information
ΠΡΟΣΟΧΗ caution
ΚΙΝΔΥΝΟΣ danger
ΑΡΓΑ slow
ΔΗΜΟΣΙΑ ΕΡΓΑ road works
ΠΑΡΚΙΝΓ parking
ΧΩΡΟΣ ΣΤΑΘΜΕΥΣΕΩΣ car park
ΑΠΑΓΟΡΕΥΤΑΙ Η ΣΤΑΘΜΕΥΣΗ
no parking
ΤΑΞΙ taxi
ΤΡΑΠΕΖΑ bank
ΤΗΛΕΦΩΝΟ telephone
ΕΚΤΟΣ ΛΕΙΤΟΥΡΓΙΑΣ out of order

How far is it? *Póso makriá íne?*
It's five minutes' walk *Íne pénde leptá me ta pódia*
It's 10 minutes by car *Íne déka leptá me avtokínito*
100 metres *ekató métra*
opposite/next to *apénandi/dípla*
junction *diastávrosi*
Where is/are...? *Pou íne...?*
Where can I find *Pou boró na vro*
a petrol station *éna venzinádiko*
a bank *mia trápeza*
a hotel? *éna xenodohío?*
How do I get there? *Pos na páo ekí?*
Can you show me where I am on the map? *Boríte na mou díxete sto hárti pou íme?*
Am I on the right road for... *Gia... kalá páo?*

No, you're on the wrong road *Óhi, pírate láthos drómo*

ON THE ROAD

Where can I hire a car? *Pou boró na nikiázo avtokínito?*
What is it insured for? *Ti asfália éhi?*
By what time must I return it? *Méhri ti óra prépi na to epistrépso?*
driving licence *díploma*
petrol *venzíni*
unleaded *amólyvdi*
oil *ládi*
Fill it up *Óso pérni*
My car has broken down *Éhi páthi vlávi to avtokinitó mou*
I've had an accident *Íha éna atíhima*
Can you check...? *Boríte na elénxete...?*
the brakes *ta fréna*
the clutch *to ambrayáz*
the engine *i mihaní*
the exhaust *i exátmisi*
the fanbelt *o imándas*
the gearbox *i tahýtites*
the headlights *ta fanária*
the radiator *to psygío*
the spark plugs *ta buzí*
the tyre(s) *ta lástiha*

TIMES AND DATES

(in the) morning *to proí*
afternoon *to apógevma*
evening *to vrádi*
(at) night *(ti) nýhta*
yesterday *htes*
today *símera*
tomorrow *ávrio*
now *tóra*
early *norís*
late *argá*
a minute *éna leptó*
five/ten *pénde/déka*

minutes *leptá*
an hour *mia óra*
half an hour *misí óra*
a quarter of an hour *éna tétarto*
at one/two (o'clock) *sti mia/stis dýo (i óra)*
a day *mia méra*
a week *mia evdomáda*
(on) Monday *(ti) deftéra*
(on) Tuesday *(tin) tríti*
(on) Wednesday *(tin) tetárti*
(on) Thursday *(tin) pémpti*
(on) Friday *(tin) paraskeví*
(on) Saturday *(to) sávato*
(on) Sunday *(tin) kyriakí*

HEALTH

Is there a chemist nearby? *Ypárhi éna farmakío edó kondá?*
Which chemist is open all night? *Pio farmakío dianikterévi?*
I don't feel well *Den esthánome kalá*
I'm ill *Íme árostos (feminine árosti)*
He/she's ill *Íne árostos/árosti*
Where does it hurt? *Pou ponái?*
It hurts here *Ponái edó*
I suffer from... *Pásko apo...*
I have a... *Ého...*
headache *ponokéfalo*
sore throat *ponólemo*
stomach ache *kilíópono*
Have you got something for travel sickness? *Éhete típota gia ti navtía?*
It's not serious *Den íne sovaró*
Do I need a prescription? *Hriázete syndagí?*
It bit me (of an animal) *Me dángose*
It stung me *Me kéntrise*
bee *mélisa*
wasp *sfíka*
mosquito *kounoúpi*
sticking plaster *lefkoplástis*
diarrhoea pills *hápia gia ti diária*

FURTHER READING

Books go in and out of print, or change imprints, with such rapidity of late that publishers are not listed here except for websites of obscure Greek presses. For most books, a web search with the author and title should suffice to dredge up its current incarnation (which these days may be a Kindle or print-on-demand edition only, or a used copy for a few pennies).

ANCIENT HISTORY AND CULTURE

Burkert, Walter **Greek Religion: Archaic and Classical**. Excellent overview of the gods and goddesses, their attributes, worship and the meaning of major festivals.
Cartledge, Paul **Cambridge Illustrated History of Ancient Greece**. Large, illustrated volume by a distinguished contemporary classicist. Also, his **The Spartans: The World of the Warrior-Heroes of Ancient Greece** reassesses this much-maligned city-state, secretive and a source of outsider speculation even in its own time.
Finley, M.I. **The World of Odysseus**. Reissued 1954 standard on just how well (or not) the Homeric sagas are borne out by archaeological facts.
Gere, Cathy **Knossos and the Prophets of Modernism**. Puts the digs at Knossos in the cultural context of their time, documenting the reciprocal effects of contemporary art and Minoan aesthetics as reconstructed by Evans's assistants, and the "blurry boundary between restorations, reconstructions, replicas and fakes".
Grimal, Pierre, ed. **Dictionary of Classical Mythology**. Still considered tops among a handful of available alphabetical gazetteers.
Hornblower, Simon **The Greek World, 479–323 BC**. The eventful period from the end of the Persian Wars to Alexander's demise; the standard university text.
Lefkowitz, Mary **Greek Gods, Human Lives: What We Can Learn from Myths**. Rather than being frivolous, immoral or irrelevant, ancient religion and its myths, in their bleak indifference of the gods to human suffering, are rated as more "grown up" than the later creeds of salvation and comfort.
Macgillivray, J. Alexander **Minotaur: Sir Arthur Evans and the Archaeology of the Minoan Myth**. Excellent demolition job by an archaeologist, on how Evans manipulated the evidence at Knossos to fit his Victorian-era prejudices.

BYZANTINE HISTORY AND CULTURE

Norwich, John Julius **Byzantium** (3 vols): **The Early Centuries, The Apogee** and **The Decline**. The most readable and masterful popular history, by a noted Byzantinologist; also available as one massive volume, **A Short History of Byantium**.
Rice, David Talbot **Art of the Byzantine Era**. Shows how Byzantine sacred craftsmanship extended from the Caucasus into northern Italy, in a variety of media.
Runciman, Steven **The Fall of Constantinople, 1453**. Still the definitive study of an event which continues to exercise modern Greek minds. His **Byzantine Style and Civilization** covers art, culture and monuments.
Ware, Archbishop Kallistos **The Orthodox Church**. Good introduction to what was, until recently, the de jure state religion of Greece.

ANTHROPOLOGY AND CULTURE

Bent, James Theodore **Aegean Islands: The Cyclades, or Life Among the Insular Greeks**. Originally published in 1881 and reissued regularly since, this remains an authoritative source on pre-tourism island customs and folklore, based on several months' winter travel.
Clark, Bruce **Twice a Stranger: How Mass Expulsion Forged Modern Greece and Turkey**. The background to the 1923 population exchanges, and how both countries are still digesting the experience three generations later. Readable and compassionate, especially the encounters with elderly survivors of the experience.
Danforth, Loring H. and Tsiaras, Alexander **The Death Rituals of Rural Greece.** Riveting, annotated photo essay on Greek funeral customs.
Du Boulay, Juliet **Portrait of a Greek Mountain Village**. Ambéli, a mountain village in northern Évvia, as it was in the mid-1960s. A sequel, Cosmos, Life, and Liturgy in a Greek Orthodox Village, explores how the Church underpins the interior lives of the villagers.
Kenna, Margaret E. **Greek Island Life: Fieldwork on Anafi**. Her 1966–7 doctoral research, reflected in her notebooks and letters home, when pre-tourism culture still survived.
Kulukundis, Elias The Feasts of Memory: Stories of a Greek Family. A journey back through time and genealogy by a diaspora Greek two generations removed from Kásos, poorest of the Dodecanese. A 2003 re-release, with an extra chapter, of his 1967 **Journey to a Greek Island**.
Llewellyn Smith, Michael **The Great Island: A Study of Crete**. Before he was a known historian (and twice ambassador to Greece), a young Llewellyn Smith wrote this, with good analysis of folk traditions and in particular Cretan song.
Papalas, Anthony J **Rebels and Radicals: Icaria 1600–2000**. The lowdown on that most peculiar of mid-Aegean islands, delving into its Ottoman past, American diaspora links, unexpected Communist affiliations and recent touristic development.
Sutton, David. **Memories Cast in Stone: The Relevance of the Past in Everyday Life**. 1990s ethnology of Kálymnos, where tenacious "traditional" practices such as dynamite-throwing paniyíria and dowry-collecting confront the new, pan-EU realities.
Tomkinson, John L. **Festive Greece: A Calendar of Traditions** (www.anagnosis.gr). Gazetter with lots of

TRANSPORT ACCOMMODATION EATING OUT ACTIVITIES A – Z LANGUAGE photos, of all the most observed feast days of the Church – and the often pagan *panigýria* attending them.

CUISINE AND WINE

Barron, Rosemary **Flavours of Greece**. The leading non-tourist-stall cookbook, with over 250 recipes.
Dalby, Andrew **Siren Feasts**. Analysis of classical and Byzantine texts shows how little Greek food has changed in three millennia.
Davidson, Alan **Mediterranean Seafood**. 1972 classic, recently re-issued, that's still the standard reference, guaranteed to end every argument as to just what that fish is on your taverna plate. Complete with recipes.
Lazarakis, Konstantinos **The Wines of Greece**. An overview, current to late 2005, of Greece's 11 recognised wine-producing regions.

MODERN HISTORY

David Brewer, **Greece: the Hidden Centuries** Greeks under Ottoman and Venetian rule, from the fall of Constantinople until the 1820s insurrection. Refreshingly revisionist work on the period, uniformly dismissed in standard (and nationalist) narratives as a new dark ages but here put in proper perspective, with many sacred cows slain along the clearly written way.
Clark, Alan **The Fall of Crete**. Breezy military history by the late, maverick English politician; good on the battles, and more critical of the command than you'd expect.
Clogg, Richard **A Concise History of Greece**. Clear, lively account of Greece from Byzantine times to 2012, with helpful maps and well-captioned artwork. The best single-volume summary; new updated edtion out January 2014.
Koliopoulos, John and Thanos Veremis **Greece, the Modern Sequel: From 1831 to the Present**. Thematic and psycho-history of the independent nation, tracing trends, first principles and setbacks.
Pettifer, James **The Greeks: the Land and People since the War**. Useful general introduction to politics, family life, food, tourism and other contemporary topics.
Potts, Jim **The Ionian Islands and Epirus**. And erudite ramble through all these islands, touching on history, popular culture and their vital relation to the mainland opposite.

Seligman, Adrian **War in the Islands**. Collected oral histories of the caique flotillas organised to raid the Axis-held Aegean islands. Detailed maps and period photos liven up the service jargon.
Woodouse, C.M. **Modern Greece: A Short History**. Spans the period from early Byzantium to the early 1980s. His **The Struggle for Greece, 1941–1949** is the best overview of that turbulent decade, and has aged well despite the brief 1990s opening of Soviet archives.

MODERN GREEK LITERATURE

Beaton, Roderick **An Introduction to Modern Greek**. Readable survey of Greek literature since independence.
A Century of Greek Poetry, 1900–2000. Well produced bilingual volume, with some lesser-known surprises alongside the big names.
Cavafy, C.P. **Collected Poems**, trans. by Edmund Keeley and Philip Sherrard or **The Complete Poems of Cavafy**, translated by Rae Dalven. Long reckoned the "standard" versions in English; 2007 translations by Evangelos Sachperoglou and Stratis Haviaras will also appeal but don't break radically new ground.
Elytis, Odysseas **Collected Poems**, **The Axion Esti**, **Selected Poems** and **Eros, Eros, Eros**. Pretty much the complete works of the Nobel laureate, in translation by George Savidis, Edmund Keeley and Olga Broumas.
Hatziyannidis, Vangelis **Four Walls**. Hatziyannidis' abiding obsessions – confinement, blackmail, abrupt disappearances – get an airing in his creepy debut novel, set on an unspecified east Aegean isle, where a reclusive landowner takes in a fugitive woman who convinces him to revive his father's honey trade – with unexpected consequences.
Kazantzakis, Nikos. Nobel laureate, woolly Marxist/Buddhist and voluntary exile, his books bear out the old maxim that classics are praised but unread. Whether in convoluted, untranslatable Greek or wooden English, Kazantzakis can be hard going. **Zorba the Greek** (*The Life and Culture of Alexis Zorbas*, in the original) is a surprisingly dark and nihilistic work, worlds away from the two-dimensionality of the film; **The Last Temptation of Christ**, filmed, provoked riots by Orthodox fanatics in 1989; **Report to Greco** explores his Cretanness; while **Christ Recrucified** *(The Greek Passion)* encompasses

the Easter drama within Christian-Muslim dynamics on Crete.
Ladas, Alexis **Falconera** (Lycabettus Press, Athens, www.lycabettus.com). Ripping good yarn, with plenty of Boy's Own action (but some convincingly well-written un-Boy's Own sex), fictionalising in part of a daring raid to interfere with Germany resupply of Crete by the British-supported Greek Raiding Schooner Flotilla, in which the author served.
Markaris, Petros **The Late-Night News** (as **Deadline in Athens**, in US), *Che Committed Suicide*. The first (1995) and third (2003) volumes of the pitch-perfect Inspector Costas Haritos series, the only ones easily available in English, revealing a grittier Greece few visitors see behind the *souvláki*-and-*syrtáki* stereotypes. You'll get a truer picture of the country from these often eerily prophetic detective thrillers than from a whole shelf of history/anthropology texts or often poor foreign correspondent reports.
Myrivilis, Stratis; trans. Peter Bien Two novels set during the 1920s on Lésvos, Myrivilis's homeland: **The Mermaid Madonna** and **The Schoolmistress with the Golden Eyes**. The cheap-and-nasty, heavily abridged paperback editions of these are worth avoiding in favour of the original 1950s full-length hardbacks, readily available on-line.
Papadiamantis, Alexandros; trans. Peter Levi **The Murderess**. Landmark social-realist novel, set on Skiáthos at the turn of the 19th/20th centuries.
Seferis, George; trans. Edmund Keeley **Collected Poems 1924–1955**; **Complete Poems**. The former has Greek-English texts on facing pages, preferable to the so-called "complete" works of Greece's other Nobel literary laureate.
Strani-Potts, Maria **The Cat of Portovecchio: Corfu Tales**. Specifically, the thinly disguised working-class district of Mandoúki during the decade after World War – with a cat as a unifying thread.

FOREIGN WRITERS ON THE ISLANDS

Carroll, Michael **An Island in Greece: On the Shores of Skopelos**. That island, plus surrounding ones, through a young boat-bum's eyes in the 1960s; essentially adopted by a leading local family, he still lives there.
De Bernières, Louis **Captain Corelli's Mandolin**. Heart-rending tragicomedy set on occupied Kefalloniá during

World War II which despite dubious politics has acquired cult status.
Durrell, Lawrence **Prospero's Cell** and **Reflections on a Marine Venus**. Corfu in the 1930s, and Rhodes in 1945–7, now feeling rather old-fashioned, alcohol-fogged and patronising of the "natives", but still entertaining enough.
Fowles, John **The Magus**. Best-seller, inspired by Fowles's spell teaching on Spétses during the 1950s, of post-adolescent manipulation, conspiracy and cock-teasing (the usual Fowles obsessions).
Green, Peter **The Laughter of Aphrodite**. Historical novel by a distinguished classicist successfully re-creates Sappho of Mytilene and her milieu.
Jinkinson, Roger **Tales from a Greek Island** and **More Tales from a Greek Island**. Stories long and short set in and around Diafáni, Kárpathos, where Jinkinson lives much of the year. Poignant, blackly funny, even revisionist about World War II heroics.
Manus, Willard **This Way to Paradise: Dancing on the Tables** (www.lycabettus.com). American expatriate's affectionate summing-up of 35-plus years living in Líndos, from its innocence to its corruption. Wonderful anecdotes of the hippie days, and walk-on parts for the famous and infamous.
Miller, Henry **The Colossus of Maroussi**. Miller takes to Corfu, the Argolid, Athens and Crete of 1939 with the enthusiasm of a first-timer in Greece; deserted archaeological sites and larger-than-life personalities.
Stone, Tom **The Summer of My Greek Taverna**. Set in a thinly disguised Kámbos of early-1980s Pátmos, this is a poignant cautionary tale for all who've ever fantasised about leasing a taverna (or buying a property) in the islands.
Travis, William **Bus Stop Symi**. Chronicles three years' residence there in the pre-tourism 1960s; fairly

insightful, though resented on the island for its artistic licence.
Unsworth, Barry **Pascali's Island**. Late-Ottoman Rhodes seen through the eyes of Basil Pascali, hapless spy and fixer.
Waller, John **Greek Walls, An Odyssey in Corfu** and **Corfu Sunset, Avrio Never Comes**. Good-natured, optimistic expats-build-and-then-renovate-a-house sagas stretching over five decades, from undiscovered island of 1966 to the new century. His more recent **Walking the Corfu Trail: With Friends, Flowers and Food** is exactly that.
Wheeler, Sarah **Evvia: Travels on an Undiscovered Island**. A five-month ramble through Évvia in the early

Send Us Your Thoughts

We do our best to ensure the information in our books is as accurate and up-to-date as possible. The books are updated on a regular basis using local contacts, who painstakingly add, amend and correct as required. However, some details (such as telephone numbers and opening times) are liable to change, and we are ultimately reliant on our readers to put us in the picture.
    We welcome your feedback, especially your experience of using the book "on the road". Maybe we recommended a hotel that you liked (or another that you didn't), or you came across a great bar or new attraction we missed.
    We will acknowledge all contributions, and we'll offer an Insight Guide to the best letters received.

Please write to us at:
    Insight Guides
    PO Box 7910
    London SE1 1WE
Or email us at:
    insight@apaguide.co.uk

1990s, juxtaposing historical/cultural musings with adventures on the ground.

ARCHAEOLOGICAL AND HIKING GUIDES

Burn, A. R. and Mary **The Living Past of Greece**. Worth toting around for the sake of lively text and clear plans; covers most major sites from Minoan to medieval.
Hetherington, Paul **The Greek Islands: Guide to the Byzantine and Medieval Buildings and Their Art**. As it says, though there are some astonishing omissions of stellar monuments like Rhodes's painted churches in favour of the obscure.
Chilton, Lance **Various walking guides** (www.marengowalks.com). Short guidelets to the best walks around various island cheap-flight destinations, accompanied by maps.
Wilson, Loraine **High Mountains of Crete**. Almost 100 walks and treks, mostly in the White Mountains but also mounts Psilorítis and Díkti, described by the most experienced foreign guide.

BOTANICAL FIELD GUIDES

Baumann, Helmut **Greek Wildflowers and Plant Lore in Ancient Greece**. As the title says; lots of interesting ethnobotanical trivia, useful photos.
Fielding, John and Nicholas Turland **Flowers of Crete** Massive volume (updated 2008) with 1,900 colour plates of the Cretan flora, much of which is found on neighbouring islands.
Huxley, Anthony, and William Taylor **Flowers of Greece and the Aegean**. The only volume dedicated to both islands and mainland, with good photos, though taxonomy is now a bit obsolete.

CREDITS

Insight Guide Credits

Distribution

UK
Dorling Kindersley Ltd
A Penguin Group company
80 Strand, London, WC2R 0RL
sales@uk.dk.com

United States
Ingram Publisher Services
1 Ingram Boulevard, PO Box 3006,
La Vergne, TN 37086-1986
ips@ingramcontent.com

Australia and New Zealand
Woodslane
10 Apollo St, Warriewood,
NSW 2102, Australia
info@woodslane.com.au

Worldwide
Apa Publications GmbH & Co. Verlag
KG (Singapore branch)
7030 Ang Mo Kio Avenue 5
08-65 Northstar @ AMK
Singapore 569880
apasin@singnet.com.sg

Printing
CTPS-China

www.insightguides.com

Project Editor
Carine Tracanelli
Series Manager
Carine Tracanelli
Author
Marc Dubin
Picture Editor/Art Editor
Tom Smyth/Shahid Mahmood
Map Production
Original cartography Berndtson &
Berndtson, updated by
Apa Cartography Department
Production
Tynan Dean and Rebeka Davies

Contributors

This new edition of *Insight Guide:
Greek Islands* was thoroughly
updated by Marc Dubin – a well-
travelled resident of London who has
a house on Sámos. Dubin also wrote
the brand new chapter on
Thessaloníki.

About Insight Guides

Insight Guides have more than
40 years' experience of publishing
high-quality, visual travel guides. We
produce 400 full-colour titles, in both
print and digital form, covering more
than 200 destinations across the
globe, in a variety of formats to meet
your different needs.

　　Insight Guides are written by
local authors who use their on-the-
ground experience to provide the
very latest information; their local
expertise is evident in the extensive
historical and cultural background
features. All the reviews in **Insight
Guides** are independent; we strive
to maintain an impartial view. Our
reviews are carefully selected to
guide to you the best places to stay
and eat, so you can be confident that
when we say a restaurant or hotel is
special, we really mean it.

Legend

City maps

Freeway/Highway/Motorway
Divided Highway
Main Roads
Minor Roads
Pedestrian Roads
Steps
Footpath
Railway
Funicular Railway
Cable Car
Tunnel
City Wall
Important Building
Built Up Area
Other Land
Transport Hub
Park
Pedestrian Area
Bus Station
Tourist Information
Main Post Office
Cathedral/Church
Mosque
Synagogue
Statue/Monument
Beach
Airport

Regional maps

Freeway/Highway/Motorway
(with junction)
Freeway/Highway/Motorway
(under construction)
Divided Highway
Main Road
Secondary Road
Minor Road
Track
Footpath
International Boundary
State/Province Boundary
National Park/Reserve
Marine Park
Ferry Route
Marshland/Swamp
Glacier   Salt Lake
Airport/Airfield
Ancient Site
Border Control
Cable Car
Castle/Castle Ruins
Cave
Chateau/Stately Home
Church/Church Ruins
Crater
Lighthouse
Mountain Peak
Place of Interest
Viewpoint

INDEX

Main references are in bold type

INSIGHT GUIDES

Travel guides, ebooks, apps and online
www.insightguides.com

INSIGHT GUIDES

INSPIRING YOUR NEXT ADVENTURE

Insight Guides offers you a range of travel guides
to match your needs. Whether you are looking for
inspiration for planning a trip, cultural information,
walks and tours, great listings, or practical advice, we
have a product to suit you.

Greek Islands: Main Ferry Routes

0   50 km

0   50 miles